Ernest Hemingway

FIVE DECADES OF CRITICISM

Ernest Hemingway

FIVE DECADES OF CRITICISM

Edited by

LINDA WELSHIMER WAGNER

Michigan State University Press
1974

★
★
★
★
★

Contents

Introduction

"FROM MY VERY FIRST NOVEL . . . I never for a moment doubted that I was the pioneer of a new era."[1] Hemingway's late reminiscence seems even more accurate now, thirteen years after his suicide, than when he wrote it early in the sixties. The smoke of the continuous critical battle provoked by his writings has begun to settle, and much recent criticism emphasizes Hemingway's role as pace-setter for the writers of not only America but also the world. It is apparently safe to claim that no other modern American writer is so widely read.

Detractors from the Hemingway legend will say that part of his phenomenal success as a writer was luck. In a sense, they are right. Hemingway was in exactly the right place—Paris—during the crucial twenties, so that his first work was published and read by the most important avant garde writers and critics of the decade. His early success was also possible because his first three books (nearly half his "major work") were published during some of America's most prosperous years, 1924 to 1929; and his ability to live from his writing made him a rarity among serious American novelists. But more important than the economics of his first decade as writer is the fact that Hemingway, as novice writer, became the protege and even the intimate of some of the century's greatest writers—Gertrude Stein, Ezra Pound, James Joyce, Ford Madox Ford. No wonder he was proud of having created a new direction in fiction. How often had he listened to Pound urge him to "Make It New"?

For Hemingway and other artists of these Paris years, developing direction in the arts was important. They believed that only through art could man change his culture ("Artists are the antennae of the race," Pound had said); and in the post-war milieu, men had even greater reason to hope for change. Art must rid the culture of its tendency to expect panaceas and happy endings; it must also teach that convention need not be prescriptive. The old ways of doing things—writing novels, worshipping gods, earning livings—need not be the only ways. Replacing a codified philosophy as the new art did, it is no wonder that—for many of the artists, at least—art came to have the importance of a religion. To Ford Madox Ford, writing was "a priest's vocation. . . . To write honestly and well was the most important thing in the world."[2] To Pound, "The mastery of any art is the work of a lifetime."[3]

Hemingway learned these lessons well. There was never any confusion in

1

his mind about the importance of his writing. He lived the life he did at least partly to continue his work. His ostensible search for adventure, for power, for prestige was usually directed toward giving himself the materials as well as the confidence in his work to begin again. His relatively few novels are testimony to the fearful existence of the man who as apprentice writer had learned how difficult it was to write anything well, much less the great literature he had set his course toward. Considering his lifetime of effort, we can forgive Hemingway the writer his evident pride in *The Old Man and the Sea,* his last finished novel, as he writes in 1952,

Whatever I learned is in the story but I hope it reads simply and straight and all the things that are in it do not show but only are with you after you have read it. . . . It's as though I had gotten finally what I had been working for all my life.[4]

If it is possible for a collection of essays to have a focus, this one aims toward presenting Hemingway as writer, as craftsman, seeking to shape his statement of beliefs about life with all the love and finesse of any gifted artisan. Important information about his early writing practices, his admiration for other writers, and his own judgments as literary critic appear in Section I, "The Development of the Writer." Section II contains five essays which survey all of Hemingway's writing, each from a different thematic perspective. Section III includes five studies of the often-discussed Hemingway style, termed variously "sweet," "omissive," and "colloquial." The concluding section is comprised of essays treating each major novel or story collection separately. Several of these essays are among the most recent published and, to indicate one trend in criticism, are formalist. But this section also includes the first criticism published on Hemingway's writing, Edmund Wilson's 1924 review of *3 Stories & 10 Poems* and *In Our Time,* a review which also emphasizes Hemingway's craft. In "Mr. Hemingway's Dry-Points," Wilson aligns the terse yet pictorial prose with the sharpest, most incisive of the engraving family, the dry-point method. The analogy would have delighted Hemingway.

Emphasis on craft, of course, need not undercut the thematic relevance of Hemingway's writing. He may have often lived outside the United States, but his work shows him, in his probing self-consciousness, to be one of the most American of authors. Trying to find his proper niche in the turn-of-the-century civilization provides much of the tension of the Nick Adams stories, as well as of many of the novels. It became Hemingway's role to record, first, the disbelief, and then the acceptance of his own realization, that nineteenth century concepts no longer would suffice. From "Indian Camp" and "Soldier's

Home" to *The Sun Also Rises,* Hemingway shares his disillusion and grows to a kind of ironic affirmation that both puzzled and disarmed the literary world. *Nihilism* was never an accurate term for Hemingway's writing; the existentialists looked back and found him already there, but with personal solutions too prescriptive to be viable for them. The solutions did seem to work for Hemingway, however, and most readers of the fifties (and earlier) admired him for his consistency.

For younger readers in the sixties, however, these same pat solutions were not only nostalgic: they were anathema. Hemingway's surety was a threat to the relativism so many people had adopted during the decade. Because of this shift in readers' attitudes (in distance not unlike the shift Hemingway's generation itself experienced during the twenties), Jay B. Hubbell finds in 1972 that "the reputation of Hemingway seems to be declining."[5] Not far, however. Hubbell also notes that a survey during the late sixties finds Hemingway No. 1 among modern American authors; just as he had been in the 1944 *Saturday Review of Literature* poll. For at least twenty-five years, Hemingway's work has been on top. He has been America's most popular novelist, both in this country and abroad;[6] and his reputation among scholars has not suffered because of his great popular success.

With his books translated into at least thirty-three other languages, Hemingway's stature seems secure; and current criticism reflects this knowledge. People have stopped questioning the authenticity of his work, and are concentrating on finding terms to express what he achieved. One of the most interesting directions in the more recent criticism is that taken by the formalist critics, who may be close to believing Hemingway's own late description of his art,

I sometimes think my style is suggestive rather than direct. The reader must often use his imagination or lose the most subtle part of my thought.[7]

No matter what the current in Hemingway criticism has been, there has never been a dearth of it. In his recent bibliography David Pownall cites over five hundred essays on Hemingway in only the past fifteen years. Such proliferation is not new. Beginning with Wilson's 1924 essay, Hemingway has received continuous comment, whether or not he was publishing new work. His career has, in that way, been unusual: his writing has not gone through the slack periods, the fall from critical favor, of the work of Fitzgerald, Faulkner, Dreiser, and countless others. So there are many fine essays and books from which to draw; there are also, unfortunately, too many writings which tell a reader more about the critic than about Hemingway's work. Probably no

American writer in history has been the victim of so much prejudiced literary study. Whether it was the interest in Freudian and Jungian criticism, or whether readers were incapable of separating Hemingway the supposedly flamboyant sportsman-drinker from Hemingway the writer, much criticism, especially during the thirties and forties, cast little light on Hemingway's writing.

Then, too, Hemingway became the victim of the "expectation fallacy." Critics thought they could predict what he would write next; and when the book or story did not fit what they had come to consider Hemingway's pattern,[8] they denounced it rather than trying to understand it. Only recently has *For Whom the Bell Tolls* been seen as the "epic" novel Hemingway intended it to be. And, as Richard Bridgman remarked about the much maligned *Across the River and Into the Trees,*

I've always thought that the *presence* of Hemingway produced quite misleading assessments of his books. For example, what if, say, Truman Capote had written *Across the River?* Mightn't it then be read as a singularly vital and revealing portrait of an aging American warrior?[9]

Of the 22 essays included here, only six have appeared in any of the other anthologies of criticism on Hemingway's work. Fifteen of the essays have been published since the author's death, eight of these within the last five years. One essay has never been published before. By selecting such relatively new materials, I have hoped to avoid the critical patterns established during Hemingway's lifetime, when the fallacies of both expectation and biography were more likely to occur.

The quality of criticism has also improved since Audre Hanneman's meticulous bibliography appeared in 1967 *(Ernest Hemingway: A Comprehensive Bibliography),* followed by Carlos Baker's capable biography, *Ernest Hemingway, A Life Story,* in 1969. In addition to these valuable books, Philip Young and Charles W. Mann have provided scholars with a suggestion of materials yet unpublished in *The Hemingway Manuscripts, An Inventory.* Considering the quantity of materials yet to be studied, scholars are learning to be somewhat prudent in their judgments.

Since Hemingway's death in 1961, four books of his writing have been published, either as new publications or as re-issues. In 1964 *A Moveable Feast* appeared, amid sounds of protest. Hemingway's memoirs of the Paris years were hardly charitable, yet his fondness for a few people—most strikingly for Pound—suggested that his treatment of others might have some bases. In 1969 most of his Spanish Civil War writing was published as *The Fifth Column and*

Four Stories of the Spanish Civil War. In 1970 the three-part novel *Islands in the Stream* appeared, to mixed reactions. Readers objected to the fairly static fish catch, sentimental love scenes, and much philosophizing about a man's relation to his children and family. Unpolished as the book is, readers never questioned the authenticity of this novel. In 1972 Philip Young edited *The Nick Adams Stories,* an interesting collection of the well-known Nick stories and other previously unpublished fragments and stories.

While there have been many reviews of these books, the basic Hemingway criticism pays slight attention to them, seeming to feel that any work not finished by Hemingway the craftsman is truly not finished, and therefore not worthy of being judged beside the acknowledged masterpieces. In one way, this attitude emphasizes the recent critical stance, that of judging Hemingway as skilled craftsman. Sheldon Grebstein's 1973 book, in fact, is titled simply *Hemingway's Craft,* and at least two other recent studies also relate style to Hemingway's themes, Richard Peterson's *Hemingway: Direct and Oblique* and Jackson Benson's *Hemingway: The Writer's Art of Self Defense.* Several new books concern style even more specifically, Chaman Nahal's *The Narrative Pattern in Ernest Hemingway's Fiction* and C. R. Longyear's *Linguistically Determined Categories of Meaning.*

Other new studies have explored entirely fresh areas (Emily Stipes Watts' 1971 *Ernest Hemingway and the Arts* and John M. Howell's compilation, *Hemingway's African Stories: The Stories, Their Sources, Their Critics*) while some others have returned to by-now familiar areas of criticism, but with new insights: Delbert E. Wylder's *Hemingway's Heroes* describes the different kinds of heroes in each novel, while Richard B. Hovey uses a Jungian approach in *Hemingway: The Inward Terrain.* Also of interest are Arthur Waldhorn's *The Reader's Guide to Ernest Hemingway* and Jackson Benson's *The Short Stories of Ernest Hemingway.*

Other recent books have attempted to complete the Hemingway picture. Matthew J. Bruccoli has edited two collections of the earliest writing—*Ernest Hemingway, Cub Reporter: Kansas City Star Stories* and *Ernest Hemingway's Apprenticeship: Oak Park 1916–1917.* Gene Z. Hanrahan's *The Wild Years* collects 73 of Hemingway's articles for the *Toronto Star,* while William White's *By-Line: Ernest Hemingway* contains 77 columns from nearly four decades. Nicholas Joost's *Ernest Hemingway and The Little Magazines: The Paris Years* and Robert O. Stephens' *Hemingway's Nonfiction: The Public Voice* are both valuable books, as is George Wickes' *Americans in Paris,* a study of writers abroad in the twenties. In *The Flesh and the Word,* Floyd Watkins places Hemingway even more directly in the company of his peers,

T. S. Eliot and William Faulkner. Granting the basic importance of Carlos Baker's pioneering *Hemingway: The Writer as Artist* (now in its fourth edition) and Philip Young's *Ernest Hemingway* (enlarged in 1966 as *Ernest Hemingway: A Reconsideration*), it is promising to have so many useful books available. There are also many collections of criticism now in print, and most recently Robert O. Stephens has edited *Ernest Hemingway,* a collection of reviews and essays contemporary with each of the major novels.

Because of the great quantity of criticism on Hemingway's work, I have chosen to omit any formal bibliography. Several valuable guides to criticism are already available. Frederick Hoffman's bibliographic essay, "Ernest Hemingway," written late in 1967, is available in *15* (now *16*) *Modern American Authors,* ed., Jackson Bryer; the Autumn, 1968, Hemingway issue of *Modern Fiction Studies* includes a 32-page bibliography of criticism compiled by Maurice Beebe and John Feaster. In 1969 the *Hemingway-Fitzgerald Annual* began publication, and has presented useful essays, notes, and bibliographic items each year. Soon to be released is David Pownall's seven-volume annotated bibliography of criticism published during the past fifteen years concerning all twentieth century writers, including approximately 500 essays on Hemingway's work.

In 1974, fifty years after Edmund Wilson's essay, the Hemingway scholar has a great deal more to go on than intuition. The only real gap in source materials now is the absence of published letters, and readier access to the unpublished writing. But even without the valuable resources available in 1974, the first fifty years of Hemingway criticism has many kinds of excellence. I am sorry only that I had to omit some very perceptive essays. My thanks to Joseph Waldmeir, Russel B. Nye, Jean Busfield, and particularly, Lyle Blair.

LINDA W. WAGNER
East Lansing, Michigan

1. "A man's Credo," *Playboy,* X, No. 1 (January 1963), 120.

2. As quoted by Arthur Mizener in *The Saddest Story, A Biography of Ford Madox Ford* (New York: The World Publishing Co., 1971), xix. The credit to Robie Macaulay writing in "The Dean in Exile: Notes on Ford Madox Ford as Teacher," *Shenandoah* (Spring 1953), 44–48.

3. *Literary Essays of Ezra Pound* (Norfolk, Conn.: New Directions Press, 1935), 10. As Alfred Kazin wrote in 1971, "More than anyone else in that great generation that believed in 'the religion of the word,' Hemingway managed, by one word after another, to make the world as linear as his prose" (*Bright Book of Life,* Boston, Little, Brown and Co., p. 6).

4. Letter to the Editors, *Life* (August 25, 1952), 124.

5. *Who Are the Major American Writers?* (Durham, N.C.: Duke University Press, 1972), 284.

6. There have been many essays and several books describing the international reactions to Hemingway's writings. The most comprehensive is Roger Asselineau's *The Literary Reputation of Hemingway in Europe*. Representative of the high respect in which Hemingway is held is Sartre's note that "The greatest literary development in France between 1929 and 1939 was the discovery of Faulkner, Dos Passos, Hemingway" (Hubbell, 168). Even the *TLS* granted Hemingway (and Faulkner and Fitzgerald) the highest of reputations (*Ibid.*, 167).

7. Hubbell, 283, 225, and 279.

8. *Playboy*, 1963, 120.

9. It seems to be a tribute to the richness of Hemingway's art that so many different "patterns" have been identified.

10. Letter from Professor Bridgman to the editor, February 6, 1973.

I. Hemingway, The Development of the Writer

HEMINGWAY'S TUTOR, EZRA POUND

HAROLD M. HURWITZ

HEMINGWAY'S INDEBTEDNESS TO Ezra Pound has never been fully explored. Those critics who have discussed it have usually confined themselves to general remarks about the value of Pound's criticism of Hemingway's early work. Although the poet's suggestions were helpful, even more important was the transference of certain attitudes and values that lay behind the criticism. This process was of profound significance in Hemingway's artistic development, for it re-enforced his dedication to his craft and aided him in discovering and defining a credo and a faith. All of this resulted primarily from the impact of Pound's character and art and was interwoven with their friendship.

Their relationship was long and uneven, but the important years for Hemingway were the postwar period in Paris, during his apprenticeship. It was roughly from 1922–1925 that he was closest to Pound, and it was during these years that Pound's advice and encouragement were of the greatest value to him. When Hemingway reached Paris in December of 1921 as a roving correspondent for the Toronto *Star Weekly*,[1] Pound was already in the center of the literary turbulence there. Settling in Paris in the spring of 1921,[2] the American poet soon assumed the role of confidant, cicerone, and literary marshal that he had created for himself in London, at the same time continuing his remarkable career as a poet, editor, and correspondent.

Hemingway admired Pound's work and was anxious to meet him. Sometime in late January or early February, 1922, they met for the first time, apparently by accident at Sylvia Beach's bookstore, where they were introduced by the proprietress.[3] According to Pound, Hemingway told him that he had traveled four thousand miles just to see him.[4]

After the initial meeting, Hemingway visited Pound at his apartment, but

Reprinted with permission from *Modern Fiction Studies,* XVII, No. 4 (Winter, 1971–2), 469–482.

came away disappointed in the man and irritated by his egocentricity. Shortly afterwards, he vented his anger in an obscene lampoon of the poet, which he showed to the French writer Lewis Galantière, whom he had met through Sherwood Anderson's letter of introduction. A few weeks later, however, Hemingway brought Pound the manuscript of one of his short stories—probably "Up in Michigan"—and the poet praised it warmly. Hemingway then informed Galantière that they "were now getting along fine. I'm teaching Pound how to box and he's helping me with my writing."[5]

By the late winter of 1922, they had become close friends, and the form and nature of their relationship had been established. In addition to criticizing Hemingway's work, Pound had become his sponsor and friend. In March of 1922, according to Charles Fenton, he sent six of Hemingway's poems to Scofield Thayer of the *Dial* and took a story for the *Little Review*.[6] Also, they spent much time together discussing writers and writing, as well as playing tennis, duelling, and boxing. Although these extraliterary activities did not add much to Hemingway's expertise, they were important in cementing the friendship and in making Hemingway receptive to criticism from Pound—perhaps because the young writer was the superior athlete and the poet a good-natured loser.[7] Wyndham Lewis' description of a Pound-Hemingway boxing match conveys the importance of the activity and the informality and closeness of the relationship. Upon entering Pound's Paris apartment for the first time, Lewis saw him furiously attacking a tall, severe handsome statue: "After a final swing at the dazzling solar plexus (parried effortlessly by the trousered statue) Pound fell back upon his settee. The young man was Hemingway. Pound got on like a house of fire with this particular statue."[8]

Although Pound was very fond of Hemingway personally, he was even more impressed with the quality of his work and was determined that his friend should receive proper recognition. Translating feeling into action, he soon launched a crusade to call attention to Hemingway's writing. A typical effort of his was described by John Peale Bishop, a willing victim of Pound's propaganda. When Bishop arrived in Paris in June, 1922 and asked Pound about American writers of talent then living there, the latter's answer, to quote Bishop, "was a taxi, which carried us . . . across the Left Bank . . . to the Rue du Cardinal Lemoine" where Hemingway lived.[9] In addition to extolling his virtues as a writer, Pound gratuitously added a story about Hemingway's being wounded in the war, buried by falling dirt, and left for four days.[10]

In July, 1922, William Bird asked the poet to supervise a series of prose booklets that he would bring out. Seeing another opportunity to get Hemingway into print, Pound decided to include him in the series. Pound commissioned the writers, chose the selections, and organized the venture, which he called an "Inquest into the state of contemporary English prose." The books selected were to be strictly modern and had "to tell the truth about *moeurs contemporains,* without fake, melodrama, conventional ending."[11] Hemingway's *in our time,* consisting of eighteen short vignettes, was the sixth and last volume in the series.

Hemingway began writing the vignettes shortly after the trunk containing almost all of his work was lost in Paris in December, 1922. In the following April, through Pound's effort, six of the sketches were published in the *Little Review.* By July he had added twelve more and delivered the manuscript to Bird. Because of delays in the printing and binding, *in our time* wasn't published until the following January.

Pound also seems to have played a minor role in the publication of *Three Stories and Ten Poems,* the first of Hemingway's books. In February, 1923, Hemingway and his wife spent several days with the Pounds at Rapallo. Among the guests were Robert McAlmon, the expatriate owner of the Contact Publishing Company. In McAlmon's version, during a discussion about writing Hemingway told him that all of his fiction, with the exception of a few stories, had recently been lost. McAlmon asked Hemingway to send him what he had left. The result of this, according to McAlmon, was the *Three Stories and Ten Poems,* published by Contact in the summer of 1923.[12]

In addition to using Pound as a sparring partner and sponsor, Hemingway began to regard him as a literary guide. For example, at this time Hemingway was reading the Russian novelists, especially Dostoyevsky. He was fascinated but puzzled, for he found them extremely moving but very prolix, seemingly contradicting Pound's strictures about economy and precision. Hemingway sought his friend's explanation for this but was startled at his reply that he had never read the Russians. Instead, he gave Hemingway some advice which he found very valuable, remembered for almost forty years, and quoted in *A Moveable Feast:* " 'Keep to the French,' Ezra said. 'You've plenty to learn there.' "[13]

During this period they were also involved in other joint efforts which drew them close and increased their mutual respect and esteem. In March, 1922, Hemingway began to help Pound with his Bel Esprit project, a plan to free Eliot from the bank so that he could concentrate on his poetry, a rather impractical scheme of voluntary contributions by practising writers.[14] In the winter of 1923, they made a walking tour of the ancient Italian battlefields, especially Piombono and Ortobello, where Hemingway described the campaigns of the medieval soldier of fortune and patron of the arts, Sigismondo Malatesta. In August of that year, at a reception for John Quinn at Pound's,

Ezra introduced Hemingway to Ford Madox Ford and got the latter to give Hemingway a position as subeditor on his projected *transatlantic review.* The post was not very satisfying, but it did give Hemingway an outlet for some of his own work as well as that of Joyce and Gertrude Stein.[15]

The frequent contacts between them ended in the summer of 1924, when Pound settled permanently in Rapallo.[16] In the following years they met rarely but maintained a continuing interest in each other's work and career. In May of 1925, Hemingway published his "Homage to Ezra," his first major tribute to the poet.[17] In it he praised Pound as a major poet and a noble human being. In 1927, Pound asked Hemingway for a contribution to his new review, *The Exile,* and Hemingway sent a short poem which was published in the first issue.

Their last meeting occurred in Paris in 1934. Joyce asked Hemingway to accompany him to dinner with Pound because he was convinced that the poet was mad and he was "genuinely frightened of him." Hemingway went with Joyce and was also alarmed at his friend's behavior. He later wrote Pound's lawyer, Julian Cornell, that the poet spoke "very erratically" throughout the evening.[18]

After Pound left Paris in 1924, he and Hemingway carried on a desultory correspondence. Some of the poet's letters were friendly, some critical, indicating by their tone either a genuine estrangement or a further decline in the poet's faculties. The last Pound-Hemingway letter in D. D. Paige's collection is a disjointed lecture on economics written to the novelist a year after the appearance of *Green Hills of Africa* in 1935. In it Pound criticizes Hemingway for not murdering usurers instead of lions. It is worth quoting in some detail as a reflection of Pound's developing monomania and as an indication of Hemingway's generosity; for, as far as we know, the novelist never answered nor allowed Pound's vituperation to destroy his respect for his achievements:

And the buggars back of the Bank of Paris are more worth killin than pussy cats, however titanic, that ain't got no guns to shoot back with, you god damn lionhunter. What wuz the pore brute doin' to you? But Mr. DeWendel, Deterding, etc. that did NOT even make peace. . . .

Why not take a crack at 'em in the only god damn part where they FEEL —god rot their testicles—in their wallet, in the buggarin bunk account.

You seen a lot, and unpleasant; but WHY WAS IT? Because some sodomitical usurer wanted to SELL the godamn blankets, and airplanes. As I am trying to indicate in my poem. . . .[19]

Despite Pound's decline and his activities in support of Mussolini during World War II, Hemingway remained loyal. He contributed financially to

Pound's defense in 1948, helped to support Dorothy Pound while she was living in Washington during her husband's confinement in St. Elizabeth's, and gave the poet $1,500 when he was released.[20] He also tried to get Pound out of St. Elizabeth's. In the New Directions booklet of tributes to the poet on his 70th birthday (1955), Hemingway wrote that he would "gladly pay tribute to Ezra, but what I would like to do is get him the hell out of St. Elizabeth's, have him given a passport and allow him to return to Italy where he is justly valued as a poet. . . ."[21] In 1958 Hemingway added the above statement to Robert Frost's successful appeal for dismissal of the charges against Pound.

Hemingway's last living comment on Pound reaffirmed his importance as a friend and as a poet. In an extended interview with George Plimpton of the *Paris Review* in the spring of 1958, Hemingway, asked to describe Pound's influence on his work, remarked rather impatiently that "Ezra was extremely intelligent on the subjects he really knew. . . . Here it is simpler and better to . . . reaffirm my loyalty to Ezra as a great poet and a loyal friend. . . ."[22]

The reasons for their mutual attraction and esteem are not hard to understand. Hemingway was looking for criticism and appreciation, and Ezra provided both. In addition, Hemingway admired Pound's work tremendously, as he indicated in his "Homage to Ezra": "Pound writes a large and distinguished share of the really great poetry that has been written by any American living or dead. . . ." Hemingway also respected the poet's purposefulness: "He has fought his fights with a very gay grimness and his wounds heal quickly. He does not believe that he came into the world to suffer. He is no masochist and that is one more reason why he is not a minor poet."

Pound, for his part, responded quickly and enthusiastically to Hemingway's talent. He felt that his young friend was really "making it new," and he unselfishly wished to see him recognized and encouraged. Eliot has explained this aspect of Pound's personality as a "passionate desire . . . to live in a period in which he could be surrounded by equally intelligent and creative minds."[23] In addition, Pound realized that he could use Hemingway's freshness and rawness as part of his crusade against the Philistines.

There are also nonliterary reasons for their closeness. In some ways their personalities were similar; both were active, energetic, and, to use Wyndham Lewis' phrase, "violently American." In his portrait of Ezra, published in 1949, Lewis, who knew Pound well, commented on the Americanness of his character: "Pound is—was always, is, must always remain, violently American. . . . the 'tough guy' that has made Hemingway internationally famous, and the 'strenuousness' of him of the Big Stick, are modes of the American ethos with which Pound is perfectly in tune."[24]

In addition, both seemed to enjoy, if not prefer, the company of compatriots. Besides Hemingway, Pound was close to George Antheil, William Bird, E. E. Cummings, Man Ray, McAlmon, and others. Hemingway kept his American ties through such friends as Bill Gorton, Donald Ogden Stewart, John Dos Passos, and Malcolm Cowley. Also, Pound's use of American dialect and Hemingway's fondness for it reflect their inveterate Americanness. Aliens in a foreign soil, they seem to have responded quickly to the native element they found in each other.

Both Pound and Hemingway had many friends in Paris, and their relationship was just one among many close ones each had. But Hemingway realized that his friendship with Pound was special and that his lessons were important. Recalling his apprenticeship in Paris in *A Moveable Feast,* Hemingway proclaimed his respect for the poet's instructions and defined his debt to him: "Ezra . . . was the man I liked and trusted the most as a critic then, the man . . . who had taught me to distrust adjectives as I would later learn to distrust certain people in certain situations. . . ."[25]

In Hemingway, Pound found the opportunity to express his genius for teaching and campaigning. Hemingway's prose was exciting; but just as thrilling to Pound was the fact that he was almost the first to discover him. In their relationship the poet was more a friend than a master, but to his everlasting credit he seemed to get more pleasure from helping to nurture Hemingway's genius than from his own work. His unselfish attitude is reflected in the advice he gave Hadley in August of 1923 as the Hemingways were leaving Paris for home. "Never try to change Hem," he told her. "Most wives try to change their husbands. With him it would be a terrible mistake."[26]

As a teacher and friend Pound's influence on Hemingway was deep, partly because Hemingway's respect for the poet made him amenable to suggestions. The literary influence is most apparent in the novelist's early work, which Pound helped to make tighter and sharper. He did this by eliminating superfluous adjectives and adverbs and by tutoring him in techniques of economy and precision. Hemingway once told Fenton that "the only work of mine that I endorse or sign as my true work is what I have published since *Three Stories and Ten Poems* and the first *In Our Time.*"[27] Since neither one has mentioned which of Hemingway's stories they discussed, one must assume from Hemingway's statement that Pound probably read and criticized the three stories—"Up in Michigan," "Out of Season," and "My Old Man"—and the *in our time* vignettes.

There are no manuscript copies of the stories with Pound's criticism, but a close examination of the revisions Hemingway made in the vignettes gives some indication of what he may have learned from the poet's advice. Fortunately, there are available several versions of chapter iii, the one beginning "Minarets stuck up in the rain out of Adrianople across the mud flats." Both Fenton and Malcolm Cowley have carefully studied the revisions, and their conclusions, which are similar, cover the ground.[28] The later versions were derived from the first three paragraphs of a story that Hemingway cabled to the *Toronto Star* from Adrianople on October 20, 1922. The same account in modified form appeared in the *Little Review* in April, 1923. The third was the one published in *in our time* in 1924. Minor changes were made in the first American *In Our Time* (1925) and in the Scribner's edition (1930).

Between the first and last, Hemingway reduced the 241 words to 121, the more than thirty descriptive adjectives to ten, and made every one of them hard and clear. In addition, he shortened the length of the sentences, changed some of the adjectives to past participles, added several present participles, and made almost all of the sentences simple and declarative. The total effect was, Cowley says, to make the reader feel he was "seeing events for themselves instead of just hearing about them."[29] Undoubtedly, much of the improvement came from his own maturity, as well as from his immersion in Gertrude Stein's work and from her criticism of his stories, but even Hemingway has admitted that Pound's help was of great value.

Another way in which Pound helped to sharpen Hemingway's style was his emphasis on and encouragement in using "le mot juste." Speaking of this period, Hemingway remarked in *Death in the Afternoon* that he found the greatest difficulty in putting "down what really happened in action; what the actual things were which produced the emotion that you experienced."[30] The right word was an essential part of that action, he realized, for it would enable him to convey the feeling of just "how it was." In the passage quoted above from *A Moveable Feast,* Hemingway credits Pound with being the "man who believed in the *mot juste*—the *one and only* correct word to use," and suggests that this was one of the lessons transmitted from poet to novelist. Although there are no records of their conversations on this subject, from Hemingway's remarks and from Pound's essays we can deduce the essence of their discussions. For example, since 1913 Pound had been advising young writers to "use no superfluous word, no adjective which does not reveal something. . . . Go in fear of abstractions."[31] It is unlikely that Hemingway would not have heard this sermon, and it is not necessary to underline its importance in his theory and practice.

There is also evidence in Hemingway's early stories and poetry that he learned a great deal about rhythm and images from Pound's advice and from his poetry. In the passage quoted from *Death in the Afternoon,* Hemingway notes that in the early days he was trying to get "the real thing, the sequence of motion and fact which made the emotion and which would be valid in a year or in ten years, or with luck and if you stated it purely enough, always. . . ." Pound had discussed these problems in his essays and resolved some of them in his verse, which Hemingway knew well. In his "Credo" from "A Retrospect," the poet had recommended the use of an "absolute rhythm . . . which corresponds to the emotion or shade of emotion to be expressed." Regarding symbols, he had remarked that "the proper and perfect symbol is the natural object. . . ."[32] It is unlikely that he would have neglected the opportunity to impress upon his young friend the importance of these literary virtues. In fact, Pound's suggestions about images and symbols may have been an important factor in Hemingway's decision to go to Spain in the spring of 1923, to see the bullfights, and to try to write about them directly, as he did in some of the early vignettes. Cowley suggests that the short "chapters" in *In Our Time* were Hemingway's attempt to apply the "doctrine of the accurate image" which he had learned from the poet.[33]

Also, from Pound's poetry the novelist seems to have gained some effective techniques for expressing irony and hostility. Many of Hemingway's early poems reveal a bitter irony that is mindful of Pound's work. This quality was probably more personal than derivative, but in Pound's verse he saw that one could effectively and artistically express anger through anticlimax and understatement. For example, Hemingway's "The Age Demanded," published in *Der Querschnitt* in February, 1925, is obviously an adaptation and imitation of Pound's "Mauberley," especially in its tone of futility and frustration:

> The age demanded that we sing
> And cut away our tongue.
> The age demanded that we flow
> And hammered in the bung.
> The age demanded that we dance
> And jammed us into iron pants.
> And in the end the age was handed
> The sort of shit that it demanded.[34]

In its indictment of the age, as well as in its use of anticlimax and colloquial idiom, "The Age Demanded" reflects the impact and appeal of Pound's viewpoint, tone, and technique. If it is true, as Fenton claims, that Hemingway's poems were the "final exercise in the completion of an apprenticeship," then his debt to Pound was profound, not only in verbal matters but in the reenforcement of an attitude and in the evolution of a style. One can see the transformation from the poetry to the prose in a passage like the following from the opening chapter of *A Farewell to Arms:* "At the start of the winter came the permanent rain and with the rain came the cholera. But it was checked and in the end only seven thousand died of it in the army." Hemingway's remarks about the influence and importance of Pound's poetry, included in a letter he wrote Ford Madox Ford in 1932, are particularly apt here:

. . . any poet born in this century or in the last ten years of the preceding century who can honestly say that he has not been influenced by or learned greatly from the work of Ezra Pound deserves to be pitied rather than rebuked. It is as if a prose writer born in that time should not have learned or been influenced by James Joyce. . . . The best of Pound's writings . . . will last as long as there is any literature.[35]

Pound also played an important role in helping Hemingway realize his goals of "making it true" and "seeing it clear." Although Hemingway was consciously striving for these effects before he met Pound, the poet proved extremely helpful by supporting and encouraging his friend's belief in the need for artistic discipline in "making it true" and in impressing upon him the value of Flaubert as a model for achieving this end.

John Peale Bishop felt that this was Pound's most important contribution to Hemingway's work. Speaking of Hemingway's debt to Twain and Anderson, Bishop, who, as we have seen, knew both Pound and Hemingway in Paris during the latter's apprenticeship, felt that neither one of his earliest influences could supply Hemingway with what he most needed then, "a training in discipline." It was Pound who did that, he asserted:

There was one school which for discipline surpassed all others: that of Flaubert. It still had many living proponents, but none more passionate than Ezra Pound. In Paris, Hemingway submitted much of his apprentice work in fiction to Pound. It came back to him blue-penciled, most of the adjectives gone. The comments were unsparing. Writing for a newspaper was not at all the same as writing for a poet.[36]

Reflecting Pound's sentiments and advice, as well as his own convictions, Hemingway frequently commented on Flaubert and discipline, perhaps most clearly in *Green Hills of Africa* where the narrator tells Kandinsky that one requisite for achieving the fourth and fifth dimensions in prose was discipline, "the discipline of Flaubert."[37]

Another result of the friendship was that it helped shape and support Hemingway's attitude towards his work, especially in the strengthening of his belief in the seriousness of the writer's function, the necessity for complete artistic integrity, and the horror of the inaccurate. It is likely that one thing that attracted Hemingway to Pound was that the latter not only shared his views on these matters but was absolutely uncompromising about them. It is hardly necessary to quote from their work to substantiate their abhorrence of literary fakery, but one typical statement from each will indicate the similarity in attitude and emphasis. "Bad art is inaccurate art," Pound wrote in *The Egoist* in 1913. "It is art that makes false reports. . . . If an artist falsifies his reports . . . in order that he may conform to the taste of his time, to the proprieties of a sovereign, to the conveniences of a preconceived code of ethics, then that artist lies."[38] Hemingway's echo of this view appears throughout his work, perhaps most succinctly in the passage mentioned above from *Green Hills of Africa.* Continuing his discussion of how one achieves the fourth and fifth dimensions, the narrator tells Kandinsky that in addition to the discipline of Flaubert one needs "the conception of what it can be and an absolute conscience as unchanging as the standard meter in Paris, to prevent faking." Given Pound's deep feelings on this subject, his missionary propensities, and the closeness of the friendship, it is unlikely that he would not have urged his views on his friend and/or supported the novelist's own convictions.

Pound's impact on Hemingway may possibly be reflected and defined in his work, for there are shades of the Poundian character in much of his fiction. As many commentators have rightly pointed out, Hemingway's heroes have had a dedication to their work that mirrors the author's commitment to his, from Jake Barnes' concern with his journalism to Santiago's devotion to fishing. But in a way the Hemingway hero is also Poundian, especially in his compulsion for perfection and his impatience with incompetence, two qualities that Hemingway seems to have particularly admired. Obvious examples of these virtues would be Frederic Henry's contempt for the officious carabinieri in *A Farewell to Arms* and Robert Jordan's fastidiousness about dynamiting techniques in *For Whom the Bell Tolls* (1940), the latter described as follows: ". . . he was lashing the grenades side by side on top of the braced blocks of explosive, winding the wire over their corrugations so they would hold tight and firm and lashing it tight; twisting it with the pliers. He felt of the whole thing and then, to make it more solid, tapped in a wedge above the grenades that blocked the whole charge firmly in against the steel."[39] What most likely happened was that Hemingway's latent respect for craftsmanship became manifest during the Paris years because of Ezra's prodding, his example, and advice, and because of Hemingway's growing commitment to his writing; and the Hemingway hero may reflect what Pound helped Hemingway to discover in himself.

In addition, many of Hemingway's minor heroes seem to have been partially modeled after Pound. The sympathetic ones not only have the poet's generosity and unselfishness, but his energy and exuberance as well. Also, they are usually treated with the humorous but loving touch he applied to Pound in his early poetry. From the novels there are resemblances to Ezra in Count Mippipopolous, the good-natured, wealthy admirer of Lady Brett in *The Sun Also Rises;* Major Valentini, the skillful, efficient surgeon in *A Farewell to Arms;* Anselmo, "the good old man" of Pablo's guerilla band in *For Whom the Bell Tolls;* and the noble, conspiratorial Grand Master of *Across the River and Into the Trees,* who shared many secrets with the Colonel, including their love of Italy, "an old country, much fought over, and always triumphant in defeat."

It is unlikely, however, that Hemingway would have made a major hero of Ezra, for he always had a realistic view of his friend's shortcomings and an awareness of the ludicrous side of his character. As early as 1924 there was a bemused note in his treatment of the poet, as the following lines from "The Soul of Spain" indicate:

> They say Ezra is the shit.
> But Ezra is nice
> Come let us build a
> Monument to Ezra.
> Good a very nice monument.

This ambivalence was intensified by Pound's treasonous activities. Although Hemingway thought he should be released from St. Elizabeth's, he could not excuse Pound's stupidity. Ezra was "a lovely poet," but a "stupid traitor," he told Harvey Breit in 1950.[40]

However, he felt that Pound's genius, integrity, and generosity outweighed his weaknesses. Both in the *Paris Review* interview and in *A Moveable Feast* he acknowledged his debt to the poet and expressed an unqualified admiration for his work. Perhaps Hemingway's respect is best seen in the fact that he never attacked Pound as he did other early friends and influences, especially Sherwood Anderson in *The Torrents of Spring,* Gertrude Stein in *Green Hills of Africa,* and Scott Fitzgerald in *A Moveable Feast.*

The most important effects of Pound's friendship with Hemingway were that it increased his self-confidence and reassured him of the importance of his work. To Hemingway, writing became not only a vocation but a faith. Pound's tireless efforts on behalf of good writing, the satisfaction he derived from his poetry, and the beauty of his art, seem to have confirmed the neophyte's belief in the importance and value of the craft. T. S. Eliot has best summed up this aspect of Pound's contribution to young writers like Hemingway: "He has cared deeply that his contemporaries and juniors should write well; he has cared less for his personal achievement than for the life of letters and art. One of the lessons to be learnt from his critical prose and from his correspondence is the lesson to care unselfishly for the art one serves."[41]

Hemingway's comments on Pound indicate that this was one of the lessons he had learned from him; and, if so, this ideal was vastly more significant for the man and his work than the "blue-penciling of adjectives" and the instructions in precision and economy which most critics have assumed were Pound's major contribution. The profound importance of this lesson is apparent in Hemingway's enduring dedication to writing and the heroic work which resulted. When he first met Ezra in 1922, Hemingway was just beginning the difficult ascent from journalism to art. The value of Pound's lessons at that time was not so much in showing him how to do it but in helping to convince him that it was worth doing.

If this thesis is correct, then the familiar concluding lines of *Death in the Afternoon,* in which Hemingway summarizes his faith and practice, can be read not only as a description of his literary credo but also as an accurate reflection of what he had either learned from the poet or had confirmed by his instructions. In this connection it is interesting to note that the tone and style, as well as the sentiment of the passage, are strikingly similar to the assertive mood and informal but positive manner of Pound's critical dicta:

The great thing is to last and get your work done and see and hear and learn and understand; and write when there is something that you know; and not before; and not too damned much after. Let those who want to save the world if you can get to see it clear and as a whole. Then any part you make will represent the whole if it's made truly. The thing to do is work and learn to make it.

1. The exact date of Hemingway's arrival in Paris is not known; but he and his wife sailed for Europe on December 8, and he wrote his first letter from Paris, to Sherwood Anderson, shortly before Christmas 1921. See Charles A. Fenton, *The Apprenticeship of Ernest Hemingway, the Early Years* (1954; rpt New York: New American Library, 1961), pp. 99–100; and Carlos Baker, *Ernest Hemingway, a Life Story* (New York: Scribner's, 1969), pp. 83–84.

2. Pound's first letter from Paris is dated April, 1921. See *The Letters of Ezra Pound, 1907–1941,* ed., D.D. Paige (New York: Harcourt, 1950), p. 166.

3. Mrs. Pound described the first meeting at Shakespeare & Co. to Michael Reck, a young friend of Pound's during his St. Elizabeth years. See Michael Reck, *Ezra Pound, A Close-Up* (New York:

McGraw-Hill, 1967), pp. 40–41. There is no mention of this encounter in Sylvia Beach's autobiography, *Shakespeare and Company* (New York: Harcourt, 1959).

4. Reck, *Ezra Pound,* p. 41.

5. This incident is recorded in Matthew Josephson's *Life among the Surrealists* (New York: Holt, 1962), p. 89.

6. *The Apprenticeship,* p. 119. According to rumor, Hemingway was angry with Thayer for not publishing his poetry and for telling him that he would never be a poet. But in a study of *The Dial,* William Wasserstrom discovered that among the staff and in the files there was "no memory or record" of receiving any poems from Hemingway or of making any comments about them. See Wasserstrom's *The Time of the "Dial"* (Syracuse: Syracuse Univ. Press, 1963), pp. 88–89, 171–172.

7. The latest assessment of Hemingway's boxing and tennis, much discussed topics, is that of Harold Loeb, the Robert Cohn of *The Sun Also Rises.* Loeb, who played tennis and boxed with him often in Paris in the twenties, recently rendered judgments of poor at tennis and only fair at boxing. See Harold Loeb, "Hemingway's Bitterness," *The Connecticut Review,* 1 (October 1967), 8–9.

8. Wyndham Lewis, "Ezra: The Portrait of a Personality," *Quarterly Review of Literature,* 5 (1949–50), 140.

9. John Peale Bishop, "Homage to Hemingway," *New Republic,* 11 Nov. 1936, p. 39.

10. John Peale Bishop, "The Missing All," *Virginia Quarterly Review,* 13 (Winter 1937), 107.

11. From Pound's postscript to his *Indiscretions* or *Une Revue des Deux Mondes* (1923), the first volume in "the inquest." Reprinted in *Pavannes and Divagations* (New York: New Directions, 1958), p. 50. For more information on the series and Hemingway's contribution to it, see *The Letters of Ezra Pound,* pp. 183–184; Fenton, *The Apprenticeship,* pp. 223–224, notes 12 and 13; and Carlos Baker, *Hemingway, The Writer as Artist,* 3rd ed. (Princeton: Princeton University Press, 1963), p. 22.

12. McAlmon described this incident in his autobiography, *Being Geniuses Together* (London: Secker & Warburg, 1938), pp. 155–156. Fenton repeats it without question, but Baker notes that "Hemingway denied this meeting" *(The Writer as Artist,* p. 15). Baker believes that the publication of *Three Stories and Ten Poems* resulted from McAlmon's trip to Spain with Hemingway in May of 1923 *(A Life Story,* p. 111).

13. (New York: Scribner's, 1964), pp. 134–135.

14. The Bel Esprit project is best described in *A Moveable Feast,* pp. 110–112.

15. For Hemingway's activities on the *transatlantic review,* see Ford's autobiography, *It Was the Nightingale* (London: Lippincott, 1933), pp. 289, 292, 295–296, 323, 333.

16. According to Mrs. Pound, they left in April, 1924, stopped in Rapallo, left for Sicily, and returned to live in Rapallo three months later (Reck, *Ezra Pound,* p. 48). The date for the itinerary had previously been unknown. Pound returned to Paris several times during 1924.

17. In *This Quarter,* 2 (May 1925), 221–225. Reprinted in *An Examination of Ezra Pound,* ed. Peter Russell (New York: New Directions, 1950), pp. 73–76.

18. Quoted in Charles Norman, *Ezra Pound* (New York: Macmillan, 1960), p. 322.

19. Dated "Rapallo, 28 November [1936]" in *The Letters of Ezra Pound,* p. 283.

20. Reck, p. 84. Pound never cashed the check. He had it framed and kept it as a souvenir.

21. The New Directions pamphlet was unobtainable, but the tribute is quoted by Jack LaZebnick, "The Case of Ezra Pound," *New Republic,* 1 April 1957, p. 17.

22. "Ernest Hemingway, The Art of Fiction," *Paris Review,* 18 (1958), 73.

23. *The Literary Essays of Ezra Pound,* ed. and intro. T.S. Eliot (London; Faber & Faber, 1954), intro. p. xii.

24. "Ezra: The Portrait of a Personality," pp. 140–141.

25. *A Moveable Feast,* p. 134.

26. Quoted in Carlos Baker, *Ernest Hemingway, A Life Story,* p. 114.

27. *The Apprenticeship of Ernest Hemingway*, p. 178.

28. *The Apprenticeship of Ernest Hemingway*, pp. 181–185; *The Sun Also Rises*, intro. Malcolm Cowley, pp. xix–xxi, in *Three Novels of Ernest Hemingway* (New York: Scribner's, 1962).

29. *The Sun Also Rises*, intro. p. xxi.

30. (New York: Scribner's, 1932), p. 2.

31. Ezra Pound, "A Few Dont's by an Imagiste," *Poetry*, 2 (1913), 201.

32. In *Pavannes and Divisions* (New York: Knopf, 1918), p. 103.

33. *The Sun Also Rises*, intro. p. xii.

34. Reprinted in *The Collected Poems of Ernest Hemingway* ("Pirated Edition": San Francisco: no publisher listed, 1960), p. 11.

35. Quoted in Baker, *A Life Story*, pp. 236, 605–606. Hemingway was responding to a request by Ford to contribute to a tribute to Pound by prominent writers, which would appear at the same time as Pound's *A Draft of XXX Cantos*.

36. "Homage to Hemingway," p. 40.

37. (New York: Scribner's, 1935), p. 27.

38. "The Serious Artist," from *The Egoist;* reprinted in *The Literary Essays of Ezra Pound*, pp. 43–44.

39. (New York: Scribner's, 1940), p. 436.

40. "Talk with Mr. Hemingway," *New York Times Book Review*, 17 Sept. 1950, p. 14.

41. *The Literary Essays of Ezra Pound*, intro. p. xii.

AN INTERVIEW WITH ERNEST HEMINGWAY

GEORGE PLIMPTON

HEMINGWAY: You go to the races?

INTERVIEWER: Yes, occasionally.

HEMINGWAY: Then you read the *Racing Form* . . . there you have the true Art of Fiction.

—Conversation in a Madrid café, May, 1954

Ernest Hemingway writes in the bedroom of his home in the Havana suburb of San Francisco de Paula. He has a special workroom prepared for him in a square tower at the southwest corner of the house, but prefers to work in his bedroom, climbing to the tower room only when "characters" drive him up there.

The bedroom is on the ground floor and connects with the main room of the house. The door between the two is kept ajar by a heavy volume listing

Reprinted with permission from *The Paris Review* 18 (Spring, 1958). 60–89.

and describing "The World's Aircraft Engines." The bedroom is large, sunny, the windows facing east and south letting in the day's light on white walls and a yellow-tinged tile floor.

The room is divided into two alcoves by a pair of chest-high bookcases that stand out into the room at right angles from opposite walls. A large and low double bed dominates one section, oversized slippers and loafers neatly arranged at the foot, the two bedside tables at the head piled seven high with books. In the other alcove stands a massive flattop desk with two chairs at either side, its surface an ordered clutter of papers and mementos. Beyond it, at the far end of the room, is an armoire with a leopard skin draped across the top. The other walls are lined with whitepainted bookcases from which books overflow to the floor, and are piled on top amongst old newspapers, bullfight journals, and stacks of letters bound together by rubber bands.

It is on the top of one of these cluttered bookcases—the one against the wall by the east window and three feet or so from his bed—that Hemingway has his "work desk"—a square foot of cramped area hemmed in by books on one side and on the other by a newspaper-covered heap of papers, manuscripts, and pamphlets. There is just enough space left on top of the bookcase for a typewriter, surmounted by a wooden reading board, five or six pencils, and a chunk of copper ore to weight down papers when the wind blows in from the east window.

A working habit he has had from the beginning, Hemingway stands when he writes. He stands in a pair of his oversized loafers on the worn skin of a lesser kudu—the typewriter and the reading board chest-high opposite him.

When Hemingway starts on a project he always begins with a pencil, using the reading board to write on onionskin typewriter paper. He keeps a sheaf of the blank paper on a clipboard to the left of the typewriter, extracting the paper a sheet at a time from under a metal clip which reads "These Must Be Paid." He places the paper slantwise on the reading board, leans against the board with his left arm, steadying the paper with his hand, and fills the paper with handwriting which in the years has become larger, more boyish, with a paucity of punctuation, very few capitals, and often the period marked with an x. The page completed, he clips it face down on another clipboard which he places off to the right of the typewriter.

Hemingway shifts to the typewriter, lifting off the reading board, only when the writing is going fast and well, or when the writing is, for him at least, simple: dialogue, for instance.

He keeps track of his daily progress—"so as not to kid myself"—on a large chart made out on the side of a cardboard packing case and set up against the wall under the nose of a mounted gazelle head. The numbers on the chart showing the daily output of words differ from 450, 575, 462, 1250, to 512, the higher figures on days Hemingway puts in extra work so he won't feel guilty spending the following day fishing on the Gulf Stream.

A man of habit, Hemingway does not use the perfectly suitable desk in the other alcove. Though it allows more space for writing, it too has its miscellany: stacks of letters, a stuffed toy lion of the type sold in Broadway nighteries, a small burlap bag full of carnivore teeth, shotgun shells, a shoe-horn, wood carvings of lion, rhino, two zebras, and a warthog—these last set in a neat row across the surface of the desk—and, of course, books. You remember books of the room, piled on the desk, bedside tables, jamming the shelves in indiscriminate order—novels, histories, collections of poetry, drama, essays. A look at their titles shows their variety. On the shelf opposite Heming-way's knees as he stands up to his "work desk" are Virginia Woolf's *The Common Reader,* Ben Ames Williams' *House Divided, The Partisan Reader,* Charles A. Beard's *The Republic,* Tarlé's *Napoleon's Invasion of Russia, How Young You Look* by one Peggy Wood, Alden Brook's *Shakespeare and the Dyer's Hand,* Baldwin's *African Hunting,* T. S. Eliot's *Collected Poems,* and two books on General Custer's fall at the battle of the Little Big Horn.

The room, however, for all the disorder sensed at first sight, indicates on inspection an owner who is basically neat but cannot bear to throw anything away—especially if sentimental value is attached. One bookcase top has an odd assortment of mementos: a giraffe made of wood beads, a little cast-iron turtle, tiny models of a locomotive, two jeeps and a Venetian gondola, a toy bear with a key in its back, a monkey carrying a pair of cymbals, a miniature guitar, and a little tin model of a U.S. Navy biplane (one wheel missing) resting awry on a circular straw place mat—the quality of the collection that of the odds and ends which turn up in a shoebox at the back of a small boy's closet. It is evident, though, that these tokens have their value, just as three buffalo horns Hemingway keeps in his bedroom have a value dependent not on size but because during the acquiring of them things went badly in the bush which ultimately turned out well. "It cheers me up to look at them," Hemingway says.

Hemingway may admit superstitions of this sort, but he prefers not to talk about them, feeling that whatever value they may have can be talked away. He has much the same attitude about writing. Many times during the making of this interview he stressed that the craft of writing should not be tampered with by an excess of scrutiny—"that though there is one part of writing that is solid and you do it no harm by talking about it, the other is fragile, and if you talk about it, the structure cracks and you have nothing."

As a result, though a wonderful raconteur, a man of rich humor, and possessed of an amazing fund of knowledge on subjects which interest him, Hemingway finds it difficult to talk about writing—not because he has few ideas on the subject, but rather that he feels so strongly that such ideas should remain unexpressed, that to be asked questions on them "spooks" him (to use one of his favorite expressions) to the point where he is almost inarticulate. Many of the replies in this interview he preferred to work out on his reading board. The occasional waspish tone of the answers is also part of this strong feeling that writing is a private, lonely occupation with no need for witnesses until the final work is done.

This dedication to his art may suggest a personality at odds with the rambunctious, carefree, world-wheeling Hemingway-at-play of popular conception. The point is, though, that Hemingway, while obviously enjoying life, brings an equivalent dedication to everything he does—an outlook that is essentially serious, with a horror of the inaccurate, the fraudulent, the deceptive, the half-baked.

Nowhere is the dedication he gives his art more evident than in the yellow-tiled bedroom—where early in the morning Hemingway gets up to stand in absolute concentration in front of his reading board, moving only to shift weight from one foot to another, perspiring heavily when the work is going well, excited as a boy, fretful, miserable when the artistic touch momentarily vanishes—slave of a self-imposed discipline which lasts until about noon when he takes a knotted walking stick and leaves the house for the swimming pool where he takes his daily half-mile swim.

INTERVIEWER: Are these hours during the actual process of writing pleasurable?

HEMINGWAY: Very.

INTERVIEWER: Could you say something of this process? When do you work? Do you keep to a strict schedule?

HEMINGWAY: When I am working on a book or a story I write every morning as soon after first light as possible. There is no one to disturb you and it is cool or cold and you come to your work and warm as you write. You read what you have written and, as you always stop when you know what is going to happen next, you go on from there. You write until you come to a place where you still have your juice and know what will happen next and you stop and try to live through until the next day when you hit it again. You have started at six in the morning, say, and may go on until noon or be through before that. When you stop you are as empty, and at the same time never empty but filling, as when you have made love to someone you love. Nothing can hurt you, nothing can happen, nothing means anything until the next day when you do it again. It is the wait until the next day that is hard to get through.

INTERVIEWER: Can you dismiss from your mind whatever project you're on when you're away from the typewriter?

HEMINGWAY: Of course. But it takes discipline to do it and this discipline is acquired. It has to be.

INTERVIEWER: Do you do any rewriting as you read up to the place you left off the day before? Or does that come later, when the whole is finished?

HEMINGWAY: I always rewrite each day up to the point where I stopped. When it is all finished, naturally you go over it. You get another chance to correct and rewrite when someone else types it, and you see it clean in type. The last chance is in the proofs. You're grateful for these different chances.

INTERVIEWER: How much rewriting do you do?

HEMINGWAY: It depends. I rewrote the ending to *Farewell to Arms*, the last page of it, thirty-nine times before I was satisfied.

INTERVIEWER: Was there some technical problem there? What was it that had stumped you?

HEMINGWAY: Getting the words right.

INTERVIEWER: Is it the rereading that gets the "juice" up?

HEMINGWAY: Rereading places you at the point where it *has* to go on, knowing it is as good as you can get it up to there. There is always juice somewhere.

INTERVIEWER: But are there times when the inspiration isn't there at all?

HEMINGWAY: Naturally. But if you stopped when you knew what would happen next, you can go on. As long as you can start, you are all right. The juice will come.

INTERVIEWER: Thornton Wilder speaks of mnemonic devices that get the writer going on his day's work. He says you once told him you sharpened twenty pencils.

HEMINGWAY: I don't think I ever owned twenty pencils at one time. Wearing down seven No. 2 pencils is a good day's work.

INTERVIEWER: Where are some of the places you have found most advantageous to work? The Ambos Mundos hotel must have been one, judging from the number of books you did there. Or do surroundings have little effect on the work?

HEMINGWAY: The Ambos Mundos in Havana was a very good place to work in. This *finca* is a splendid place, or was. But I have worked well everywhere. I mean I have been able to work as well as I can under varied circumstances. The telephone and visitors are the work destroyers.

INTERVIEWER: Is emotional stability necessary to write well? You told me once that you could only write well when you were in love. Could you expound on that a bit more?

HEMINGWAY: What a question. But full marks for trying. You can write any time people will leave you alone and not interrupt you. Or rather you can if you will be ruthless enough about it. But the best writing is certainly when you are in love. If it is all the same to you I would rather not expound on that.

INTERVIEWER: How about financial security? Can that be a detriment to good writing?

HEMINGWAY: If it came early enough and you loved life as much as you loved your work it would take much character to resist the temptations. Once writing has become your major vice and greatest pleasure only death can stop it. Financial security then is a great help as it keeps you from worrying. Worry destroys the ability to write. Ill health is bad in the ratio that it produces worry which attacks your subconscious and destroys your reserves.

INTERVIEWER: Can you recall an exact moment when you decided to become a writer?

HEMINGWAY: No, I always wanted to be a writer.

INTERVIEWER: Philip Young in his book on you suggests that the traumatic shock of your severe 1918 mortar wound had a great influence on you as a writer. I remember in Madrid you talked briefly about his thesis, finding little in it, and going on to say that you thought the artist's equipment was not an acquired characteristic, but inherited, in the Mendelian sense.

HEMINGWAY: Evidently in Madrid that year my mind could not be called very sound. The only thing to recommend it would be that I spoke only briefly about Mr. Young's book and his trauma theory of literature. Perhaps the two concussions and a skull fracture of that year had made me irresponsible in my statements. I do remember telling you that I believed imagination could be the result of inherited racial experience. It sounds all right in good jolly post-concussion talk, but I think that is more or less where it belongs. So until the next liberation trauma, let's leave it there. Do you agree? But thanks for leaving out the names of any relatives I might have implicated. The fun of talk is to explore, but much of it and all that is irresponsible should not be written. Once written you have to stand by it. You may have said it to see whether you believed it or not. On the question you raised, the effects of wounds vary greatly. Simple wounds which do not break bone are of little account. They sometimes give confidence. Wounds which do extensive bone and nerve damage are not good for writers, nor anybody else.

INTERVIEWER: What would you consider the best intellectual training for the would-be writer?

HEMINGWAY: Let's say that he should go out and hang himself because he finds that writing well is impossibly difficult. Then he should be cut down without mercy and forced by his own self to write as well as he can for the rest of his life. At least he will have the story of the hanging to commence with.

INTERVIEWER: How about people who've gone into the academic career? Do you think the large numbers of writers who hold teaching positions have compromised their literary careers?

HEMINGWAY: It depends on what you call compromise. Is the usage that of a woman who has been compromised? Or is it the compromise of the statesman? Or the compromise made with your grocer or your tailor that you will pay a little more but will pay it later? A writer who can both write and teach should be able to do both. Many competent writers have proved it could be done. I could not do it, I know, and I admire those who have been able to. I would think though that the academic life could put a period to outside experience which might possibly limit growth of knowledge of the world. Knowledge, however, demands more responsibility of a writer and makes writing more difficult. Trying to write something of permanent value is a full-time job even though only a few hours a day are spent on the actual writing. A writer can be compared to a well. There are as many kinds of wells as there are writers. The important thing is to have good water in the well and it is better to take a regular amount out than to pump the well dry and wait for it to refill. I see I am getting away from the question, but the question was not very interesting.

INTERVIEWER: Would you suggest newspaper work for the young writer? How helpful was the training you had with the *Kansas City Star?*

HEMINGWAY: On the *Star* you were forced to learn to write a simple declarative sentence. This is useful to anyone. Newspaper work will not harm a young writer and could help him if he gets out of it in time. This is one of the dustiest clichés there is and I apologize for it. But when you ask someone old tired questions you are apt to receive old tired answers.

INTERVIEWER: You once wrote in the *transatlantic review* that the only reason for writing journalism was to be well paid. You said: "And when you destroy the valuable things you have by writing about them, you want to get big money for it." Do you think of writing as a type of self-destruction?

HEMINGWAY: I do not remember ever writing that. But it sounds silly and violent enough for me to have said it to avoid having to bite on the nail and make a sensible statement. I certainly do not think of writing as a type of self-destruction though journalism, after a point has been reached, can be a daily self-destruction for a serious creative writer.

INTERVIEWER: Do you think the intellectual stimulus of the company of other writers is of any value to an author?

HEMINGWAY: Certainly.

INTERVIEWER: In the Paris of the twenties did you have any sense of "group feeling" with other writers and artists?

HEMINGWAY: No. There was no group feeling. We had respect for each other. I respected a lot of painters, some of my own age, others older—Gris, Picasso, Braque, Monet, who was still alive then—and a few writers: Joyce, Ezra, the good of Stein. . . .

INTERVIEWER: When you are writing, do you ever find yourself influenced by what you're reading at the time?

HEMINGWAY: Not since Joyce was writing *Ulysses.* His was not a direct influence. But in those days when words we knew were barred to us, and we had to fight for a single word, the influence of his work was what changed everything, and made it possible for us to break away from the restrictions.

INTERVIEWER: Could you learn anything about writing from the writers? You were telling me yesterday that Joyce, for example, couldn't bear to talk about writing.

HEMINGWAY: In company with people of your own trade you ordinarily speak of other writers' books. The better the writers the less they will speak about what they have written themselves. Joyce was a very great writer and he would only explain what he was doing to jerks. Other writers that he respected were supposed to be able to know what he was doing by reading it.

INTERVIEWER: You seem to have avoided the company of writers in late years. Why?

HEMINGWAY: That is more complicated. The further you go in writing the more alone you are. Most of your best and oldest friends die. Others move away. You do not see them except rarely, but you write and have much the same contact with them as though you were together at the café in the old days. You exchange comic, sometimes cheerfully obscene and irresponsible letters, and it is almost as good as talking. But you are more alone because that is how you must work and the time to work is shorter all the time and if you waste it you feel you have committed a sin for which there is no forgiveness.

INTERVIEWER: What about the influence of some of these people—your contemporaries—on your work? What was Gertrude Stein's contribution, if any? Or Ezra Pound's? Or Max Perkins'?

HEMINGWAY: I'm sorry but I am no good at these post-mortems. There are coroners literary and nonliterary provided to deal with such matters. Miss Stein wrote at some length and with considerable inaccuracy about her influence on my work. It was necessary for her to do this after she had learned to write dialogue from a book called *The Sun Also Rises.* I was very fond of her and thought it was splendid she had learned to write conversation. It was no new thing to me to learn from everyone I could, living or dead, and I had no idea it would affect Gertrude so violently. She already wrote very well in other ways. Ezra was extremely intelligent on the subjects he really knew. Doesn't this sort of talk bore you? This backyard literary gossip while washing out the dirty clothes of thirty-five years ago is disgusting to me. It would be different if one had tried to tell the whole truth. That would have some value. Here it is simpler and better to thank Gertrude for everything I learned from her about the abstract relationship of words, say how fond I was of her, reaffirm my loyalty to Ezra as a great poet and a loyal friend, and say that I cared so much for Max Perkins that I have never been able to accept that he is dead. He never asked me to change anything I wrote except to remove certain words which were not then publishable. Blanks were left, and anyone who knew the words would know what they were. For me he was not an editor. He was a wise friend and a wonderful companion. I liked the way he wore his hat and the strange way his lips moved.

INTERVIEWER: Who would you say are your literary forebears—those you have learned the most from?

HEMINGWAY: Mark Twain, Flaubert, Stendhal, Bach, Turgenev, Tolstoi, Dostoevski, Chekhov, Andrew Marvell, John Donne, Maupassant, the good Kipling, Thoreau, Captain Marryat, Shakespeare, Mozart, Quevedo, Dante, Vergil, Tintoretto, Hieronymus Bosch, Breughel, Patinier, Goya, Giotto, Cézanne, Van Gogh, Gauguin, San Juan de la Cruz, Góngora—it would take a day to remember everyone. Then it would sound as though I were claiming an erudition I did not possess instead of trying to remember all the people who have been an influence on my life and work. This isn't an old dull question. It is a very good but a solemn question and requires an examination of conscience. I put in painters, or started to, because I learn as much from painters about how to write as from writers. You ask how this is done? It would take another day of explaining. I should think what one learns from composers and from the study of harmony and counterpoint would be obvious.

INTERVIEWER: Did you ever play a musical instrument?

HEMINGWAY: I used to play cello. My mother kept me out of school a whole year to study music and counterpoint. She thought I had ability, but I was absolutely without talent. We played chamber music—someone came in to play the violin; my sister played the viola, and mother the piano. That cello —I played it worse than anyone on earth. Of course, that year I was out doing other things too.

INTERVIEWER: Do you reread the authors of your list—Twain, for instance?

HEMINGWAY: You have to wait two or three years with Twain. You remember too well. I read some Shakespeare every year, *Lear* always. Cheers you up if you read that.

INTERVIEWER: Reading, then, is a constant occupation and pleasure.

HEMINGWAY: I'm always reading books—as many as there are. I ration myself on them so that I'll always be in supply.

INTERVIEWER: Do you ever read manuscripts?

HEMINGWAY: You can get into trouble doing that unless you know the author personally. Some years ago I was sued for plagiarism by a man who claimed that I'd lifted *For Whom the Bell Tolls* from an unpublished screen scenario he'd written. He'd read this scenario at some Hollywood party. I was there, he said, at least there was a fellow called "Ernie" there listening to the reading, and that was enough for him to sue for a million dollars. At the same time he sued the producers of the motion pictures *North West Mounted Police* and the *Cisco Kid,* claiming that these, as well, had been stolen from that same unpublished scenario. We went to court and, of course, won the case. The man turned out to be insolvent.

INTERVIEWER: Well, could we go back to that list and take one of the painters—Hieronymus Bosch, for instance? The nightmare symbolic quality of his work seems so far removed from your own.

HEMINGWAY: I have the nightmares and know about the ones other people have. But you do not have to write them down. Anything you can omit that you know you still have in the writing and its quality will show. When a writer omits things he does not know, they show like holes in his writing.

INTERVIEWER: Does that mean that a close knowledge of the works of the people on your list helps fill the "well" you were speaking of a while back? Or were they consciously a help in developing the techniques of writing?

HEMINGWAY: They were a part of learning to see, to hear, to think, to feel and not feel, and to write. The well is where your "juice" is. Nobody knows what it is made of, least of all yourself. What you know is if you have it, or you have to wait for it to come back.

INTERVIEWER: Would you admit to there being symbolism in your novels?

HEMINGWAY: I suppose there are symbols since critics keep finding them.

If you do not mind I dislike talking about them and being questioned about them. It is hard enough to write books and stories without being asked to explain them as well. Also it deprives the explainers of work. If five or six or more good explainers can keep going why should I interfere with them? Read anything I write for the pleasure of reading it. Whatever else you find will be the measure of what you brought to the reading.

INTERVIEWER: Continuing with just one question on this line: One of the advisory staff editors wonders about a parallel he feels he's found in *The Sun Also Rises* between the dramatis personae of the bull ring and the characters of the novel itself. He points out that the first sentence of the book tells us Robert Cohn is a boxer; later, during the *desencajonada,* the bull is described as using his horns like a boxer, hooking and jabbing. And just as the bull is attracted and pacified by the presence of a steer, Robert Cohn defers to Jake who is emasculated precisely as is a steer. He sees Mike as the picador, baiting Cohn repeatedly. The editor's thesis goes on, but he wondered if it was your conscious intention to inform the novel with the tragic structure of the bullfight ritual.

HEMINGWAY: It sounds as though the advisory staff editor was a little bit screwy. Who ever said Jake was "emasculated precisely as is a steer"? Actually he had been wounded in quite a different way and his testicles were intact and not damaged. Thus he was capable of all normal feelings as a *man* but incapable of consummating them. The important distinction is that his wound was physical and not psychological and that he was not emasculated.

INTERVIEWER: These questions which inquire into craftsmanship really are an annoyance.

HEMINGWAY: A sensible question is neither a delight nor an annoyance. I still believe though that it is very bad for a writer to talk about how he writes. He writes to be read by the eye and no explanations nor dissertations should be necessary. You can be sure that there is much more there than will be read at any first reading and having made this it is not the writer's province to explain it or to run guided tours through the more difficult country of his work.

INTERVIEWER: In connection with this, I remember you have also warned that it is dangerous for a writer to talk about a work in progress, that he can "talk it out" so to speak. Why should this be so? I only ask because there are so many writers—Twain, Wilde, Thurber, Steffens, come to mind—who would seem to have polished their material by testing it on listeners.

HEMINGWAY: I cannot believe Twain ever "tested out" *Huckleberry Finn* on listeners. If he did they probably had him cut out good things and put in the bad parts. Wilde was said by people who knew him to have been a better talker than a writer. Steffens talked better than he wrote. Both his writing and his talking were sometimes hard to believe, and I heard many stories change as he grew older. If Thurber can talk as well as he writes he must be one of the greatest and least boring talkers. The man I know who talks best about his own trade and has the pleasantest and most wicked tongue is Juan Belmonte, the matador.

INTERVIEWER: Could you say how much thought-out effort went into the evolvement of your distinctive style?

HEMINGWAY: That is a long-term tiring question and if you spent a couple of days answering it you would be so self-conscious that you could not write. I might say that what amateurs call a style is usually only the unavoidable awkwardnesses in first trying to make something that has not heretofore been made. Almost no new classics resemble other previous classics. At first people can see only the awkwardness. Then they are not so perceptible. When they show so very awkwardly people think these awkwardnesses are the style and many copy them. This is regrettable.

INTERVIEWER: You once wrote me that the simple circumstances under which various pieces of fiction were written could be instructive. Could you apply this to "The Killers"—you said that you had written it, "Ten Indians" and "Today Is Friday" in one day—and perhaps to your first novel *The Sun Also Rises?*

HEMINGWAY: Let's see. *The Sun Also Rises* I started in Valencia on my birthday, July 21st. Hadley, my wife, and I had gone to Valencia early to get good tickets for the *feria* there which started the 24th of July. Everybody my age had written a novel and I was still having a difficult time writing a paragraph. So I started the book on my birthday, wrote all through the *feria,* in bed in the morning, went on to Madrid and wrote there. There was no *feria* there, so we had a room with a table and I wrote in great luxury on the table and around the corner from the hotel in a beer place in the Pasaje Alvarez where it was cool. It finally got too hot to write and we went to Hendaye. There was a small cheap hotel there on the big long lovely beach and I worked very well there and then went up to Paris and finished the first draft in the apartment over the sawmill at 113 rue Notre Dame des Champs six weeks from the day I started it. I showed the first draft to Nathan Asch, the novelist, who then had quite a strong accent and he said "Hem, vaht do you mean saying you wrote a novel? A novel huh. Hem, you are riding a trahvel buch." I was not too discouraged by Nathan and rewrote the book, keeping in the travel (that was the part about the fishing trip and Pamplona) at Schruns in the Vorarlberg at the Hotel Taube.

The stories you mention I wrote in one day in Madrid on May 16 when it snowed out the San Isidro bullfights. First I wrote "The Killers," which I'd tried to write before and failed. Then after lunch I got in bed to keep warm and wrote "Today Is Friday." I had so much juice I thought maybe I was going crazy and I had about six other stories to write. So I got dressed and walked to Fornos, the old bullfighters' café, and drank coffee and then came back and wrote "Ten Indians." This made me very sad and I drank some brandy and went to sleep. I'd forgotten to eat and one of the waiters brought me up some bacalao and a small steak and fried potatoes and a bottle of Valdepeñas.

The woman who ran the pension was always worried that I did not eat enough and she had sent the waiter. I remember sitting up in bed and eating, and drinking the Valdepeñas. The waiter said he would bring up another bottle. He said the señora wanted to know if I was going to write all night. I said no, I thought I would lay off for a while. Why don't you try to write just one more, the waiter asked. I'm only supposed to write one, I said. Nonsense, he said. You could write six. I'll try tomorrow, I said. Try it tonight, he said. What do you think the old woman sent the food up for?

I'm tired, I told him. Nonsense, he said (the word was not nonsense). You tired after three miserable little stories. Translate me one.

Leave me alone, I said. How am I going to write it if you don't leave me alone. So I sat up in bed and drank the Valdepeñas and thought what a hell of a writer I was if the first story was as good as I'd hoped.

INTERVIEWER: How complete in your own mind is the conception of a short story? Does the theme, or the plot, or a character change as you go along?

HEMINGWAY: Sometimes you know the story. Sometimes you make it up as you go along and have no idea how it will come out. Everything changes as it moves. That is what makes the movement which makes the story. Sometimes the movement is so slow it does not seem to be moving. But there is always change and always movement.

INTERVIEWER: Is it the same with the novel, or do you work out the whole plan before you start and adhere to it rigorously?

HEMINGWAY: *For Whom the Bell Tolls* was a problem which I carried on each day. I knew what was going to happen in principle. But I invented what happened each day I wrote.

INTERVIEWER: Were the *Green Hills of Africa, To Have and Have Not,* and *Across the River and into the Trees* all started as short stories and developed into novels? If so, are the two forms so similar that the writer can pass from one to the other without completely revamping his approach?

HEMINGWAY: No, that is not true. The *Green Hills of Africa* is not a novel but was written in an attempt to write an absolutely true book to see whether the shape of a country and the pattern of a month's action could, if truly presented, compete with a work of the imagination. After I had written it I wrote two short stories, "The Snows of Kilimanjaro" and "The Short Happy Life of Francis Macomber." These were stories which I invented from the knowledge and experience acquired on the same long hunting trip one month of which I had tried to write a truthful account of in the *Green Hills. To Have and Have Not* and *Across the River and into the Trees* were both started as short stories.

INTERVIEWER: Do you find it easy to shift from one literary project to another or do you continue through to finish what you start?

HEMINGWAY: The fact that I am interrupting serious work to answer these questions proves that I am so stupid that I should be penalized severely. I will be. Don't worry.

INTERVIEWER: Do you think of yourself in competition with other writers?

HEMINGWAY: Never. I used to try to write better than certain dead writers of whose value I was certain. For a long time now I have tried simply to write the best I can. Sometimes I have good luck and write better than I can.

INTERVIEWER: Do you think a writer's power diminishes as he grows older? In the *Green Hills of Africa* you mention that American writers at a certain age change into Old Mother Hubbards.

HEMINGWAY: I don't know about that. People who know what they are doing should last as long their heads last. In that book you mention, if you look it up, you'll see I was sounding off about American literature with a humorless Austrian character who was forcing me to talk when I wanted to do something else. I wrote an accurate account of the conversation. Not to make deathless pronouncements. A fair per cent of the pronouncements are good enough.

INTERVIEWER: We've not discussed character. Are the characters of your work taken without exception from real life?

HEMINGWAY: Of course they are not. *Some* come from real life. Mostly you invent people from a knowledge and understanding and experience of people.

INTERVIEWER: Could you say something about the process of turning a real-life character into a fictional one?

HEMINGWAY: If I explained how that is sometimes done, it would be a handbook for libel lawyers.

INTERVIEWER: Do you make a distinction—as E. M. Forster does—between "flat" and "round" characters?

HEMINGWAY: If you describe someone, it is flat, as a photograph is, and from my standpoint a failure. If you make him up from what you know, there should be all the dimensions.

INTERVIEWER: Which of your characters do you look back on with particular affection?

HEMINGWAY: That would make too long a list.

INTERVIEWER: Then you enjoy reading over your own books—without feeling there are changes you would like to make?

HEMINGWAY: I read them sometimes to cheer me up when it is hard to write and then I remember that it was always difficult and how nearly impossible it was sometimes.

INTERVIEWER: How do you name your characters?

HEMINGWAY: The best I can.

INTERVIEWER: Do the titles come to you while you're in the process of doing the story?

HEMINGWAY: No. I make a list of titles *after* I've finished the story or the book—sometimes as many as 100. Then I start eliminating them, sometimes all of them.

INTERVIEWER: And you do this even with a story whose title is supplied from the text—"Hills Like White Elephants," for example?

HEMINGWAY: Yes. The title comes afterwards. I met a girl in Prunier where I'd gone to eat oysters before lunch. I knew she'd had an abortion. I went over and we talked, not about that, but on the way home I thought of the story, skipped lunch, and spent that afternoon writing it.

INTERVIEWER: So when you're not writing, you remain constantly the observer, looking for something which can be of use.

HEMINGWAY: Surely. If a writer stops observing he is finished. But he does not have to observe consciously nor think how it will be useful. Perhaps that would be true at the beginning. But later everything he sees goes into the great reserve of things he knows or has seen. If it is any use to know it, I always try to write on the principle of the iceberg. There is seven eighths of it under water for every part that shows. Anything you know you can eliminate and it only strengthens your iceberg. It is the part that doesn't show. If a writer omits something because he does not know it then there is a hole in the story.

The Old Man and the Sea could have been over a thousand pages long and had every character in the village in it and all the processes of how they made their living, were born, educated, bore children, etc. That is done excellently and well by other writers. In writing you are limited by what has already been done satisfactorily. So I have tried to learn to do something else. First I have tried to eliminate everything unnecessary to conveying experience to the reader so that after he or she has read something it will become a part of his or her experience and seem actually to have happened. This is very hard to do and I've worked at it very hard.

Anyway, to skip how it is done, I had unbelievable luck this time and could convey the experience completely and have it be one that no one had ever conveyed. The luck was that I had a good man and a good boy and lately writers have forgotten there still are such things. Then the ocean is worth writing about just as man is. So I was lucky there. I've seen the marlin mate and know about that. So I leave that out. I've seen a school (or pod) of more than fifty sperm whales in that same stretch of water and once harpooned one nearly sixty feet in length and lost him. So I left that out. All the stories I know from the fishing village I leave out. But the knowledge is what makes the underwater part of the iceberg.

INTERVIEWER: Archibald MacLeish has spoken of a method of conveying experience to a reader which he said you developed while covering baseball games back in those *Kansas City Star* days. It was simply that experience is communicated by small details, intimately preserved, which have the effect of indicating the whole by making the reader conscious of what he had been aware of only subconsciously. . . .

HEMINGWAY: The anecdote is apocryphal. I never wrote baseball for the *Star*. What Archie was trying to remember was how I was trying to learn in Chicago in around 1920 and was searching for the unnoticed things that made emotions such as the way an outfielder tossed his glove without looking back to where it fell, the squeak of resin on canvas under a fighter's flat-soled gym shoes, the gray color of Jack Blackburn's skin when he had just come out of stir and other things I noted as a painter sketches. You saw Blackburn's strange color and the old razor cuts and the way he spun a man before you knew his history. These were the things which moved you before you knew the story.

INTERVIEWER: Have you ever described any type of situation of which you had no personal knowledge?

HEMINGWAY: That is a strange question. By personal knowledge do you mean carnal knowledge? In that case the answer is positive. A writer, if he is any good, does not describe. He invents or *makes* out of knowledge personal and impersonal and sometimes he seems to have unexplained knowledge which could come from forgotten racial or family experience. Who teaches the homing pigeon to fly as he does; where does a fighting bull get his bravery, or a hunting dog his nose? This is an elaboration or a condensation on that stuff we were talking in Madrid that time when my head was not to be trusted.

INTERVIEWER: How detached must you be from an experience before you can write about it in fictional terms? The African air crashes, for instance?

HEMINGWAY: It depends on the experience. One part of you sees it with complete detachment from the start. Another part is very involved. I think there is no rule about how soon one should write about it. It would depend on how well adjusted the individual was and on his or her recuperative powers. Certainly it is valuable to a trained writer to crash in an aircraft which burns. He learns several important things very quickly. Whether they will be of use to him is conditioned by survival. Survival, with honor, that outmoded and all-important word, is as difficult as ever and as all-important to a writer. Those who do not last are always more beloved since no one has to see them in their long, dull, unrelenting, no quarter given and no quarter received, fights that they make to do something as they believe it should be done before they die. Those who die or quit early and easy and with very good reason are preferred because they are understandable and human. Failure and well-disguised cowardice are more human and more beloved.

INTERVIEWER: Could I ask you to what extent you think the writer should concern himself with the sociopolitical problems of his times?

HEMINGWAY: Everyone has his own conscience and there should be no rules about how a conscience should function. All you can be sure about in a political-minded writer is that if his work should last you will have to skip the politics when you read it. Many of the so-called politically enlisted writers change their politics frequently. This is very exciting to them and to their political-literary reviews. Sometimes they even have to rewrite their viewpoints . . . and in a hurry. Perhaps it can be respected as a form of the pursuit of happiness.

INTERVIEWER: Has the political influence of Ezra Pound on the segregationalist Kasper had any effect on your belief that the poet ought to be released from St. Elizabeth's Hospital?[1]

HEMINGWAY: No. None at all. I believe Ezra should be released and allowed to write poetry in Italy on an undertaking by him to abstain from any politics. I would be happy to see Kasper jailed as soon as possible. Great poets are not necessarily girl guides nor scoutmasters nor splendid influences on youth. To name a few: Verlaine, Rimbaud, Shelley, Byron, Baudelaire, Proust, Gide, should not have been confined to prevent them from being aped in their thinking, their manners or their morals by local Kaspers. I am sure that it will take a footnote to this paragraph in ten years to explain who Kasper was.

INTERVIEWER: Would you say, ever, that there is any didactic intention in your work?

HEMINGWAY: Didactic is a word that has been misused and has spoiled. *Death in the Afternoon* is an instructive book.

INTERVIEWER: It has been said that a writer only deals with one or two ideas throughout his work. Would you say your work reflects one or two ideas?

HEMINGWAY: Who said that? It sounds much too simple. The man who said it possibly *had* only one or two ideas.

INTERVIEWER: Well, perhaps it would be better put this way: Graham Greene said in one of these interviews that a ruling passion gives to a shelf of novels the unity of a system. You yourself have said, I believe, that great writing comes out of a sense of injustice. Do you consider it important that a novelist be dominated in this way—by some such compelling sense?

HEMINGWAY: Mr. Greene has a facility for making statements that I do not possess. It would be impossible for me to make generalizations about a shelf of novels or a wisp of snipe or a gaggle of geese. I'll try a generalization though. A writer without a sense of justice and of injustice would be better off editing the year book of a school for exceptional children than writing novels. Another generalization. You see; they are not so difficult when they are sufficiently obvious. The most essential gift for a good writer is a built-in, shock-proof, shit detector. This is the writer's radar and all great writers have had it.

INTERVIEWER: Finally, a fundamental question: namely, as a creative writer what do you think is the function of your art? Why a representation of fact, rather than fact itself?

HEMINGWAY: Why be puzzled by that? From things that have happened and from things as they exist and from all things that you know and all those you cannot know, you make something through your invention that is not a representation but a whole new thing truer than anything true and alive, and you make it alive, and if you make it well enough, you give it immortality. That is why you write and for no other reason that you know of. But what about all the reasons that no one knows?

George Plimpton

---

1. As this issue went to press a Federal Court in Washington, D.C., dismissed all charges against Pound, clearing the way for his release from St. Elizabeth's. [April 18, 1958—ED.]

ERNEST HEMINGWAY, LITERARY CRITIC

DANIEL FUCHS

I

THOUGH THE CRITICS have found many things to praise in Hemingway, his mind was seldom one of them. Dwight Macdonald, in a funny if unoriginal essay, seems to express the consensus in saying that there is little evidence of thought in his writing, that for all his sureness of "instinct" as a writer, he strikes one as not particularly intelligent.[1] And Leslie Fiedler points to a pervasive humorlessness, a shortcoming of mind, in him as a writer.[2] If the critics have been sharks to Hemingway's Santiago, it is also a case of man bites shark. Who more proudly flaunted his contempt of them? Who was the first to make megalomania part of the novelist's personal style—as if critical intelligence were exercised only by those who live life all the way from the neck up? Yet Hemingway was a writer whose diction, whose tone, whose very existence as an artist imply a relationship with literary culture no less certain than that of the mythical New York beasts he excoriates.[3] I am not speaking of his characteristic literary ideas, his typical confrontations, his dilemmas and resolutions, the topography of his fictional world, about which much has been said, but of a more purely speculative function in which a particular prose or literary position or artist's reputation is under scrutiny, whether in direct comment or tangential remark. Though this is an admittedly bookish approach to Hemingway, it is one he has still to gain by, and the very fact that it can be congenial indicates a kind of resilience to his intelligence that is not often associated with it. He was a critic in spite of himself. What is more, he had a more than tacit commitment to a particular cast of literary mind which in terms of his own preferences constitutes a tradition; this commitment makes clear the extent and quality of his humor.

For all his one-time modernity, for all his appropriation of a unique style, for all his Bohemianism, Hemingway is in a literary tradition as old as the novel itself. If we are looking for illustrious forefathers we may go as far back as *Don Quixote*. Leicester Hemingway, in his biographical reminiscence, re-

Reprinted with permission from *American Literature,* XXXVI (January 1965), 431–451.

calls the following: "Ernest said there had been some wonderful men in the recent human past. These included Cervantes, Cellini and the Elizabethans."[4] And in *Death In the Afternoon* Hemingway tells us that he has "cared for" Cervantes, one of the very few writers who wrote before the nineteenth century whom he has made a point of complimenting.[5] Another is Fielding. He seems to have known Fielding well and felt the presence of a somehow kindred spirit to the extent that he quotes parts of the preface to *Joseph Andrews* as introductory squibs in his parody of Anderson, *The Torrents of Spring*. More than this, Fielding is the only author on Hemingway's fullest list of "musts" for young writers who wrote before the nineteenth century.[6] Along with the expected works of Stendhal, Flaubert, Tolstoy, we find him singling out *Joseph Andrews* and *Tom Jones* as part of the novel's most distinguished pedigree. His preference for Fielding should not surprise us, since he sees the unheroic hero in the world of his imagining and consistently mistrusts the elevated, the mystical, the glorious, the grand. In attacking Waldo Frank's *Virgin Spain* as "bedside mysticism"[7] he makes a remark which all innovators of realistic fiction would applaud: "All bad writers are in love with the epic."[8] (The comic epic in prose is another thing.) Parody, mistrust of the heroic, Cervantes, Fielding. The point I wish to make in this essay is that Hemingway is in what may be called the novel in burlesque tradition—burlesque conceived in its broadest range of sense, from explicit parody to implicit criticism. Hemingway is one of those writers who would not have written so well had others not written so poorly or, as the case may be, so differently, one of those novelists for whom the novel has been, among other things, literary criticism. Flaubert, Joyce, Mark Twain —all of whom he held in the highest regard—are others. All of these gave a new meaning to the word realism.

Ezra Pound once remarked that Hemingway is pre-eminently the wiseguy,[9] and though Delmore Schwartz dismisses this as an extravagance, Pound is here, as he often is, profoundly right about a literary peer. Hemingway's prose is indeed motivated by a comic contempt of standard English in its aspect of respectability, gentility, polite euphemism, though it never forgets it in its aspect of biblical plainness and repetition. Furthermore, as we shall have occasion to see, his wiseguy intransigence is manifest so often in the way he builds a scene, conceives a character, projects a vision, that it, as much as anything else, marks his characteristic style. This is at the heart of his critical sense. When this is understood, Macdonald's remarks, say, about Hemingway's affinity to his "opposites . . . Stendhal and Tolstoi—interesting that he should feel awed by them—who had no style at all, no effects"—will be easily countered. For example, what writer could we associate more with the battle

initiations of Fabrice del Dongo and Nickolai Rostov than Hemingway? Hemingway's joke, his *Kunst,* lies in showing that things as they really are are
different from what they are like in story books and political speeches, that the
writer's duty is to cut away the imaginative deadwood, that realism is so often,
in Tolstoy's phrase, "making things strange," that the wiseguy can be the
source of an unexpected, bracing wisdom. Hemingway's distinction as a writer
is that he considered this insight not only as matter but as manner. Macdonald
speaks of him as if his writing were separable from his mind, which may be
the reason he finds so little intelligence in him.

Hemingway, in short, like Cervantes, Fielding, Stendhal, Flaubert, Mark
Twain, and Joyce, writes what is in this sense an anti-literary literature. Like
that of many of the modernists of the twenties, Hemingway's work was at first
hardly considered literature at all. Reminiscing about the early Paris days, he
considers "all of the stories back in the mail that came in through a slit in the
saw mill door, with notes of rejection that would never call them stories, but
always anecdotes, sketches, contes, etc."[10] The genteel American response to
his work was typified by his parents. His mother (a reader of Walter Scott who
named her summer place "Windemere") and father returned *In Our Time* and
were "bewildered and shocked" by *The Sun Also Rises.*[11] One need only teach
In Our Time to observe even now the curious mixture of reverence and
confusion in response to it.

Hemingway did not write better prose than that which appears in the *In
Our Time* sequence (he has, of course, done worse), and it is this prose which
registers as clearly as any his wiseguy stance. "On the Quai at Smyrna," which
is an introductory sketch, exhibits a tension between the comfortable, genteel
English of the English captain who is narrator and the war experience which
it cannot seem to contain. Listening to the dispossessed women, he says, "The
strange thing was . . . [how] they screamed at that time." They would be
"quieted" by the searchlight: "That always did the trick." The dead ones had
to be "cleared off" the pier. One was a "most extraordinary case"—the one
whose legs drew stiff. Where English is capable of recording the shock of war
it is in a Gulliver-like recording of detail. The euphemism, the detachment of
the captain's manner is painfully modified by what he actually sees. But the
captain seems to be aware of the inability of his language to express his feelings.
Hence his irony in describing the harbor: "There were plenty of nice things
floating around in it. That was the only time in my life I got so I dreamed about
things." In his nervous matter-of-factness the Englishman sounds like a
grown-up Huck Finn. "The Greeks were nice chaps too. When they evacuated
they had all their baggage animals they couldn't take with them so they just

broke their forelegs and dumped them into the shallow water. . . . It was all a pleasant business. My word yes a most pleasant business." The final turn of the screw is that his casual, genteel manner explodes in his face as his intended irony becomes indistinguishable from it.

This opening sketch about the Greco-Turkish war is connected to the final vignette in which Hemingway, or a surrogate, is interviewing the Greek king. A tension exists between the grim realities of revolutionary politics and the inanities of genteel conversation. Perhaps the best example of this deflationary technique is the Chapter IV vignette.[12]

It was a frightfully hot day. We'd jammed an absolutely perfect barricade across the bridge. It was simply priceless. A big old wrought-iron grating from the front of a house. Too heavy to lift and you could shoot through it and they would have to climb over it. It was absolutely topping. They tried to get over it, and we potted them from forty yards. They rushed it, and officers came out alone and worked on it. It was an absolutely perfect obstacle. Their officers were very fine. We were frightfully put out when we heard the flank had gone, and we had to fall back.

Here again Hemingway observes the inadequacies of a language not equipped to deal with the destructive realities, an Englished language echoing from afar the terms of hunting and country festivities. Though the language is English, the way it is scrutinized is American. That the barricade is "perfect . . . simply priceless . . . absolutely topping" does not blend well with the murderous activity in which the English are both agents and victims. Then, too, being "frightfully put out" when the flank goes is something of a different order from a frightfully hot day. The docility of the language intensifies the panic, all of which is to the writer's credit. It may well be, as Carlos Baker informs us, that Hemingway is here imitating the speech of his friend Captain E. E. Dorman-Smith. But the use he is making of it has little relevance to friendship.

The most sustained piece Hemingway has done in this vein is the rarely noticed story, "A Natural History of the Dead." In conception a small *tour de force,* it is a montage of two violently dissonant prose styles: the first we are to take as standard English; the second as vintage Hemingway. The standard English style is not identifiable as the style of any of the four stooges named —W. H. Hudson, Gilbert White, Bishop Stanley, and Mungo Park: rather it is a mock-gentleman style which attempts to give us the essence of the English clubman's adventure story. The wiseguy irony implicit is that naturalistic adventure should be rendered so unadventurously, so prissily, as if Africa were an extension of the club. Mungo Park is quoted in pastiche; the stiff-upper-lip confidence of his prose is almost indistinguishable from Hemingway's parody.

When that persevering traveller, Mungo Park, was at one period of his course fainting in the vast wilderness of an African desert, naked and alone, considering his days as numbered and nothing appearing to remain for him to do but to lie down and die, a small moss-flower of extraordinary beauty caught his eye. "Though the whole plant," says he, "was no larger than one of my fingers, I could not contemplate the delicate confirmation [*sic*] of its roots, leaves and capsules without admiration. Can that Being who planted, watered and brought to perfection, in this obscure part of the world, a thing which appears of so small importance, look with unconcern upon the situation and suffering of creatures formed after his own image? Surely not. Reflections like these would not allow me to despair; I started up and, disregarding both hunger and fatigue, travelled forward, assured that relief was at hand; and I was not disappointed."[13]

In Hemingway's story Park is always "that persevering traveler" and he perseveres because, like Bishop Stanley, he knows that the study of Natural History is linked with an increase in faith, in "the protecting eye of that Providence." Park, who starts out (attempting to ascertain the course of the Niger) in a blue coat with yellow buttons and ends up two and a half years later naked, drinking at a trough between two cows, is more subject to despair than Hemingway will allow. Parody, however, is not known for its qualities of fairness. There is, in fact, a somewhat unwarranted calm about the Scot's prose and manner. It contrasts sharply with the hysteria, the *nada,* which Hemingway chillingly conveys in the second half of the story (after some funny transitions). Nor is Park's prose designed to record things memorably; an elephant is a "powerful and docile creature," a native a "poor untutored slave."

War is what Hemingway is talking about in the story. When he writes, "Let us therefore see what inspiration we may derive from the dead," he is attempting a *reductio* of the providential: "One wonders what that persevering traveler, Mungo Park, would have seen on a battlefield in hot weather to restore his confidence . . . and have any such thoughts as Mungo Park about those formed in His own image." Associating the providential and the idea of an ennobling death weighted with significance with the so-called Humanist literary movement, which in a mock-footnote he calls "an extinct phenomenon," Hemingway flaunts his first-hand experience of war like so many medals. If Hemingway's accusation that the Humanists were "dead in their youth of choice" is hysterical (it has its ironic point, e.g., Irving Babbitt arriving at his willed, fixed position in his twenties), few would dispute his feeling that the violence at the center of contemporary experience is one of the things that makes the Humanist categories seem inadequate. Moreover, the entire piece can be seen in terms of the old realistic priority placed on actuality.

The last section of the piece, all dialogue, emerges as the last refinement in actually being there. In this dialogue the writer records not only the disintegration of abstraction but of language as well. It need hardly be said that the negation expressed in the story does not leave the reader with a sense of all problems solved. What Hemingway succeeded in doing is making his reader more sharply aware of a dubious prose and the too comfortable assumptions supporting it. He has referred to this brutal story as being "written in popular style and . . . designed to be the Whittier's *Snow Bound* of our time." No "angels near at hand" in this frozen cave, no "harmless novel" this, but rather the mind of the writer engaged in the typical modernist stripping away of empty forms.

Probably the most famous passage in Hemingway does precisely this as it at the same time reminds us that this stripping down can be the underside of the coherence one may achieve in the face of its nihilistic potential. Frederic Henry tells us that abstract words like glory, honor, and courage seemed obscene beside the concrete names of villages. Hemingway's work can be seen as an attempt to redefine the actuality these abstractions might have. Pound could easily perceive the satiric thrust which this task inevitably entailed. He had written to Harriet Monroe that good writing needs ideas derived from seeing life in arrangement, the design in life as it exists, not the trying to see life according to an idea.[14] Pound taught his friends to go in fear of abstraction. Polite English became a victim. One of the characteristics of the twenties is that it gave rise to a number of highly stylized literary languages, testimony to the belief that the language, the civilization, needed reappraisal. The assumption that any writer uses English as if he were inventing it is much more relevant to the production of that era than it is to that of our own day. It is part of the orthodoxy of modernism.

II

Hemingway's disenchantment with polite English is generalized into a pervasive Anglophobia. Often this is fairly explicit, as in Frederic Henry's conversation with Count Greffi.

> "Oh, but when you are tired it will be easier for you to talk English."
> "American."
> "Yes. American. You will please talk American. It is a delightful language."[15]

This distinction between American and English is something which Hemingway felt deeply, if hyperbolically. It is, of course, more than a difference in diction and syntax. His very name—Hemingway—was to his wry sense of things too right-sounding, too English; he liked to be called Hemingstein and would sometimes sign his name in letters with even greater comic distortion. For Hemingway "English" often serves as a shorthand for the storybook ending, the providential, the public display, the political rhetoric, the disguise of privileged class, the pseudo-chivalric manner, the exacerbating euphemism of gentility. Occasionally the Hemingway hero will fall into it to his embarrassment as when Frederic Henry is told by Catherine that her fiancé was killed in the battle of the Somme. "It was a ghastly show," he says. "Were you there?" she asks. "No," he replies.[16] In *The Sun Also Rises* a Mrs. Braddocks introduces Robert Prentiss, a rising new novelist from New York by way of Chicago who had, Jake Barnes tells us, "some sort of an English accent." Jake's disgust is immediately evident. Prentiss asks Jake if he finds "Paris amusing?" and Jake is obviously angered. "Oh, how charmingly you get angry. I wish I had that faculty," says Prentiss, adding to Jake's animal repugnance of him. When Brett tries to brighten his mood he tells her that it has been a "priceless" evening. Brett herself is called Lady Brett when Jake holds her in contempt, when he considers her Englishness: "Brett had a title too. Lady Ashley. To Hell with Brett. To Hell with you, Lady Ashley."[17] And in *The Torrents of Spring,* we are given to believe that it is characteristically English to grace hastily the distinguished new Englishman, the dying Henry James, with the Order of Merit.[18] Similarly, the English tourist is the most removed for Hemingway, the most unreal. Arriving at the festival in Pamplona is a "sightseeing car . . . with twenty-five Englishwomen in it. They sat in the big, white car and looked through their glasses at the fiesta. . . . The fiesta absorbed even the Biarritz English so that you did not see them unless you passed close to a table." Of course, they are absurd at the bullfight: "The Biarritz crowd did not like it. They thought Romero was afraid."[19]

Some of Hemingway's best friends are English—or some of his most amiable characters: Harris in *The Sun Also Rises,* for one ("Take Harris. Still Harris was not of the upper classes," Jake notes). (Catherine Barkley is Scottish, not English. When asked by Rinaldi if she loved England, she replies: "Not too well. I'm Scotch, you see.") It is the English in their aspect of decadent aristocracy that consistently elicit Hemingway's deflationary wit. "When you were with the English," Jake says, "you got into the habit of using English expression in your thinking. The English spoken language—the upper classes, anyway—must have fewer words than the Eskimo."[20] And the Hemingway hero must be some sort of expert on languages with few words. Nor is this aggression typical of only the younger Hemingway. No Hemingway hero is more contemptuous of the English than Colonel Cantwell of *Across the*

River and Into the Trees: " 'My lady has called twice,' the concierge said in English. Or whatever that language should be called we all speak, the Colonel thought. Leave it at English. That is about what they have left. They should be allowed to keep the name of the language." His young lady friend wants to learn "American." The Colonel's anti-English feelings are perhaps even more intense in his account of Montgomery: "I have seen him come into an hotel and change from his proper uniform into a crowd-catching kit to go out in the evening to animate the populace . . . he is a British General. Whatever that means." Cantwell adds to this description of "Field Marshal Bernard Law Montgomery" the information that he knew he was not great.[21]

It is as if the English were the source of most civilized evasions and distortions, a severe case, a monolithic instance of what Lawrence calls mental consciousness. Hemingway, too—in a parallel which does not imply an identity—encountered the dominant culture with disgust and aggression, countering respectability with an aesthetic primitivism, an intellectual Bohemianism. There is a balance in his work between primitivism and culture, between the physical ordeal, the victory of the code character and the brooding though anti-rational intelligence of the hero. He is, in Richard Chase's phrase, a highbrow-lowbrow;[22] or, to put it another way, he is a redskin half-paleface. He portrays defiance and grace in terms which are more than physical, making a raid upon a faltering cultural style. His Anglophobia is not to be strictly equated with a hatred of all things English so much as it is to be understood as a symbol of the failure of a gentility which results in a turning from life.

What is most inimical to Hemingway is the tradition of American literature he identifies as English. He maintains that "Emerson, Hawthorne, Whittier and Company wrote like exiled English colonials from an England of which they were never a part to a newer England that they were making. Very good men with small, dried and excellent wisdom of Unitarians; men of letters; Quakers with a sense of humor." What is perhaps most valuable in Hemingway's judgment is the clarity of his rejection in relation to his own writing. "All these men were gentlemen or wished to be. They were all very respectable. They did not use the words that people always have used in speech, the words that survive in language. Nor would you gather they had bodies. They had minds, yes. Nice, dry, clean minds."[23] If there is a broad truth in Hemingway's remarks it is of the kind that resides in John Jay Chapman's hyperbolic remark that the one thing a man in the future would not be able to know from our mid-nineteenth century writers (with Hawthorne an obvious exception here too) is that there were two sexes in America. But even the broad truth should not have completely blinded him to the fact that Emerson, albeit in a very different way, was very much engaged in the transformation of cultural values, in defining what was new world and how the new world was superior to the old. Extravagant as Hemingway's judgment may seem to be, it is more or less the going judgment of the polite, occasional, literary, picturesque, Europe-imitating schoolroom poets.

III

Hemingway's criticism comprehends, then, not only a renovation of language but in many cases an involvement with and judgment of other writers. *The Torrents of Spring,* the spirited but slight parody of Anderson in the role of victim of abstraction, almost succeeds in being as funny as *Dark Laughter* often is; it is a minor instance, more important as rehearsal than performance. Hemingway's confrontation of other writers was not merely in the vein of parody nor merely a presence in his minor work. The power of *A Farewell to Arms* is the power of negation, a negation which can be understood as his expression of ideas and evaluation of literary reputations that were very much in the air in the twenties. Carlos Baker mentions Hardy in connection with this novel; an explicit connection can be drawn. The sense of an indifferent cosmos, or even a cruel President of the Immortals underlies the work. The grim confusion of tragedy and farce is also Hardyesque. But Hemingway delineates this confusion in a burlesque dimension. He presents the brutal war as a series of jokes—it never happened this way in the books (except those of Stendhal, Tolstoy, Crane). Frederic Henry is no hero, not even a soldier, but an ambulance driver. And even in this capacity it does not matter whether he supervises the removal of the sick or not. The transference worked better when he was not there. Hurt in battle, he is "blown up while . . . eating cheese." Even if he had had notions of military glory he tells us that his gun jumped so sharply that there was no question of hitting anything. The Italian army itself is disorganized and disenchanted and appears like something out of a comic opera. The soldiers' helmets are not uniform; most of them are too big and come down almost over the ears of the men who wear them. The one "legitimate hero," Moretti, "bored everyone he met with his stories." The Italians fire on themselves. Frederic Henry is suspected of being a German in Italian uniform—the only alternative is the separate peace, the way of the anti-hero. And there is "Oh love, let us be true." But this is a Hardy-cum-Hemingway universe. The illomen rain, Catherine's fatalistic feeling about it, the sad, haunting folk refrain (O, western wind), the irrational fear justified by the indifference of the universe, the miscast woman made for a good providence —all these bring Henry to a Hardyesque explanation with a Hemingway twist:

"If people bring so much courage to this world the world has to kill them to break them, so of course it kills them. The world breaks everyone and afterward many are strong at the broken places. But those that will not break it kills. It kills the very good and the very gentle and the very brave impartially." Or again, Henry on a modest version of the President of the Immortals: "They threw you in and told you the rules and the first time they caught you off base they killed you."[24]

If Hemingway's nihilism at this point seems lyrical at best or juvenile at worst, it gains in stature by comparison. Henry himself makes the judgments for us in his conversation with Count Greffi as the subject turns to war books. Greffi speaks first:

"There is 'Le Feu' by a Frenchman, Barbusse. There is 'Mr. Britling Sees Through It [*sic*].' "
"No, he doesn't."
"What?"
"He doesn't see through it. Those books were at the hospital."
"Then you have been reading?"
"Yes, but nothing any good."
"I thought 'Mr. Britling' a very good study of the English middle-class soul."
"I don't know about the soul."[25]

In the introduction to *Men at War* Hemingway adds to this: "The only good war book to come out during the last war was 'Under Fire' by Henri Barbusse. He was the first one to show us, the boys who went from school or college to the last war, that you could protest in anything besides poetry, the gigantic useless slaughter in generalship that characterized the Allied conduct of the war from 1915 to 1917 . . . when you came to read it over to try to take something permanent and representative from it the book did not stand up. Its greatest quality was his courage in writing the book when he did. They had learned to tell the truth without screaming."[26]

Since both *Under Fire* and *Mr. Britling Sees It Through* ran through several printings in a short time in the United States, Frederick Henry was alluding to well-known books. Barbusse's sensational tone, his egalitarian grievances, his operatic manner, his pacifist editorializing—all give us something of the war that Hemingway does not. But in point of fable, answerable style, sustained psychological portraiture, and accuracy of observation, Hemingway has mastered a subject in part from noticing the shortcomings of Barbusse.

He thinks more kindly of him, however, than of H. G. Wells. Britling, an exemplary Britisher, a man of letters who inhabits the England of "Old John Bull," who considers the backstreets of London "an excrescence," and who believes that "one does not love women, one loves children," is of the genteel, complacent, mental sort that Hemingway likes to abuse. Britling, who despite ominous signs cannot imagine a world war, thinks of the Sarajevo murders as "something out of 'The Prisoner of Zenda.' " The war does break out, and Britling, responding to the narrator's call for a disciplined and clarified will, becomes a special constable. He rationalizes the war as the way the world reconstructs itself and the length of it by the notion that too brief a struggle might lead to a squabble for plunder. The protracted war brings nothing but the death of Mr. Britling's son, his subsequent breakdown, and, finally, his recovery with a wish for a world-federal-republic. If God means anything, thinks Britling, he means tenderness. Wells's novel suggests more than it dramatizes, and its appeal was largely a matter of timeliness. We are given a picture of complacency shattered. Some of the actuality of war is conveyed through the letters of Britling's son. Britling does, in Wells's view, see it through. Henry's point seems to be that he literally did not see much of it at all, or did only from the grandstands. And if Britling's hopeful internationalism and grasping at deity are illustrative of his middle-class soul, these are, for Henry, pale abstractions compared to the experience he has lived through. Henry's mistrust of abstraction, including the middle-class soul, obviously does not blind us to the fact that Britling's ideas are indeed alternatives. The literary point, however, is that in the novel they are almost offhand suggestions. Hemingway is typically associating writing well with telling the truth, the kind of truth *A Farewell to Arms* reveals.

Neither of these novels is important enough to focus Hemingway's main ideas very well. It would take his grappling with writers of greater moment to him than Barbusse and Wells for him to get at the center of his literary position. We have already encountered one of them.

IV

In 1925, Carl Van Doren, writing in the *Century Magazine,* spoke of "two men who have lately divided between them the honors of literary eminence" in England and France: Thomas Hardy and Anatole France.[27] How much of these then giant figures had Hemingway read? There is a juvenilia sketch done in the style of France called "A Divine Gesture,"[28] in which God, as much a tyrant as France's Ialdabaoth, convinces his wormlike followers that they must not squirm in dissent. The mingling of the mundane and the theological, the satire of religion with anti-Catholic emphasis, the non-representational quality of a whimsical idea-narrative indicate that Hemingway knew about *The Revolt of the Angels* even if he had not read it.

There is explicit mention of Anatole France and Hardy in *The Sun Also Rises.* Frances, Cohn's impatient mistress, is angry with him:

"You're thirty-four. Still, I suppose that is young for a great writer. Look at Hardy. Look at Anatole France. He died just a little while ago. Robert doesn't think he's any good though. Some of his French friends told him."[29]

Again the allusion to acknowledged greatness, this time with a difference. From the vantage point of the extreme right, the extreme left, and surrealism, new French writers pointed to Anatole France's vulnerability. For the Americans in Paris, the culture hero whose aesthetic would be the most serious indictment of France was Flaubert. Hemingway has said that he was "the one that we believed in, loved without criticism."[30] His control, his clarity, his rage, his irony—all of these were instructive to the advance-guard expatriates who were indifferent to the loosely strung idea-narratives, the insistent abstraction of the politically-minded later France.

There is a good deal of pastiche in *The Sun Also Rises,* with burlesque references to Mencken and Brooks among the most transparent.[31] There is, moreover, another allusion to Anatole France which is now somewhat obscure but particularly instructive. Bill Gorton tells Jake about "irony and pity"— "They're mad about it in New York"—words which were sacred to Anatole France. Bill and Jake are in Burguete for fishing and Jake is digging for the worms. Bill, thinking of Anatole France, fancies Jake a capitalist type:

"I saw you out of the window," he said. "Didn't want to interrupt you. What were you doing? Burying your money?"

"You lazy bum!"

"Been working for the common good? Splendid. I want you to do that every morning. . . ."

"Work for the good of all." Bill stepped into his underclothes. "Show irony and pity."

I started out of the room with the tackle bag, the nets, and the rod case. . . .

"Aren't you going to show a little irony and pity?"

I thumbed my nose.

"That's not irony."

As I went downstairs I heard Bill singing, "Irony and Pity. When you're feeling . . . Oh, Give them Irony and Give them Pity. Oh, give them Irony. When they're feeling . . . Just a little irony. Just a little pity . . ." He kept on singing until he came downstairs. The tune was: "The

Bells are Ringing for Me and My Gal." I was reading a week-old Spanish
paper.

"What's all this irony and pity?"

"What? Don't you know about Irony and Pity?"

"No. Who got it up?"

"Everybody. They're mad about it in New York. It's just like the Fratellinis used to be."[32]

The passage spoofs a well-known Anatolian phrase, the source of which would
have been much more familiar to literary men of the twenties than it is to us
today. It is from the important prose ramble, *The Garden of Epicurus.*

The more I think over human life the more I am persuaded we ought to
choose Irony and Pity for its assessors and judges, as the Egyptians called upon
the goddess Isis and the goddess Nephtys on behalf of their dead. Irony and
Pity are both of good counsel; the first with her smiles makes life agreeable;
the other sanctifies it with her tears. The Irony I invoke is no cruel deity. She
mocks neither love nor beauty. She is gentle and kindly disposed. Her mirth
disarms anger and it is she who teaches us to laugh at rogues and fools, whom
but for her we might be so weak as to hate.[33]

Any discussion of France's irony is complicated by the fact that there are,
generally speaking, three phases of it. The irony of *The Crime of Sylvester
Bonnard,* an early work, is indeed indulgent and smiling. In *The Garden of
Epicurus,* however, as in the contemporaneous *At the Sign of the Reine Pé-
dauque,* the indulgence is more willed than felt. What is genuinely present is
a disarmingly playful nihilism bordering on despair. Though there is still a
verbal, or somewhat more than verbal, balancing of irony and pity in *The
Garden of Epicurus,* by the time France writes the works which now seem his
best or at least most popular, *Penguin Island* and *The Revolt of the Angels,*
irony stands pretty much alone, stripped of indulgence. It is a bitter irony,
the logical extension of the nihilism of *The Garden of Epicurus.* It is hardly
likely, then, that "irony and pity" would be understood by literary men in the
twenties in its earlier, gentle incarnation. *The Garden of Epicurus* must have
been considered in the same context as the later works, a temptation to a
despair it was only too easy to feel. Bill Gorton initiates the spoof and he is
not only a good friend or even an alter ego, but a symbol of Jake's health.

If irony and pity were the rage in New York, or anything resembling it,
Hardy, too, most explicitly in *The Dynasts,* would be a reason why. Though
Hemingway would never dream of a spirit world, even as an artistic device,
the Spirit of the Pities and the Spirits Ironic express a sense of life that

paralleled and lent imaginative impetus to post-war themes. As we have seen, *A Farewell to Arms* is an expression of this world view. What does relate Hemingway to writers so very different from him as France and Hardy is the pose of the Ecclesiast. Solomon was an old man when he expressed the dim, retrospective view (France and Hardy were always old), but this did not inhibit the young American who, it is clear, had just cause for a pessimistic view. The discrepancy between venerable wisdom and eternal youth is one that would become telling when Hemingway would get only chronologically older.

Irony *is* an important element in Hemingway's fiction; and pity, too, is a subject for his defining. The irony may be the old irony of fate that we get in Catherine's death or Jake's wound or the sharks that plague Santiago. But more characteristic is irony as a matter of tone, as something controlled by Hemingway. That is, the spectatorial irony of France and Hardy, passive with some aggression on the one hand, cruel with some remission on the other, arises out of a sense of loss, a meaninglessness, which Hemingway and his surrogate heroes must do something about to survive. The older fatalism is replaced by stoicism; despite the threat of disintegration, the hero controls. To be sure, the hero is not a consummate expression of the mores and dominant conventions of his society; he finds his integrity in the face of them. But where the irony of Hardy and Anatole France issued into the absurd, the irony of Hemingway is, more characteristically, a sober naming of the ridiculous. The first implies loss, the second a minimal gain. The first is universal in tendency, the second is more expressive of particular men at a particular historical moment. If Jake lacks much conviction, and the worst are full of passionate intensity, the difference between Jake and a character like Krebs, in "Soldiers Home," should be underscored. Jake's negation is selective (though sometimes provincial), a fact which itself implies a vantage point of stabilizing intelligence. Jake is, certainly, an observer; but he is also an actor in a novel whose lessons of morality and style are by now so clear that it emerges as Ernest Hemingway's Morality Play. As an observer, Jake is collaterally related to the straight-man voyagers of eighteenth-century fiction who indirectly expressed the irony of the author. The things they so factually observe! This, of course, is part of the central technical inspiration in *Huckleberry Finn;* as everyone knows, Hemingway owes much to Mark Twain's peculiarly American expression of it (the sensitive, responsible though apparently amoral initiate, the leaving of society, the violence giving over to bad dreams, the mistrust of abstraction, the deflation of the chivalric, the vernacular voice, the lonely equilibrium of self—though Jake is aware of any ironies and not mainly the agent for their indirect expression). It is also related to Flaubert's exemplary irony, which is at base nothing more than his being painfully, mockingly present in a world whose most common occurrences have their own kind of incredibility. The most common meaning the word now possesses in relation to literature is the one which originates in the venerable split between the writer and a society he knows only too well. The code characters notwithstanding, the real hero in Hemingway is his prose and those characters who are a surrogate for the disillusioned irony it expresses. His concept of the hero, accordingly, is one of his burlesque elements. Jake, for example, is not a great lover or a formidable fighter or a thinker who prospers in the rational order derived from a contemplation of disorder. His hero is the private, passive, ultimately modest man, a hero of abnegation, the very precariousness of whose selfhood qualifies him for minimal saintliness, for disinterested action. Yet, if the hero does not win, neither does he lose. If one may pursue the figure, he holds life to a draw, with, among others of a very different stamp, the almost feminine virtues of sensitivity, sympathy, intuition (he is sometimes afraid of the dark and even cries!). Hemingway's criticism of language, then, is also a criticism of personal style, just as it is a criticism of cultural assumptions. His characteristic irony, like that of the novelists in burlesque already named, involves a persistent attitude toward culture, toward books. This is nowhere more apparent than in *The Sun Also Rises.*

At Princeton Robert Cohn "read too much"; in Hemingway's world this is analogous to drinking too much. Cohn lives in a fantasy world.

He had been reading W. H. Hudson. That sounds like an innocent occupation, but Cohn had read and reread "The Purple Land." "The Purple Land" is a very sinister book if read too late in life. It recounts splendid imaginary amorous adventures of a perfect English gentleman in an intensely romantic land, the scenery of which is very well described. For a man to take it at thirty-four as a guide-book to what life holds is about as safe as it would be for a man of the same age to enter Wall Street direct from a French convent, equipped with a complete set of the more practical Alger books. Cohn, I believe, took "The Purple Land" as literally as though it had been an R. G. Dun report. You understand me, he made some reservations, but on the whole the book to him was sound.[34]

(Cohn's suggestion that he and Jake go off to South America together shows that he had not grasped Hudson's "loner" psychology very well.) If Hardy and Anatole France were a too apparent temptation to despair, W. H. Hudson represented a rainbow evasion of difficult considerations. Should it seem that Jake has too easy game in ridiculing *The Purple Land,* it is to be remembered that Hudson was considered one of the best writers of English prose by no less a judge than Ford Madox Ford.[35] First published in 1885, it was popular enough to be issued in The Modern Library in 1916. This does not prevent one from sharing Jake's opinion of the book. Richard Lamb's tendency to treat women as part of the local color, his wide-eyed primitivism, his political myopia, would support Jake's ironic view. And if Jake is not joking in saying that the scenery is very well described, perhaps he should be: "great plains smiling with everlasting spring; ancient woods; swift beautiful rivers; ranges of blue hills stretching away to the dim horizon. And beyond those fair slopes, how many leagues of pleasant wilderness are sleeping in the sunshine, where the wild flowers waste their sweetness and no plough turns the fruitful soil."[36]

Hudson's sentimentality, his too easy preference for the inanimate to the human, are symptomatic of the lack of personal responsibility that marks his narrator's debonair adventures. Cohn would be attracted. Jake, one of Hemingway's moral scorekeepers, would not be. Cohn is more of a throwback to the chivalric hero than is the flighty Richard Lamb. When we are almost ready to prefer Cohn's idealized preferences to the broken relationships of everyone else, we need only recall that Cohn is usually wrong in his judgments of others. "I don't believe she could marry anybody she didn't like," he says of Brett. "She's done it twice," Jake answers. Cohn is "ready to do battle for his lady love." Because "he was so sure that Brett loved him. He was going to stay, and true love would conquer all."[37] Part of Cohn's sentimentality is that he can love a woman only in an "affair." Brett is ultimately unattainable, hence desirable. In this sense she is a lost generation Dulcinea, nowhere nearly as perfect as Cohn imagines her to be. Cohn may be seen as a mean, distant relative of Don Quixote; his windmills are ladies, his giants the romanticizing of them. There must be a way other than schoolboy chivalry to dispel the cosmic ironies.

Though the ironies have excluded Jake from the final consummation, they cannot entirely reduce him. His decency remains intact. Though he has suffered a temporary collapse due to Brett's receptivity to all comers, the consequences of this receptivity are not something he could have entirely foreseen. He does what he can to keep Romero from her. The last line of the book— "Isn't it pretty to think so?"—is a sign of Jake's sanity as well as his irony; it names Brett as another who, although she gave up Romero, lives essentially in fantasy. Despite the gloom of much of the book, a good part of it is pervaded by high spirits stemming from the peace of nature and the self-possession of those who have a clear object of ridicule. It should come as no great surprise that Hemingway regarded the book "as in part a humorous one";[38] or that he regarded the lost generation tag as splendid bombast.

Burlesque novelists in the past have often had more to sustain them—a return to happy normalcy, a love for the thing burlesqued. Hemingway has only an attenuated connection with this kind of affirmation; when it is made it is made most typically through the code characters who, in effect, ritualistically overcome a physical crisis analogous to the psychological one that confronts the hero. They overcome the ironies; they are not merely marionettes; their pain has meaning; they help to redefine glory, honor, courage. Hemingway's art is in this way confessional, yet the use of this adjective makes us hasten to add that he has less to say about the meaning of mental suffering. It is this, not the question of whether he had an intelligent encounter with culture, that renders him vulnerable. Hemingway *has* run Huck Finn through life, or part of life; he has stopped short of a maturity that would put him in the same ring with the greatest novelists—as he himself admits in his deferential remarks about Tolstoy. If Hemingway now reads, at times, too much like a classic writer of the twenties, if the artifice of understatement is once again giving over to a more open *cri de coeur,* if it is thought that the ironic brilliance of aesthetic realism fosters a paucity of human commitment, if it is felt that Hemingway sold the Romantic self short, if irony itself is viewed as the emblem of a Bohemian intransigence which the writer can no longer afford—whether he feels that there is no viable Bohemian community or he feels that identification with our most characteristic suffering is the way of transcending it it is a tribute to him that a number of our recent novelists, Norman Mailer and Saul Bellow for example, still think of him as an angel to wrestle with, a father to kill. Considering the narrowness, even the exclusiveness, of his vision, it has had considerable endurance, attributable in good measure to the fact that he made his encounter with literature an inextricable part of it.

1. Dwight Macdonald, "Ernest Hemingway," *Encounter,* XVIII, 116–117 (Jan., 1962).

2. Leslie Fiedler, "Hemingway in Ketchum," *Partisan Review,* XXIX, 396, 398 (Summer, 1962).

3. For his most extreme statement on "New York literary reviews," see Hemingway's preface to Elio Vittorini's *In Sicily.* Nowhere in his work is there such a density of, shall we say, humanistic tropes.

4. Leicester Hemingway, *My Brother, Ernest Hemingway* (Cleveland, 1962), p. 171.

5. *Death in the Afternoon* (New York, 1932), p. 73.

6. *Esquire,* IV, 21, 174a, 174b (Oct., 1935).

7. *Death in the Afternoon,* p. 53.

8. *Ibid.,* pp. 35–36.

9. Quoted by Delmore Schwartz in *Ernest Hemingway: The Man and His Work,* ed. John K. M. McCaffery (Cleveland and New York, 1950), p. 114.

10. *Green Hills of Africa* (New York, 1935), p. 70.

11. *My Brother, Ernest Hemingway,* p. 100.

12. *The Short Stories of Ernest Hemingway* (New York, 1953), pp. 87–88, 113.

13. *Ibid.,* pp. 440–441.

14. From a letter of Ezra Pound to Harriet Monroe, in the Harriet Monroe collection in the University of Chicago Library, dated Dec. 15, 1915. Paraphrased with permission of the University of Chicago Library.

15. *A Farewell to Arms* (New York, 1929), p. 269.

16. *Ibid.,* pp. 18–19.

17. *The Sun Also Rises* (New York, 1926), pp. 21, 30.

18. *The Hemingway Reader* (New York, 1953), p. 51.

19. *Op. cit.,* pp. 205, 217.

20. *Ibid.,* p. 149.

21. *Across the River and Into the Trees* (New York, 1951), pp. 195, 206, 134.

22. *The Democratic Vista* (New York, 1958), p. 52.

23. *Green Hills of Africa,* p. 21. Longfellow, too, is fair game: "Someone with English blood has written, 'Life is real, life is earnest, and the grave is not its goal.' And where did they bury him? And what became of the reality of his earnestness?" The apparent objection is to Longfellow's abstract, moralizing quality. Yet the shrill, juvenile quality of the nihilism here expressed makes one think of Longfellow's virtues.

24. *A Farewell to Arms,* pp. 259, 338.

25. *Ibid.,* p. 270.

26. *Men at War,* ed. Ernest Hemingway (New York, 1942), p. 9.

27. *Century Magazine,* CX, 419 (Jan. 25, 1925).

28. *Double Dealer,* III, 267–268 (May, 1922).

29. *Op. cit.,* pp. 50–51.

30. *Green Hills of Africa,* p. 71.

31. See pp. 43, 115. Also worth noting is Jake's mention of A. E. W. Mason in that it expresses the old realistic ridicule of the marvelous: "I was reading a wonderful story about a man who had frozen in the Alps and then fallen into a glacier and disappeared, and his bride was going to wait twenty-five years exactly for his body to come out on the moraine, while her true love waited too" (p. 120). Jake also reads from Turgenieff's "A Sportsman's Sketches," which, in its unobtrusive craftsmanship, clarifies and makes sober: "I had read it before but it seemed quite new. The country became quite clear and the feeling of pressure in my head seemed to loosen" (p. 147).

32. *Ibid.,* pp. 113–114. The Fratellinis are the continental circus act. For Mencken and Brooks, see pp. 43, 115.

33. *The Garden of Epicurus,* trans. Alfred Allison (New York, 1923), p. 112.

34. *Op. cit.,* p. 9.

35. Hemingway includes *Far Away and Long Ago* in his list of exemplary prose works in *Esquire* for October, 1935.

36. *The Purple Land* (New York, 1916), p. 12.

37. *Op. cit.,* pp. 178, 199.

38. Charles Fenton, *The Apprenticeship of Ernest Hemingway* (New York, 1954), p. 203.

HEMINGWAY, THE *CORRIDA,* AND SPAIN

KENETH KINNAMON

On December 8, 1921, Ernest Hemingway and his first wife sailed for Paris. At the age of twenty-two he had already decided to become a writer, and Paris offered a better environment for his apprenticeship than Kansas City, Toronto, or Chicago.[1] Instead of the customary landing at Cherbourg, however, he followed the longer route to Spain and then north to Paris by rail. As he had not had an opportunity to visit Spain while in Europe during World War I, he was now seeing it for the first time. His reaction was immediate and intense. Soon after his arrival in Paris, he wrote back to Sherwood Anderson in Chicago, "You ought to see the Spanish coast. Big brown mountains looking like tired dinosaurs slumped down into the sea."[2] Shortly afterward he used the same simile in a dispatch to the Toronto *Star Weekly* describing Vigo, the town where he had landed. In terms of his later literary production, it seems appropriate that he should have landed in Spain when he came to Europe to begin his serious career.

Of Hemingway's seven novels to date, four have had in whole or in part Spanish or Spanish-American settings. *The Sun Also Rises* takes place both in France and in Spain, but the emotional center of the book is in the section dealing with the fiesta in Pamplona; indeed, the British title is *Fiesta.* It is true that Key West and the Gulf of Mexico form more of the background of *To Have and Have Not* than does Cuba; but Cuban revolutionary activity and intrigue, if not quite a vital thematic element, certainly provide important counterpoint both to the predicament of Harry Morgan and the "have-nots" and to that of Richard Gordon and the "haves." *For Whom the Bell Tolls,* of course, is set entirely in Spain. Finally, *The Old Man and the Sea* returns to the Cuban scene and has for protagonist a Cuban fisherman. In addition to these novels—three of which are certainly among Hemingway's best four—the Spanish or Spanish-American scene has been treated in his book on *tauroma-*

Reprinted with permission from *Texas Studies in Literature and Language,* I (Spring 1959), 44–61.

quia, Death in the Afternoon, in roughly twenty-five per cent of his published short stories, including such important ones as "The Undefeated" and "A Clean, Well-Lighted Place," and in much of his miscellaneous journalism. If one judges by quantity alone, then, it is obvious that for almost the whole of his artistic career Hemingway has been fascinated by the scene and character of Spain and parts of Spanish America.

Surprisingly little effort has been made to isolate and examine the Spanish influence on Hemingway. The neglect is surprising because this influence has penetrated deep into the origins of his art and his world view, far deeper than most critics have noticed or been willing to allow. The Spanish background in Hemingway has more important functions than merely to serve as a playground for lost generation wastrels, a laboratory for the study of civil war and revolution, or a fishing resort. Hemingway has so completely assimilated certain aspects of the Spanish temperament that they have become—perhaps unconsciously on his part—a determining factor in his conception of morality (at best idiosyncratic and at worst vulgar or barbaric to many non-Spanish readers), his theory of tragedy, and the characteristic type of his hero. An account of the effects of his contacts with the Spanish environment and character on his work should clarify the crucial result of his expatriation—that it has involved, to a remarkable degree, alienation from American and assimilation of Spanish values.

Hemingway saw his first bullfights in the summer of 1922, but he did not begin his serious study of the *corrida* until the following summer. At first his purpose was simply to provide himself with an appropriate subject for his apprenticeship; as he later recalled in *Death in the Afternoon,* he "was trying to learn to write, commencing with the simplest things, and one of the simplest things of all . . . is violent death." And he took with him to Spain a stereotyped preconception of what he was going to see: "I thought they would be simple and barbarous and cruel and that I would not like them, but that I would see certain definite action which would give me the feeling of life and death that I was working for." But he quickly discovered the inadequacy of his preconceptions and the mistake he had made in choosing the bullfight as one of "the simple things" to write about: "I found the definite action; but the bullfight was so far from simple and I liked it so much that it was much too complicated for my then equipment for writing to deal with and, aside from four very short sketches, I was not able to write anything about it for five years—and I wish I would have waited ten."[3]

Actually, Hemingway wrote about the bullfight almost immediately. In October, 1923, he sent two articles to the Toronto *Star Weekly.* The title of the first, "Bullfights not sport but tragedy," shows that he had already divested himself of the basic misconception about the spectacle that the uninitiated American holds. In addition to these two pieces of journalism, Hemingway also put the bullfight to artistic use in his second published volume, *in our time,* which appeared in the spring of 1924. Six, not four as he later remembered, of the eighteen short sketches in this volume are about the bullfight. All but one of these deal with the least attractive aspects of the *fiesta brava*—gorings of men and horses, cowardly bulls, prolonged and messy kills, a bullfighter drunk the morning before a fight, and the death of a bullfighter. But the sketches also introduce two *toreros* who were among Hemingway's favorites, Nicanor Villalta, whose magnificent kill is the subject of the only sketch showing the bullfight as art, and Maera, who was later eulogized in *Death in the Afternoon* and became a prototype of the Hemingway hero. The sketches as a whole are remarkable for the close accuracy of the descriptions by an *aficionado* of such short standing and for the concentration on sequence of event with the accompanying eschewal of overtly expressed emotion that marks much of Hemingway's best writing.

But the bullfight had become more for Hemingway than merely a subject for literary finger exercises. It had become a profound spiritual experience, perhaps the most profound of all. In the late spring of 1924, he wrote sardonically in the *transatlantic review,* "Since seeing his first bull-fight, Mr. William Bird, the publisher, no longer finds it necessary to read the cabled base-ball reports from New York."[4] Later in the same year, he quoted approvingly a remark made by Picasso to Donald Ogden Stewart, "You know it's absolutely the only thing left in the world. Bul [*sic*] fighting that is." Hemingway's interest, however, had no missionary leanings. Initiation into the brotherhood of *afición* seemed to entail a conspiracy toward the exclusion of the merely curious, and he feared that an invasion of tourists would spoil the fiesta at Pamplona. Therefore, he reasoned, "the more people that think it is terrible, brutal degrading relic of etc. the better."[5]

This cultistic tendency of Hemingway as *aficionado* also receives explicit statement in *The Sun Also Rises* (1926), his first serious novel:

He [the hotel owner, Montoya] always smiled as though bullfighting were a very special secret between the two of us; a rather shocking but really very deep secret that we knew about. He always smiled as though there were something lewd about the secret to outsiders, but that it was something that we understood. It would not do to expose it to people who would not understand.

The acceptance of Jake Barnes as a colleague by Spanish *aficionados* is not an easy process; it even involves a ritualistic tactile confirmation:

They were always very polite at first, and it amused them very much that I should be an American. Somehow it was taken for granted that an American could not have aficion. He might simulate it or confuse it with excitement, but he could not really have it. When they saw that I had aficion, and there was no password, no set questions that could bring it out, rather it was a sort of oral spiritual examination with the questions always a little on the defensive and never apparent, there was this same embarrassed putting the hand on the shoulder, or a "Buen hombre." But nearly always there was the actual touching. It seemed as though they wanted to touch you to make it certain.[6]

The almost mystical, certainly spiritual, fellowship of *aficion* for the bullfight was the bond which cemented Jake's relationship with Spain, and we are justified by Jake's role in the novel as well as by the biographical facts of this period of the novelist's life in assuming that the same bond cemented Hemingway's early relationship with Spain. In considering his later Spanish themes, it is extremely important to remember that the bullfight was the first center of Hemingway's Spanish world.

The only completely admirable character in *The Sun Also Rises* is the young matador, Pedro Romero, whom Hemingway patterned after the contemporary Niño de la Palma and named for a great eighteenth-century matador. Thus the bullfighter had become a prototype of the Hemingway hero very early. The moral stature of Romero is most vividly pointed up by the rivalry between him and Robert Cohn for Lady Brett Ashley. The rivalry culminates in a fist fight in which Cohn, although the physical victor, suffers complete moral defeat. And it is Romero who is responsible at least passively for Brett's only moral victory, which is achieved when she renounces him in order not to be "one of these bitches that ruins children." Furthermore, Romero is admirable because he is an artist with a brilliant future in the bull ring, a man with a métier, in contrast to Cohn, Brett, Mike, and even Jake himself, people either without a métier or unsuccessful in it and with no future at all. Finally, Romero is heroic because his way of living is extremely intense; he telescopes experience in much the same way that Robert Jordan was later to do in *For Whom the Bell Tolls*. As Jake tells Cohn early in the novel, "Nobody ever lives their life all the way up except bull-fighters." Cohn, however, whose own abnormality lies in his constant but unsuccessful quest for experience, replies, "I'm not interested in bull-fighters. That's an abnormal life."[7] The irony of this dialogue is that for Jake and Hemingway the life of the *torero* is not abnormal but supernormal, for it is the only one in which a man can be an artist through the exertion of skill and physical and moral courage in the face of what Hemingway himself was later to call the ultimate reality, death.

A great deal of Romero's stature, however, is due to his youth and his innocence. Like Paco of "The Capital of the World," he is, "as the Spanish phrase has it, full of illusions." Also, he is a *torero* before the first goring, and thus largely an unknown quantity. The case is very different for the *torero* in the first story of Hemingway's next book, *Men Without Women* (1927). In this story the matador is Manuel García, whose name is the same as that of the actual matador called Maera mentioned above. "The Undefeated" discloses some of the seamiest sides of bullfighting—the ruthless and mercenary promoter, the contemptuous waiters in cheap restaurants, the bored and supercilious critic, the unsympathetic and insulting crowd. The central figure, Manuel García, is a matador long past his prime but compelled to continue fighting by his sense of honor, his pride in his profession, and his illusory rationalization that he is still capable of making a comeback. After wangling a contract to appear as a substitute at a nocturnal *corrida,* he engages the services of a skillful old picador, Zurito. Understanding his friend's compulsion to return to the ring, the old picador agrees to appear with him on the condition that he will give up the profession if the *corrida* is not successful. Manuel's work in the ring is valiant and supremely honest, although he does not maintain full control of the bull and has lost most of his art. When he tries to make the kill, four times the sword strikes bone and fails to penetrate.[8] Although each time he goes in over the horn well and his lack of success is attributable simply to bad luck, the crowd unjustly begins to throw things from the stands. Along with the usual cushions, these things include his own sword, which had rebounded into the crowd after his last attempt at the kill, and an empty champagne bottle, evidently thrown by the bored bullfight critic. On the fifth attempt Manuel is gored. Afterwards in the infirmary Zurito, according to their agreement, starts to cut off Manuel's *coleta,* the small pigtail that bullfighters wear on the back of their heads as a badge of the profession. Manuel feels that he must keep his *coleta* intact in order to maintain his honor and self-respect, and Zurito, understanding his friend's feeling, says, "I won't do it. I was joking."[9] On the operating table from which he will not arise, Manuel continues to insist that he "was going good" in the ring before the goring, maintaining to the end his honor and refusing to accept defeat. It is in this sense that he is "The Undefeated."

Very early Hemingway was fascinated by the Spanish characteristic of refusing to accept defeat in a situation justifying surrender and by that refusal achieving a kind of victory. The first example of this characteristic in action was Pedro Romero's fist fight with Robert Cohn in *The Sun Also Rises.* The latest example is that of Santiago in *The Old Man and the Sea.* Hemingway's treatments of this theme appear throughout almost the whole course of his literary career, and the theme itself provides us with an important key to an understanding of his interpretation of the Spanish character.

Another story in *Men Without Women* is of major importance in indicating the shift away from American and toward Spanish values which had begun to take place in Hemingway beginning in 1922. This is "Banal Story." On one level it represents a reversion to Hemingway's satirical talent, which had been prominently manifested in his high-school journalism as well as in *The Torrents of Spring.* The early satirical novel has little connection with Spain except for one curious parallel. The epigraph to Chapter I is the following quotation from Fielding's preface to *Joseph Andrews:* "The only source of the true Ridiculous (as it appears to me) is affectation."[10] Hemingway may or may not have been aware that this quotation is in a direct line of descent from an epigram by Spain's greatest writer, Cervantes: "Toda afectación es mala." At any rate, the point of Hemingway's satire in "Banal Story" on Americans who try to "live the full life of the mind" by seeking romance and intellectual stimulation in the escapist world of such magazines as *The Forum* is that they are guilty of affectation and insincerity. But in sharp dramatic contrast to these Americans, "stretched flat on a bed in a darkened room in his house in Triana, Manuel García Maera lay with a tube in each lung, drowning with the pneumonia . . . Bull-fighters were very relieved he was dead, because he did always in the bull-ring the things they could only do sometimes."[11] It is evident that Maera had become a prototype of the undefeated Hemingway hero.

Maera is given extended treatment in *Death in the Afternoon.* A *banderillero* in the *cuadrilla* of the great Juan Belmonte, Maera left Belmonte and became a matador when he was refused an increase in salary.[12] After a close analysis of the development of Maera's style and an assessment of the final achievement of his art, Hemingway relates an incident very similar to that of Maera's fictional projection in "The Undefeated." Maera dislocates his wrist in attempting to make the kill, but after several more unsuccessful efforts he finally succeeds, although all the while the pain in his arm has been almost unbearable. He also dies a Hemingwayesque death:

Anyway he died that winter in Seville with a tube in each lung, drowned with pneumonia that came to finish off the tuberculosis. When he was delirious he rolled under the bed and fought with death under the bed dying as hard as a man can die. I thought that year he hoped for death in the ring but he would not cheat by looking for it. You would have liked him, Madame. Era muy hombre.

This is one of the few times that Hemingway speaks Spanish to his old lady in *Death in the Afternoon.* For Hemingway, "era muy hombre" is the supreme compliment, and it could only be expressed in Spanish. When the old lady asks him if Maera had been "mean about money," as Belmonte had, the author replies,

He was not. He was generous, humorous, proud, bitter, foul-mouthed and a great drinker. He neither sucked after intellectuals nor married money. He loved to kill bulls and lived with much passion and enjoyment although the last six months of his life he was very bitter. He knew he had tuberculosis and took absolutely no care of himself; having no fear of death he preferred to burn out, not as an act of bravado, but from choice.

This catalog of virtues, together with "a valor that was so absolute and such a solid part of him that it made everything easy that he understood,"[13] comprises those most important for a Hemingway hero. Maera's death, which occurred in 1924, continued to haunt Hemingway for a long time afterward. It is necessary to emphasize the year, for only *Three Stories and Ten Poems* and *in our time* appeared before it. Thus Hemingway's contact with Maera came exactly when the writer was developing the values and attitudes which would appear in his fiction as well as in *Death in the Afternoon.* Maera did in fact exert a strong formative influence on these values and attitudes.

Death in the Afternoon is, in part, exactly what the author wrote he intended it to be in a bibliographical note at the end of the book: "It is intended as an introduction to the modern Spanish bullfight and attempts to explain that spectacle both emotionally and practically." Also, Hemingway wrote, it "is not intended to be either historical or exhaustive."[14] We need only to glance at a work that is historical and exhaustive, José María de Cossío's monumental study in three huge volumes, *Los toros: Tratado técnico e histórico,* to realize that the brief period of ten years from 1922 to 1932, filled as it was with other activities and other writing, was much too short for Hemingway to gain a really sound scholarly knowledge of all aspects of the complex subject. But as an introduction to the *fiesta brava* for the non-Spanish reader, *Death in the Afternoon* is excellent, much better than any other book of similar intention in English, including the many that have followed it and borrowed from it.

Hemingway knew the bullfight from the inside as well as from the stands.

In addition to his friendship with Maera and other bullfighters as well as with Spanish *aficionados,* and in addition to his own brief attempts at amateur bullfighting, which included the celebrated *quite* that saved John Dos Passos a serious goring, Hemingway was a close personal friend of the American matador, Sidney Franklin, whom he met early in August, 1929. Franklin in his autobiography gives a humorous and engaging account of their friendship. On first meeting Hemingway, he suspected that the unkempt writer was a tramp looking for a handout. Even after Hemingway introduced himself, Franklin did not recognize the name; indeed, the bullfighter did not learn of the writer's fame until after a month of constant companionship, and then only from a common friend. But from the first meeting Franklin was highly impressed by Hemingway's modesty, his knowledge of wines, his insistence on paying his own way, and, most of all, his knowledge of the bullfight. "As we chatted," Franklin writes of their first meeting,

I realized that this fellow had a choice selection of English terms for bullfighting which up until then I had been at a loss to translate. And he used them very casually, as though it were old stuff with him . . . He was the first person who spoke to me in American English who appeared to have a deep understanding of the business . . . I drew our conversation into channels which would show me just how much he knew about bullfighting. And, little by little, he amazed me. He was familiar with events and instances which only a deep and sincere student of the subject could know about.

Hemingway accompanied Franklin and his *cuadrilla,* living in the same hotel suites with them, for the remainder of the 1929 season and all of the 1930 season. Hemingway and Franklin even worked out a system of signals whereby Hemingway gave the bullfighter instructions from behind the *barrera.* Franklin later generously commented, "This direction from him was the cause of my meteoric rise."[15] The experience was extremely valuable to Hemingway, for it gave him an even deeper insight into the psychology of bullfighters and added to his large store of practical information about the bullfight.

It has been necessary to emphasize the intensity of Hemingway's personal interest in the bullfight, his close association with the institution, and his careful study of the art for almost ten years before the publication of *Death in the Afternoon,* because critics have seldom been willing to accept the book on its own terms. This reluctance is part of the larger question of the difference between Hispanic and Anglo-Saxon culture, for the *fiesta brava* has never been successful outside of Spanish-speaking countries. This is also to say that the emotions and temperament of a non-Hispanic *aficionado* have to some degree been Hispanicized. This statement is notably true in the case of Hemingway. As a result, the condemnations of *Death in the Afternoon* by non-Hispanic critics who are not *aficionados* have been largely on moral grounds. These critics have usually ignored the problem of whether the book succeeds in its primary aim of introducing "the modern Spanish bullfight . . . both emotionally and practically." A notorious example is Max Eastman in his article, "Bull in the Afternoon." There have even been critics who have attempted to imply that Hemingway's reaction to the bullfight is that of a vulgar American rather than a Spaniard. Thus Harry Levin, in an otherwise excellent essay on Hemingway's style, writes,

Where are his limitations? What are his values? We may well discover that they differ from our assumptions, when he shows us a photograph of a bullfighter close to a bull, and comments: "If there is no blood on his belly afterwards you ought to get your money back." We may be ungrateful to question such curiosity . . . it may well spring from the American zest of the fan who pays his money to reckon the carnage. When Spain's great poet, García Lorca, celebrated the very same theme, averting his gaze from the spilling of the blood, his refrain was *"Que no quiero verla!"* ("I don't want to see it!").[16]

The picture Mr. Levin refers to is one of Nicanor Villalta in a *derechazo* pass with the *muleta* in which the bull passes so closely that it brushes blood from its bleeding shoulder onto the unharmed body of the bullfighter. The poem in which Mr. Levin says García Lorca "celebrated the very same theme" is "Llanto por Ignacio Sánchez Mejías," an elegy on the death of a famous matador killed by a goring in the ring. What García Lorca did not want to see was not the blood of the bull on the man as evidence of a close pass, but rather "la sangre / de Ignacio sobre la arena" ("the blood / of Ignacio on the sand"), hardly, one would think, "the very same theme" as that of Hemingway, who many times in *Death in the Afternoon* explicitly insists that the bullfight is an artistic and emotional failure when a bullfighter is gored.

But Mr. Levin very rightly implies that Hemingway's values are different from "ours." They are different precisely in that they are Hispanicized. The truth of this statement is evident on almost every page of *Death in the Afternoon,* but nowhere, perhaps, is it more so than in those parts which discuss death:

Some one with English blood has written: "Life is real; life is earnest, and the grave is not its goal." And where did they bury him? and what became of the reality and the earnestness? The people of Castille have great common sense. They could not produce a poet who would write a line like that. They know death is the unescapable reality, the one thing any man may be sure of; the only security; that it transcends all modern comforts and that with it you do not need a bathtub in every American home, nor, when you have it, do you need the radio. They think a great deal about death and when they have a religion they have one which believes that life is much shorter than death. Having this feeling they take an intelligent interest in death and when they can see it being given, avoided, refused and accepted in the afternoon for a nominal price of admission they pay their money and go to the bull ring.[17]

That Hemingway has had exactly the same kind of interest in death is obvious from the biographical facts, although to call this interest an obsession is to state the case much too strongly, and to construe his career as a deliberate quest for death, as was done after the African airplane crashes, is ridiculous.

Paradoxically, perhaps, this awareness of the inevitability of death in the end for man is, together with the creation of plastic beauty, what provides the supreme emotional appeal of bullfighting culminating in the death of the bull. Hemingway describes this appeal extremely well:

Now the essence of the greatest emotional appeal of bullfighting is the feeling of immortality that the bullfighter feels in the middle of a great faena and that he gives to the spectators. He is performing a work of art and he is playing with death, bringing it closer, closer, closer, to himself, a death that you know is in the horns because you have the canvas-covered bodies of the horses on the sand to prove it. He gives the feeling of his immortality, and, as you watch it, it becomes yours. Then when it belongs to both of you, he proves it with the sword.[18]

The perfect bullfight is thus one in which death in the form of a brave bull is conquered artistically and valiantly, thereby allowing the bullfighter and, vicariously, the spectators to make a gesture of defiance at their own ultimate fate, even a temporary victory over it. In this way a perfect bullfight provided a norm around which Hemingway developed his idea of the morally undefeated. It cannot be emphasized too strongly that the idea developed from a Spanish ritual.

Among the most enlightening of the many digressions in *Death in the Afternoon* are those which deal with Spanish painting. Goya, Velázquez, and El Greco comprise the great trio of painters whom Hemingway admires and evaluates. He has a vast admiration for each of them, although Goya is clearly the favorite. Although made a bit uneasy by his suspicion that El Greco was a homosexual, Hemingway is not speaking ironically when he says that the painter should redeem for the tribe the various types of perversion represented by Gide, Wilde, and Whitman.[19] Velázquez draws Hemingway's special attention because of the importance the painter gave to his art per se. But Goya receives Hemingway's highest praise, probably because his artistic aims were very much like the novelist's own:

Goya did not believe in costume [unlike Velázquez] but he did believe in blacks and in grays, in dust and in light, in high places rising from plains, in the country around Madrid, in movement, in his own cojones, in painting, in etching, and in what he had seen, felt, touched, handled, smelled, enjoyed, drunk, mounted, suffered, spewed-up, lain-with, suspected, observed, loved, hated, lusted, feared, detested, admired, loathed, and destroyed. Naturally no painter has been able to paint all that but he tried.[20]

Thus Goya is an ideal example of what Hemingway thinks the artist must be, a man who puts into his art what he knows and "the way it was." But Goya is also, like Maera, a type of the Hemingway hero, especially in his appetite for experience. Furthermore, Hemingway is attracted to Goya because two of the painter's basic themes, bullfighting and war, are the writer's own.

One of the articles of Goya's faith, Hemingway asserts, was a belief in his own *cojones.* Why, one wonders, would not the words "heart" or "guts" describe the concept just as well? The answer is not only that Hemingway wanted to stress the quality of masculinity as a major component of courage, but also that he had come to formulate his basic attitudes in Spanish terms; indeed, his attitudes from 1922 to 1932 were becoming progressively more Hispanicized. According to Spanish folklore, which Hemingway accepts in this respect, human courage resides in the *cojones.* In the explanatory glossary at the end of *Death in the Afternoon,* he says of *cojones* that "a valorous bullfighter is said to be plentifully equipped with these."[21] The protagonists of each subsequent Hemingway novel are all plentifully equipped by the novelist with *cojones.*

It is important to note that *Death in the Afternoon* is filled with many of the abstract words which had been so odious to Frederic Henry in *A Farewell to Arms.* Spain, as it were, had restored Hemingway's faith in the reality of the qualities that these abstract words signify, a faith that had been lost after World War I because the qualities did not seem real in a non-Spanish setting and among people who were not Spanish-speaking. "In Spain," Hemingway writes, "honor is a very real thing. Called pundonor, it means honor, probity, courage, self-respect and pride in one word. Pride is the strongest characteris-

tic of the race and it is a matter of pundonor not to show cowardice." Hemingway is completely convinced of the reality of the quality, and he realizes the
difficulty of conveying the reality to his non-Spanish audience, among whom
honor is only a word: "This honor thing is not some fantasy that I am trying
to inflict on you . . . I swear it is true. Honor to a Spaniard, no matter how
dishonest, is as real a thing as water, wine, or olive oil. There is honor among
pickpockets and honor among whores. It is simply that the standards differ."[22]
And although their standards often differ from conventional ones, Hemingway's heroes all have a strong sense of honor.

Hemingway's most famous use of a Spanish word, of course, is that of
nada in "A Clean, Well-Lighted Place," which appeared in the March, 1933,
issue of *Scribner's Magazine,* only a little more .than five months after the
publication of *Death in the Afternoon.* The critics have rightly considered this
story central to Hemingway's world view, and a few of them have pointed out
the important idea of *cojones* as man's defense against *nada.* Robert Penn
Warren, for example, gets to the heart of the matter when he writes, "The
violent man is the man taking an action appropriate to the realization of the
fact of nada. He is, in other words, engaged in the effort to discover human
values in a naturalistic world."[23] And while it is perfectly true that the *nada-*
concept is a compelling symbol of the emptiness and anarchy of life in the
twentieth century, the critics have not sufficiently emphasized that the concept
takes its rise from a specific Spanish setting and is expressed by a Spanish word.

Hemingway was away from Spain during most of the middle thirties, but
his interest in the bullfight did not wane. In January, 1937, he and Sidney
Franklin attempted unsuccessfully to bring to fruition a plan of several years'
standing to introduce bullfights to Cuba. But even more important matters
were now claiming Hemingway's attention, for Spain had been in the grips of
a civil war for six months. Having obtained a contract as a war correspondent
for the North American Newspaper Alliance, Hemingway sailed from New
York in February.

The Spanish Civil War and its aftermath proved fruitful for both his
journalism and his serious literary output. From May, 1938, to February,
1939, he published four stories, "Old Man at the Bridge," "The Denunciation," "The Butterfly and the Tank," and "Night Before Battle," as well as
his second play, *The Fifth Column,* and a film sound track, *The Spanish Earth.*
Of the stories, only "Old Man at the Bridge" has subsequently been published
in a collection. The other three stories center around Chicote's Bar in Madrid,
which had been one of Hemingway's haunts before the war. "The Denunciation" tells of a Fascist who appears in Chicote's during the siege of the city.

He is recognized only by the narrator of the story, obviously Hemingway himself, and by an old waiter. After an inner struggle and a plea for justification from the narrator, the waiter telephones the authorities to denounce the Fascist. The narrator, unwilling to see the death of the Fascist, whom he had known and liked in the old days before the war, leaves the bar knowing that the denunciation was necessary for the cause of the Republic but receiving little satisfaction from that knowledge. The story is important as an early example of Hemingway's mixed feelings toward the war. On the one hand, he realized that at one extreme fanaticism and at the other a cold-blooded cynicism were necessary for the successful prosecution of the conflict; but on the other hand, many of his friends were on the side of the Fascists, and, like Robert Jordan in *For Whom the Bell Tolls,* he had been closer to the people of Navarre, now one of Franco's strongholds, than to any other people of Spain.

All of these four stories, as well as a slightly later one, "Under the Ridge," are reportorial in character. "The Butterfly and the Tank" and "Night Before Battle" turn on the taut nerves and dangerous tension of a city under constant bombardment. "Under the Ridge," frankly autobiographical, points out the Spanish distrust of foreigners and emphasizes also the sinister ruthlessness of the Russian Communists and their lack of any real understanding of the Spanish people, a point which was to receive extended treatment in *For Whom the Bell Tolls.* "Old Man at the Bridge," the best story of the group, is a vivid and touching presentation in miniature of the brutal impact of the war on the many neutral Spaniards. The old man of the title is a refugee from the village of San Carlos, where he had been a keeper of animals. The bridge over the Ebro River is for him a dead end: " 'I am without politics,' he said. 'I am seventy-six years old. I have come twelve kilometers now and I think now I can go no further.' " Puzzled and dazed by the chaos of events which he cannot understand, the old man is left at the bridge to fall into the hands of the enemy, a victim and a symbol of the betrayal of Spain: "There was nothing to do about him. It was Easter Sunday and the Fascists were advancing toward the Ebro. It was a gray overcast day with a low ceiling so their planes were not up. That and the fact that cats know how to look after themselves was all the good luck that old man would ever have."[24]

The Fifth Column, as Hemingway was later to admit,[25] is a failure as a work of art. Even in his preface to the play, he seems apologetic and dissatisfied: "While I was writing the play the Hotel Florida, where we lived and worked, was struck by more than thirty high explosive shells. So if it is not a good play perhaps that is what is the matter with it." But it does have the vivid atmospheric accuracy of the stories and the journalism of the period, however contrived and melodramatic the characters are. The protagonist, Philip Rawlings, is a counterespionage agent for the Republican forces in Madrid. Rawlings, in contrast to Robert Jordan of *For Whom the Bell Tolls,* actually cares little about the Spanish people. He is a professional Communist who has pledged himself to a continual war against fascism. His political duty compels him to break off an affair with Dorothy Bridges, an American magazine correspondent. The "moral," Hemingway wryly writes in the preface, "is that people who work for certain organizations have very little time for home life."[26] The difference in moral stature between Robert Jordan and Philip Rawlings, one is tempted to think, is in direct proportion to their devotion to the people of Spain.

It is *For Whom the Bell Tolls,* of course, that is the most important product of Hemingway's experience with the Spanish Civil War. Although politically he had been wholeheartedly on the side of Republican Spain, the novel carefully eschews the tempting trap of partisanship. The Marxist critics, who had confidently presumed during the conflict that Hemingway was in their camp, deplored the novel because it was not propagandistic. Alvah Bessie, for example, writing in *New Masses,* accused Hemingway of having "written a novel of Spain without the Spanish people" because he attacked the French Communist leader, André Marty, and because he led "the untutored reader to believe that the role of the Soviet Union in Spain was sinister and reprehensible."[27] Such judgments appear ludicrous enough today, for, as Carlos Baker has pointed out, *For Whom the Bell Tolls* is "a work of fiction whose moral values transcended political affiliations."[28]

The objections of Arturo Barea, however, cannot be so lightly passed over. Señor Barea, a distinguished novelist in his own right as well as a Spaniard active in the Civil War for the Loyalists, maintains that *For Whom the Bell Tolls* is finally an artistic failure because it does not present a true picture of the Spanish people at war. The basic reason for this failure, he holds, is that "Hemingway has understood the emotions which our 'people as a whole' felt in the bull-ring, but not those which it felt in the collective action of war and revolution." Barea points out that the extremely provincial peasants from Castille would never have submitted to the leadership of the degenerate Pablo and the gypsy Pilar. Neither the cynical massacre of the village Fascists nor the multiple rape of Maria would have been possible as a collective action, for "the brutal violence of Spaniards . . . is always individual."[29] Finally, Maria's extreme innocence of even the rudiments of kissing is completely unreal in a rural girl, but her offering herself to Robert Jordan without being asked would have immediately caused her to lose the respect of the other members of the band.

One feels extremely uncomfortable in replying to a man so ideally situated to evaluate the fidelity of Hemingway's picture of the Spanish people at war as Señor Barea. Certain things, however, may be pointed out. Señor Barea is correct in his unwillingness to accept Maria on realistic terms. In many respects she is the most unsatisfactory character in the book. The motivation for her affair with Robert Jordan is insufficient and finally unconvincing. Except for prostitutes, Hemingway's Spanish world, centered around the bullfight, has excluded women. Maria's dreamlike quality is probably a reflection of this exclusion. But something is to be said for Maria as a symbol. She represents the Spanish land, which remains innocent and fresh and lovely despite its rape by the Fascists. The most satisfactory intercourse of Jordan and Maria takes place not in his sleeping bag, but in the idyllic mountain meadow: "They were walking through the heather of the mountain meadow and Robert Jordan felt the brushing of the heather against his legs . . . felt the sun on his head, felt the breeze from the snow of the mountain peaks cool on his back and, in his hand, he felt the girl's hand firm and strong, the fingers locked in his." Maria is felt in exactly the same way as the country and the weather are felt. Her hair is repeatedly described as the color of wheat, the same wheat, one supposes, that Jake Barnes and Bill Gorton had seen on the way to Pamplona. The most concrete sensuous impressions conveyed of the actual sexual act are "the smell of heather crushed and the roughness of the bent stalks under her head and the sun bright on her closed eyes." Afterwards, too, Robert Jordan "was lying on his side, his head deep in the heather, smelling it and the smell of the roots and the earth and the sun came through it and it was scratchy on his bare shoulders and along his flanks." As he lies there he sees across the meadow a hawk hunting. In the beautifully nostalgic last chapter of *Death in the Afternoon,* hawks are among the very last mementos of Spain that Hemingway evokes. Finally, the earth moves during their intercourse. This earth, it must be remembered, was the Spanish earth. I do not mean to imply that Hemingway consciously drew the parallel between Maria and the Spanish land, but the parallel is none the less present. In an elegaic article for *New Masses* in 1939 entitled "On the American Dead in Spain," Hemingway had written, "For our dead are a part of the earth of Spain now and the earth of Spain can never die."[30] It is exactly in this sense that Jordan, waiting for death, is correct when he tells Maria at the end of the novel, "There is no good-by, *guapa,* because we are not apart."[31]

According to Hemingway's own critical principles, however, symbols cannot operate successfully unless there is complete truth of presentation on the realistic level. The failure of Maria as a character may be ascribed to her failure to meet this requirement. The other Spanish characters in *For Whom the Bell Tolls* are generally types, not symbols. Here Señor Barea seems to have mistaken Hemingway's intention. It is difficult to believe Barea's implication that Hemingway sinned through ignorance in grouping together Pablo and Pilar with the peasants of Castille, for Hemingway has always been conscious of the intense regionalism of the Spaniard, even in war,[32] and his corresponding distrust of outsiders. But Hemingway had to sacrifice a minor point of psychological propriety in order to gain the more important objective of national scope. The microcosm of the guerilla band is intended to represent the macrocosm of the whole Spanish people.

For Whom the Bell Tolls is finally successful in presenting Spain and her people in war primarily because its author maintains exactly the right proportion between emotional involvement and detached objectivity. The reader's final picture of the Spanish character as revealed in the novel is very similar to one of Robert Jordan's own assessments: "What a people they have been. What sons of bitches from Cortez, Pizarro, Menéndez de Avila all down through Enrique Lister to Pablo. And what wonderful people. There is no finer and no worse people in the world. No kinder and no crueler."[33] Needless to say, this picture does not represent the complete Spanish character, that compound of paradoxes, but it is a large and important part of the whole. Hemingway later said of *For Whom the Bell Tolls,* "It was everything I had learned about Spain for eighteen years."[34] What he had learned was the essential nature of the Spanish character, and the long process of learning had formed some of his most basic attitudes and values and had provided the materials for a major portion of his writing.

Since 1941 Hemingway has made his permanent home in Cuba. He appears now to be spiritually at home only in a Spanish-speaking environment. It is futile to speculate as to what course his writing will take in the future, although his last two novels both have for protagonists men who share their author's Hispanic attitudes and values. This statement may at first glance seem strange in the case of Richard Cantwell, but one needs only to recall the description of Maera to realize how well the mantle of the Spanish bullfighter has fallen on the shoulders of the American colonel. And although the meaning of *The Old Man and the Sea* is universal, it is conceived strictly in Spanish-American terms. In this novel the Hemingway hero has achieved a new serenity without the sacrifice of valor; it is almost as if Santiago were a combination of the *cojones* of Maera and the mellow beauty of Rafael Gómez, El Gallo. To gain a full view of the development of the attitudes underlying Hemingway's art, one must of course take into account many other factors, but the dominant element has been Spanish.

1. For a suggestive discussion of Hemingway's reasons for going to Paris, see Charles A. Fenton, *The Apprenticeship of Ernest Hemingway* (New York, 1954), pp. 115–117.

2. Quoted in Fenton, pp. 118–119.

3. *Death in the Afternoon* (New York, 1932), pp. 2, 3.

4. "And to the United States," I (1924), 377.

5. "Pamplona Letter," *transatlantic review*, II, 301.

6. *The Sun Also Rises* (New York, 1926), pp. 135, 136.

7. *Ibid.*, pp. 254, 10.

8. In *Death in the Afternoon* Hemingway recounts a similar incident which happened to Manuel García Maera. This fact and the fact that the names are the same indicate fairly certainly that Hemingway patterned his fictional character after the real matador.

9. *The Fifth Column and the First Forty-nine Stories* (New York, 1938), p. 363.

10. *The Hemingway Reader*, ed. Charles Poore (New York, 1953), p. 25.

11. *The Fifth Column and the First Forty-nine Stories*, p. 459.

12. Hemingway's vast admiration for Maera, a personal friend, seems to have led him to distort the facts. Actually, Maera had been a matador before he joined Belmonte's *cuadrilla*, although he did not reach the highest rank in his profession until after he had left Belmonte, having acquired by that time a vast knowledge of bulls and bullfighting. See José María de Cossío, *Los toros: Tratado técnico e histórico*, III (Madrid, 1943), p. 343.

13. *Death in the Afternoon*, pp. 82, 82–83, 78.

14. *Ibid.*, p. 517.

15. *Bullfighter from Brooklyn* (New York, 1952), pp. 173, 179.

16. "Observations on the Style of Ernest Hemingway," *Kenyon Review*, XIII (1951), 606.

17. *Death in the Afternoon*, p. 266.

18. *Ibid.*, p. 213.

19. Hemingway is quoted as follows on El Greco's "View of Toledo": "This is the best picture in the Museum for me, and Christ knows there are some lovely ones." See Lillian Ross, "How Do You Like It Now, Gentlemen?" *The New Yorker*, XXVI (May 13, 1950), 58.

20. *Death in the Afternoon*, p. 205.

21. *Ibid.*, p. 428.

22. *Ibid.*, pp. 91, 92.

23. "Hemingway," *Literary Opinion in America*, ed. Morton Dauwen Zabel (New York, 1951), p. 448.

24. *The Fifth Column and the First Forty-nine Stories*, pp. 177, 178.

25. Carlos Baker, *Hemingway: The Writer as Artist* (Princeton, 1952), p. 235n.

26. *The Fifth Column and the First Forty-nine Stories*, pp. v, vi.

27. "Hemingway's 'For Whom the Bell Tolls'," XXXVII (November 5, 1940), 26.

28. Baker, *op. cit.*, p. 238.

29. "Not Spain But Hemingway," *Horizon*, III (May, 1941), 352.

30. XXX (February 14), 3.

31. *For Whom the Bell Tolls* (New York, 1940), pp. 158, 159, 464.

32. See, e.g., "Hemingway Reports Spain," *New Republic,* XCV (June 8, 1938), 125–126.

33. *For Whom the Bell Tolls,* pp. 354–355.

34. Quoted in Malcolm Cowley, "A Portrait of Mister Papa," *Ernest Hemingway: The Man and His Work,* ed. John K. M. McCaffery (Cleveland, 1950), p. 53.

II. The Work, Studies of the Work as a Whole

ERNEST HEMINGWAY

ROBERT PENN WARREN

IN MAY, 1929, in *Scribner's Magazine,* the first installment of *A Farewell to Arms* appeared. The novel was completed in the issue of October, and was published in book form the same year. Ernest Hemingway was already regarded, by a limited literary public, as a writer of extraordinary freshness and power, as one of the makers, indeed, of a new American fiction. *A Farewell to Arms* more than justified the early enthusiasm of the connoiseurs for Hemingway, and extended his reputation from them to the public at large. Its great importance was at once acknowledged, and its reputation has survived through the changing fashions and interests of many years.

What was the immediate cause of its appeal? It told a truth about the first world war, and a truth about the generation who had fought it and whose lives, because of the war, had been wrenched from the expected pattern and the old values. Other writers had told or were to tell similar truths about this war. John Dos Passos in *Three Soldiers,* E. E. Cummings in *The Enormous Room,* William Faulkner in *Soldier's Pay,* Maxwell Anderson and Laurence Stallings in *What Price Glory?* All these writers had presented the pathos and endurance and gallantry of the individual caught and mangled in the great anonymous mechanism of a modern war fought for reasons that the individual could not understand, found insufficient to justify the event, or believed to be no reasons at all. And *A Farewell to Arms* was not the first book to record the plight of the men and women who, because of the war, had been unable to come to terms with life in the old way. Hemingway himself in *The Sun Also Rises,* 1926, had given the picture of the dislocated life of young English and American expatriates in the bars of Paris, the "lost generation," as Gertrude Stein defined them. But before that, F. Scott Fitzgerald, who had been no nearer to the war than

Reprinted with permission from Robert Penn Warren, *Selected Essays* (N.Y.: Random House, 1951), 80–118.

an officer's training camp, had written of the lost generation. For the young people about whom Fitzgerald wrote, even when they were not veterans and even when their love stories were enacted in parked cars, fraternity houses, and country clubs and not in the cafés and hotels of Paris, were like Hemingway's expatriates under the shadow of the war and were groping to find some satisfaction in a world from which the old values had been withdrawn. Hemingway's expatriates had turned their backs on the glitter of the Great Boom of the 1920's, and Fitzgerald's young men were usually drawn to the romance of wealth and indulgence, but this difference is superficial. If Hemingway's young men begin by repudiating the Great Boom, Fitzgerald's young men end with disappointment in what even success has to offer. "All the sad young men" of Fitzgerald—to take the title of one of his collections of stories—and the "lost generation" of Hemingway are seekers for landmarks and bearings in a terrain for which the maps have been mislaid.

A Farewell to Arms, which appeared ten years after the first world war and on the eve of the collapse of the Great Boom, seemed to sum up and bring to focus an inner meaning of the decade being finished. It worked thus, not because it disclosed the end results that the life of the decade was producing —the discontents and disasters that were beginning to be noticed even by unreflective people—but because it cut back to the beginning of the process, to the moment that had held within itself the explanation of the subsequent process.

Those who had grown up in the war, or in its shadow could look back nostalgically, as it were, to the lost moment of innocence of motive and purity of emotion. If those things had been tarnished or manhandled by the later business of living, they had, at least, existed, and on a grand scale. If they had been tarnished or manhandled, it was not through the fault of the individual who looked back to see the image of the old simple and heroic self in Frederic or Catherine, but through the impersonal grindings of the great machine of the universe. *A Farewell to Arms* served, in a way, as the great romantic alibi for a generation, and for those who aped and emulated that generation. It showed how cynicism or disillusionment, failure of spirit or the worship of material success, debauchery or despair, might have been grounded in heroism, simplicity, and fidelity that had met unmerited defeat. The early tragedy could cast a kind of flattering and extenuating afterglow over what had come later. The battlefields of *A Farewell to Arms* explained the bars of *The Sun Also Rises*— and explained the young Krebs, of the story "Soldier's Home," who came back home to a Middle-Western town to accept his own slow disintegration.

This is not said in disparagement of *A Farewell to Arms.* It is, after all, a compliment to the hypnotic force of the book. For the hypnotic force of the book was felt from the first, and it is not unusual for such a book to be relished by its first readers for superficial reasons and not for the essential virtues that may engage those who come to it later.

In accounting for the immediate appeal of *A Farewell to Arms,* the history of the author himself is of some importance. In so far as the reader knew about Ernest Hemingway in 1929, he knew about a young man who seemed to typify in his own experience the central experience of his generation. Behind the story of *A Farewell to Arms* and his other books there was the shadow of his own story that could stamp his fiction with the authenticity of a document and, for the more impressionable, with the value of a revelation. He could give an ethic and a technique for living, even in the face of defeat or frustration, and yet his own story was the story that we have always loved: the American success story.

He was born in Oak Park, Illinois, in the Middle West—that region which it was fashionable to condemn (after Mencken and Sinclair Lewis) as romance-less, but which became endowed, paradoxically enough, with the romance of the American average. His father was a physician. There were two boys and four girls in the family. In the summers the family lived in northern Michigan, where there were Indians, and where lake, streams, and forests gave boyhood pursuits their appropriate setting. In the winters he went to school in Oak Park. He played football in high school, ran away from home, returned and, in 1917, graduated. After graduation he was for a short time a reporter on the *Kansas City Star,* but the war was on and he went to Italy as a volunteer ambulance driver. He was wounded and decorated, and after his recovery served in the Italian army as a soldier. For a time after the war he was a foreign correspondent for the *Toronto Star,* in the Near East.

In the years after the war Hemingway set about learning, quite consciously and with rigorous self-discipline, the craft and art of writing. During most of his apprenticeship he lived in Paris, one of the great number of expatriates who were drawn to the artistic capital of the world to learn to be writers, painters, sculptors, or dancers, or simply to enjoy on a low monetary exchange the freedom of life away from American or British conventions. "Young America," writes Ford Madox Ford, "from the limitless prairies leapt, released, on Paris. They stampeded with the madness of colts when you let down the slip-rails between dried pasture and green. The noise of their advancing drowned all sounds. Their innumerable forms hid the very trees on the boulevards. Their perpetual motion made you dizzy." And of Hemingway himself: "He was presented to me by Ezra [Pound] and Bill Bird and had rather the aspect of an Eton-Oxford, huskyish young captain of a midland regiment of His Britannic Majesty. . . . Into that animated din would drift Hemingway, balancing on the point of his toes, feinting at my head with hands as large as hams and relating sinister stories of Paris landlords. He told them with singularly choice words in a slow voice."[1]

The originality and force of Hemingway's early stories, published in little magazines and in limited editions in France, were recognized from the first by many who made their acquaintance. The seeds of his later work were in those stories of *In Our Time,* concerned chiefly with scenes of inland American life and a boy's growing awareness of that life in contrast to vivid flashes of the disorder and brutality of the war years and the immediate post-war years in Europe. There are both contrast and continuity between the two elements of *In Our Time.* There is the contrast between the lyric rendering of one aspect of the boyhood world and the realistic rendering of the world of war, but there is also a continuity, because in the boyhood world there are recurring intimations of the blackness into which experience can lead even in the peaceful setting of Michigan.

With the publication of *The Sun Also Rises,* in 1926, Hemingway's work reached a wider audience, and at the same time defined more clearly the line his genius was to follow and his role as one of the spokesmen for a generation. But *A Farewell to Arms* gave him his first substantial popular success and established his reputation. It was a brilliant and compelling novel; it provided the great alibi; it crowned the success story of the American boy from the Middle West, who had hunted and fished, played football in high school, been a newspaper reporter, gone to war and been wounded and decorated, wandered exotic lands as a foreign correspondent, lived the free life of the Latin Quarter of Paris, and, at the age of thirty, written a best seller—athlete, sportsman, correspondent, soldier, adventurer, and author.

It would be possible and even profitable to discuss *A Farewell to Arms* in isolation from Hemingway's other work. But Hemingway is a peculiarly personal writer, and for all the apparent objectivity and self-suppression in his method as a writer, his work, to an uncommon degree, forms a continuous whole. One part explains and interprets another part. It is true that there have been changes between early and late work, that there has been an increasing self-consciousness, that attitudes and methods that in the beginning were instinctive and simple have become calculated and elaborated. But the best way to understand one of his books is, nevertheless, to compare it with both earlier and later pieces and seek to discern motives and methods that underlie all of his work.

Perhaps the simplest way into the whole question is to consider what kind of world Hemingway writes about. A writer may write about his special world merely because he happens to know that world, but he may also write about that special world because it best dramatizes for him the issues and questions that are his fundamental concerns—because, in other words, that special world has a kind of symbolic significance for him. There is often—if we discount mere literary fashion and imitation—an inner and necessary reason for the writer's choice of his characters and situations. What situations and characters does Hemingway write about?

They are usually violent. There is the hard-drinking and sexually promiscuous world of *The Sun Also Rises;* the chaotic and brutal world of war, as in *A Farewell to Arms, For Whom the Bell Tolls,* many of the inserted sketches of *In Our Time,* the play *The Fifth Column,* and some of the stories; the world of sport, as in "Fifty Grand," "My Old Man," "The Undefeated," "The Snows of Kilimanjaro"; the world of crime, as in "The Killers," "The Gambler, the Nun, and the Radio," and *To Have and Have Not.* Even when the situation of a story does not fall into one of these categories, it usually involves a desperate risk, and behind it is the shadow of ruin, physical or spiritual. As for the typical characters, they are usually tough men, experienced in the hard worlds they inhabit, and not obviously given to emotional display or sensitive shrinking—men like Rinaldi or Frederic Henry of *A Farewell to Arms,* Robert Jordan of *For Whom the Bell Tolls,* Harry Morgan of *To Have and Have Not,* the big-game hunter of "The Snows of Kilimanjaro," the old bullfighter of "The Undefeated," or the pugilist of "Fifty Grand." Or if the typical character is not of this seasoned order, he is a very young man, or boy, first entering the violent world and learning his first adjustment to it.

We have said that the shadow of ruin is behind the typical Hemingway situation. The typical character faces defeat or death. But out of defeat or death the character usually manages to salvage something. And here we discover Hemingway's special interest in such situations and characters. His heroes are not squealers, welchers, compromisers, or cowards, and when they confront defeat they realize that the stance they take, the stoic endurance, the stiff upper lip mean a kind of victory. If they are to be defeated they are defeated upon their own terms; some of them have even courted their defeat; and certainly they have maintained, even in the practical defeat, an ideal of themselves— some definition of how a man should behave, formulated or unformulated— by which they have lived. They represent some notion of a code, some notion of honor, that makes a man a man, and that distinguishes him from people who merely follow their random impulses and who are, by consequence, "messy."

In case after case, we can illustrate this "principle of sportsmanship," as Edmund Wilson has called it, at the center of a story or novel. Robert Jordan, in *For Whom the Bell Tolls*, is somehow happy as he lies, wounded, behind the machine gun that is to cover the escape of his friends and his sweetheart from Franco's Fascists. The old bullfighter, in "The Undefeated," continues his incompetent fight even under the jeers and hoots of the crowd, until the bull is dead and he himself is mortally hurt. Francis Macomber, the rich young sportsman who goes lion-hunting in "The Short, Happy Life of Francis Macomber," and who has funked it and bolted before a wounded lion, at last learns the lesson that the code of the hunter demands that he go into the bush after an animal he has wounded. Brett, the heroine of *The Sun Also Rises*, gives up Romero, the young bullfighter with whom she is in love, because she knows she will ruin him, and her tight-lipped remark to Jake, the newspaper man who is the narrator of the novel, might almost serve as the motto of Hemingway's work: "You know it makes one feel rather good deciding not to be a bitch."

It is the discipline of the code that makes man human, a sense of style or good form. This applies not only in isolated, dramatic cases such as those listed above, but is a more pervasive thing that can give meaning, partially at least, to the confusions of living. The discipline of the soldier, the form of the athlete, the gameness of the sportsman, the technique of an artist can give some sense of the human order, and can achieve a moral significance. And here we see how Hemingway's concern with war and sport crosses his concern with literary style. If a writer can get the kind of style at which Hemingway, in *Green Hills of Africa*, professes to aim, then "nothing else matters. It is more important than anything else he can do." It is more important because, ultimately, it is a moral achievement. And no doubt for this reason, as well as for the reason of Henry James's concern with cruxes of a moral code, he is, as he says in *Green Hills of Africa*, an admirer of the work of Henry James, the devoted stylist.

But to return to the subject of Hemingway's world: the code and the discipline are important because they can give meaning to life that otherwise seems to have no meaning or justification. In other words, in a world without supernatural sanctions, in the God-abandoned world of modernity, man can realize an ideal meaning only in so far as he can define and maintain the code. The effort to do so, however limited and imperfect it may be, is the characteristically human effort and provides the tragic or pitiful human story. Hemingway's attitude on this point is much like that of Robert Louis Stevenson in "Pulvis et Umbra":

Poor soul, here for so little, cast among so many hardships, filled with desires so incommensurate and so inconsistent, savagely surrounded, savagely descended, irremediably condemned to prey upon his fellow lives: who should have blamed him had he been of a piece with his destiny and a being merely barbarous? And we look and behold him instead, filled with imperfect virtues . . . an ideal of decency, to which he would rise if it were possible; a limit of shame, below which, if it be possible, he will not stoop. . . . Man is indeed marked for failure in his effort to do right. But where the best consistently miscarry how tenfold more remarkable that all should continue to strive; and surely we should find it both touching and inspiriting, that in a field from which success is banished, our race should not cease to labor. . . . It matters not where we look, under what climate we observe him, in what stage of society, in what depth of ignorance, burthened with what erroneous morality; by campfires in Assiniboia, the snow powdering his shoulders, the wind plucking his blanket, as he sits, passing the ceremonial calumet and uttering his grave opinions like a Roman senator; on ships at sea, a man inured to hardship and vile pleasures, his brightest hope a fiddle in a tavern and a bedizened trull who sells herself to rob him, and he for all that, simple, innocent, cheerful, kindly like a child, constant to toil, brave to drown, for others; . . . in the brothel, the discard of society, living mainly on strong drink, fed with affronts, a fool, a thief, the comrade of thieves, and even here keeping the point of honor and the touch of pity, often repaying the world's scorn with service, often standing firm upon a scruple, and at a certain cost, rejecting riches:—everywhere some virtue cherished or affected, everywhere some decency of thought or carriage, everywhere the ensign of man's ineffectual goodness! . . . under every circumstance of failure, without hope, without help, without thanks, still obscurely fighting the lost fight of virtue, still clinging, in the brothel or on the scaffold, to some rag of honor, the poor jewel of their souls! They may seek to escape, and yet they cannot; it is not alone their privilege and glory, but their doom; they are condemned to some nobility. . . .

Hemingway's code is more rigorous than Stevenson's and perhaps he finds fewer devoted to it, but, like Stevenson, he can find his characteristic hero and characteristic story among the discards of society, and, like Stevenson, is aware of the touching irony of that fact. But for the moment the important thing in the parallel is that, for Stevenson, the world in which this drama of pitiful aspiration and stoic endurance is played out, is apparently a violent and meaningless world—"our rotary island loaded with predatory life and more drenched with blood . . . than ever mutinied ship, scuds through space."

Neither Hemingway nor Stevenson invented this world. It had already appeared in literature before their time, and that is a way of saying that this cheerless vision had already begun to trouble men. It is the world we find pictured (and denied) in Tennyson's "In Memoriam"—the world in which human conduct is a product of "dying Nature's earth and lime." It is the world pictured (and not denied) in Hardy and Housman, a world that seems to be presided over by blind Doomsters (if by anybody), as Hardy put it in his poem "Hap," or made by some brute and blackguard (if by anybody), as Housman put it in his poem "The Chestnut Casts Its Flambeaux." It is the world of Zola or Dreiser or Conrad or Faulkner. It is the world of, to use Bertrand Russell's phrase, "secular hurryings through space." It is the God-abandoned world, the world of Nature-as-all. We know where the literary men got this picture. They got it from the scientists of the nineteenth century. This is Hemingway's world, too, the world with nothing at center.

Over against this particular version of the naturalistic view of the world, there was, of course, an argument for Divine Intelligence and a Divine purpose, an argument that based itself on the beautiful system of nature, on natural law. The closely knit order of the natural world, so the argument ran, implies a Divine Intelligence. But if one calls Hemingway's attention to the fact that the natural world is a world of order, his reply is on record in a story called "A Natural History of the Dead." There he quotes from the traveler Mungo Park, who, naked and starving in an African desert, observed a beautiful little moss-flower and meditated thus:

Can the Being who planted, watered, and brought to perfection, in this obscure part of the world, a thing which appears of so small importance, look with unconcern upon the situation and suffering of creatures formed after his own image? Surely not. Reflections like these would not allow me to despair: I started up and, disregarding both hunger and fatigue, travelled forward, assured that relief was at hand; and I was not disappointed.

And Hemingway continues:

With a disposition to wonder and adore in like manner, as Bishop Stanley says [the author of *A Familiar History of Birds*], can any branch of Natural History be studied without increasing that faith, love and hope which we also, everyone of us, need in our journey through the wilderness of life? Let us therefore see what inspiration we may derive from the dead.

Then Hemingway presents the picture of a modern battlefield, where the bloated and decaying bodies give a perfect example of the natural order of chemistry—but scarcely an argument for faith, hope, and love. That picture is his answer to the argument that the order of nature implies meaning in the world.

In one of the stories, "A Clean, Well-Lighted Place," we find the best description of what underlies Hemingway's world of violent action. In the early stages of the story we see an old man sitting late in a Spanish café. Two waiters are speaking of him.

> "Last week he tried to commit suicide," one waiter said.
> "Why?"
> "He was in despair."
> "What about?"
> "Nothing."
> "How do you know it was nothing?"
> "He has plenty of money."

The despair beyond plenty of money—or beyond all the other gifts of the world: its nature becomes a little clearer at the end of the story when the older of the two waiters is left alone, reluctant too to leave the clean, well-lighted place:

> Turning off the electric light he continued the conversation with himself. It is the light of course but it is necessary that the place be clean and pleasant. You do not want music. Certainly you do not want music. Nor can you stand before a bar with dignity although that is all that is provided for these hours. What did he fear? It was not fear or dread. It was a nothing that he knew too well. It was all a nothing and a man was nothing too. It was only that and light was all it needed and a certain cleanness and order. Some lived in it and never felt it but he knew it all was nada y pues nada y nada y pues nada. Our nada who art in nada, nada be thy name thy kingdom nada thy will be nada in nada as it is in nada. Give us this nada our daily nada and nada us our nada as we nada our nadas and nada us not into nada but deliver us from nada; pues nada. Hail nothing full of nothing, nothing is with thee. He smiled and stood before a bar with a shining steam pressure coffee machine.
> "What's yours?" asked the barman.
> "Nada."

At the end the old waiter is ready to go home:

> Now, without thinking further, he would go home to his room. He would lie in bed and finally, with daylight, he would go to sleep. After all, he said to himself, it is probably only insomnia. Many must have it.

And the sleepless man—the man obsessed by death, by the meaninglessness of the world, by nothingness, by nada—is one of the recurring symbols in the work of Hemingway. In this phase Hemingway is a religious writer. The despair beyond plenty of money, the despair that makes a sleeplessness beyond insomnia, is the despair felt by a man who hungers for the sense of order and assurance that men seem to find in religious faith, but who cannot find grounds for his faith.

Another recurring symbol is the violent man. But the sleepless man and the violent man are not contradictory; they are complementary symbols. They represent phases of the same question, the same hungering for meaning in the world. The sleepless man is the man brooding upon nada, upon chaos, upon Nature-as-all. (For Nature-as-all equals moral chaos; even its bulls and lions and kudu are not admired by Hemingway as creatures of conscious self-discipline; their courage has a meaning only in so far as it symbolizes human courage.) The violent man is the man taking an action appropriate to the realization of the fact of nada. He is, in other words, engaged in the effort to discover human values in a naturalistic world.

Before we proceed with this line of discussion, it might be asked, "Why does Hemingway feel that the quest necessarily involves violence?" Now, at one level, the answer to this question would involve the whole matter of the bias toward violence in modern literature. But let us take it in its more immediate reference. The typical Hemingway hero is the man aware, or in the process of becoming aware, of nada. Death is the great nada. Therefore whatever code or creed the hero gets must, to be good, stick even in the face of death. It has to be good in the bull ring or on the battlefield and not merely in the study or lecture room. In fact, Hemingway is anti-intellectual, and has a great contempt for any type of solution arrived at without the testings of immediate experience.

So aside from the question of a dramatic sense that would favor violence, and aside from the mere matter of personal temperament (for Hemingway describes himself on more than one occasion as obsessed by death), the presentation of violence is appropriate in his work because death is the great nada. In taking violent risks man confronts in dramatic terms the issue of nada that is implicit in all of Hemingway's world.

But to return to our general line of discussion. There are two aspects to this violence that is involved in the quest of the Hemingway hero, two aspects that seem to represent an ambivalent attitude toward nature.

First, there is the conscious sinking into nature, as we may call it. On this line of reasoning we would find something like this: if there is at center only nada, then the only sure compensation in life, the only reality, is gratification of appetite, the relish of sensation.

Continually in the stories and novels one finds such sentences as this from *Green Hills of Africa:* ". . . drinking this, the first one of the day, the finest one there is, and looking at the thick bush we passed in the dark, feeling the cool wind of the night and smelling the good smell of Africa, I was altogether happy." What is constantly interesting in such sentences is the fact that happiness, a notion that we traditionally connect with a complicated state of being, with notions of virtue, of achievement, etc., is here equated with a set of merely agreeable sensations. For instance, in "Cross-Country Snow," one of the boys, George, says to the other, Nick, who in story after story is a sort of shadow of Hemingway himself, "Maybe we'll never go skiing again, Nick." And Nick replies, "We've got to. It isn't worth while if you can't." The sensations of skiing are the end of life. Or in another story, "Big Two-Hearted River: Part II," a story that is full of the sensation-as-happiness theme, we find this remark about Nick, who has been wading in a trout stream: "Nick climbed out onto the meadow and stood, water running down his trousers and out of his shoes, his shoes squelchy. He went over and sat on the logs. He did not want to rush his sensations any." The careful relish of sensation—that is what counts, always.

This intense awareness of the world of the senses is, of course, one of the things that made the early work of Hemingway seem, upon its first impact, so fresh and pure. Physical nature is nowhere rendered with greater vividness than in his work, and probably his only competitors in this department of literature are William Faulkner, among the modern, and Henry David Thoreau, among the older American writers. The meadows, forests, lakes, and trout streams of America, and the arid, sculpturesque mountains of Spain, appear with astonishing immediacy, an immediacy not dependent upon descriptive flourishes. But not only the appearance of landscape is important; a great deal of the freshness comes from the discrimination of sensation, the coldness of water in the "squelchy" shoes after wading, the tangy smell of dry sagebrush, the "cleanly" smell of grease and oil on a field piece.[2] Hemingway's appreciation of the aesthetic qualities of the physical world is important, but a peculiar poignancy is implicit in the rendering of those qualities; the beauty of the physical world is a background for the human predicament, and the very relishing of the beauty is merely a kind of desperate and momentary compensation possible in the midst of the predicament.

This careful relishing of the world of the senses comes to a climax in drinking and sex. Drink is the "giant-killer," the weapon against man's thought of nada. And so is sex, for that matter, though when sexual attraction achieves the status of love, the process is one that attempts to achieve a meaning rather than to forget meaninglessness in the world. In terms of drinking and sex, the typical Hemingway hero is a man of monel-metal stomach and Homeric prowess in the arts of love. And the typical situation is love, with some drinking, against the background of nada—of civilization gone to pot, of war, or of death—as we get it in all of the novels in one form or another, and in many of the stories.

It is important to remember, however, that the sinking into nature, even at the level of drinking and mere sexuality, is a self-conscious act. It is not the random gratification of appetite. We see this quite clearly in *The Sun Also Rises* in the contrast between Cohn, who is merely a random dabbler in the world of sensation, who is merely trying to amuse himself, and the initiates like Jake and Brett, who are aware of the nada at the center of things and whose dissipations, therefore, have a philosophical significance. The initiate in Hemingway's world raises the gratification of appetite to the level of a cult and a discipline.

The cult of sensation, as we have already indicated, passes over very readily into the cult of true love, for the typical love story is presented primarily in terms of the cult of sensation. (*A Farewell to Arms,* as we shall see when we come to a detailed study of that novel, is closely concerned with this transition.) Even in the cult of true love it is the moment that counts, and the individual. There is never any past or future to the love stories, and the lovers are always isolated, not moving within the framework of obligations of an ordinary human society. The notion of the cult—a secret cult composed of those who have been initiated into the secret of nada—is constantly played up.

In *A Farewell to Arms,* for instance, Catherine and Frederic are two against the world, a world that is, literally as well as figuratively, an alien world. The peculiar relationship between Frederic and the priest takes on a new significance if viewed in terms of the secret cult. We shall come to this topic later, but for the moment we can say that the priest is a priest of Divine Love, the subject about which he and Frederic converse in the hospital, and that Frederic himself is a kind of priest, one of the initiate in the end, of the cult of profane love. This same pattern of two against the world with an understanding confidant or interpreter, reappears in *For Whom the Bell Tolls* —with Pilar, the gypsy woman who understands "love," substituting for the priest of *A Farewell to Arms.*

The initiates of the cult of love are those who are aware of nada, but their effort, as members of the cult, is to find a meaning to put in place of the nada. That is, there is an attempt to make the relationship of love take on a religious significance in so far as it can give meaning to life. This general topic is not new with the work of Hemingway. It is one of the literary themes of the nineteenth century—and has, as a matter of fact, a longer history than that.

If the cult of love arises from and states itself in the language of the cult of sensation, it is an extension of the sinking-into-nature aspect of the typical Hemingway violence; but in so far as it involves a discipline and a search for a "faith," it leads us to the second aspect of the typical violence.

The violence, although in its first aspect it represents a sinking into nature, at the same time, in its second aspect, represents a conquest of nature, and of nada in man. It represents such a conquest, not because of the fact of violence, but because the violence appears in terms of a discipline, a style, and a code. It is, as we have already seen, in terms of a self-imposed discipline that the heroes make one gallant, though limited, effort to redeem the incoherence of the world: they attempt to impose some form upon the disorder of their lives, the technique of the bullfighter or sportsman, the discipline of the soldier, the fidelity of the lover, or even the code of the gangster, which, though brutal and apparently dehumanizing, has its own ethic. (Ole Anderson, in "The Killers," is willing to take his medicine without whining, and even recognizes some necessity and justice in his plight. Or the dying Mexican, in "The Gambler, the Nun, and the Radio," refuses to squeal despite the detective's argument: "One can, with honor, denounce one's assailant.")

If it is said that Frederic in *A Farewell to Arms* does not, when he deserts, exhibit the discipline of the soldier, the answer is simple: his obligation has been constantly presented as an obligation to the men in his immediate command, and he and the men in his command have never recognized an obligation to the total war—they recognize no meaning in the war and are bound together only by a squad sense and by their immediate respect for each other; when Frederic is separated from his men his obligation is gone. His true obligation then becomes the fidelity to Catherine.

The discipline, the form, is never quite capable of subduing the world, but fidelity to it is part of the gallantry of defeat. By fidelity to it the hero manages to keep one small place "clean" and "well-lighted," and manages to retain, or achieve for one last moment, his dignity. There should be, as the old Spanish waiter reflects, a "clean, well-lighted place" where one could keep one's dignity at the late hour.

We have said earlier that the typical Hemingway character is tough and, apparently, insensitive. But only apparently, for the fidelity to a code, to the discipline, may be the index to a sensitivity that allows the characters to see, at moments, their true plight. At times, and usually at times of stress, it is the tough man in the Hemingway world, the disciplined man, who is actually aware of pathos or tragedy. The individual toughness (which may be taken to be the private discipline demanded by the world) may find itself in conflict with the natural human reactions; but the Hemingway hero, though he may be aware of the claims of the natural reaction, the spontaneous human emotion, cannot surrender to it because he knows that the only way to hold on to the definition of himself, to "honor" or "dignity," is to maintain the discipline, the code. For example, when pity appears in the Hemingway world—as in "The Pursuit Race"—it does not appear in its maximum but in its minimum manifestation.

What this means in terms of style and method is the use of understatement. This understatement, stemming from the contrast between the sensitivity and the superimposed discipline, is a constant aspect of the work, an aspect that was caught in a cartoon in the *New Yorker.* The cartoon showed a brawny, muscle-knotted forearm and a hairy hand that clutched a rose. It was entitled "The Soul of Ernest Hemingway." Just as there is a margin of victory in the defeat of the Hemingway characters, so there is a little margin of sensitivity in their brutal and apparently insensitive world. Hence we have the ironical circumstance—a central circumstance in creating the pervasive irony of Hemingway's work—that the revelation of the values characteristic of his work arises from the most unpromising people and the most unpromising situations—the little streak of poetry or pathos in "The Pursuit Race," "The Killers," "My Old Man," "A Clean, Well-Lighted Place," or "The Undefeated." We have a perfect example of it in the last-named story. After the defeat of the old bullfighter, who is lying wounded on an operating table, Zurito, the picador, is about to cut off the old fellow's pigtail, the mark of his profession. But when the wounded man starts up, despite his pain, and says, "You couldn't do a thing like that," Zurito says, "I was joking." Zurito becomes aware that, after all, the old bullfighter is, in a way, undefeated, and deserves to die with his coleta on.

This locating of the poetic, the pathetic, or the tragic in the unpromising person or situation is not unique with Hemingway. It is something with which we are acquainted in a great deal of our literature since the Romantic Movement. In such literature, the sensibility is played down, and an antiromantic surface sheathes the work; the point is in the contrast. The impulse that led Hemingway to the simple character is akin to the one that drew Wordsworth to the same choice. Wordsworth felt that his unsophisticated peasants were more honest in their responses than the cultivated man, and were therefore more poetic. Instead of Wordsworth's peasant we have in Hemingway's work the bullfighter, the soldier, the revolutionist, the sportsman, and the gangster; instead of Wordsworth's children we have the young men like Nick, the person just on the verge of being initiated into the world. There are, of course, differences between the approach of Wordsworth and that of Hemingway, but there is little difference on the point of marginal sensibility. In one sense, both are anti-intellectual, and in such poems as "Resolution and Independence" or "Michael" one finds even closer ties.

I have just indicated a similarity between Wordsworth and Hemingway on the grounds of a romantic anti-intellectualism. But with Hemingway it is far more profound and radical than with Wordsworth. All we have to do to see the difference is to put Wordsworth's Preface to the *Lyrical Ballads* over against any number of passages from Hemingway. The intellectualism of the eighteenth century had merely put a veil of stereotyped language over the world and a veil of snobbism over a large area of human experience. That is Wordsworth's indictment. But Hemingway's indictment of the intellectualism of the past is that it wound up in the mire and blood of 1914, to 1918; that it was a pack of lies leading to death. We can put over against the Preface of Wordsworth, a passage from *A Farewell to Arms:*

I was always embarrassed by the words sacred, glorious, and sacrifice and the expression in vain. We had heard them, sometimes standing in the rain almost out of earshot, so that only the shouted words came through, and had read them, on proclamations that were slapped up by billposters over other proclamations, now for a long time, and I had seen nothing sacred, and the things that were glorious had no glory and the sacrifices were like the stockyards at Chicago if nothing was done with the meat except to bury it. There were many words that you could not stand to hear and finally only the names of places had dignity. . . . Abstract words such as glory, honor, courage, or hallow were obscene beside the concrete names of villages, the numbers of roads, the names of rivers, the numbers of regiments and the dates.

I do not mean to say that the general revolution in style, and the revolt against the particular intellectualism of the nineteenth century, was a result of the first world war. As a matter of fact, that revolt was going on long before the war, but for Hemingway, and for many others, the war gave the situation a peculiar depth and urgency.

Perhaps we might scale the matter thus: Wordsworth was a revolutionist —he truly had a new view of the world—but his revolutionary view left great tracts of the world untouched; the Church of England, for instance. Arnold and Tennyson, a generation or so later, though not revolutionists themselves, are much more profoundly stirred by the revolutionary situation than ever Wordsworth was; that is, the area of the world involved in the debate was for them greater. Institutions are called into question in a more fundamental way.

But they managed to hang on to their English God and their English institutions. With Hardy, the area of disturbance has grown greater, and what can be salvaged is much less. He, like the earlier Victorians, had a strong sense of community to sustain him in the face of the universe that was for him, as not finally for Arnold and Tennyson, unfriendly, or at least neutral and Godless. But his was a secret community, different from that of social institutions. It was a human communion that, as a matter of fact, was constantly being violated by institutions. Their violation of it is, in fact, a constant source of subject matter and a constant spring of irony. Nevertheless, Hardy could refer to himself as a meliorist. He could not keep company with Wordsworth or Tennyson or Arnold; and when Hardy, having been elected an Honorary Fellow of Magdalene College, Cambridge, was to be formally admitted, the Master, Doctor Donaldson (as we know from A. C. Benson's *Diary*) was much afraid that Hardy might dislike the religious service. The occasion, however, went off very well, even though Hardy, after impressing the Master with his knowledge of ecclesiastical music, did remark, "Of course it's only a sentiment to me now." Hardy listened to a sermon by the Archdeacon of Zanzibar, who declared that God was "a God of *desire*—who both hated and loved—not a mild or impersonal force." But even though Hardy could not accept the God of the Bishop of Zanzibar, he still had faith in the constructive power of the secret community.

Now, in Hemingway we see something very like Hardy's secret community, but one much smaller, one whose definition has become much more specialized. Its members are those who know the code. They recognize each other, they know the password and the secret grip, but they are few in number, and each is set off against the world like a wounded lion ringed round by waiting hyenas (*Green Hills of Africa* gives us the hyena symbol—the animal whose death is comic because it is all hideously "appetite": wounded, it eats its own intestines). Furthermore, this secret community is not constructive; Hemingway is no meliorist. In fact, there are hints that somewhere in the back of his mind, and in behind his work, there is a kind of Spenglerian view of history: our civilization is running down. We get this most explicitly in *Green Hills of Africa:*

A continent ages quickly once we come. The natives live in harmony with it. But the foreigner destroys, cuts down the trees, drains the water, so that the water supply is altered and in a short time the soil, once the sod is turned under, is cropped out and, next, it starts to blow away as it has blown away in every old country and as I had seen it start to blow in Canada. The earth gets tired of being exploited. A country wears out quickly unless man puts back in it all his residue and that of all his beasts. When he quits using beasts and uses machines, the earth defeats him quickly. The machine can't reproduce, nor does it fertilize the soil, and it eats what he cannot raise. A country was made to be as we found it. We are the intruders and after we are dead we may have ruined it but it will still be there and we don't know what the next changes are. I suppose they all end up like Mongolia.

I would come back to Africa but not to make a living from it. . . . But I would come back to where it pleased me to live; to really live. Not just let my life pass. Our people went to America because that was the place for them to go then. It had been a good country and we had made a bloody mess of it and I would go, now, somewhere else as we had always had the right to go somewhere else and as we had always gone. You could always come back. Let the others come to America who did not know that they had come too late. Our people had seen it at its best and fought for it when it was well worth fighting for. Now I would go somewhere else.

This is the most explicit statement, but the view is implicit in case after case. The general human community, the general human project, has gone to pot. There is only the little secret community of, paradoxically enough, individualists who have resigned from the general community, and who are strong enough to live without any of the illusions, lies, and big words of the herd. At least, this is the case up to the novel *To Have and Have Not,* which appeared in 1937. In that novel and in *For Whom the Bell Tolls,* Hemingway attempts to bring his individualistic hero back to society, to give him a common stake with the fate of other men.

But to return to the matter of Wordsworth and Hemingway. What in Wordsworth is merely simple or innocent is in Hemingway violent: the gangster or bullfighter replaces the leech-gatherer or the child. Hemingway's world is a more disordered world, and the sensibility of his characters is more ironically in contrast with their world. The most immediate consideration here is the playing down of the sensibility as such, the sheathing of it in the code of toughness. Gertrude Stein's tribute is here relevant: "Hemingway is the shyest and proudest and sweetest-smelling storyteller of my reading." But this shyness manifests itself in the irony. In this, of course, Hemingway's irony corresponds to the Byronic irony. But the relation to Byron is even more fundamental. The pity is valid only when it is wrung from the man who has been seasoned by experience. Therefore a premium is placed on the fact of violent experience. The "dumb ox" character, commented on by Wyndham Lewis, represents the Wordsworthian peasant; the character with the code of the tough guy, the initiate, the man cultivating honor, gallantry, and reckless-ness, represents the Byronic aristocrat.

The failures of Hemingway, like his successes, are rooted in this situation. The successes occur in those instances where Hemingway accepts the essential limitations of his premises—that is, when there is an equilibrium between the dramatization and the characteristic Hemingway "point," when the system of ironies and understatements is coherent. On the other hand, the failures occur when we feel that Hemingway has not respected the limitations of his premises —that is, when the dramatization seems to be "rigged" and the violence, therefore, merely theatrical. The characteristic irony, or understatement, in such cases, seems to be too self-conscious. For example, let us glance at Hemingway's most spectacular failure, *To Have and Have Not.* The point of the novel is based on the contrast between the smuggler and the rich owners of the yachts along the quay. But the irony is essentially an irony without any center of reference. It is superficial, for, as Philip Rahv indicates, the only difference between the smuggler and the rich is that the rich were successful in their buccaneering. The revelation that comes to the smuggler dying in his launch—"a man alone ain't got no . . . chance"—is a meaningless revelation, for it has no reference to the actual dramatization. It is, finally, a failure in intellectual analysis of the situation.

There is, I believe, a good chance that *For Whom the Bell Tolls* will not turn out to be Hemingway's best novel (an honor I should reserve for *A Farewell to Arms*) primarily because in this most ambitious of the novels Hemingway does not accept the limitations of his premises. I do not mean to imply that it is on a level with *To Have and Have Not.* There is a subtler irony in the later novel. I have pointed out that the irony in *To Have and Have Not* is that of the contrast between the smuggler and the rich in the yachts along the pier; that is, it is a simple irony, in direct line with the ostensible surface direction of the story. But the irony in *For Whom the Bell Tolls* runs counter to the ostensible surface direction of the story. As surface, we have a conflict between the forces of light and the forces of darkness, freedom versus fascism, etc. Hero and heroine are clearly and completely and romantically aligned on the side of light. We are prepared to see the Fascist atrocities and the general human kindness of the Loyalists. It happens to work out the other way. The scene of horror is the massacre by the Loyalists, not by the Fascists. Again, in the attack on El Sordo's hill by the Fascists, we are introduced to a young Fascist lieutenant, whose bosom friend is killed in the attack. We are suddenly given this little human glimpse—against the grain of the surface. But this incident, we discover later, is preparation for the very end of the novel. We leave the hero lying wounded, preparing to cover the retreat of his friends. The man who is over the sights of the machine gun as the book ends is the Fascist lieutenant, whom we have been made to know as a man, not as a monster. This general ironical conditioning of the overt story line is reflected also in the attitude of Anselmo, who kills but cannot believe in killing. In other words, the irony here is much more functional, and more complicated, than that of *To Have and Have Not;* the irony affirms that the human values may transcend the party lines.

Much has been said to the effect that *To Have and Have Not* and *For Whom the Bell Tolls* represent a basic change of point of view, an enlargement of what I have called the secret community. Now no doubt that is the intention behind both books, but the temper of both books, the good one and the bad one, is the old temper, the cast of characters is the old cast, and the assumptions lying far below the explicit intention are the old assumptions.

The monotony and self-imitation, into which Hemingway's work some-times falls, are again an effect of a failure in dramatization. Hemingway, apparently, can dramatize his "point" in only one basic situation and with only one set of characters. He has, as we have seen, only two key characters, with certain variations from them by way of contrast or counterpoint. His best women characters, by the way, are those who most nearly approximate the men; that is, they embody the masculine virtues and point of view characteris-tic of Hemingway's work.

But the monotony is not merely a monotony deriving from the characters as types; it derives, rather, from the limitations of the author's sensibility, which seems to come alive in only one issue. A more flexible sensibility, one capable of making nicer discriminations, might discover great variety in such key characters and situations. But Hemingway's successes are due, in part at least, to the close co-ordination that he sometimes achieves between the char-acter and the situation, and the sensibility as it reflects itself in the style.

The style characteristically is simple, even to the point of monotony. The characteristic sentence is simple, or compound; and if compound, there is no implied subtlety in the co-ordination of the clauses. The paragraph structure is, characteristically, based on simple sequence. There is an obvious relation between this style and the characters and situations with which the author is concerned—a relation of dramatic decorum. (There are, on the other hand, examples, especially in the novels, of other, more fluent, lyrical effects, but even here this fluency is founded on the conjunction *and;* it is a rhythmical and not a logical fluency. And the lyrical quality is simply a manifestation of that marginal sensibility, as can be demonstrated by an analysis of the occasions on which it appears.)

But there is a more fundamental aspect of the question, an aspect that involves not the sensibility of the characters but the sensibility of the author. The short, simple rhythms, the succession of coordinate clauses, the general lack of subordination—all suggest a dislocated and ununified world. The figures who live in this world live a sort of hand-to-mouth existence perceptually, and conceptually they hardly live at all. Subordination implies some exercise of discrimination—the sifting of reality through the intellect. But in Hemingway we see a romantic anti-intellectualism.

In Wordsworth, too, we see this strain of anti-intellectualism. He, too, wishes to clear away the distorting sophistications of the intellect, and to keep his eye on the object. The formulations of the intellect create the "veil of familiarity" that he would clear away. His mode, too, was to take unpromising material and reveal in it the lyric potentiality. He, too, was interested in the margin of sensibility. He, too, wished to respect the facts, and could have understood Hemingway's rejection of the big abstract words in favor of "the concrete names of villages, the numbers of roads, the names of rivers, the numbers of regiments and the dates."

The passage from *A Farewell to Arms* from which the above quotation comes is, of course, the passage most commonly used to explain the attitude behind Hemingway's style. But we can put with it other passages of a similar import, and best of all a sentence from the story "Soldier's Home." Krebs, the boy who has been through the war and who comes back home to find himself cut off from life, had "acquired the nausea in regard to experience that is the result of untruth or exaggeration." He is a casualty, not of bullet or bayonet, but of the big, abstract words. Hemingway's style is, in a way, an attempt to provide an antidote for that "nausea."

A Farewell to Arms is a love story. It is a compelling story at the merely personal level, but it is much more compelling and significant when we see the figures of the lovers silhouetted against the flame-streaked blackness of war, of a collapsing world, of nada. For there is a story behind the love story. That story is the quest for meaning and certitude in a world that seems to offer nothing of the sort. It is, in a sense, a religious book; if it does not offer a religious solution it is nevertheless conditioned by the religious problem.

The very first scene of the book, though seemingly casual, is important if we are to understand the deeper motivations of the story. It is the scene at the officers' mess where the captain baits the priest. "Priest every night five against one," the captain explains to Frederic. But Frederic, we see in this and later scenes, takes no part in the baiting. There is a bond between him and the priest, a bond that they both recognize. This becomes clear when, after the officers have advised Frederic where he should go on his leave to find the best girls, the priest turns to him and says that he would like to have him to go to Abruzzi, his own province:

"There is good hunting. You would like the people and though it is cold it is clear and dry. You could stay with my family. My father is a famous hunter."
"Come on," said the captain. "We go whorehouse before it shuts."
"Goodnight," I said to the priest.
"Goodnight," he said.

In this preliminary contrast between the officers, who invite the hero to go the brothel, and the priest, who invites him to go to the cold, clear, dry country, we have in its simplest form the issue of the novel.

Frederic does go with the officers that night, and on his leave he does go to the cities, "to the smoke of cafés and nights when the room whirled and you needed to look at the wall to make it stop, nights in bed, drunk, when you knew that that was all there was, and the strange excitement of waking and not knowing who it was with you, and the world all unreal in the dark and so exciting that you must resume again unknowing and not caring in the night, sure that this was all and all and all and not caring." Frederic, at the opening of the novel, lives in the world of random and meaningless appetite, knowing that it is all and all and all, or thinking that he knows that. But behind that there is a dissatisfaction and disgust. Upon his return from his leave, sitting in the officers' mess, he tries to tell the priest how he is sorry that he had not gone to the clear, cold, dry country—the priest's home, which takes on the shadowy symbolic significance of another kind of life, another view of the world. The priest had always known that other country.

He had always known what I did not know and what, when I learned it, I was always able to forget. But I did not know that then, although I learned it later.

What Frederic learns later is the story behind the love story of the book.

But this theme is not merely stated at the opening of the novel and then absorbed into the action. It appears later, at crucial points, to define the line of meaning in the action. When, for example, Frederic is wounded, the priest visits him in the hospital. Their conversation makes even plainer the religious background of the novel. The priest has said that he would like to go back after the war to the Abruzzi. He continues:

"It does not matter. But there in my country it is understood that a man may love God. It is not a dirty joke."

"I understand."

He looked at me and smiled.

"You understand but you do not love God."

"No."

"You do not love Him at all?" he asked.

"I am afraid of him in the night sometimes."

"You should love Him."

"I don't love much."

"Yes," he said. "You do. What you tell me about in the nights. That is not love. That is only passion and lust. When you love you wish to do things for. You wish to sacrifice for. You wish to serve."

"I don't love."

"You will. I know you will. Then you will be happy."

We have here two important items. First, there is the definition of Frederic as the sleepless man, the man haunted by nada. Second, at this stage in the novel, the end of Book I, the true meaning of the love story with Catherine has not yet been defined. It is still at the level of appetite. The priest's role is to indicate the next stage of the story, the discovery of the true nature of love, the "wish to do things for." And he accomplishes this by indicating a parallel between secular love and Divine Love, a parallel which implies Frederick's quest for meaning and certitude. And to emphasize further this idea, Frederic, after the priest leaves, muses on the high, clean country of the Abruzzi, the priest's home that has already been endowed with the symbolic significance of the religious view of the world.

In the middle of Book II (chapter xviii), in which the love story begins to take on the significance that the priest had predicted, the point is indicated by a bit of dialogue between the lovers.

"Couldn't we be married privately some way? Then if anything happened to me or if you had a child."

"There's no way to be married except by church or state. We are married privately. You see, darling, it would mean everything to me if I had any religion. But I haven't any religion."

"You gave me the Saint Anthony."

"That was for luck. Some one gave it to me."

"Then nothing worries you?"

"Only being sent away from you. You're my religion. You're all I've got."

Again, toward the end of Book IV (chapter xxxv), just before Frederic and Catherine make their escape into Switzerland, Frederic is talking with a friend, the old Count Greffi, who has just said that he thought H. G. Wells's novel

Mr. Britling Sees It Through a very good study of the English middleclass soul. But Frederic twists the word *soul* into another meaning.

"I don't know about the soul."
"Poor boy. We none of us know about the soul. Are you *Croyant?*"
"At night."

Later in the same conversation the Count returns to the topic:

"And if you ever become devout pray for me if I am dead. I am asking several of my friends to do that. I had expected to become devout myself but it has not come." I thought he smiled sadly but I could not tell. He was so old and his face was very wrinkled, so that a smile used so many lines that all gradations were lost.
"I might become very devout," I said. "Anyway, I will pray for you."
"I had always expected to become devout. All my family died very devout. But somehow it does not come."
"It's too early."
"Maybe it is too late. Perhaps I have outlived my religious feeling."
"My own comes only at night."
"Then too you are in love. Do not forget that is a religious feeling."

So here we find, again, Frederic defined as the sleepless man, and the relation established between secular love and Divine Love.

In the end, with the death of Catherine, Frederic discovers that the attempt to find a substitute for universal meaning in the limited meaning of the personal relationship is doomed to failure. It is doomed because it is liable to all the accidents of a world in which human beings are like the ants running back and forth on a log burning in a campfire and in which death is, as Catherine says just before her own death, "just a dirty trick." But this is not to deny the value of the effort, or to deny the value of the discipline, the code, the stoic endurance, the things that make it true—or half true—that "nothing ever happens to the brave."

This question of the characteristic discipline takes us back to the beginning of the book, and to the context from which Frederic's effort arises. We have already mentioned the contrast between the officers of the mess and the priest. It is a contrast between the man who is aware of the issue of meaning in life and those who are unaware of it, who give themselves over to the mere flow of accident, the contrast between the disciplined and the undisciplined. But the contrast is not merely between the priest and the officers. Frederic's friend, the surgeon Rinaldi, is another who is on the same "side" of the contrast as the priest. He may go to the brothel with his brother officers, he may even bait the priest a little, but his personal relationship with Frederic indicates his affiliations; he is one of the initiate. Furthermore, he has the discipline of his profession, and, as we have seen, in the Hemingway world, the discipline that seems to be merely technical, the style of the artist or the form of the athlete or bullfighter, may be an index to a moral value. "Already," Rinaldi says, "I am only happy when I am working." (Already the seeking of pleasure in sensation is inadequate for Rinaldi.) This point appears more sharply in the remarks about the doctor who first attends to Frederic's wounded leg. He is incompetent and does not wish to take the responsibility for a decision.

Before he came back three doctors came into the room. I have noticed that doctors who fail in the practice of medicine have a tendency to seek one another's company and aid in consultation. A doctor who cannot take out your appendix properly will recommend to you a doctor who will be unable to remove your tonsils with success. These were three such doctors.

In contrast with them there is Doctor Valentini, who is competent, who is willing to take responsibility, and who, as a kind of mark of his role, speaks the same lingo, with the same bantering, ironical tone, as Rinaldi—the tone that is the mark of the initiate.

So we have the world of the novel divided into two groups, the initiate and the uninitiate, the aware and the unaware, the disciplined and the undisciplined. In the first group are Frederic, Catherine, Rinaldi, Valentini, Count Greffi, the old man who cut the paper silhouettes "for pleasure," and Passini, Manera, and the other ambulance men in Frederic's command. In the second group are the officers of the mess, the incompetent doctors, the "legitimate hero" Ettore, and the "patriots"—all the people who do not know what is really at stake, who are deluded by the big words, who do not have the discipline. They are the messy people, the people who surrender to the flow and illusion of things. It is this second group who provide the context of the novel, and more especially the context from which Frederic moves toward his final complete awareness.

The final awareness means, as we have said, that the individual is thrown back upon his private discipline and his private capacity to endure. The hero cuts himself off from the herd, the confused world, which symbolically appears as the routed army at Caporetto. And, as Malcolm Cowley has pointed out,[3] the plunge into the flooded Tagliamento, when Frederic escapes from the battle police, has the significance of a rite. By this "baptism" Frederic is reborn into another world; he comes out into the world of the man alone, no longer supported by and involved in society.

Anger was washed away in the river along with my obligation. Although that ceased when the carabiniere put his hands on my collar. I would like to have had the uniform off although I did not care much about the outward forms. I had taken off the stars, but that was for convenience. It was no point of honor. I was not against them. I was through. I wished them all the luck. There were the good ones, and the brave ones, and the calm ones and the sensible ones, and they deserved it. But it was not my show any more and I wished this bloody train would get to Maestre and I would eat and stop thinking.

So Frederic, by a decision, does what the boy[4] Nick does as the result of the accident of a wound. He makes a "separate peace." And from the waters of the flooded Tagliamento arises the Hemingway hero in his purest form, with human history and obligation washed away, ready to enact the last phase of his appropriate drama, and learn from his inevitable defeat the lesson of lonely fortitude.

This is not the time to attempt to give a final appraisal of Hemingway's work as a whole or even of this particular novel—if there is ever a time for a "final" appraisal. But we may touch on some of the objections which have been brought against his work.

First, there is the objection that his work is immoral or dirty or disgusting. This objection appeared in various quarters against *A Farewell to Arms* at the time of its first publication. For instance, Robert Herrick wrote that if suppression were to be justified at all it would be justified in this case. He said that the book had no significance, was merely a "lustful indulgence," and smelled of the "boudoir," and summarized his view by calling it "garbage."[5] That objection has, for the most part, died out, but its echoes can still be occasionally heard, and now and then at rare intervals some bigot or high-minded but uninstructed moralist will object to the inclusion of *A Farewell to Arms* in a college course.

The answer to this moralistic objection is fundamentally an answer to the charge that the book has no meaning. The answer would seek to establish the fact that the book does deal seriously with a moral and philosophical issue, which, for better or worse, does exist in the modern world in substantially the terms presented by Hemingway. This means that the book, even if it does not end with a solution that is generally acceptable, still embodies a moral effort and is another document of the human effort to achieve ideal values. As for the bad effect it may have on some readers, the best answer is perhaps to be found in a quotation from Thomas Hardy, who is now sanctified but whose most famous novels, *Tess of the D'Urbervilles* and *Jude the Obscure*, once suffered the attacks of the dogmatic moralists, and one of whose books was burned by a bishop:

> Of the effects of such sincere presentation on weak minds, when the courses of the characters are not exemplary and the rewards and punishments ill adjusted to deserts, it is not our duty to consider too closely. A novel which does moral injury to a dozen imbeciles, and has bracing results upon intellects of normal vigor, can justify its existence; and probably a novel was never written by the purest-minded author for which there could not be found some moral invalid or other whom it was capable of harming.[6]

Second, there is the objection that Hemingway's work, especially of the period before *To Have and Have Not,* has no social relevance, that it is off the main stream of modern life, and that it has no concern with the economic structure of society. Critics who hold this general view regard Hemingway, like Joseph Conrad and perhaps like Henry James, as an exotic. There are several possible lines of retort to this objection. One line is well stated in the following passage by David Daiches if we substitute the name of Hemingway for Conrad:

> Thus it is no reproach to Conrad that he does not concern himself at all with the economic and social background underlying human relationships in modern civilization, for he never sets out to study those relationships. The Marxists cannot accuse him of cowardice or falsification, because in this case the charge is not relevant [though it might be relevant to *To Have and Have Not* or to *For Whom the Bell Tolls*]. That, from the point of view of the man with a theory, there are accidents in history, no one can deny. And if a writer chooses to discuss those accidents rather than the events which follow the main stream of historical causation, the economic, or other, determinist can only shrug his shoulder and maintain that these events are less instructive to the students than are the major events which he chooses to study; but he cannot accuse the writer of falsehood or distortion.[7]

That much is granted by one of the ablest critics of the group who would find Hemingway an exotic. But a second line of retort would fix on the word *instructive* in the foregoing passage, and would ask what kind of instruction, if any, is to be expected of fiction, as fiction. Is the kind of instruction expected of fiction in direct competition, at the same level, with the kind of instruction offered in Political Science I or Economics II? If that is the case, then out with Shakespeare and Keats and in with Upton Sinclair.

Perhaps *instruction* is not a relevant word, after all, for this case. This is a very thorny and debatable question, but it can be ventured that what good fiction gives us is the stimulation of a powerful image of human nature trying to fulfill itself, and not instruction in an abstract sense. The economic man and political man are important aspects of human nature and may well constitute part of the *materials* of fiction. Neither the economic nor the political man is the complete man; other concerns may still be important enough to engage the attention of a writer—such concerns as love, death, courage, the point of honor, and the moral scruple. A man has to live with other men in terms not only of economic and political arrangements but also of moral arrangements; and he has to live with himself, he has to define himself. It can truly be said that these concerns are all interrelated in fact, but it might be dangerously dogmatic to insist that a writer should not bring one aspect into sharp, dramatic focus.

And it might be dangerously dogmatic to insist that Hemingway's ideas are not relevant to modern life. The mere fact that they exist and have stirred a great many people is a testimony to their relevance. Or to introduce a variation on that theme, it might be dogmatic to object to his work on the ground that he has few basic ideas. The history of literature seems to show that good artists may have very few *basic* ideas. They may have many ideas, but the ideas do not lead a life of democratic give-and-take, of genial camaraderie. No, there are usually one or two basic, obsessive ones. Like Savonarola, the artist may well say: *"Le mie cose erano poche e grandi."* And the ideas of the artist are grand simply because they are intensely felt, intensely realized—not because they are, by objective standards, by public, statistical standards, "important." No, that kind of public, statistical importance may be a condition of their being grand but is not of the special essence of their grandeur. (Perhaps not even the condition—perhaps the grandeur inheres in the fact that the artistic work shows us a parable of meaning—how idea is felt and how passion becomes idea through order.)

An artist may need few basic ideas, but in assessing his work we must introduce another criterion in addition to that of intensity. We must introduce the criterion of area. An artist's basic ideas do not operate in splendid isolation; to a greater or lesser degree, they prove themselves by their conquest of other ideas. Or again differently, the focus is a focus of experience, and the area of experience involved gives us another criterion of condition, the criterion of area. Perhaps an example would be helpful here. We have said that Hemingway is concerned with the scruple of honor, that this is a basic idea in his work. But we find that he applies this idea to a relatively small area of experience. In fact, we never see a story in which the issue involves the problem of definition of the scruple, nor do we ever see a story in which honor calls for a slow, grinding, day-to-day conquest of nagging difficulties. In other words, the idea is submitted to the test of a relatively small area of experience, to experience of a hand-picked sort, and to characters of a limited range.

But within that range, within the area in which he finds congenial material and in which competing ideas do not intrude themselves too strongly, Hemingway's expressive capacity is very powerful and the degree of intensity is very great. He is concerned not to report variety of human nature or human situation, or to analyze the forces operating in society, but to communicate a certain feeling about, a certain attitude toward, a special issue. That is, he is essentially a lyric rather than a dramatic writer, and for the lyric writer virtue depends upon the intensity with which the personal vision is rendered rather than upon the creation of a variety of characters whose visions are in conflict among themselves. And though Hemingway has not given—and never intended to give—a documented diagnosis of our age, he has given us one of the most compelling symbols of a personal response to our age.

1. Introduction to the Modern Library edition of *A Farewell to Arms.*

2. Commented on by Ford Madox Ford in his introduction to the Modern Library edition of *A Farewell to Arms.*

3. Introduction to the *Portable Hemingway,* The Viking Press. In this general connection one may consider the strategic advantage that Hemingway has in that it is the Italian army from which his hero deserts. If his hero had, for instance, deserted from the American army, the American reader's resistance to accepting the act would have been much greater—the reader's own immediate loyalties, etc., would have been betrayed by Frederic's act. And by the same token the resistance to the symbolic meaning of the act—the resigning from society—would have been much greater. The reader is led to accept the act because the desertion is from a "foreign" army. The point is indicated in a passage of dialogue between Frederic and Catherine. Frederic complains that he doesn't want them to have to live in secret and on the run like criminals.

"I feel like a criminal. I've deserted from the army."

"Darling, *please* be sensible. It's not deserting from the army. It's only the Italian army."

It may be objected that since Hemingway himself saw service on the Italian front it is only natural that his story should be laid there and that by consequence the fact has no symbolic significance and no significance as fictional strategy. But the fact that circumstances of personal history dictated the setting of the story does not prevent the author from seizing on and using the advantages inherent in the situation.

4. *In Our Time,* chapter vi.

5. "What Is Dirt?" *Bookman,* November, 1929.

6. "The Profitable Reading of Fiction," in *Life and Art, Essays, Notes and Letters.*

7. For a contrary view of the work of Conrad, see my essay on p. 31 *(Selected Essays).*

THE OTHER HEMINGWAY

ALAN HOLDER

IT SEEMS TO BE the general consensus of Hemingway criticism that his women characters fall into one of two categories, either that of the bitch who threatens to rob the Hemingway male of his strength and integrity, or that of the dream girl, a mindless creature who makes no demands upon her man and who exists only to satisfy his (sexual) needs; in his pleasure is her fulfillment. Both creatures are regarded as the product of a "masculine" sensibility, one which is jealous of its freedom, anxious to safeguard its virility, engaged most deeply by experiences that are far removed from home and hearth, from domesticity and fatherhood, a sensibility to which the female is essentially peripheral.[1] There is a good deal of truth in this description; indeed, it is an accurate representation of the "major" Hemingway. However, there are certain elements in his work that refuse to be fitted into this formula. We need to refine our conception of his treatment of women and the implications of that treatment; we need to recognize and acknowledge the other Hemingway.

In effect, a step towards such recognition was taken by Carlos Baker when he noted the distinct *pull* of domesticity evident in some of Hemingway's fiction; the dissolution of marriage through death or divorce generates a feeling of despair in such stories as "A Canary for One," "Homage to Switzerland," and "In Another Country."[2] (We might remember that Hemingway himself could never permit one of his own marriages to come to an end without soon plunging into another.) But even in these stories the focus is on the *man's* unhappiness. On certain other occasions, however, Hemingway has been able to widen his focus to include woman among those "whom things are done to." The same writer who has displayed a deep hostility toward the female has at times been able to perceive that she can sometimes be more sinned against than sinning, that she has legitimate demands which his males either ignore or refuse to meet, that she can rightfully lay claim to an existence that does not begin and end with coition in a hotel bedroom or a sleeping bag. What we get

Reprinted with permission from *Twentieth Century Literature* (1963), 153–157.

then is a reining in of Hemingway's tendency to look at the woman through the eyes of the abstracted male, and a consequent tension in the work as a whole between that attitude and a tendency to empathize with the woman. To be sure, that empathy, demonstrated chiefly in the short stories, has not produced any notable female characters, but it has brought into Hemingway's fiction a certain self-criticism of his dominant attitudes.

"The Short Happy Life of Francis Macomber," the work that is placed first in the collected edition of Hemingway's short stories,[3] gives us the classic portrait of the bitch who destroys her man. But one of the very first stories that Hemingway ever published, "Up in Michigan," is a tale of the victimization of a young woman by an insensitive self-centered male. Liz Horton desires, in part, the sexual attentions of Jim Gilman, but she is hardly prepared for his rough approach or for his indifference to her after the act of intercourse. "She was cold and miserable and everything felt gone." She shakes Jim, who has gone to sleep. "Jim stirred and curled a little tighter." (pp. 85–86) Hemingway presents the action with characteristic lack of explicit comment, but his sympathy with Liz is unmistakable. The story is decidedly not a "nostalgic" evocation of boyhood as Leslie Fiedler would have us believe.[4]

Three out of the next four pieces that follow "Up in Michigan" in the collected edition may be said to constitute a "childbirth" sequence, which again centers on the victimization of woman, this time by the combined forces of biology and war. (The fourth piece, "Chapter I," may be taken as a contrasting portrait of male insouciance in time of war.) One of these works, the vignette that serves as "Chapter II," describes refugees of the Greco-Turkish war fleeing in carts. There is a woman in one of these carts "having a kid, with a young girl holding a blanket over her and crying. Scared sick looking at it." (p. 97) In "On the Quai at Smyrna" the narrator seems unable to escape his memories of the women refugees who refused to give up their dead babies: "You didn't mind the women who were having babies as you did those with the dead ones." (p. 88) But one Hemingway character in this sequence does mind the agony of childbirth, the husband of "Indian Camp," who, horrified at his wife's protracted labor pains which are marked by her screams, cuts his throat. The sensibility that this act indicates, one extremely responsive to the woman's pain (and one perhaps that is pierced with guilt at having brought it upon her), seems very much akin to the sensibility that created "Up in Michigan" and the following sequence in the first place. Fiedler has said of Hemingway that "there is no writer to whom childbirth more customarily presents itself as the essential catastrophe." But in Fiedler's view this is an expression of Hemingway's rejection "of maturity and of fatherhood . . ."[5]

Though this remark applies to other of Hemingway's works, there is no such rejection present in these childbirth scenes, but only an empathy with woman's plight, a horror at the ultimate outrage of childbirth that is visited upon her (cf. the closing pages of *A Farewell to Arms*).

Moreover, along with the rejection of fatherhood in Hemingway, we can find a rejection of that rejection. How damning a portrait we get in "Hills Like White Elephants" and *To Have and Have Not* of the man who wants his woman to serve solely as the source of his sexual pleasure, who denies her the motherhood that she desires. In the story, the nameless man keeps assuring his wife (or mistress) that the abortion he wants her to undergo is " 'really an awfully simple operation . . . It's not really an operation at all.' " Once it is performed they will be " 'happy' " again. (p. 275) In *To Have and Have Not*, Richard Gordon's wife is permitted to voice what is perhaps the most extended and bitter condemnation of the male in all of Hemingway. She says to her husband:

Everything I believed in and everything I cared about I left for you because you were so wonderful and you loved me so much that love was all that mattered. Love was the greatest thing, wasn't it? Love was what we had that no one else had or could ever have. . . . Slop. Love is just another dirty lie. Love is ergoapiol pills to make me come around because you were afraid to have a baby. Love is quinine and quinine and quinine until I'm deaf with it. Love is that dirty aborting horror that you took me to. Love is my insides all messed up. It's half catheters and half whirling douches. I know about love. Love always hangs up behind the bathroom door. It smells like lysol. To hell with love. . . . I'm through with love. Your kind of picknose love. You writer.[6]

"You writer"—used here as a kind of culminating epithet in this savage tirade, the phrase may well be revealing, a striking self-criticism on the part of Hemingway, a writer whose ideal women are willing to settle for sex, pure and simple. (It is implied that Gordon's wife is a Catholic who does not feel truly married to him because the ceremony was not performed in the Church. Hemingway's commitment to Catholicism, qualified as it was, may have been enough to strengthen his guilt at having created an image of ideal love divorced from parenthood.)

Richard Gordon and the nameless man in "Hills Like White Elephants" represent an advanced stage of the insensitivity to woman's needs that Hemingway had depicted earlier in "Cat in the Rain." The wife in that story wishes to rescue a cat attempting to shelter itself from the rain, and to keep it as her own. This is part of a larger desire for a domesticity and femininity she is being deprived of. Unlike her husband, who does not want her to let it grow, she is not happy with her short hair; she is tired of " 'looking like a boy.' " (p. 169) Absorbed in his reading, he is indifferent to her yearnings and finally tells her to " 'shut up and get something to read.' " (p. 170) The padrone of the hotel in which they are staying presents her with a cat, showing a greater consideration for her than her husband displays.

A grotesque version of the insensitive husband occurs in "An Alpine Idyll" (published the same year as "Hills Like White Elephants"). The narrator has been skiing for "too long" and is glad to get down into the valley and away from "the unnatural high mountain spring." (pp. 344–345) But once in the valley he is told of a farmer's wife who had died some months before and whose frozen corpse, propped upright, was used by her husband as a lantern post. Philip Young is quite right when he locates the story's significance in the narrator's lack of response to this bit of pastoral gothic (although Young does not particularly concern himself with what it is the narrator is not responding to). In Young's view, the Hemingway protagonist, repeatedly confronted with the terrible, shows himself in this story to be building up a protective shell around himself; he is becoming less vulnerable to the world's horrors.[7] However, to go beyond this interpretation, Hemingway may mean us to associate the acquisition of this protection with the narrator's protracted skiing, thereby making the point that the process of hardening has been allowed to go too far. For the narrator is even less sensitive than the peasant. The latter, made aware that he had done wrong, was ashamed. The narrator and his friend, after hearing of the atrocity, merely agree that it's time to eat. Victimization of the woman has been carried to an extreme here and has been met by an equally extreme insensitivity. It might be noted that this story was published along with "Cross-Country Snow," where the world of skiing and male companionship was set in opposition to the world of domesticity and fatherhood encroaching on Nick Adams. In that story Hemingway seemed to favor the masculine world. But in "An Alpine Idyll" he may be suggesting that the narrator, presumably Nick, has indeed been skiing too long, that his immersion in an exclusively male world has crippled his capacity for natural response, this capacity being tested, appropriately enough, by an outrage committed against a woman.

What the foregoing pages have tried to show is that the "male" temperament that has fashioned the two principal female types in Hemingway has not been allowed to operate unabashedly; that Hemingway has displayed what is not generally attributed to him, a capacity to question some of his own deepest responses towards women. The tension between those impulses and the criticism that Hemingway himself subjects them to is most subtly, and perhaps most profoundly, expressed in "Now I Lay Me," a work that has not received adequate critical scrutiny, though it is often referred to by students of Hemingway. (One is tempted to call it the archetypal Hemingway story, employing as it does a number of that writer's basic subjects: the appeal of fishing, the wounding of the protagonist, the insomnia that expresses a metaphysical malaise, the rejection of the female.)

The story is written in the first person with the narrator (who may again be taken as Nick Adams) telling of the various devices he used to get through the sleepless nights after he was wounded. He recalled the streams he had fished as a boy and fished them again in his mind. He thought of the people he had known and tried to recall everything that had ever happened to him. One of the incidents he remembered was seeing his mother destroy his father's collection of Indian arrowheads, an act that had angered her husband. (In *Love and Death in the American Novel,* Fiedler alludes twice to this event, suggesting that the mother here is the prototype of all of Hemingway's fearsome women.[8]) It was Nick's memory of this incident that rendered ironic the assurance of his orderly that marriage "would fix up everything," including his insomnia. (p. 371) The orderly's assertion set Nick to thinking of all the girls he had known and "what kind of wives they would make." Finally, however, he went back to thinking of trout fishing because he found that the girls eventually became blurred in his mind "and all became rather the same," while the streams preserved their individual features and he could always find "something new about them." (p. 371)

All these details cohere into the classical Hemingway pattern: woman regarded as lacking any essential interest, except when she assumes the role of destroyer (or sexual convenience), woman rejected in favor of a male pursuit undertaken alone or with a chosen companion. This is undoubtedly the main current of feeling that runs through the story. But there are other details that serve to check this current and to set up complicating eddies of meaning.

Among the things that Nick remembers are the contents of the attic in his boyhood home, including the jars of snakes and other specimens that his father had collected when *he* was a boy and had preserved in alcohol, "the alcohol sunken in the jars so the backs of some of the snakes and specimens were exposed and had turned white . . ." (p. 365) The image is not a pleasant one; the specimens have been preserved beyond their time. As a matter of fact, Nick remembers that the jars were eventually destroyed in a fire in the back yard when the family moved to a new house designed and built by the mother.

The reference to this burning occurs just before Nick's memory of the destruction of his father's Indian relics. To a certain extent the two incidents are parallel—in both cases the father's possessions are destroyed, and the designing of the house by the mother suggests, as did the destruction of the arrowheads, her dominance over her husband. But Hemingway precludes the emergence of a perfect parallel between the two events by having his narrator forget who burned the jars. Moreover, the ugliness of the snakes makes their destruction seem natural and desirable. Indeed, is there not the implication here that the father has tried to cling too long to the relics of his boyhood, that he has displayed an unhealthy regression? And is not the narrator himself repeating this pattern, turning away from thoughts of girls with a boy's contempt and choosing instead to think of trout streams? One would hesitate to suggest that this pattern is recognized as regression by Hemingway were it not for the outrageous sexual pun in the title (just as there is a pun relating to sex in the title of a later story, "The Sea Change"). On one level, the phrase "Now I Lay Me" is an ironic reference to the child's bedtime prayer, ironic because the narrator cannot sleep and because his war experience has brought him in some respects a long way from childhood. But in addition is there not a word play here on "lay"? For the narrator has continued to reject women; he tells us at the end of the story that he has never married. What we have seen him doing in the story (and what he has presumably continued doing) is turning in on himself in an effort to sustain himself, indulging in what we might call mental masturbatory activity centered not on the erotic but on fishing! That Hemingway himself views this as a perverted self-sufficiency is suggested by his having included among Nick's memories the time when he could find no worms, no bait at all, and he "had to cut up one of the trout [he] had caught and use him for bait." (p. 364) Here the fishing has become perverted. Like the narrator it has turned in on itself to sustain itself.

The story, then, presents us with a sick protagonist. We should credit Hemingway with perceiving the sickness. Even while expressing his hostility toward woman and his complementary desire to flee from her into fishing, he was able to stand back from himself and question the validity of that hostility and of that retreat.

1. One of the most recent and most cogently stated examples of this view is to be found in Leslie Fiedler's *Love and Death in the American Novel* (New York, 1960).

2. See Carlos Baker, *Hemingway: The Writer as Artist* (Princeton, 1956), pp. 136–139.

3. The edition in question is that issued by Charles Scribner's Sons (New York, 1953). All subsequent references to the stories will cite the pagination of that edition and be included in the text of the essay.
4. Fiedler, p. 304.
5. *Ibid.*, pp. 305–306.
6. Ernest Hemingway, *To Have and Have Not* (New York, 1937), pp. 185–186.
7. See Philip Young, *Ernest Hemingway* (New York, 1952), pp. 31–32.
8. Fiedler, pp. 307, 321.

THE STILL CENTER OF HEMINGWAY'S WORLD

BEONGCHEON YU

IN 1935 HEMINGWAY WROTE: "When you have loved three things all your life, from the earliest you can remember; to fish, to shoot and, later, to read; and when, all your life, the necessity to write has been your master, you learn to remember and, when you think back you remember more fishing and shooting and reading than anything else and that is a pleasure." In discussing the development of Hemingway as a personal artist we need not be reminded of his uncommon interest in fishing and hunting. If we add to this list two more items, war and bullfighting, we find Hemingway's world already solidly established, not an altar to the Muses but an arena for the celebration of life. The general festive mood emanating from this arena has in effect disturbed the mindful as much as it has enthralled the mindless. For instance, Edmund Wilson voiced profound misgivings about Hemingway's view of "life as a sport"; D.S. Savage in turn found his world altogether devoid of "religion, morality, politics, culture, or history," that is, anything distinctively human; and Leon Edel also denounced his art as "an evasion of life." Their tone of exasperation derives mainly from what they consider to be Hemingway's lack of high seriousness.

On the other hand, many critics have come to Hemingway's defense, calling his art a cult of the senses, excitement, ecstasy, action, and death, one critic going so far as to label him an existentialist. Whether in defense or attack, it is apparent that no treatment of his art can bypass the question of sports in his world as of no consequence. Hemingway refuses to treat sports as hobbies,

Reprinted with permission from *Phoenix* (Korea), XII (Spring 1968), 15–44.

pastime, or recreation; they are high seriousness to him, occupying the center of his world, not its periphery. His art is an attempt to accept sports as arts and restore to them their original dignity. And to have a correct view of sports in Hemingway's world, one must proceed from inside, for that approach alone can reveal what it is that fascinates him as a man and as an artist.

I

It is a critical commonplace to point out the decisive significance of war in the birth of Hemingway the novelist. He himself called his war experience "something quite irreplaceable." Whatever he meant by this, we can at least say that if war turned this lover of fishing and hunting into an "aficionado," a lover of bullfighting, it also turned a lover of reading into an artist. To him bullfighting was an art, not a sport; indeed the only art where the artist is made aware of the precious brevity of life in the face of death. When Robert Cohn complains that his life is "going so fast" and that he is "not really living it," Jake Barnes, apparently speaking for the author, declares: "Nobody ever lives their life all the way up except bullfighters." If one is not born to be a matador, the next best thing, then, is to be an aficionado capable of appreciating the matador's art and putting in words the whole truth, the absolute truth about it.

The case in point is the Pamplona scene which occupies the second half of *The Sun Also Rises,* and as the climax of the entire novel suggests its ultimate significance. (It is well to note that the novel was called *Fiesta* in both Germany and England, a title perhaps not as catching as the American title, but equally significant.) The journey from Paris to Pamplona is the pilgrimage to life's center. What it suggests is that life is still possible in Spain. All the major characters in the novel undertake this journey, and at its end they, willingly or not, are drawn in and swept along in the vortex of the festival as it unifies diverse and often conflicting human factors into a universal celebration of life. The scene reminds one of Hawthorne's Roman carnival and Forster's Krishnan festival. They are all alike in that they are also religious festivals, but what is unique about this Spanish fiesta is that it finally centers around the bullring where the pilgrims come to participate in the rites of death.

This is not to say that everyone present is capable of understanding the strange rites of death. A mere handful of people are capable of this, such as Jake, Bill, and Montoya the hotel proprietor,—a small group of aficionados. Also significant in this connection is Jake's and Bill's fishing interlude at Burguete, on their way to Pamplona. Only they go through this preparatory rite,—no other characters join Jake and Bill. This merely accentuates the well-known contrast between the initiated and the uninitiated, that is, Jake, Bill, and Montoya on one hand and Cohn, Mike, and Brett, on the other. But what norm is it that determines this difference between the initiated and the uninitiated? And who is the chief priest embodying the norm itself? It is bullfighting that gives the vital pulse to this celebration of life, and it is a bullfighter who serves as the chief priest. That is, it is Romero in this particular instance. Around Romero, literally and symbolically, occupying the center of the arena there form two circles, inner and outer. And in the inner stand Jake, Bill, Montoya, and other aficionados, and in the outer, Cohn, Mike, Brett, and many others, but all turning their intent eyes toward the center, where Romero stands alone in stillness performing his priestly rite under the Spanish sun.

The Pamplona festival is thus not the background of the novel against which characters appear, but really its culminating drama in which the matador performs the solemn ritual of death, while allowing others to participate according to their varied capacity for perceiving the mysteries involved. Hemingway describes all of Romero's bullfights with such care that some may accuse him of indulging in description for its own sake. His sense of drama is most apparent in the way Jake narrates Romero's three appearances in the ring, devoting only one paragraph to his first day, two pages to his second, and ten pages to his last, which also falls on the last day of the fiesta.

His account of Romero's first appearance is factual,—typical Hemingway:

> It was a good bull-fight. Bill and I were very excited about Pedro Romero. Montoya was sitting about ten places away. After Romero had killed his first bull Montoya caught my eye and nodded his head. This was a real one. There had not been a real one for a long time. Of the other two matadors, one was very fair and the other was passable. But there was no comparison with Romero, although neither of his bulls was much.

The bullfight on the second day is "much better," Romero being "the whole show." It is "all Romero," completely overshadowing the other two matadors. As Jake points out to Brett, bullfighting is something that is "going on with a definite end," and "less of a spectacle with unexplained horrors." With a closer look at Romero's cape-work which never wastes the bull, Jake describes the veronica, the touchstone of all cape-work:

> Romero never made any contortions, always it was straight and pure and natural in line. The others twisted themselves like corkscrews, their elbows raised, and leaned against the flanks of the bull after his horns had passed, to give a faked look of danger. Afterward, all that was faked turned bad and gave

an unpleasant feeling. Romero's bull-fighting gave real emotion, because he kept the absolute purity of line in his movements and always quietly and calmly let the horns pass him close each time. He did not have to emphasize their closeness. Brett saw how something that was beautiful done close to the bull was ridiculous if it were done a little way off. I told her how since the death of Joselito all the bull-fighters had been developing a technic that simulated this appearance of danger in order to give a fake emotional feeling, while the bull-fighter was really safe. Romero had the old thing, the holding of his purity of line through the maximum of exposure, while he dominated the bull by making him realize he was unattainable, while he prepared him for the killing.

And finally the third day: We are given still a closer look at Romero's masterful suertes. Standing in the center between Belmonte and Marcial, this 19-year-old Romero shows "the old thing," "greatness" while Belmonte is merely imitating himself and Marcial imitating Belmonte. Born bullfighter, Romero seems to love bullfighting, even his bulls. Following his first quite Romero now faces the bull:

Romero smiled. The bull wanted it again, and Romero's cape filled again, this time on the other side. Each time he let the bull pass so close that the man and the bull and the cape that filled and pivoted ahead of the bull were all one sharply etched mass. It was all so slow and so controlled. It was as though he were rocking the bull to sleep. He made four veronicas like that, and finished with a half-veronica that turned his back on the bull and came away toward the applause, his hand on his hip, his cape on his arm, and the bull watching his back going away.

Next with his own bulls, Romero is "perfect." His first bull does not see well. Finding out how badly its vision is impaired, Romero works accordingly. His style is not brilliant but only perfect, implying that it can be brilliant, even when not perfect, not vice versa. Now contrasting Romero's "classical" with Belmonte's and Marcial's decadent style, Jake also is at his best as an aficionado:

Out in the center of the ring, all alone, Romero was going on with the same thing, getting so close that the bull could see him plainly, offering the body, offering it again a little closer, the bull watching dully, then so close that the bull thought he had him, offering again and finally drawing the charge and then, just before the horns came, giving the bull the red cloth to follow with that little, almost imperceptible, jerk that so offended the critical judgment of the Biarritz bull-fight experts.

As Jake says, all this is like a course in bullfighting. "All the passes he [Romero] linked up, all completed, all slow, templed and smooth. There were no tricks and no mystifications. There was no brusqueness." Then comes the killing, which Hemingway elsewhere calls the moment of truth:

The bull was squared on all four feet to be killed, and Romero killed directly below us. He killed not as he had been forced to by the last bull, but as he wanted to. He profiled directly in front of the bull, drew the sword out of the folds of the muleta and sighted along the blade. The bull watched him. Romero spoke to the bull and tapped one of his feet. The bull charged and Romero waited for the charge, the muleta held low, sighting along the blade, his feet firm. Then without taking a step forward, he became one with the bull, the sword was in high between the shoulders, the bull had followed the low-swung flannel, that disappeared as Romero lurched close to the left, and it was over.

There is nothing bloody about the whole business. Romero in a black suit standing alone with his bull in the sun-lit arena—he is the very image of a master bullfighter performing his art to perfection. This is the moment of truth, the absolute moment. About him there is something impersonal, a quality akin to God. It is a moment when one becomes convinced of his own immortality. (Romero in fact says: "I'm never going to die.") In this stillness at the heart of violence Romero stands with no thoughts of either his entanglement with Brett or his ugly scene with Cohn. As he stands in the ring, he is altogether inaccessible and unassailable. Only those very few aficionados, such as Jake, can have a glimpse of the supreme moment. It is this vision of light that awaits those chosen wastelanders at the end of their pilgrimage; it is also the moment of triumph for Hemingway the artist, for he can make his readers *experience* the moment.

Death in the Afternoon (1932) is Hemingway's attempt to analyze this experience and re-affirm this glimpse of the supreme moment. While inevitably failing to recapture the perfect, the absolute, and the impersonal moment of *The Sun Also Rises,* this book sufficiently reveals what Hemingway finds in bullfighting. Much like Melville on cetology, Hemingway explores every possible aspect of his subject. He points out repeatedly that bullfighting is not a sport in the Anglo-Saxon sense of the word. Bullfighting really is "a tragedy," and as such it is an art, a ritual. And the bullfighter is therefore an artist who performs his suertes, killing his bull, healthy, mature and experienced, and fond of action—within the limits of fifteen minutes. To execute all this to perfection in the way tradition prescribes, a bullfighter must be a master of his art in all of its aspects. He must be a complete artist, not a specialist. Of this, Hemingway writes:

What is needed in bullfighting to-day is a complete bullfighter who is at the same time an artist to save it from the specialists; the bullfighters who can do only one thing, and who do it superlatively, but who require a special, almost made-to-order bull to bring their art to its highest point or, sometimes, to be able to have any art at all. What it needs is a god to drive the half-gods out. But waiting for a messiah is a long business and you get many fake ones. There is no record in the Bible of the number of fake messiahs that came before Our Lord, but the history of the last ten years of bullfighting would record little else.

All considered, there is little doubt but that Romero is "a complete bullfighter who is at the same time an artist," "a god to drive the half-gods out."[1]

As an art bullfighting is no exception to what can be said of art in general. The ideal bullfighter can never be made; he must be born—he must be born with what Hemingway calls genius. And by perfecting his art through knowledge and practice this potential bullfighter becomes a complete one. If art can be defined as a proper way of doing a certain thing at a proper moment, bullfighting is an art in its most elementary sense. More than in any other art, it is vitally important to act correctly in the face of death. In bullfighting, it is technical perfection that enables its performer to act in intense intimacy with death. From constant exposure to death comes that classical quality of impersonality. Romero talks of his work as "something altogether apart from himself," a virtue which a perennial undergraduate like Cohn will never learn. It is a state of detachment well beyond mere devotion or mere cynicism.

If *Death in the Afternoon* is Hemingway's analysis of bullfighting as an aficionado, *Green Hills of Africa* (1935) is then an account of his conscious experiment to apply to hunting what he learned from the art of bullfighting. This time he is no longer a spectator but an actor himself. A lover of hunting all his life, he is on familiar grounds. By pursuing big game on African safaris he can now enact the "real emotion" of bullfighting. After all, bullfighting, as he discovers, is not the only art where the artist is exposed to death. In big game hunting, too, the hunter is in the same danger. And to act rightly in this self-imposed danger he must also be a complete hunter, a complete artist.

On one occasion Hemingway feels "rotten sick" over a sable bull which he hit but did not kill. As he explains, it is not a feeling of guilt. He does not mind killing anything, any animal so long as he does it "cleanly," since they all must die anyway and his interference with the nightly and seasonal killing that goes on all the time is "very minute." What really bothers him is that as a hunter, as a would-be perfect hunter, he made a "lousy" mistake for which he cannot excuse himself. And his lousy mistake is that he shot at the whole animal instead of at the right place. It happened because at the moment he was too excited and in his over-confidence omitted "one of the steps in how it is done." Ignoring the right way of shooting at the right place, he simply tried to take the shortcut. The master hunter never skips any of the steps; when he seems to do so, it is only because his technique is so perfect and natural that it is no longer visible. As Hemingway states in his Spanish book, technique, which he calls the bastard name, is always most visible in its imperfection. On another occasion he is more successful in downing a rhino. Why he is this time becomes apparent as he describes the moment of shooting: "I was watching, freezing myself deliberately inside, stopping the excitement as you close a valve, going into that impersonal state you shoot from." Perfect control means perfect execution, and in this moment of truth in hunting there is no excitement; there is only detachment.

Neither account is complete, to be sure. For that matter, *Death in the Afternoon* itself, though comprehensive, is never complete as an exposition of the ideal and supreme norm Romero represents, because it is the kind of state which even art at its best can do no more than glimpse,—unless it is a prose capable of what Hemingway calls "a fourth and fifth dimension." This perfect, absolute, and impersonal moment which endows man with a sense of immortality is a world which fascinates an aficionado like Jake, but which remains forever alien to Cohn and his ilk.

Yet what this state signifies should be empirically real and self-evident, if viewed from a tradition which accepts the fundamental unity of all human creative activities. As a matter of fact, this moment of truth resembles the Taoist state of *wei wu wei* (inaction) or the Zen state of *mushin, muga,* or *munen* (no-mindness). (There is no need to try to make a Taoist or a Zennist of Hemingway.) Since the state in question is a universal experience, it may suffice to enumerate some of its main characteristics.[2] First, this state is realized only when all human techniques are exhausted or perfected; in this sense it can be said that the state is beyond technique, for the ultimate state of activity is inactivity itself. Second, this state is thoroughly impersonal as is a state of detachment. Third, this state is fundamentally mystical in that in it subject becomes one with object as Romero becomes one with his bull. It transcends the human antagonism between good and evil, right and wrong; it is a stage of one mind, or no-mind; it has no room for thought which only knows discrimination, but trusts what Zen calls the wisdom of the body.[3]

Fourth, this state can never be verbally transmitted, and every artist must learn his art anew, as suggested in the Buddha's flower sermon and also in Chuang Tzu's story about an aged wheelwright.[4] In the same spirit Hemingway, discussing the importance of the individual bullfighter in the tradition of his art, declares that "all art is only done by the individual."

Furthermore, Taoism holds that there is a mysterious power common to all arts and crafts. The wheelwright, carpenter, butcher, bowman, and swimmer, as Arthur Waley points out, "achieve their skill not by accumulating facts concerning their art, nor by the energetic use either of muscles or outward senses; but through utilizing the fundamental kinship which, underneath apparent distinctions and diversities, unites their own Primal Stuff to the Primal Stuff of the medium in which they work."[5] Zen, which has much in common with Taoism, also holds the same view about this kinship that unites all arts and crafts, ranging from painting, gardening, poetry, tea ceremony, architecture, Noh drama, to archery, judo, puppetry, fencing and the like. Especially instructive in this connection is Dr. Suzuki's study of the impact of Zen upon Japanese culture. In his chapters on swordsmanship he calls it an art, a deadly art in which a man's life depends on whatever move he makes—just as in bullfighting. In the same context he refers to what is basically common to both swordsmanship and bullfighting. In addition to their intrinsic value, all these arts, as Dr. Suzuki observes, serve as highly effective means of spiritual enlightenment. It is in this sense that the arts regain their original dignity, becoming rituals.[6]

II

As in *Death in the Afternoon* Hemingway attempts to recapture in nonfictional form a glimpse of Romero's ideal state, in *Green Hills of Africa* he seeks in personal terms to experience that state. In both works he strives to turn the instinctive into the conscious. The significance of both works lies in the persistent genealogy of Romero which Hemingway sought to acclimatize in fiction —in the four novels since the 1930's—with varying degrees of success. Harry Morgan, for example, scoffs at Johnson's "sloppy way to fish," and Colonel Cantwell defines a "jerk" as "a man who has never worked at his trade *(oficio)* truly, and is presumptuous in some annoying way." But neither of them can come up to the height of Romero; Morgan, though capable of manhood, has little chance because not only is he caught deep in the socio-economic mesh but stands on the wrong side of the fence; whereas Colonel Cantwell too often indulges in nostalgia, a state of mind incapable of transcendence. Only in Robert Jordan and Santiago does Hemingway come very close to realizing his artistic dream. This may account largely for the artistic excellence of *For Whom the Bell Tolls* and *The Old Man and the Sea.*

Although *For Whom the Bell Tolls* and *A Farewell to Arms* usually are lumped together as war novels, they have very little in common.

There is a world's difference between Henry, who dismisses the war as a "rotten" game and laughs off death, and Jordan, who believes in his "work," has his "greatest gift"—a capacity for "actual happiness before action," and faces his approaching death. While only in their escape into Switzerland do Henry and Catherine attain their separate peace, Jordan and Maria accept the conditions of the war. Although Henry is supposedly a volunteer as is Jordan, one wonders what in the first place motivated Henry to join the army ambulance service. His escape, whatever his justification in terms of his love for Catherine, is rather absurd. What is obvious is that whereas Henry is a victim of illusions, Jordan goes beyond them, accepts his self-imposed "discipline," and performs his "duty" with his eyes wide open—fully aware of the ultimate futility of his mission. Unlike Henry, Jordan is a descendant of Romero; he is a Romero at war.

For Romero's fifteen minutes in the bullring, Jordan has three days to live; and this he knows and resolves to make the most of. His love for Maria merely dramatizes his sense of commitment, and he is grateful for this as he says to himself: "I suppose it is possible to live as full a life in seventy hours as in seventy years." (This echoes Jake's reply to Cohn that only bullfighters live their life "all the way up.") Again to Agustín, Jordan explains: "What we do not have is time. Tomorrow we must fight. To me that is nothing. But for the Maria and me it means that we must live all of our life in this time." Henry's flight with Catherine is altogether out of the question as far as Jordan is concerned. Thus at the consummation of their love he decries "all the way now" in a mystic ecstasy: "Come now, now, for there is no now but now. Yes, now. Now, please now, only now, not anything else only this now, and where are you and where am I and where is the other one, and not why, not ever why, only this now; and on and always please then always now, always now, for now always one now."[7]

But Jordan is no Romeo; he is no blind lover. He is a Romero who smiles in the midst of his veronica. Pilar is right when, upon meeting Jordan, she is struck by his detached manner and remarks that he is "smart," "smart and cold," and "very cold in the head." Jordan assures Agustín that the capture of Segovia the provincial capital is possible with the bridge blown "correctly." Well aware that to skip one step will ruin the whole mission, he proceeds with alertness and precision, and equally meticulously readjusts the plan to each

new factor creating the slightest change in the situation—to such an extent that
Pilar curses in exasperation: "Thou and thy perfection." Instructing Agustín
now in position, he says: "*Pues,* to load. To aim it. To shoot it. Nothing more."
Later, giving his last instructions to Anselmo, a hunter who hates killing,
Jordan details this advice: "When thou firest, take a rest and make very sure.
Do not think of it as a man but as a target, *de acuerdo?* Do not shoot at the
whole man but at a point. Shoot for the exact center of the belly—if he faces
thee. At the middle of the back, if he is looking away. Listen, old one. When
I fire if the man is sitting down he will stand up before he runs or crouches.
Shoot then. If he is still sitting down shoot. Do not wait. But make sure. Get
to within fifty yards. Thou art a hunter. Thou hast no problem."

In the final moment Jordan takes his position behind the trunk of a
pinetree on the hillside, above the road and the bridge. Through his Zeiss 8-
power glasses he takes the last look at the sentry box. His vision catches
everything that happens down there, not missing the slightest stir. He recognizes the sentry's familiar face now shaved cleanly, wearing the same knitted
stocking cap, his sunken cheeks and prominent cheekbones, his bushy eye-
brows growing together in the center, and his sleepy yawning; he also records
how the sentry takes out his tobacco pouch and a packet of papers and rolls
himself a cigaret; how, the light failing to work, he goes over to the brazier,
leans over, reaches inside, brings up a piece of charcoal, juggles it in one hand
while he blows on it, then lights the cigaret and tosses the lump of charcoal
back into the brazier. Right after that, when Jordan ceases to think, he lies still
—so intent that a passing squirrel curiously keeps glancing back at him. And
when the moment of action arrives he works—"placing, bracing, wedging,
lashing tight with wire, thinking only of demolition, working fast and skillfully
as a surgeon works." (This "as a surgeon works" may remind us of Dr. Rinaldi
who says he is happy when he is working.)

So far as the mission itself is concerned, Jordan is a complete success,
though he subsequently dies. From start to finish he proves true to his reputation as a bridge demolition expert, and every move he makes is "very scientific," as General Golz says from hearsay. Yet neither about the mission nor
about the entire war does Jordan have any illusions, such as some of his
guerrilla comrades cherish. He joined the war from his love of the country and
its people, and his belief in the Republic; he is under Communist discipline for
the duration of the war merely because in this instance the Communists offer
"the best discipline and the soundest and sanest" for the execution of the war,
and he accepts this discipline as a means whereby he can do his duty, not just
to the cause but specifically to himself. This he re-affirms while facing death
alone: "Each one does what he can." Or looking down the hill slope he says:

"I hate to leave it, is all. I hate to leave it very much and I hope I have done some good in it. I have tried to with what talent I had." Awaiting his last moment, he says again: *"One thing well done can make—,"* and takes "a good long look" at everything, the earth he loves. Jordan loved well, fought well, and died well; in short, he lived well.

If Jordan's three-day mission to death compresses man's seventy year cycle, it is also a slow-motion view of Romero's fifteen minute encounter with death in the bullring. Much the same can be said of *The Old Man and the Sea.* In this novella, however, there is no glamor of war, love, and death. Yet Santiago is another Robert Jordan who believes in his work, in his discipline, not just for the duration of the war but for his life; ultimately he is another Pedro Romero at deep sea fishing, performing what he is born for, unexpectedly at the risk of his life, all alone—far away from the applauding audience. Santiago demonstrates the necessity and the reality of heroism in the every day work of a humble fisherman. If there is any glamor about him, it must be the glamor of the unglamorous.

Hemingway deliberately removes all trappings from Santiago's world, and at the same time subjects him to extremes where he must rely on nothing but his own resources. He is alone, venturing beyond the normal boundary of safe fishing; fishing out of season—in September.

Then, he is made to fight the biggest fish he has ever encountered, and fights well for hours, mustering whatever he has at his disposal. But his victory does not last long in the face of carnivorous sharks attacking his trophy. Another battle ensues with his left hand cramped (too late to regret he hasn't trained it as well as his right hand), aggravating his fatigue and hunger, and virtually depriving him of any kind of rest. Not only that, but he has broken his tiller, and lost club, oar, knife, and even rope and harpoon. Nor does he have any glaring cause such as Jordan's. On top of all this, Santiago is an old man, lacking the youthful muscle on which he can stake his life, the masculinity or virility so vital to the common image of the Hemingway character. Never before has Hemingway gone thus far in baring the stage for his hero's action to be seen in such allegorical simplicity.

But Santiago survives. Santiago survives on account of his Romero qualities. First of all, he ever insists on technical precision. As he says: "Every day is a new day. It is better to be lucky. But I would rather be exact. Then when luck comes you are ready." Exactness is preferable to luck. He also convinces himself that there is always hope so long as he can keep his head "clear." Holding the line softly between the thumb and forefinger of his right hand, he knows what is going on down deep underneath water:

This time it was a tentative pull, not solid nor heavy, and he knew exactly what it was. One hundred fathoms down a marlin was eating the sardines that covered the point and the shank of the hook where the hand-forged hook projected from the head of the small tuna.

The old man held the line delicately, and softly, with his left hand, unleashed it from the stick. Now he could let it run through his fingers without the fish feeling any tension.

It is Romero rocking his bull to sleep. Not only does Santiago know exactly what to do as the fish moves, but he tries to do whatever he wants to do to perfection. We might repeat Pilar's curse on Jordan: "Thou and thy perfection." On the second day of his fight with the marlin Santiago hopes to be "worthy of the great DiMaggio who does all things perfectly even with the pain of the bone spur in his heel." And when the fight is over he says with a fond look at the dead fish: "It was the only way to kill him." Santiago knows what is the best way to kill, and furthermore how to go about it, and thus proves himself to be a peer of his great DiMaggio.

Santiago is meant to be a master fisherman, and there is every good reason why Hemingway chose an old man as his hero. Were he a young fisherman, there would always be the possibility that he relied on his muscle rather than his art, even if he were highly competent. Santiago may no longer have his youthful muscle, but, in addition to his art, he has the wisdom of the body which compensates for his want of physical strength. As a seasoned fisherman Santiago knows how to exercise his skill with wisdom, always mindful to preserve his primal energy, which a young fisherman and for that matter any young man tends to ignore or forget. This accounts for the fact that the old man often exhausts himself less quickly than a young man would, even granting equal technical competency to both. This must be what Hemingway meant when he said in speaking of the bullfighter's physical strength: "Strength is of little use except at the actual moment of killing."[8] What really matters is not physical youth but inner youth, and that Santiago abounds in the latter is shown by his repeated invocation of Manolin, and especially his recurring vision of young lions on the African shore.

Santiago admits that he excells the marlin only in two respects: "tricks" and "resolution." If tricks mean whatever resources man is capable of, namely. his art, resolution, likewise, means his will to do whatever he was born for. The same holds for Robert Jordan, who knows exactly what to do and how to do it and by his own life proves his willingness to accept whatever his self-imposed discipline demands of him. His repeated words, such as "gift," "talent," "duty," and "work," all indicate his measure of awareness. But his mission is only a temporary vocation as he qualifies it for the duration of the war. Here is what draws Santiago away from Jordan and nearer to Romero. Just as Romero is a professional bullfighter, so is Santiago a professional fisherman. If the term "professional" connotes slickness, or something narrow as specialization, we might say that just as Romero is a born bullfighter, so is Santiago a born fisherman. While we merely suspect Romero to be such, Santiago repeatedly reassures himself that fishing is what he was born to perform. Indeed, fishing is his vocation, and his calling. (At this point we may recall St. James, Santiago's namesake, that martyred apostle who began his vocation as a humble fisherman on the Sea of Galilee.) And it is this sense of duty to one's vocation, to one's own self that explains why the idea never even occurs to Santiago to quit the whole thing and return to the village.

As Santiago fights sharks,

It is silly not to hope, he thought. Besides I believe it is a sin. Do not think about sin, he thought. There are enough problems now without sin. Also I have no understanding of it.

I have no understanding of it and I am not sure that I believe in it. Perhaps it was a sin to kill the fish. I suppose it was even though I did it to keep me alive and feed many people. But then everything is a sin. Do not think about sin. It is much too late for that and there are people who are paid to do it. Let them think about it. You were born to be a fisherman as the fish was born to be a fish. San Pedro was a fisherman as was the father of the great DiMaggio.

This unconditional acceptance of one's own position in the scheme of things is as rare as are genuine masters in any field of human activity. But this singularly echoes the spirit that sustained the medieval guild of artisans, creators of many of the works which we today call art works. It also echoes the caste system by which the *Bhagavad-Gita* rests every individual's salvation *in* this world on the perfect performance of his own *dharma*(duty).[9] And both traditions urge man to pursue his vocation for its own sake. This is what happens to Santiago as he returns home carrying only the white skeleton of the great fish. A winner takes nothing. Early in the story as Manolin reports that the Yankees have lost that day, Santiago retorts: "That means nothing. That great DiMaggio is himself again." The same we may say of Santiago's loss. Santiago is himself again.[10]

This examination of Romero in the bullring, Jordan on the war mission, and Santiago at deep sea fishing—all from the best of Hemingway's works—brings to light at least two points of significance. First, the symbolic norm of *The Sun Also Rises* is Romero, who separates the characters of awareness from those of unawareness, the initiated from the uninitiated, and the disciplined from the undisciplined. Jordan and Santiago are not descendants of Jake Barnes, but really descendants of Romero, contrary to what has been generally assumed. If Romero is Hemingway's glimpse of the ideal norm, Jordan and Santiago are his most notable successes in the attempt to concretize the ideal in the world of fiction. Second, in *The Sun Also Rises* Hemingway stands by Jake Barnes as an aficionado; but once through his two technical books, *Death in the Afternoon* and *Green Hills of Africa,* he becomes convinced of the authenticity and significance of his glimpse. This increasing awareness of the unitive nature of sports, and his confidence in handling it on a fuller scale, may account for a salient change in his narrative technique. Although *The Sun Also Rises* (and *A Farewell to Arms*) uses the first person narrative method, what we know of Romero is always secondhand through Jake Barnes; although, on the other hand, both *For Whom the Bell Tolls* and *The Old Man and The Sea,* ironically, use the third person narrative method, we are taken into the inner world of their heroes, a fact which indicates that the author himself is now within their worlds because he can be one with these heroes. His new intimacy naturally suggests and at the same time evolves from his increasing use of the stream-of-consciousness technique, which proves more effective than any other method of narration, and the confiding tone deepens as we move from Jordan to Santiago. If this indicates the culmination of Hemingway's studied simplicity, it also marks the meeting of Hemingway the man and Hemingway the artist, that is, Hemingway as a personal artist.

III

Too often in the past we have uncritically used the term, the Hemingway character or hero. It is time to take a fresh look at this problem. From one fact alone, that Hemingway's career covers nearly four decades, it is reasonable to expect some sort of shift in the so-called Hemingway character, and in truth there is a dramatic shift between the early and the later characters, with the 30's serving as a turning point. All of his early characters dread darkness; some suffer insomnia. Pressed by Captain Paravicini, Nick Adams admits: "I'm all right. I can't sleep without a light of some sort. That's all I have now" ("A Way You'll Never Be"). The same fear continues haunting him when he is back home: "I myself did not want to sleep because I had been living for a long time with the knowledge that if I ever shut my eyes in the dark and let myself go, my soul would go out of my body." This is the result of his war experience. As he explains, "I had been that way for a long time, ever since I had been blown up at night and felt it go out of me and go off and then come back"

("Now I Lay Me"). Jake Barnes expresses the same fear when he confesses that in the dark things look differently, and that for six months he "never slept with the electric light off." Frederic Henry is no exception: asked by the priest whether he is not afraid of God, Henry concedes curtly that he is afraid of Him "in the dark." And this fear of darkness reaches its nadir in that well-known short story, "A Clean, Well-Lighed Place," which came out in 1933, and the idea of nada punctuates the story with great force.

Yet the moment this fear of darkness reaches its nadir, the state of nada, the Hemingway characters experience a sudden release from it, as though they had a vision of light. None of his later heroes, Harry Morgan, Robert Jordan, Col. Cantwell, and Santiago, complains about this fear of darkness which unnerves his characters. Instead, these later heroes, especially Jordan and Santiago, constantly repeat their open sesame: Do not think. Rather than an effort to evade the thought of darkness, it indicates their awareness that there is really no time for thought since their situation demands their complete response, and that thought itself upsets their very possibility of perfect execution. This fact certainly corresponds to the significant emergence of Romero's descendants in Hemingway's fiction. What all this suggests is that they are the result of Hemingway's attempts to free these early heroes from the fear of darkness and of nada, its ultimate state.

This fear of darkness finally is the fear of death, the known impersonator of nada or nothingness. It is the fear of death that induces the wounded Nick Adams to "keep near the street lights" as he walks home at night through the cold, deserted streets of Milan. As he states: "I was very much afraid to die, and often lay in bed at night by myself, afraid to die and wondering how I would be when I went back to the front again" ("In Another Country"). It is the fear of death that keeps the old man haunting that "clean, well-lighted place," and also turns a good guerrilla revolutionist like Pablo into a coward (Pablo admits to Pilar: "I am afraid to die"). But when the fear of darkness vanishes from the later Hemingway heroes, so does their fear of death, although more of them must die lonely deaths. Death is still there as is darkness, but now they have learned to live with darkness, and consequently with death.

Much has been made of Hemingway's interest in death, and it has been labelled in various ways: the cult of death, a death-wish, an obsession with death, and the like. H.E. Bates goes so far as to assert that "in reality Hemingway has only one theme—death," and ventures his speculation: "Perhaps no Protestant can pretend to understand the Catholic mind, and it is from Catholicism, perhaps, that Hemingway's constant preocupation with the theme of death arises." In this there is much truth. In *Death in the Afternoon,* while

designating the Castilian awareness of death as great common sense, Hemingway scoffs at some Englishman who said: "Life is real; life is earnest, and the grave is not its goal." The Spanish, Hemingway points out, think a great deal about death and when they have a religion they have one which believes that life is much shorter than death. Their intelligent interest in death also accounts for their interest in bullfighting; and there is nothing obsessive or morbid about their interest in death. As he declares in the same place, death is "the unescapable reality, the only thing any man may be sure of; the only security"; and it transcends all. Thus, death needs to be accepted as an integral part of life, as it is accepted by the classical heroes who must descend to Hades. It would seem no exaggeration to state that with Hemingway death occupies the center of life, and that it awaits you from whichever point you may start. It is this presence of death that not only completes life but also makes it intensely precious. Such an acceptance of death, such an awareness of its presence is not the same as courting death as many critics said in their premature obituary on Hemingway of 1954; it is rather "the proximity of death," to use the term Hemingway on that occasion offered as a corrective of the above view.

Thus considered, the image of Romero standing alone in the sunlit bull-ring (Hemingway says there is no bullfighting without the sun) facing the bull, the carrier of death, becomes poignantly symbolic. His encounter with death, which is the climax of the whole fiesta, is the very heart of the celebration of life. The moment consummates an ecstatic embrace of life and death. In his act of killing, life's rebellion against death, Romero becomes almost a god; it is the moment of immortality as Hemingway takes pains to point out in *Death in the Afternoon*.

In "A Natural History of the Dead" in the same book, Hemingway also states that "most men die like animals, not men." That is, in their manner of death few men are distinguishable from animals. If this manner of death separates man from animal, it is also the fear of death that separates the coward from the brave. When Catherine corrects Henry's quotation that "the coward dies a thousand deaths, the brave but one," by saying that "the brave dies perhaps two thousand deaths if he's intelligent. He simply doesn't mention them," Henry admits that he is not brave and says: "I don't know. It's hard to see inside the head of the brave." Whether or not Hemingway came to see inside the head of the brave, it is apparent that he continued interested in this problem and much like the *Gawain* poet held the fear of death as the ultimate test of manhood. The meaning of his African story, "The Short Happy Life of Francis Macomber" (1936), depends much on this fear of death. What else makes a coward of this accomplished sportsman?

Margaret need not remind him that he is a coward unless she really means it as a calculated insult. It is not mere shame that he feels in him; it is "cold, hollow fear," the fear like "a cold slimy hollow in all the emptiness where once his confidence had been." He is a coward not simply because he ignored the code of hunting as he did by trying to shoot from the moving car, proposing to leave a wounded lion unfinished, and running away from the final show-down, but because now in the range of death his old confidence proved to be shallow and false, and was completely shattered. Hemingway feels that the fear of death cannot be tolerated merely because it is natural with man. It is not a matter of physical prowess as many critics suggest, but akin to a matter of spiritual prowess; rather, it precedes both in the sense that death, as Hemingway states, is the only thing man can be sure of, and the only security. When Macomber suggests that the wounded lion be left behind the river banktrees, Wilson snaps: "You mean pretend to ourselves he hasn't been hit?" By the same token one cannot pretend that death does not exist. Macomber's confidence is shallow and false because it excludes from life the fact of death. If there is a difference between him and Jordan or Santiago, it is that neither Jordan nor Santiago pretends, even though both, and Santiago in particular, since he is entirely on his own, could have easily abandoned the whole venture and retreated in safety.

But a transformation comes over Macomber as this fear of death vanishes on the next day when they get ready to shoot buffalos. Wilson says that a wounded lion is "going to charge," which may apply to Macomber, too. Francis himself does not know how this happens any more than Hemingway, but the point is that when it comes over you you know it. To his own surprise Macomber finds that for the first time in his life he feels wholly fearless, and that instead of fear, he experiences a feeling of definite elation. This "wild unreasonable happiness" he confides to Wilson: "Something happened in me after we first saw the buff and started after him. Like a dam bursting. It was pure excitement," and then adds: "I feel absolutely different." Proposing to try another lion, he declares: "I'm really not afraid of them now. After all, what can they do to you?" To this Wilson responds: "That's it. Worst one can do is kill you." But Macomber must prove it by his act, and knowing how crucial such a proof of Macomber's transformation is to the success of his story, Hemingway almost steps inside his character. He describes Macomber and Wilson as they turn in the direction the shouting gunbearer points to:

. . . they saw him coming out of the bush sideways, fast as a crab and the bull coming, nose out, mouth tight closed, blood dripping, massive head straight out, coming in a charge, his little pig eyes bloodshot as he looked at them. Wilson, who was ahead, kneeling shooting, and Macomber, as he fired, unhearing his shot in the roaring of Wilson's gun, saw fragments like slate burst from the huge boss of the horns, and the head jerked, he shot again at the wide nostrils and saw the horns jolt again and fragments fly, and he did not see Wilson now and, aiming carefully, shot again with the baffalo's huge bulk almost on him and his rifle almost level with the on-coming head, nose out, and he could see the little wicked eyes and the head started to lower and he felt a sudden white-hot, blinding flash explode inside his head and that was all he ever felt.

In this description of the split-second happening there is nothing hazy and confusing,—one of the best examples of Hemingway's art that can arrest a moment with absolute clarity. His character also now lives up to his standards. Besides Margaret's shooting, the fact that his vision can catch all this is proof of his transformation. If he can see the on-rushing buffalo at such a slow motion pace, it is safe to say that he can also shoot it down. (Hence the importance of the visual imagery in Hemingway's works.) It is a momentary glimpse into Romero's masterful suertes in the ring. And this glimpse insures Macomber's initiation into manhood, though it means death to him. Even if he hadn't been killed, he would not have been the same Macomber any longer. And this happens, significantly, when he has reached the age of thirty-five, the mid-point of his life. The moment is worth the price he pays. He dies like a man.

It is of course important to note Hemingway's gradual shift of interest from spectator sports (including bullfighting) to participant sports. Despite this shift, however, the fact still remains that none of his favorite sports is a collective activity, or what we call team work. Whether hunting, fishing, or even bullfighting, strictly speaking, one must play solo. Behind this fact lies Hemingway's conviction that in the game of death, the last one that man is expected to play, he must also play solo; and that every man must die alone, which is as absolute as the fact of death itself. At first thought, it may seem highly illogical that in the 30's, Hemingway's alleged collectivistic period, he both produced books like *Death in the Afternoon* and *Green Hills of Africa,* and wrote so much about death in his fictional work. But this illogicality is merely superficial.

Take for instance *For Whom the Bell Tolls* (1940), the culmination of Hemingway's diverse concerns as man and artist during the decade, a work which exalts the spirit of collective solidarity. One almost suspects that the real intention of the author may be the irony that the ultimate salvation is not on a collective but still on an individual basis; that in this age of mass salvation man still dies alone. Once Jordan realizes that death is inevitable, he urges his comrades to proceed while he is covering their escape and when Maria insists on remaining with him, Jordan declares: "Nay, rabbit. Listen. That people cannot die together. Each one must die alone." His is a voice of a man without a woman; and it is something more than that. It also suggests that dying is a lonely act. All along Jordan is aware of impending death, as everyone should be sooner or later. It is this awareness that makes him roll seventy years into three days, intent on living to the hilt. Thrice in the novel, at the opening, at the close, and in the middle Jordan finds himself lying flat on the brown, pine-needled floor of the forest, listening to his heartbeat with serenity, fullness, and intensity, as if he were determined to experience every moment of his own death. As he has just completed his military mission, he is going to enact his own death with equal perfection. He dies his death, one of the most lonely and therefore beautiful deaths in modern American literature, showing that dying is also an art and a ritual.

The various deaths of Catherine, Macomber, Harry, Harry Morgan, Jordan, Col. Cantwell, and many unnamed characters may tempt us to agree with H.E. Bates that Hemingway really has only one theme—death. But this is not the whole truth, for death is but one of Hemingway's twin themes. Hemingway takes such an absorbing interest in death because he takes such an absorbing interest in life. By accepting death as the center of life one completes life. Mastery of life presupposes mastery of death, and mastery of death signals mastery of life. It was Socrates who said that those who tackle philosophy aright are simply and solely practising dying, practising death all the time, but nobody sees it. Hemingway would also agree with Socrates but wonder if "sports" should replace "philosophy." But even to Socrates' "philosophy" he may have no special objection since with Socrates it is no academic matter, but eminently an art of living. From the fact that Hemingway takes death as seriously as life and thereby restores their oneness, it follows that his interest in death is not really a matter of obsession. In his treatment of death there is little that suggests obsession and morbidity. His view of death is thoroughly sane—sane to the point of assuming a classical dimension.

If Hemingway is sarcastic of academic disciplines, it is because they strive to achieve a false kind of detachment, excluding death from life, and also because they create all breeds of specialists, not complete artists. If, likewise, he seems to exalt trades, sports, and their masters as he does, it is because they are all artists, maintaining their original wholeness. Edmund Wilson's characterization of Hemingway's view of life as a sport is not altogether wrongheaded if we understand the real import of life as a sport in terms of the Hindu concept of *lila* or the comparable Renaissance concept of the cosmic dance. Life is a sport, a cosmic dance, a divine celebration in which everyone is invited to join, playing his part to perfection. Hence the importance of his role in this perpetual dance, and of Hemingway's repeated emphasis on discipline, duty, trade, and so forth. In contrast to Jordan and Santiago, who perform their roles perfectly, Harry, the hero of "The Snows of Kilimanjaro" (1936), is a failure, though Helen assures him that he has "lost nothing," and that he is "the most complete man" she has ever seen. As he admits to himself, now facing death, he failed to perform his duty to write of the world and its people in change, namely his time. Neglecting his vocation as a writer he failed to live properly, let alone perfectly.

In stressing the art of living Hemingway aligns himself with the American tradition of Emerson, Thoreau, and James. In more than one way Hemingway calls for comparison with Henry James. Hemingway once said: "I wonder what Henry James would have done with the materials of our time." His expressed admiration for James may, to many, seem incongruous, to say the least. Yet on closer look, there are many concerns which both writers share, besides their dedication to the art of fiction. As Carlos Baker pointed out, these are the American in Europe, or the contrast between the old and the new world, the artist in society, and the buried, unlived life that haunts its unwilling recollector. Montoya, the hotel owner of Pamplona, values Jake Barnes all the more because he has known very few American "aficionados," meaning that few Americans are capable of "aficion"; Pop, a white hunter in *Green Hills of Africa,* also says that "No one knows how to behave in America." And another hunter Wilson is baffled by what he calls "the great American boy-men." This matter of conduct relates directly to the matter of life as the largest art everyman must perform in his own way. Considered in this context the theme of the artist in society cannot be separated from another theme of the unlived life. In expanding the meaning of art as far as to include the art of living, James and Hemingway are at one. Within their thematic frameworks both choose significant moments and significant events which may illuminate the degrees of awareness their respective characters possess. There is of course the difference that if James chooses a quiet crisis, Hemingway chooses a violent one because if to James knowledge is a form of action, to Hemingway action is a form of knowledge. Indeed, the art of living may epitomize the central concern of both novelists, and their art dramatizes what they chose from the kind of life they personally knew best.

. Viewed from inside, Hemingway's art emerges as a wholly integrated world. Now we can see the relationship of the fourfold base of his art: the Hemingway character, the Hemingway situation, the Hemingway style, and the Hemingway philosophy. Despite their complex texture, they are the outgrowth of one most elemental root that is his vision of life and death. This may also account for the disaster many young writers suffered whenever they attempted to imitate his art. Their failure is inevitable in that they attempt to imitate what is so personal and beyond imitation, and in that all artists are inimitable at their best. Imitation, even when possible, is no better than a surface mimickery without any genuine value to the imitator's art.

Such danger is not to his imitators alone; there is also another kind of danger an artist must beware of when he over-refines his art as "style," "pose," and "ritual," for his excessive concern for form often freezes the expanding horizons of his own creative world. For instance, his philosophy of death, naturally enough, tends to simplify everything. This is what has disturbed some critics and artists. Sean O'Faolain, while conceding that Hemingway is "the only modern writer of real distinction for whom the Hero does in some form still live," nevertheless pointed out that he has "wisely and shrewdly chosen his ground and his gamut in accordance with his instinct for what he can do and cannot do," and registered his complaint that "he has not done something quite different." Similarly, Faulkner called Hemingway "a very fine talent, a man who knows exactly how to do what he wants to do." Elaborating on this, Faulkner stated: "I thought that he found out early what he could do and he stayed inside of that. He never did try to get outside the boundary of what he really could do and risk failure. He did what he really could do marvelously well, first rate." And he designated this as "not success but failure." This is an aspect of Hemingway's art that drew the general charge against the narrow range of his world. Compared with Faulkner's art, this point is quite obvious. As Faulkner guessed, it is possible that these limitations are really self-imposed ones. In 1936, advising a young writer, Hemingway said: "Listen, there is no use writing anything that has been written before unless you can beat it. What a writer in our time has to do is write what hasn't been written before or beat dead men at what they have done." Assuming that this is the very same precept young Hemingway accepted with his characteristic single-mindedness, it is more than probable that he concentrated more on "what hasn't been written before," than on beating "dead men at what they have done." He did succeed in it well, so well that it is unlikely that he will ever be beaten at what he has done.

Where he cleared the ground, he built an arena in celebration of life, exalted every moment of it to the height of art and ritual, and created the world of the eternal now. But his celebration of life has little to do with the common cult of the enjoyment of life which pervades the modern outlook on life in every phase; it runs counter to this anemic version of the hedonistic cult; it poses a serious criticism to a society which often turns "vocation" into "occupation," and "art" into "science"; a society which often reduces morality to sexual morality; and a society which often accepts money as its sole incentive. In his stress on devotion to one's own calling, on the man-without-woman, and on the winner-take-nothing, Hemingway's art may still inspire man in his struggle to remain free, independent, and whole. In all this he may be alien in the modern world, yet he belongs to the traditional world, in spite of the apparent contemporaneity of his art as a whole. Like many other artists, Hemingway has his moments of relapse when he imitates himself, but at his best he is supreme, adding his "fifth dimension" to our conventional world. Here is his unique contribution to the tradition of letters in particular and of man in general. Contrasting Goya and Velasquez with El Greco, Hemingway once said: "You can only judge a painter by the way he paints the things he believes in or cares for and the things he hates." That is, artists must be judged on their own terms. If we accept Hemingway's own terms, we should appreciate the best he can offer us, his vision that enables us to see anew our existence in its nakedness.

1. Cf. "Though Pedro Romero bore the name of an eighteenth-century matador, he was clearly a fictional projection of Ninõ de la Palma in his great period before a series of bad horn-wounds damaged his nerve" (Carlos Baker, *Hemingway: The Writer as Artist* [Princeton, 1952], p. 78). That Romero is an altogether idealized figure is evident in view of Hemingway's unflattering account of Ninõ de la Palma. See *Death in the Afternoon,* pp. 85–90.

2. For further information on the subject, see Alan W. Watts, *The Way of Zen* (New York, 1957); D.T. Suzuki, *Zen and Japanese Culture* (New York, 1957); and Nancy W. Ross, ed., *The World of Zen: An East-West Anthology* (New York, 1960). The Taoist doctrine of *wei wu wei* is best illustrated by Chuang Tzu's numerous stories. See Arthur Waley, *Three Ways of Thoughts in Ancient China* (Anchor ed, New York). Romero in action especially reminds us of Chuang Tzu's story about the Royal Carver Ting whose skill resembles that of dancing (Waley, pp. 47–48). Hemingway also records his delight at M'Cola's beautiful use of a knife *(Green Hills of Africa,* pp. 235–36).

3. The term "an instinctive wisdom of the body" is used by Robert Linssen in *Living Zen* (London, 1954), as quoted in *The World of Zen,* p. 291. Cf. "His [Manuel's] instincts and his knowledge worked automatically, and his brain worked slowly and in words. He knew all about bulls. He did not have to think about them. He just did the right thing. His eyes noted things and his body performed the necessary measures without thought. If he thought about it, he would be gone" ("The Undefeated").

4. Of the secret of his trade which is beyond book-learning, the wheelwright says: "It is a thing that cannot be put into words; there is an art in it that I cannot explain to my son." See Waley, *Three Ways.*, pp. 15–16.

5. See Waley, *The way and its Power* (New York, 1958), pp. 58–59. For the relationship between Taoism and Zen, and their unitive view of arts, see Watts, Ross and Suzuki. Emerson, paraphrasing Goethe, also says in "Natures": "The wise man, in doing one thing, does all; or, in the one thing he does rightly, he sees the likeness of all which is done rightly." For the Zen aspect of Emerson's thought, see Robert Detweiler, "Emerson and Zen," *American Quarterly*, XIV (Fall, 1962), 422–38.

6. It is in one of his chapters on swordsmanship that Suzuki quotes at length from Juan Belmonte's "The Making of a Bullfighter" (*The Atlantic Monthly*, CLIX [February 1937]), and points out the basic similarity between swordsmanship and bullfighting (*Zen and Japanese Culture*, pp. 117–20).

7. With reference to Hemingway's statement about "a fourth and fifth dimension," F.I. Carpenter relates his mystic concept of time to the philosophical thought of William James, Gertrude Stein, Henri Bergson, and P.D. Ouspensky ("Hemingway Achieves the Fifth Dimension," Carlos Baker ed., *Hemingway and His Critics* [New York, 1961], pp. 192–201). Considering the similarity between Ouspensky's "the perpetual now" and Zen's "the eternal present" (Watts' phrase), we perhaps need not be as specific as Carpenter in pinning down Hemingway's source.

8. When asked what physical exercise he takes to keep his strength up for bullfighting, Rafael Gomez is said to have responded thus: "What do I want with strength, man? The bull weighs half a ton. Should I take exercises for strength to match him? Let the bull have the strength" (*Death in the Afternoon*, p. 21).

9. The *Gita's* central message, "do your dharma without thoughts of reward," has been likened to the Taoist doctrine of inaction. That thoughts of reward interfere with the perfect execution of a work is psychologically evident. See Juan Belmonte's aforementioned article, "The Making of a Bullfighter," and Shigeyoshi Takano, "The Psychology of Swordplay" (*The World of Zen*, pp. 292–93).

10. In Hemingway's article, "On the Blue Water" (*Esquire*, V, April 1936), there is a short episode about an old fisherman's struggle which already anticipates *The Old Man and the Sea*. The fisherman in this version is "half-crazy from his loss' when rescued. This article is included in *Esquire's First Sports Reader* (pp. 63–70).

HEMINGWAY'S ESTHETIC AND ETHICAL SPORTSMEN

JOHN REARDON

IN *Death in the Afternoon* Hemingway makes two very similar statements. In the first he is talking about writing: "I was trying to write then and I found the greatest difficulty, aside from knowing truly what you really felt, rather

Reprinted with permission from *The University Review*, XXXIV (October 1967), 13–23.

than what you were supposed to feel, and had been taught to feel, was to put down what really happened in action . . ."[1] In the second he is talking about bullfighting: "people will know the first time they go, if they go open-mindedly and only feel those things they actually feel and not the things they think they should feel, whether they will care for bullfights or not." (10)

This marked similarity of observation and expression about writing and bullfighting is, in Hemingway, more than coincidental. With a frequency that makes coincidence impossible, the language which he uses to describe the craft of the bullfighter, the hunter, the fisherman he also uses to describe the craft of the writer and, beyond that, the ethical attitudes of his heroes. He constructs a metaphorical pattern that at times approaches allegory. For example, in his interview with Lillian Ross in 1950 he talked about writing in terms of base-ball: "If they [the critics] can do you harm, let them do it. It is like being a third baseman and protesting because they hit line drives at you. Line drives are regrettable, but to be expected."[2] His use of the sports simile is not, as Miss Ross makes it seem, mere bravado. For to play baseball, to hunt, fight bulls, to engage in any athletic activity in the correct way is in Hemingway's world a physical expression of that value which is involved in writing which will not cheat and in ethical attitudes which will not lie.

For over thirty years, however, writers have criticized Hemingway for his preoccupation with mere physical violence for its own sake and with despair about ethical values. Typical of these critics is Ivan Kashkeen who insisted that "his courage was the aimless courage of despair, that the obsession of death was taking hold of him, that again and again he was writing of the end—the end of love, the end of life, the end of hope, the end of all."[3]

As late as 1956 that critic was still attacking Hemingway for "the same old tragedy of craftsmanship passionately serving art for art's sake,"[4] and for making a "separate peace" in the early thirties because "he frequented bull fights in Spain, went hunting in Africa, took to fishing, settled in Florida, and did hardly any writing for seven years." (163) What Hemingway did write between 1929 and 1936 was, however, more important than Kashkeen and the others realized; for *Death in the Afternoon* (1932) and *Green Hills of Africa* (1935) are works in which Hemingway presented not only the surface action of the bullfight and the hunt but his deeper concern for the technique of art and the substance of moral belief. The books are, in part, nonfiction recapitula-tions of what the author felt about how to write and how to live.

Hemingway has very few artist fables in which he permits writers or painters to express his esthetic principles.[5] His artists are not artists of the beautiful butterfly as are Hawthorne's or of the well-made canvas as are Henry

James'. They are, rather, artists of the physical act. Nor does Hemingway have moral fables of the kind Hawthorne created so admirably. His ethical attitudes, however, can be seen taking shape in the behavior of his sportsmen. Hemingway's unified vision carries all three levels—sport, art, ethic—at one time; and when he is talking about one, his words often apply to the other two as well.

In *Death in the Afternoon* the author, using the term "artist-bullfighter," indicates that bullfighting is not one of the major arts only because it is impermanent. (14,99) That the bullfighter lives intensely, lives as Hemingway sought to live himself and to make many of his characters live, there can be no doubt. "Nobody ever lives their life all the way up except bullfighters," Jake Barnes comments. Hemingway constantly sees a relationship between what happens to a bullfighter facing a bull and what happens to a man facing a blank page or a hero facing a difficult experience. Repeatedly, a chapter of *Death in the Afternoon* begins by talking about bullfighting but ends in a discussion of writing. The book itself begins and ends talking about writing. And though it is an eminent manual of the *corrida* it is also the manual of a man learning how to write and how to evaluate his experience.

The bullfighter, the writer, the hero must work by a pure technique, with control and grace and the courage to get close to that upon which he can create truly—to that which, if he lapses in his technique, can defeat and destroy him. Romero in *The Sun Also Rises* might, in the Hemingway metaphor, be writing a good book or living a good life rather than killing a bull: "Romero never made any contortions, always it was straight and pure and natural in line. The others twisted themselves like corkscrews, their elbows raised, and leaned against the flanks of the bull after his horns had passed, to give a fake look of danger. Afterward, all that was faked turned bad and gave an unpleasant feeling. Romero's bull-fighting gave real emotion, because he kept the absolute purity of line in his movements and always quietly and calmly let the horns pass him close each time. He did not have to emphasize their closeness. Brett saw how something that was beautiful done close to the bull was ridiculous if it were done a little way off."

The technique which Romero developed in his bullfighting and later Santiago developed in his fishing Hemingway was always seeking to develop in his art—a technique which was straight and pure and natural. Similarly, his heroes, like Nick Adams, Jake Barnes, and Colonel Cantwell, though they exist close to the horns of the bull, must never make any contortions, must seek to know real emotion by keeping an absolute purity in their attitude and behavior.

The talent and training of a sportsman is very like the talent and training of an artist in Hemingway's view. He points out in *Death in the Afternoon* that "bullfighters grow up, unencouraged, having a natural talent as acrobats or jockeys or even writers have . . ." (269), that "you cannot learn to be a full matador any more than you can learn to be a major-league ballplayer, an opera singer, or a good professional boxer. You can learn to play baseball, to box, or to sing, but unless you have a certain degree of genius you cannot make your living at baseball or boxing or singing in opera." (88)

The sportsman or artist, then, and they are mentioned together in just this way throughout Hemingway, must be educated and trained properly to make use of his natural talent. The training is a painful process. The apprentice bullfighter, Hemingway insists, must not be pampered or protected from the big and often deadly bulls which the stars refuse. The potential artist of the *corrida* "who has learned to fight with the yearlings, acquired a good pure style, and then perfects his technique and learns bulls by going through the hell of facing the huge, rejected, sometimes defective, supremely dangerous bulls . . . will have the perfect education for a bullfighter if his enthusiasm and his courage are not gored out of him." (165)

The writer too had to sustain his enthusiasm and his courage during his period of training when he was learning what he truly felt rather than what he was supposed to feel, and what facts and actions produced that feeling, and how he might express it in a way that will not cheat it and will last. Certainly a writer must not be protected from difficult and painful experience if he is to know truly of what he writes. Hemingway always insisted that his active life was necessary so that he might have something meaningful to write: "In going where you have to go, and doing what you have to do, and seeing what you have to see, you dull and blunt the instrument you write with. But I would rather have it bent and dulled . . . and know that I had something to write about, than have it bright and shining and nothing to say, or smooth and well-oiled in the closet, but unused."[6] Then when the time comes that instrument can be put on the grindstone again and used against significant material.

Like the sportsman and artist, the hero in the ethical realm must get his training by facing devastating experience, must emerge with courage, enthusiasm, and the awareness of the nature of his enemy, must develop techniques which will not cheat or cheapen his integrity and experience, and must live fully with an appetite for that which he finds is valuable. What the hero must face, however, is not a bull or a blank page; it is rather that destructive force against which he measures his stature as a man. It is the force which made Jake Barnes impotent, killed Catherine Barkley, hunted Ole Anderson, and stripped the great marlin.

Hemingway frequently used the pronoun "they," personifying this force, making it an enemy the hero must face by predicament and duty as in *A Farewell to Arms:* "You did not know what it was all about. You never had time to learn. They threw you in and told you the rules and the first time they caught you off base they killed you."[7] He employed similar baseball imagery when talking about writing. "That's the hard league to play in. The ball is standard, the ball parks vary somewhat, but they are all good. There are no bad bounces. Alibis don't count. Go out and do your stuff. You can't do it? Then don't take refuge in the fact that you are a local boy or a rummy, or pant to crawl back into somebody's womb, or have the con or the old râle. You can do it or you can't do it in that league I am speaking of."[8]

Philip Young has traced the apprenticeship of the Hemingway hero in the Nick Adams stories. It is, no doubt, the experience which Nick Adams has— in "Indian Camp," "Ten Indians," "The Killers"—which makes him able to "live in it" when he comes to be Jake Barnes. Jake himself has been gored in the greatest of all contests—war. He has passed through an apprenticeship of pain and despair to emerge on the other side into a craftsmanship of courage and devotion. Jake can now proceed to live in it knowing the values. Thus he becomes the *aficionado.* And those people he respects also know the values, not only of the bullfight, but of things in general.

Count Mippipopolous, who has himself traveled much and has been wounded in his apprenticeship, says: "You see Mr. Barnes, it is because I have lived very much that now I can enjoy everything so well . . . That is the secret. You must get to know the values." Similarly, in describing matadors Hemingway advocates a tough-minded sophistication derived from experience: "The cynical ones are the best companions. But the best of all are the cynical ones when they are still devout; or after; when having been devout, then cynical, they become devout again by cynicism. Juan Belmonte is an example of the last stage." (*Death in the Afternoon,* 59) Belmonte, Hemingway's hero-bullfighter, corresponds to the Hemingway hero who has learned what things are like and can act with a true knowledge of the forces which oppose him and of the behavior he must maintain so that he might live or die with the grace and poise with which Belmonte fights bulls.

To be sure, if Jake Barnes had not been pained much and wounded he could not have understood so well the bullfighting of Romero, and if the Count had not "lived very much" he could not "know the values." It is necessary that one have experience if he is to truly understand, if he is to have *afición* for bullfighting, or writing, or living in general. Then he can help sustain high endeavor. "A bullfighter will not be better than his audience very long. If they prefer tricks to sincerity they soon get the tricks. If a really good bullfighter is to come and remain honest, sincere, without tricks and mystifications, there must be a nucleus of spectators that he can play for when he comes." (*Death in the Afternoon,* 163) For the spectators at the bull ring, like the readers of a book, "finally, when they have learned to appreciate values through experience what they seek is honest and true, not tricked, emotion and always classicism and purity of execution. . . ." (12) They are those who have "the sense of the tragedy and ritual of the fight so that the minor aspects are not important except as they relate to the whole. Either you have this or you have not . . . ." (9)

On the literary level it is, I suspect, this you-have-it-or you-have-not attitude which has given rise to the extremes of response to the art of Ernest Hemingway himself. For he needs his *aficionado* just as a bullfighter does. The in-group of Hemingway characters extends itself to an in-group of Hemingway readers. If members of the audience are disturbed by the violence, bored by the ritual, sickened by the blood, made suspicious by the mannerism, embarrassed by the phallus, then they simply will not care for the work of art—indeed they may resent it with a good deal of fervor. And Hemingway would probably insist that they should, like those who do not care for bullfights, "avoid those horrible sights which so disgust foreigners and tourists."[9] In Hemingway, foreigners and tourists are nearly always insensitive outsiders, those who cannot appreciate the tragedy of the bull ring, the skeleton of the fish, or the short but happy life. They are the people who use words like sacred, glorious, sacrifice, who close clean well-lighted cafés early because they are all confidence, and who carry home a canary for one. They are not aficionados and thus cannot know the values because they have neither the talent nor the training.

Old Santiago has said, "A man can be destroyed but not defeated," and Hemingway's obsession with knowing the values, finding the genuine in sport or art or ethic, is essentially a defense against being defeated. When one employs bad technique he drops his defense and becomes subject to forces which will not only destroy him but defeat him as well. In *Green Hills of Africa,* after having "gut shot" a sable antelope bull and then lost its track, Hemingway chastises himself: "I was thinking about the bull and wishing to God I had never hit him. Now I had wounded him and lost him . . . Tonight he would die and the hyenas would eat him, or, worse, they would get him before he died, hamstringing him and pulling his guts out while he was alive . . . I felt a son of a bitch to have hit him and not killed him. I did not mind killing anything, any animal, if I killed it cleanly . . ."[10] The author said earlier in the same book: "Since I still loved to hunt I resolved that I would only shoot as long as I could kill cleanly and as soon as I lost that ability I would stop." (148) He may have decided that he had, indeed, lost that ability, one morning in Montana. Losing that ability in the hunt meant defeat: the sable is left to the mercy of the hyenas.

Interestingly hyenas and other scavengers have always had a symbolically horrid role in Hemingway's world. He despises the ugliness of these parasites and destroyers. They are repugnant throughout *Green Hills of Africa,* and they haunt the last days of the writer who has sold his integrity in "The Snows of Kilimanjaro," becoming for him the stinking embodiment of an ignoble death. Their counterparts in the sea, the sharks, tear Santiago's great and beautiful fish which he caught by going out too far.

Writers who have, justly I think, pointed out a parallel between Santiago, his fish, and the sharks, and Hemingway, his work, and the critics, might add another dimension of the hunter, his sable, and the hyenas. But beyond that there seems to be a parallel pertinent to the Hemingway hero generally and, as I have implied above, to Hemingway himself. The hyenas, the sharks are the animal manifestations of that great force which the killers represent in the human realm. They are the force which seeks to defeat the hero, the man of courage, of integrity. By giving up the hunt the hunter obviously is destroyed, but he remains undefeated.

In his endeavor to sustain the integrity of his killing or his creating, the Hemingway sportsman-artist-hero is always faced with the problem of time. If he is to kill or create truly, his endeavors must not be hurried. Hemingway discusses this problem in *Green Hills of Africa* relating it to the artist as well as the hunter: "It is not pleasant to have a time limit by which you must get your kudu or perhaps never get it, nor even see one. It is not the way hunting should be. It is too much like those boys who used to be sent to Paris with two years in which to make good as writers or painters after which, if they had not made good, they could go home and into their father's business. The way to hunt is for as long as you live against as long as there is such and such an animal; just as the way to paint is as long as there is you and colors and canvas, and to write as long as you can live and there is pencil and paper or ink or any machine to do it with, or anything you care to write about, and you feel a fool, and you are a fool, to do it any other way." (11–12)

As he mentioned to Lillian Ross in 1950, "Time is the least thing we have of," and though the artist learns in "quicker ratio" than most men, "there are some things which cannot be learned quickly and time, which is all we have, must be paid heavily for their acquiring." (*Death in the Afternoon,* 192) In his African book he continues: "But here we were, now, caught by time, by the season, and by the running out of our money, so that what should have been as much fun to do each day . . . was being forced into that most exciting perversion of life; the necessity of accomplishing something in less time than should truly be allowed for its doing." (12)

Writers too are forced by circumstances into perversions which hurry them and mar their efforts. "First, economically. They make money. It is only by hazard that a writer makes money although good books always make money eventually. Then our writers when they have made some money increase their standard of living and they are caught. They have to write to keep up their establishments, their wives, and so on, and they write slop. It is not slop on purpose but because it is hurried." (*Green Hills of Africa,* 23) Nor must the hero hurry his appreciations, as the writer and sportsman must avoid hurrying their labors. He must relish the taste of good food, the drinking of good wine, the satisfaction of a good country, the love of a woman he loves, the kinesthetic pleasure of activity. If he is to be sure that what he does is of value and will last he must be responsible every moment of his life, just as a Henry James' hero is responsible, never to let down. He must live in a constant slow tension to distinguish the true from the false.

There are places in Hemingway's stories as there are in *The Ambassadors* or in *Huckleberry Finn* when action suddenly ceases and one concentrates on the fulfilling moment. The description of Spain's countryside in *The Sun Also Rises,* while Robert Cohn sleeps, is one of the longest and most famous of these, but they abound. In "Cross Country Snow" Nick Adams "looked up the hill. George was coming down in telemark position, kneeling; one leg forward and bent, the other trailing; his sticks hanging like some insect's thin legs, kicking up puffs of snow as they touched the surface and finally the whole kneeling trailing figure coming round in a beautiful right curve, crouching, the legs shot forward and back, the body leaning out against the swing, the sticks accenting the curve like points of light; all in a wild cloud of snow." One must have time for such detail as this which for the writer is meant to convey what he truly felt and for the hero is that which is true to feel.

The artist must work not only unhurriedly and with absolute attention, but like the sportsman and the hero, with the coverage of loneliness. In *Green Hills of Africa* Hemingway insisted: "The more people the less game you'll see. You should hunt kudu alone." (209) And he also said: "Writers should work alone. They should see each other only after their work is done, and not too often then." (21)

As late as 1954 he made a similar pronouncement in his Nobel Prize speech: "Writing at its best is a lonely life. Organizations for writers palliate the writer's loneliness, but I doubt if they improve his writing. He grows in public stature as he sheds his loneliness and often his work deteriorates. For he does his work alone, and if he is a good enough writer, he must face eternity or the lack of it each day."

Over twenty years earlier Hemingway had said much the same thing in his book about bullfighting: "All art is only done by the individual. The individual is all you ever have and all schools only serve to classify their members as failures. The individual, the great artist, when he comes, uses everything that has been discovered or known about his art up to that point . . . and then the great artist goes beyond what has been done or known and makes something of his own." (99–100)

It is because he must "make something of his own" while facing "eternity or the lack of it" that the artist's creation is so extraordinary and lonely an act. "How simple the writing of literature would be," he said in his Nobel Prize speech, "if it were only necessary to write in another way what has been well written. It is because we have had such great writers in the past that a writer is driven far out past where he can go, out to where no one can help him." Hemingway had made the same point earlier: Santiago must go out far, past where he should go, where no one can help him, in his lonely and creative quest for the marlin, and so does the leopard near the summit of Kilimanjaro.

In the same way the hero, by his own method for getting at the truth, must go beyond what has been known (and for him proved false) and must face eternity or the lack of it. The Hemingway hero faces the loneliness which so many other American heroes have faced and which Thornton Wilder called, in reference to Thoreau, "the American loneliness." Suspecting all secondhand truths, American authors as uncongenial as Emerson and Hawthorne, Mark Twain, and Henry James have sought as Thoreau did "to live so sturdily and Spartan-like as to put to rout all that was not life, to cut a broad swath and shave close, to drive life into a corner, and reduce it to its lowest terms . . ." Unless one does this he might be subject to that which can cheat and mystify.

So in *The Sun Also Rises* the Monastery at Roncesvalles is "a remarkable place." "It isn't the same as fishing, though, is it?" For it is in the personal experience of fishing that one discovers what is good and beautiful and trust-worthy, not in the monastery. Morality must constantly stand the test of individual experience, and that which is of value in Hemingway's world arises, no less empirically than at Walden Pond, or in Lambert Strethers' Paris, or on Huck Finn's Mississippi, out of the experience of an individual who is essentially alone and far out in a moral no-man's land. Thus in *Death in the Afternoon* the author points out: "So far about morals, I know only that what is moral is what you feel good after and what is immoral is what you feel bad after . . ."

Such morality is not so cold-blooded and self-indulgent as it might at first glance appear, nor is it as cynical as critics have argued. The Hemingway hero is an ethical empiricist, or as Carlos Baker calls him, a pragmatist. His attitude is, in fact, like Huck Finn's when that boy asks: "What's the use of learning to do right when it's troublesome to do right and ain't no trouble to do wrong, and the wages is just the same?" And his response is the same as Huck's: "I couldn't answer that. So I reckoned I wouldn't bother no more about it, but after this do whichever come handiest at the time." Whatever comes handiest at the time is what you feel good about; it is a morality defined in experience when you are alone and far out, a morality based on what you truly felt rather than what you were supposed to feel, and one about which there is no faking and nothing that will go bad afterwards.

In Hemingway's world, one is always in great danger when he is alone and far out. In order to protect himself he must know the rules, must avoid at all cost cheating, and must work with only the most slow skilled technique. And then if one has good luck he will fall into the rhythm of doing things well; he will be in a state when all things seem to fall beautifully into place for him. Jake Barnes fishes well (as does Nick Adams in "The Big Two-Hearted River"), almost with the rhythm and pattern of ritual, and he is the one who best understands the beautifully patterned ritual of Romero's bullfighting. Macomber has learned how to behave beautifully in the ritual of his last and only creative act. Though one must not talk about it too much for fear of breaking the spell, Hemingway indicates that he himself had found an ecstatic rhythm in *Green Hills of Africa:* "I knew that I was shooting well and I had the feeling of well being and confidence that is so much more pleasant to have than to hear about." (55)

The same need for ritual and rhythm seems to be related to the act of writing. In spite of all that happened to him and his family during the time he was writing *A Farewell to Arms*—the difficult birth of his son by Caesarian section, the suicide of his father—"much more vividly I remember living in the book and making up what happened in it every day. Each day . . . I stopped when I was still going good and when I knew what would happen next. The fact that the book was a tragic one did not make me unhappy since I believed that life was a tragedy and knew it could only have one end. But finding you were able to make something up; to create truly enough so that it made you happy to read it; and to do this every day you worked, was something that gave a greater pleasure than I have ever known. Beside it nothing else mattered."[11]

It is this ability to sustain pure technique and find the ecstasy of creation which provides the greatest pleasure one can know. It provides a feeling "you can never feel in any other way than by yourself. That something I cannot yet define completely but the feeling comes when you write well and truly of something and know impersonally you have written in that way and those who are paid to read it and report on it do not like the subject so they say it is all a fake, yet you know its value absolutely . . ." For its value is eternal; it is experienced mystically; and it is objectified in *Green Hills of Africa* in Hemingway's description of the Gulf Stream:

when, on the sea, you are alone with it and know that this Gulf Stream you are living with, knowing, learning about, and loving, has moved, as it moves, since before man, and that it has gone by the shorelines of that long, beautiful, unhappy island since before Columbus sighted it and that the things you find out about it, and those that have always lived in it are permanent and of value because that stream will flow, as it has flowed, after the Indians, after the Spaniards, after the British, after the Americans and after all the Cubans and the systems of governments, the richness, the poverty, the martyrdom, the sacrifice and the venality and the cruelty are all gone . . .[12]

Trying to comprehend this "one single, lasting thing—the stream," giving it form in physical, literary, or ethical accomplishment, is the great achievement and happiness of the sportsman-artist-hero. One can perceive that which is lasting in terrain, in animal action, in works of art, in human behavior, and perhaps most poignantly at the moment when life and death meet, when the bull and the bullfighter, with grace and beauty, at the moment of truth, become one.

Thus in Hemingway's world, one can live by the rules one writes prose by or fights bulls by. Philip Young has noted about Hemingway: "All he wanted, he said, was to know how to live. Later he said that all he wanted was to write well. Any discrepancy which might appear to exist between these two statements is illusory."[13] Hemingway's people, whether they be sportsmen, or artists, or heroes without specific occupation, have passed through traumatic experiences and emerge into a devotion to a code. This code permeates all aspects of their life and is reflected in all their conduct and perceptions. It is

that high development of the experienced man—manners—wherein are fused
into integrity one's physical, social, esthetic, and ethical attitudes and behavior. He controls himself and confronts his destiny within the framework of
those manners, and thereby saves himself from being defeated—though he is
very likely to be destroyed.

Hemingway is, of course, not unique as a writer whose characters undergo
an indoctrination by pain into some sort of permeating wisdom. The theme is
ancient. But he shares with relatively few—mostly those who are concerned
positively with manners—the desire to shape beyond despair and cynicism, a
pattern of conduct in essence devout. In the difficulty of facing the destructive
force, the Hemingway hero lives by a pattern of manners which is the concrete
manifestation of his general moral vision, and which serves him in large and
small experience, in facing a charging bull or drinking a glass of wine.

One can observe then how Hemingway's enjoyment of a good wine can
apply metaphorically to good art and good living as well: "In wine, most
people at the start prefer sweet vintages, Sauternes, Graves, Barsac and spar-
kling Burgundy because of their picturesque quality while later they would
trade all these for a light but full and fine example of the Grand crus of Medoc
though it may be in a plain bottle without label, dust, or cobwebs, with nothing
picturesque, but only its honesty and delicacy and the light body of it on your
tongue, cool in your mouth and warm when you have drunk it. So in bullfighting." And so, it would seem, in most other things in Hemingway's world.
Certainly Delmore Schwartz need not have apologized for being "pretentious
or astounding" when he said that among novelists Hemingway "most resembles Jane Austen, who was also interested in a special kind of conduct."[14]

But more than he resembles Jane Austen, Hemingway resembles Henry
James in this respect. Like James, Hemingway could see no distinction between a way of art and a way of life. Like James's heroes, Hemingway's have
a special sensibility; manners to both represent an outward manifestation of
an inner wisdom, an ultimate fusion of the spirit of a man with the actions of
a man. They become as well the means whereby a man or a writer can express
his individuality without vulgarity or egotism, his sense of values without
pretension or sentimentality. As Hemingway put it in *Death in the Afternoon:*
"The matador, if he knows his profession, can increase the amount of danger
of death that he runs exactly as much as he wishes. He should, however,
increase this danger, *within the rules provided for his protection.* In other words
it is to his credit if he does something that he knows how to do in a highly
dangerous but still geometrically possible manner. It is to his discredit if he
runs danger through ignorance, through disregard of the fundamental rules,

through physical or mental slowness, or through blind folly. The matador must dominate the bulls by knowledge and science. In the measure in which this domination is accomplished with grace will it be beautiful to watch." (21)

It is not strange, therefore, that Hemingway has been attacked by some critics on much the same terms as James. It is assumed that both these writers, concerned as they were with craftsmanship, with manners that become almost mannerisms in the heroes, with manner that becomes almost mannerism in the art, with closed societies, with special sensibilities, were merely advocates of art for art's sake. They were not. But they did believe in subduing a general feeling about art and life into a fairly rigid code exemplified by individual characters, precise enough to be called an "art of living."

Both had that rare and remarkable ability to make the concrete action of a character in a novel—whether the character be a gentleman over a tea cup or a matador in an arena—emblematic of a whole way of art and way of life. It is essentially this fusion of the physical-esthetic-ethical in one action by one unified vision which Hemingway shares with Henry James—in spite of the vastly different stories each tells. That is why Hemingway praises James, and seems to puzzle or surprise readers when he does, as one of only three "good" American authors.

In *Green Hills of Africa* Hemingway said, "there is a fourth and fifth dimension that can be gotten" in prose. What these dimensions are has often seemed to puzzle critics. I believe the fourth dimension is esthetic; the fifth ethical. These added dimensions occur obviously with the other three; they emerge from the story metaphorically, almost allegorically. Thus is Hemingway's sportsman the physical manifestation of the writer, who is the esthetic manifestation of the hero, who is the ethical manifestation of the code. A prose which contains all five dimensions is possible to a writer who is "serious enough and has luck," he said. Hemingway was always serious about writing and he was, I think, often lucky.

1. Ernest Hemingway, *Death in the Afternoon* (New York, 1932), p. 2. Subsequent references to this work will be made to this edition.

2. Lillian Ross, "How Do You Like It Now, Gentlemen?" *The New Yorker,* May 13, 1950, p. 41.

3. Ivan Kashkeen, "Ernest Hemingway: A Tragedy of Craftsmanship" (1935), in *E. H.: The Man and His Work,* ed. John K. M. McCaffery (New York, 1950), p. 93. Originally in *International Literature* (U.S.S.R.), (1935).

4. Ivan Kashkeen, "Alive in the Midst of Death" (1956), in *Hemingway and His Critics,* ed. Carlos Baker, American Century Series (New York, 1961), p. 178. Originally in *Soviet Literature,* (1956).

5. Carlos Baker discusses "The Snows of Kilimanjaro" as an artist fable, equating Hemingway's position in that with Henry James' position in "The Lesson of the Master." See Carlos Baker, *Hemingway, the Writer as Artist,* 2nd ed. (Princeton, 1956), p. 192.

6. Ernest Hemingway, "Preface" in *The Short Stories of Ernest Hemingway* (New York, 1938), vii.

7. Ernest Hemingway, *A Farewell to Arms* (New York, 1949), p. 338.

8. In Malcolm Cowley, "A Portrait of Mister Papa," *Life,* January 10, 1949, p. 101.

9. Hemingway quotes this in *Death in the Afternoon* from a decree passed by the Spanish government to protect the horses. The goring of these animals was that which most offended the unindoctrinated or unsympathetic members of the audience. Ironically, these padded protectors "in no way decrease the pain suffered by the horses; they take much of the bravery from the bull . . . and they are the first step toward the suppression of the bullfight." (7–8).

10. Ernest Hemingway, *Green Hills of Africa,* Scribners (New York, 1935), p. 271–2. Subsequent references to this work will be made to this edition.

11. See Hemingway's introduction to the illustrated edition of *A Farewell to Arms* (New York, 1948), pp. vii-viii.

12. *Green Hills of Africa,* pp. 148–150. This sentence, which runs over 400 words, is the longest sentence in Hemingway. In it the author equates the Gulf Stream on which he fished, and Santiago fished, with the stream of history and time and finally with that eternity which the artist must face when he creates.

13. Philip Young, *Ernest Hemingway,* (New York, 1952), 179.

14. Delmore Schwartz, "Ernest Hemingway's Literary Situation" (1938), in McCaffery, p. 117. Originally in *Southern Review,* III (Spring, 1938).

CONFITEOR HOMINEM:
ERNEST HEMINGWAY'S RELIGION OF MAN

JOSEPH WALDMEIR

IN RECENT YEARS, critics have become increasingly suspicious that it is necessary to read Ernest Hemingway's work on the symbolic as well as on the story level in order to gain a full appreciation of its art.[1] Since the publication of *The Old Man and the Sea,* the suspicion has become first an awareness, then a certainty. Of all Hemingway's work, this one demands most to be read on both levels; and the story, its details, its method of presentation, are sufficiently similar to the balance of his work as to suggest strongly the possibility of a

Reprinted with permission from *PMASAL,* XLII, (1956), 277–281.

similar reading and perhaps a similar interpretation.

The Old Man and the Sea is, as story, very good Hemingway. It is swiftly and smoothly told; the conflict is resolved into a struggle between a man and a force which he scarcely comprehends, but which he knows that he must continue to strive against, though knowing too that the struggle must end in defeat. The defeat is only apparent, however, for, as in "The Undefeated," it becomes increasingly clear throughout the story that it is not victory or defeat that matters but the struggle itself. Furthermore, *The Old Man and the Sea,* while reasserting the set of values, the philosophy which permeates all of Hemingway, is built upon the great abstractions—love and truth and honor and loyalty and pride and humility—and again speaks of the proper method of attaining and retaining these virtues, and of the spiritual satisfaction inevitably bestowed upon their holder.

The Christian religious symbols running through the story, which are so closely interwoven with the story in fact as to suggest an allegorical intention on Hemingway's part, are so obvious as to require little more than a listing of them here. The Old Man is a fisherman, and he is also a teacher, one who has taught the boy not only how to fish—that is, how to make a living—but how to behave as well, giving him the pride and humility necessary to a good life. During the trials with the great fish and with the sharks his hands pain him terribly, his back is lashed by the line, he gets an eyepiercing headache, and his chest constricts and he spits blood. He hooks the fish at noon, and at noon of the third day he kills it by driving his harpoon into its heart. As he sees the second and third sharks attacking, the Old Man calls aloud " 'Ay,' " and Hemingway comments: "There is no translation for this word and perhaps it is just such a noise as a man might make, involuntarily, feeling the nail go through his hand and into the wood."[2] On landing, the Old Man shoulders his mast and goes upward from the sea toward his hut; he is forced to rest several times on his journey up the hill, and when he reaches the hut he lies on the bed "with his arms out straight and the palms of his hands up."[3]

The Christian symbolism so evident here shifts from man to fish—a legitimate symbol for Christ since the beginning of Christianity, as it was a legitimate religious symbol before Christianity—and back to man throughout the story. This apparent confusion is consistent not only within the Hemingway philosophy as an example of the sacrificer-sacrificed phenomenon (a point which I will discuss later in this paper) but within formal Christianity as well, if the doctrine of the Trinity be accepted. Furthermore, the phenomenon itself closely parallels the Roman Catholic sacrifice of the Mass, wherein a fusion of the priest-man with Christ takes place at the moment of Transubstantiation.

Along with the Christ symbols, reinforcing them, but depending on them for its importance, is a rather intricate numerology. It is not formalized—neither is the numerology of Christianity—but it is carefully set forth.

Three, seven, and forty are key numbers in the Old and New Testaments, and in the religion, and Hemingway makes a judicious use of them. The Old Man, as the story opens, has fished alone for forty-four famine days and with the boy for forty more. The Old Man's trial with the great fish lasts exactly three days; the fish is landed on the seventh attempt; seven sharks are killed; and, although Christ fell only three times under the Cross, whereas the Old Man has to rest from the weight of the mast seven times, there is a consistency in the equal importance of the numbers themselves.

But, once it has been established that *The Old Man and the Sea* may be read on the symbolic as well as on the story level, a new problem presents itself, a problem which grows out of the nature of the symbolic level and out of the disturbing realization that the two levels exist harmoniously in the work. I think that the problem may best be expressed by two questions which the discerning reader must have asked himself as he put *The Old Man and the Sea* down: Is the story, as it appears at first glance to be, a Christian allegory? Has the old master tough guy decided, in the words of Colonel Cantwell, "to run as a Christian"? If neither of these questions can be answered with an un-qualified affirmative—and I submit that they cannot—then a further question must be asked: Just what is the book's message?

The answer assumes a third level on which *The Old Man and the Sea* must be read—as a sort of allegorical commentary by the author on all his previous work, by means of which it may be established that the religious overtones of *The Old Man and the Sea* are not peculiar to that book among Hemingway's works, and that Hemingway has finally taken the decisive step in elevating what might be called his philosophy of Manhood to the level of a religion.

Two aspects of the total work, including *The Old Man and the Sea,* must be considered at this point in order to clarify the above conclusion on the one hand, and to answer the questions concerning Hemingway's Christianity on the other.

The first of these aspects is Hemingway's concern with man as man, with man in his relation to things of this world almost exclusively. The other world, God, does not often enter into the thoughts, plans, or emotions of a Heming-way character. God exists—most of the characters are willing to admit His existence, or at least, unwilling to deny it—but not as an immanent Being, not ever benevolent or malevolent.

God is sometimes prayed to by the Hemingway hero at moments of crisis, but His aid or succor are never depended upon, never really expected. Thus we have Jake Barnes in the Cathedral at Pamplona, on the eve of his great trial, praying for everybody he can think of, for good bullfights and good fishing; and as he becomes aware of himself kneeling, head bent, he

was a little ashamed, and regretted that I was such a rotten Catholic, but realized that there was nothing I could do about it, at least for awhile, and maybe never, but that anyway it was a grand religion, and I only wished I felt religious and maybe I would the next time. . . .[4]

And thus, too, we have the Old Man, who, after twenty-four hours of his monumental struggle have passed, prays for heavenly assistance mechanically, automatically, thinking, "I am not religious," and "Hail Marys are easier to say than Our Fathers." And after forty-five hours, he says:

"Now that I have him coming so beautifully, God help me to endure. I'll say a hundred Our Fathers and a hundred Hail Marys. But I cannot say them now."
Consider them said, he thought, I'll say them later.[5]

But when the struggle is ended and the full ironic impact of his "victory" is clear, he asks himself what it was that beat him, and answers, "Nothing . . . I went out too far."[6]

He who depends too heavily on prayer, or for that matter on any external aids when faced with a crisis, is not very admirable to Hemingway. In *Death in the Afternoon,* when he wants to describe the unmanliness of a "cowardly bullfighter" girding himself for action, Hemingway places him in church

in his bullfighting clothes to pray before the fight, sweating under the armpits, praying that the bull will embiste, that is, charge frankly and follow the cloth well; oh blessed Virgin that thou wilt give me a bull that will embiste well, blessed Virgin, give me that bull, blessed Virgin, that I should touch this bull in Madrid to-day on a day without wind; promising something of value or a pilgrimage, praying for luck, frightened sick. . . .[7]

A man must depend upon himself alone in order to assert his manhood, and the assertion of his manhood, in the face of insuperable obstacles, is the complete end and justification of his existence for a Hemingway hero. The Old Man *must* endure his useless struggle with the sharks; Manuel, in "The Undefeated," *must,* in spite of his broken wrist and a terrible goring, go in on the bull six times and accept the horn at last; Jake *must* continue to live as "well" and "truly" and "honestly" as he is able in spite of his overwhelming frustration. And each must face his struggle alone, with no recourse to other-worldly help, for only as solitary individuals can they assert their manhood.

And significantly they must go it alone without regard to otherworldly blame. As far as sin is concerned, Jake would probably say along with the Old Man, "Do not think about sin. It is much too late for that and there are people who are paid to do it. Let them think about it."[8] And Manuel would probably nod agreement.

However, in spite of such obvious rejections of otherworldly Christianity in his affirmation of Manhood, Hemingway has formulated as rigid a set of rules for living and for the attainment of Manhood as can be found in any religion. These rules, along with the detailed procedure for their application, constitute the second aspect of Hemingway's total work to be considered in this paper.

The rules are built upon the great abstractions mentioned above. They are so bound up with the procedure for their application that the procedure itself might be considered to be a rule—or better, that neither rules nor procedure exist without one another. Hemingway's philosophy of Manhood is a philoso-phy of action; a man is honest when he acts honestly, he is humble when he acts humbly, he loves when he is loving or being loved. Thus, taking an awareness of the rules as he has taken an awareness of the abstractions for granted, Hemingway concerns himself primarily with the presentation of procedure. The procedure is carefully outlined; it is meticulously detailed. If no part of it is overlooked or sloughed off, it must result in a satisfying experience almost in and of itself.

This procedure, this ritual—for such is what the procedure actually amounts to—is most clearly evident in Hemingway's treatment of the bullfight. *Death in the Afternoon* is devoted to an evaluation of the manhood of various bullfighters on the basis of their ability to abide by the rules, and to a description of the ritual by means of which they prove possession and communicate the satisfaction to be gained from a proper performance of function to the spectator. War, the prize ring, fishing, hunting, and making love are some of the other celebrations by means of which Hemingway's religio-philosophy of Man is conveyed. But the bullfight is the greatest because, besides possessing, as the others do also, a procedure inviolate, intimately related to the great abstractions, it always ends in death. It assumes the stature of a religious sacrifice by means of which a man can place himself in harmony with the universe, can satisfy the spiritual as well as the physical side of his nature, can atone for the grievous omissions and commissions of his past, can purify and elevate himself in much the same way that he can in any sacrificial religion. The difference between Hemingway's religion of man and formal religion is simply—yet profoundly—that in the former the elevation does not extend beyond the limits of this world, and in the latter, Christianity for example, the ultimate elevation is totally otherworldly.

The bullfighter is in a sense a priest, performing the sacrifice for the sake of the spectator as well as for his own sake, giving each that "feeling of life and death and mortality and immortality" which Hemingway described in *Death in the Afternoon,* and, as does the Roman Catholic priest on the ideal level, the bullfighter actually places his own life in jeopardy. This curious phenomenon of the sacrificer gambling on becoming the sacrificed serves to clarify the terms of Hemingway's system, rather than, as at first glance it might seem, to confuse them. The bullfighter recognizes the possibility and imminence of death when he steps into the ring, and he must face it bravely. He must perform the sacrifice cleanly, with one true stroke, preserving both his honor and the bull's dignity. If he kills out of malice or out of fear his actions will show it, and the spectator will be distracted from concentration upon the sacrifice to awareness of the man, and no satisfaction will result.

There must be a cognizance of death both from the standpoint of killing and from that of being killed; there must be more than a cognizance actually; there must be an acceptance. Knowledge of death's inevitability so that he does not react to its immediacy, coupled with unconcern for the possibilities of life after death, are necessary attributes of the ideal bullfighter. His aim can extend no further than the great abstractions themselves, how he earns them and how he communicates them. He must realize that it is not *that* one dies but *how* one dies that is important. And equally important, that it is not *that* one kills but *how* one kills.

It is not only in his treatment of the bullfight that this second aspect of Hemingway's total work is evident, though there it may be most immediately apparent. The abstractions, the rules, the ritual, the sacrifice dominate the details of *The Old Man and the Sea* as they dominate those of "The Undefeated" and *The Sun Also Rises.*[9] We are told carefully, painstakingly, how the Old Man performs his function as fisherman; how he prepares for the hoped-for struggle:

Before it was really light he had his baits out and was drifting with the current. One bait was down forty fathoms. The second was at seventy-five and the third and fourth were down in the blue water at one hundred and one hundred and twenty-five fathoms. Each bait hung head down with the shank of the hook inside the bait fish, tied and sewed solid and all the projecting part of the hook, the curve and the point, was covered with fresh sardines. Each sardine was hooked through both eyes so that they made a half-garland on the projecting steel.

. . . Each line, as thick around as a big pencil, was looped onto a green-sapped stick so that any pull or touch on the bait would make the stick dip and each line had two forty-fathom coils which could be made fast to the other spare coils so that, if it were necessary, a fish could take out over three hundred fathoms of line.[10]

We are told how he hooks the fish and secures the line, waiting suspensefully for the fish to turn and swallow the bait, then waiting again until it has eaten it well, then striking, "with all the strength of his arms and the pivoted weight of his body," three times, setting the hook; then placing the line across his back and shoulders so that there will be something to give when the fish lunges, and the line will not break. We are told specifically, in terms reminiscent of such descriptions of the bullfight, how the kill is made:

The old man dropped the line and put his foot on it and lifted the harpoon as high as he could and drove it down with all his strength, and more strength he had just summoned, into the fish's side just behind the great chest fin that rose high in the air to the altitude of a man's chest. He felt the iron go in and he leaned on it and drove it further and then pushed all his weight after it.[11]

The immanence of death for the sacrificer as well as for the sacrificed, and his total disregard of its possibility, are made clear at the climax of the struggle when the Old Man thinks: "You are killing me, fish . . . Come on and kill me. I do not care who kills who."[12]

It is at this point I think that the questions asked earlier in this paper can be answered. Has Hemingway decided to "run as a Christian"? I think not; the evidence in *The Old Man and the Sea,* with the exception of the Christian symbolism, indicates that he is no more Christian now than he was when he wrote *The Sun Also Rises.* But the Christian symbolism *is* in the book, and it *does* appear to constitute a Christian religious allegory. Yes, but on a superficial level. The religious allegory, attached to the two aspects of the total body of Hemingway's work as they appear in *The Old Man and the Sea,* which have been the subject of most of my discussion thus far, actually constitute a third level on which *The Old Man and the Sea* must be read—as the allegorical interpretation of the total body of the work.

I said above that Hemingway is no more Christian now than he was thirty years ago; it has been my intention in this paper to show that he was *no less religious* thirty years ago than he is now. The evidence which I have presented adds up to something more than a philosophy or an ethic, the two terms which have most often been used to describe Hemingway's world view; it adds up to what I would call a Religion of Man. Hemingway did not turn religious to write *The Old Man and the Sea.* He has always been religious, though his religion is not of the orthodox, organized variety. He celebrates, he has always celebrated, the Religion of Man; *The Old Man and the Sea* merely celebrates it more forcefully and convincingly than any previous Hemingway work. It is the final step in the celebration. It is the book which, on the one hand, elevates the philosophy to a religion by the use of allegory, and on the other, by being an allegory of the total body of his work, enables us to see that work finally from the point of view of religion.

1. The two most recent comprehensive examinations of Hemingway symbolism are: Carlos Baker, *Hemingway: The Writer as Artist* (Princeton: Princeton University Press, 1952), and Philip Young, *Ernest Hemingway* (New York: Rinehart, 1952).

2. Ernest Hemingway, *The Old Man and the Sea* (New York: Scribner, 1952), p. 118.

3. *Ibid.,* p. 134.

4. Hemingway, *The Sun Also Rises* (New York: Scribner, 1926), pp. 99–100.

5. *The Old Man and the Sea,* p. 96.

6. *Ibid.,* p. 133.

7. Hemingway, *Death in the Afternoon* (New York: Scribner, 1932), p. 90.

8. *The Old Man and the Sea,* p. 116. Hemingway has always had a deep respect for Christians —provided they *live* like Christians. His great abstractions are also great Christian virtues; and when he finds a believer, such as the priest in *A Farewell to Arms* or Anselmo in *For Whom the Bell Tolls,* who lives in accord with the abstractions, he praises him as "a Christian," and adds, for the benefit of the hypocritical, "something very rare in Catholic countries."

There is no evidence of intentional blasphemy in any of his work; the deeply religious are frequently exalted, not in the terms of Christianity, but in Hemingway's own terms. In the one-act play, "Today is Friday," Christ's Manhood is given far greater importance than His Godhead with no blasphemous overtones. The First Soldier, speaking for Hemingway and offering the highest praise he is capable of, answers, "He was pretty good in there today," each time the cynical Second Soldier minimizes Christ's manliness. The words are not only directly addressed to the cynic, but indirectly to the emotionally disturbed Third Soldier as well, who has had a religious experience which the First cannot share, but which he comprehends and sympathizes with.

9. With the possible exception of sacrifice, they dominate the details of *Across the River and Into the Trees* as well. If examined in terms of the religion of Manhood, this is not as unsuccessful a book as most critics have claimed. It gives those members of the Order who realize that they will die a natural death a way to meet the problem of dying. Colonel Cantwell still enjoys many of the things that have contributed to the happiness of his life—the beauties of nature and art, the taste of good food and drink, the pleasures of hunting, the give and take of sexual love—and in memory he can experience again the pleasure of fulfilling a soldier's duties.

The reviewers have looked upon this preparation for dying as little more than nostalgic sentimentalism; but even granting that the story tends in this direction, it still fits neatly into the Hemingway religio-philosophical mold. At its climax there is the usual refusal to turn to the supernatural, a more pointed refusal than ever: "You going to run as a Christian?" the Colonel asks himself, and answers, "Maybe I will get Christian toward the end. Yes, he said, maybe you will. Who wants to make a bet on that?" (p. 291)

10. *The Old Man and the Sea,* pp. 33–34.
11. *Ibid.,* pp. 103–104.
12. *Ibid.,* p. 102.

III. The Work, Studies of Method and Language

THE SWEET STYLE OF ERNEST HEMINGWAY

PAUL GOODMAN

IT IS AN EXAGGERATION to say that the language determines the metaphysics of the tribe and what people can think—the so-called "Whorfian hypothesis." Language is checked by unverbalized experience. Language itself is plastic and says new things when necessary. People do manage to communicate across the barrier of language and culture, e.g., I get something out of Homer, Genesis, and Confucius. And in the problems of philosophy, we can usually think away the language of previous thinkers and still find a real problem for ourselves.

But we can put Whorf's thesis in a more modest form that is more rewarding: a style of speech is a hypothesis about how the world is. When speakers adopt a style, they are already saying something substantive. A good style, colloquial and literary, is one that is adequate to cope with, that "saves," a wide range of experience, omitting nothing indispensable. It proves itself as a way of being, it does not break down, it is believable.

This view is similar to the newer philosophy of linguistic analysis that has developed out of linguistic positivism. Instead of treating popular metaphysics as nonsense in which people are stuck, and to which prophylaxis must be applied, linguistic analysis takes common speech as a repository of vast empirical experience of curious matters by the community, just as the common law is the embodied wisdom of the Anglo-Saxon people (such as it is). The philosophical problem is to decipher exactly what is being said; in colloquial sentences, what do people *mean* when they say "mind," "cause," "responsibility," "good," "bad," and so forth?

Reprinted with permission from *The New York Review of Books*, XVII, No. 11 (December 30, 1971), 27–28.

Literary style is a convenient object for this kind of analysis. It is usually less subtle than excellent colloquial speech, but it is recorded and it provides large coherent wholes to examine. Let us look briefly at a famous modern style, Hemingway's, and single out one of its dominant hypotheses.

It is a passive style. The characters, including the narrator, are held off in such a way—"alienated," as Brecht puts it—that they influence nothing; events happen to them. The actions that they initiate—the story consists entirely of actions that they initiate—do not add up to actualizing them; it is one thing after another. Yet neither do the actions betray and doom them, as in ancient stories of Fate, for that would impart a meaning, a tragic meaning, to the world. Rather, the events turn out to be happenings.

Needless to say, the passivity of people in contemporary society, with its high technology and centralized organization, has been the prevailing theme of naturalistic fiction for over a century. But Hemingway takes the theme at a deeper level. His stories are located in nonindustrial scenes, often in fairly primitive places, and they are about activities that are even spectacularly individualistic and active, dangerous sports, smuggling, soldiers on the loose. The characters come on with a heavy preponderance of active verbs. And the effect is passive. Unlike the naturalists who show how men are puppets of the institutions, and *by* showing it inject their own activity, often political, into the prose, Hemingway contrives by his style, by what he tells and what he avoids telling, to show that happening-to-one is the nature of things. (Psychoanalytically, the passivity has been internalized.)

Here are two passages from *The Sun Also Rises,* published in 1926 when Hemingway was twenty-eight. The first is the end of a description, similar to others in the book. The characters have driven up a high mountain and it is cold.

The bus leveled down onto the straight line of a road that ran to Burguete. We passed a crossroads and crossed a bridge over a stream. The houses of Burguete were along both sides of the road. There were no side-streets. We passed the church and the school-yard, and the bus stopped. We got down and the driver handed down our bags and the rod-case. A carabineer in his cocked hat and yellow leather cross straps came up.

"What's in there?" he pointed to the rod-case.

I opened it and showed him. He asked to see our fishing-permits and I got them out. He looked at the date and then waved us on.

"Is that all right?" I asked.

"Yes. Of course."
We went up the street, past the whitewashed stone houses.

The other passage is the climax of action of the novel, the bullfight.

When he had finished his work with the muleta and was ready to kill, the crowd made him go on. They did not want the bull killed yet, they did not want it to be over. Romero went on. It was like a course in bull fighting. All the passes he linked up, all completed, all slow, templed and smooth. There were no tricks and no mystifications. There was no brusqueness. And each pass as it reached the summit gave you a sudden ache inside. The crowd did not want it ever to be finished.

The bull was squared on all four feet to be killed, and Romero killed directly below us. He killed not as he had been forced to by the last bull, but as he wanted to. He profiled directly in front of the bull, drew the sword out of the muleta and sighted along the blade. The bull watched him. Romero spoke to the bull and tapped one of his feet. The bull charged and Romero waited for the charge, the muleta held low, sighting along the blade, his feet firm. Then without taking a step forward, he became one with the bull, the sword was in high between the shoulders, the bull had followed the low slung flannel, that disappeared as Romero lurched clear to the left, and it was over. The bull tried to go forward, his legs commenced to settle, he swung from side to side, hesitated, then went down on his knees, and. . . . Handkerchiefs were waving all over the bull-ring. The President looked down from the box and waved his handkerchief. . . .

These passages are, of course, artfully different—within the narrow range of language that Hemingway uses. The short, active, declarative sentences of the description are increasingly connected by "and" in the action, accelerating the tempo; finally there are only commas, speed of speech. In the climactic sentence "Then without taking a step, etc.," the syntax is allowed to break down. The description has a natural randomness, as things turn up, including the pointless dialogue with the carabineer. In the action every sentence is pointed to the climax.

In both passages, Hemingway uses the repetitions that are his favorite glue. But in the description they are more freely scattered and oddly equivocal in syntax: "road," "cross-roads," "cross-straps," "crossed," "sides of the road," "side-streets," "leveled down," "got down," "handed down." In the action, the repetitions follow more directly and are univocal, urgent, plangent: "They did not want," "they did not want it over," "he wanted to"; "killed," "killed," "killed"; "directly below us," "directly in front of the bull";

"charged," "waited for the charge"; "handkerchiefs were waving," "waved his handkerchief."

Nevertheless, the two passages have overwhelmingly in common the chief characteristic of Hemingway's style early and mature: the persons are held at arm's length, there is no way to get inside them or identify with them, it is happening to them. (But note that the events do not happen to the prose; rather the prose influences the events. For instance, it is because the driver handed *down* the bags and *ended* with the rod-case that the carabineer came *up* and pointed to the rod-case.)

In a description of arriving in a new place, it is plausible for events to happen to a person; but in the passages of action it is almost uncanny—and this is why this is a remarkable style—how we still seem to hear, "It happened that the crowd did not want," or even "it happened to the crowd that it did not want"; "it happened to Romero that he wanted," "it happened that he profiled," "it happened to him that the bull charged," and "it happened that he met the charge." This has gotten to be the style of "objective" journalism, but it was writers like Hemingway who invented the style for the journalists. The verbs are active and the sentences declarative, but since the *persons* do not do it, we feel that they do not *do* it. And this is how the author has plotted it in the preceding pages anyway.

The narrator too is mesmerized by what he is telling. The effect is not at all like the impressionism of Virginia Woolf, for she lets us experience the first-person knower, who grows. Rather, as I have said, it is like the Brechtian "alienation," which Hemingway achieves more consistently than Brecht.[1]

That we exist in a meaningless universe—vanity of vanities—is the theme of *The Sun Also Rises* with its motto and title taken from Ecclesiastes; and this novel, though not powerful, is authentic through and through. In Hemingway's later works, the more romantic or adventurous themes are betrayed by the passive style. (*The Old Man and the Sea* has some authenticity, but the style is richer.) Ideally, the style of any work should be the style *of* that work, a unique language saying what the whole work wants to say. But of course with Hemingway and most of us, our style is our way of being in the world in general rather than for just this one book. We are wise to choose our subjects according to what we *can* say. In the best cases, we choose on the borderline and learn to say more. Hemingway played it a little too safe.

To make my point, let me contrast this passive style with a powerful active style. I unfairly choose a very great passage. Here is the exordium of the opening section of *The Decline and Fall of the Roman Empire*.

For three long chapters Gibbon has been describing and (more or less) extolling the Roman Empire under the Antonines, its extent, its power, its prosperity, its arts, its institutions and civil peace, the occasional beneficence of its rulers. He concludes,

But the empire of the Romans filled the world, and, when that empire fell into the hands of a single person, the world became a safe and dreary prison for his enemies. The slave of Imperial despotism, whether he was condemned to drag his gilded chain in Rome and the senate, or to wear out a life of exile on the barren rock of Seriphus, or the frozen banks of the Danube, expected his fate in silent despair. To resist was fatal, and it was impossible to fly. On every side he was encompassed with a vast extent of sea and land, which he could never hope to traverse without being discovered, seized, and restored to his irritated master. Beyond the frontiers, his anxious view could discover nothing, except the ocean, inhospitable deserts, hostile tribes of barbarians, of fierce manners and unknown language, or dependent kings, who would gladly purchase the emperor's protection by the sacrifice of an obnoxious fugitive. "Wherever you are," said Cicero to the exiled Marcellus, "remember that you are equally within the power of the conqueror."

Whether in his enlightened awareness or in his Enlightenment prejudice, there is no doubt that Gibbon is in complete control of the vast scene and appropriates it for the reader. In each sentence he exhausts the alternative situations, the possibilities of action, the geographical space of the world. The ideas are many and not repeated, the motion is rapid for an elegant style, yet he gives us all the balances and parallels and even a chiasmus. Without losing speed, he builds to longer sentences, grander territory, bleaker scenery, and more desperate gloom. Yet, though he has the story in his grip, he is by no means cold or detached; he does not strangle himself. Nearly every sentence has something sarcastic or spiteful—"safe prison," "gilded chain in the senate," "irritated master," "obnoxious fugitive." He is not talking about an abstraction; we are made to identify with that hyperactive, and balked, victim. And in the book the plotted place of this bitter outburst, after the (rather) golden narration that precedes, is like a blow.

Return now to Hemingway and his narrow range. It is not surprising that a succession of short active indicative sentences produces passivity. We turn to each verb after it has struck. There is not enough syntactical leeway for the author or reader to become engaged either actively or contemplatively, or as one who desires, or one who interprets. An advantage of the style is that it is in close contact with the facts being told, since there is no intermediary of indirect discourse, point of view, subordination, explanation. This is its aptness for journalistic reporting. A disadvantage is that it can rapidly become boring, as Hemingway often is, because it is hard to make the bits add up and there is increasing resistance to taking the bits in. When Hemingway is good, he provides glue, repetitions, or leading tones like the rod-case.

But Hemingway certainly also used the style hoping to tell simple, down-to-earth experience, and in this crucial respect the style doesn't work, since it is not how we experience. I have elsewhere made the same point against taking short active indicative sentences as the syntactical kernels of all sentences. The world that is told by them is not primary experience, which is more elaborately and globally structured, and we see that when such sentences are actually spun out, the effect is human passivity. To derive all sentences from short active sentences, as Chomsky does in his basic grammar, must be wrong, because this is not how uncorrupted speakers are in the world, especially children.

But we must then ask a further question: If Hemingway's style is so persistently passive in effect, how can it cope with enough of human life to be viable? I can think of four ways in which Hemingway countervails the passive effect of his prose.

First, obviously, is the violent *macho* activism of the characters and events he couches in the prose, nothing but bullfighters, warriors, gun-packing gangsters, hunters of big animals and big fish. But this becomes real thin real soon. One begins to psychoanalyze it simply because there is nothing else to do with it. One wishes that the chosen sport was baseball, with teammates, or that he wrote about equally manly tasks like farming or carpentry, so that there could be some product more interesting than a corpse.

Second, he knows better. There is a unique sentence in *The Sun Also Rises* that is a most peculiar development of the accustomed style. The whole passage is a deviation. A man has been killed on the street by a bull being driven to the ring, and a waiter at the café comments that it's a stupid kind of fun and not for him. The narrator says,

The bull who killed Vicente Girones was named Bocanegra, was number 118 of the bull-breeding establishment of Sanchez Taberno and was killed by Pedro Romero as the third bull of that same afternoon. His ear was cut by popular acclamation and given to Pedro Romero, who, in turn, gave it to Brett, who wrapped it in a handkerchief belonging to myself, and left both ear and handkerchief, along with a number of Muratti cigarette-stubs, shoved far back in the drawer of the bedtable that stood beside her bed in the Hotel Montoya, in Pamplona.

This unusually long and uncharacteristically complex sentence is the only spunky sentence in the book, and one of the few in Hemingway's work. It tells of a rebellious, not passive, response: bitter contempt. Once the short active sentences are brought synoptically together, the effect is to write them off, to tell the world off. But though he *knows* this, Hemingway cannot follow it up, so that the passage is merely sentimental—sentimentality is feeling or "significance" more than the plot warrants. Instead he goes on to the bullfight and, as if on the rebound, to the one overwritten paragraph in the book, "Pedro Romero had the greatness, etc.," which is hopelessly sentimental. Instead of taking his own rage as meaningful, Hemingway makes a desperate bid to find a hero, an agent. It doesn't wash.

The rejected theme reappears years later, however, as the rueful message of *The Old Man and the Sea,* that you try like the devil and bring back bones. The later book is not spunky, it rationalizes; but it is a fairly hard look at Hemingway himself.

(Incidentally, the bull's ear that Brett leaves behind with the cigarette butts, embarrassedly in the back of the drawer, is the real literary probability for her walking out on the young bullfighter in the end, and not the lofty renunciation that some of the critics seem to read. What *does* one do with shitty underwear or a bull's ear, in a hotel?)

A third way in which Hemingway countervails the passive hypothesis of his style is his stoical ethic. It appears not in the subject matter or the prose, but in the plotting: the people are loyal, they endure, they go it alone. This ethic is surely why he was so popular and seemed to be a major writer during his era. He gave people something to live on with, when the conditions were so absurd. But he did not have enough intellect to assert a lasting ethical position.

My impression is that young people today do not find him "existential" enough. I have heard young people seriously ask what difference it would make if the human race vanished utterly. Hemingway would have been shocked by such an attitude, as I am. Put it this way: normally, we would expect characters in novels, especially toward the end, to do something, influence events. In Hemingway's novels the characters are done to, but at least they *are* done to by the events, they are engaged in them. In many recent novels, however, the characters just "make the scene," they are not engaged in the events but are like tourists. Or they con the scene like hipsters. They seem to have infinite time. Hemingway understood that people get worn out, grow old.

But therefore—yin and yang—in contemporary writing, there is a flood of very personal reporting of *actual* political events in which the authors have taken part. More passionate and reflective than objective journalism, less plotted and universal than poetic fiction, this has become a new genre since it fills the need of the times. So far as I have read, Barbara Deming is the best. Mailer is an interesting transitional writer; he is caught in an ethic partly Hemingway and partly hipster. He gravitates to the new subject matter, but he is not committed to its actions and therefore he becomes decorative. (Reminds me of Carlyle.)

In my opinion, Hemingway's work will last, not because of his stoical ethic but because of something in his style. It is sweetness. It appears more frequently in books later than *The Sun Also Rises,* especially in *A Farewell to Arms.* When it appears, the short sentences coalesce and flow, and sing— sometimes melancholy, sometimes pastoral, sometimes personally embarrassed in an adult, not an adolescent, way. In the dialogues, he pays loving attention to the spoken word. And the writing is meticulous; he is sweetly devoted to writing well. Most everything else is resigned, but here he makes an effort, and the effort produces lovely moments. The young, since they read poorly, do not dig that *writing* is his "existential" act. As Spinoza would say it, for a writer his writing is intellect in action, his freedom, whereas the themes he is stuck with, his confusion, his audience are likely to be his human bondage.

---

1. In one of his aphorisms, Kafka says, "I have long since fallen under the wheels—comfortingly enough." But in his stories he persists in asking why; he feels insulted. The effect is not comfortingly passive but painfully restive.

ERNEST HEMINGWAY

RICHARD BRIDGMAN

I

AROUND 1916, when Ernest Hemingway first addressed himself to the art of writing, the American vernacular still had not found a secure place in

Reprinted with permission from Richard Bridgman, *The Colloquial Style in America* (N.Y.: Oxford University Press, 1966), 195–230.

prose fiction. Ring Lardner was mechanically exploiting it for satirical purposes, Sherwood Anderson was trying to use its supposititious honesty with indifferent success, and it looked as if the reserves of power Mark Twain had discovered in the vernacular were lost again. The job of shaping the vernacular for general service, of giving substance to Gertrude Stein's lessons in abstraction, or conversely, of imposing aesthetic form on eccentric colloquial material remained undone. To Hemingway fell the task of joining the two lines leading from Henry James and Mark Twain.

Hemingway opened his career in the Oak Park high school newspaper, writing clever imitations of Ring Lardner, who was himself then writing for another local paper, the Chicago *Tribune*. As late as 1918 when he was serving in Italy, Hemingway still indulged in Lardnerian pastiche. "Well Al we are here in this old Italy and now that I am here I am not going to leave it. Not at all if any. And that is not no New Years revolution Al but the truth."[1] But after Hemingway was wounded, he dropped the hampering cynicism inherent in Lardner's style. Hemingway wrote Maxwell Perkins that he had "not been at all hardboiled since July 8, 1918—on the night on which I discovered that that also was vanity."[2]

Charles Fenton has shown us how Hemingway's early work as a newspaperman and foreign correspondent helped to prune his style. Whether it was the style sheet of the Kansas City *Star* demanding "Avoid the use of adjectives, especially such extravagant ones as *splendid, gorgeous, grand, magnificent*" ("The best rules I ever learned for the business of writing"), or the economy demanded in transmitting one's stories by transatlantic cables ("Isn't it a great language?"),[3] the demand for concision bore steadily down upon Hemingway throughout his apprentice years. This, coupled with his intense desire to render "what really happened in action"[4] and to exorcise the commercial smugness and sentimentality which he felt deliberately sought to obscure life as he had known it, naturally led Hemingway to admire *Huckleberry Finn.*

Aside from Hemingway's own tribute to that book then, it should come as no surprise to hear Philip Young propose that "throughout [*Huckleberry Finn*] there is the same simplicity of rhythm, vocabulary and sentence structure that we associate with Hemingway. Hemingway's effects of crispness, clarity and a wonderful freshness are there."[5] At the same time we must be prepared to qualify radically the kind of simplicity we are willing to acknowledge is present. Both Gertrude Stein and Sherwood Anderson are proof enough that limitation of vocabulary and simplification of syntax are not in themselves sufficient to earn clarity and directness. In fact, short of servile imitation, it is hard to see how the construction and management of these qualities *could* be learned directly from Mark Twain. Carlos Baker, after noting similarities between Hemingway and Mark Twain, commented, "No influence is alleged. What Hemingway found effective in Twain was whatever corroborated his own point of view about the writer's obligation to truth" (op. cit., p. 181).

Much of my own view of Hemingway's stylistic relationship to his predecessors is an elaboration of Baker's. We know that Hemingway came to Paris with a predilection for the Midwestern vernacular and that this was already linked in his style with extensive journalistic experience. But as we shall see, he needed the schooling he received from Gertrude Stein and Ezra Pound, not to speak of the secondary influences and examples of Conrad, Crane, Ford, Joyce, and others then living in Europe, before he could draw much profit from Mark Twain's example. Once Hemingway's mind was fixed upon the discipline of form, once his attention was brought to the surface and structure of his prose, once, in short, he was equipped with technical theory, he could then understand his enthusiasm for *Huckleberry Finn* and make something of it.

Hemingway's first published book, *Three Stories and Ten Poems* (Summer 1923), lays down the significant lines of his stylistic progress. The loss of a suitcase containing a year's work accounts in part for the symbolic aptness of the three stories.[6] But, in addition, the evidence provided in both *in our time* (Spring 1924) and *In Our Time* (Fall 1925) shows that Hemingway was consciously testing various approaches and stylistic techniques. He rarely repeated an experiment that failed to advance him stylistically. Even if a particular tack succeeded—as "My Old Man" did—Hemingway abandoned it unless it contributed to the construction of a satisfactory stylistic conveyance for his meaning. "My Old Man," if not directly derived from Sherwood Anderson, is close enough to be "fairly described as Andersonian."[7] It is the account of the career and death of a dishonest jockey seen through the eyes of his son, and it seems to be the only story Hemingway ever told in the voice of a child, although some of the Nick Adams stories concern boyhood experiences. The second of the three stories, "Up in Michigan," uses Gertrude Stein's insistent repetition and dictional simplification to describe an act of seduction among the closest American equivalent to peasants. "Up in Michigan" is Hemingway's sole venture into a past preceding his birth and therefore unknown to him. The third story, "Out of Season," represents vintage Hemingway in the 'twenties, for it combines a European background, fishing, and a strained American marital relationship. Its one jarring stylistic note is the sardonically reiterated designation of the male principal—"the young gentleman." When Hemingway was assured of his footing on the slippery ground of style he became better able to control his satirical impulse. But however familiar the stance of "Out of Season" may seem through the perspective of hindsight, Hemingway could not be certain in 1923 that it was the one he needed, and so he continued to experiment.

Sherwood Anderson can be dismissed quickly as a stylistic guide for the young journalist. He was a friend to Hemingway, a counselor, a correspondent, a model of seriousness, an admirer—"a young fellow of extraordinary talent"[8] —and he suggested possible sources for thematic material, especially those of sexual frustration and childhood misery. But as John Peale Bishop observed, what neither Mark Twain nor Sherwood Anderson "could supply was a training in discipline."[9] Anderson had identified an area of sensual life worth exploration and to express it he had adopted a potentially useful version of the vernacular. What he could not manage, however, was a scrupulous concentration either upon that area or upon his language. Knowing where the material lay but not how to express it, Anderson was at once a valuable and an irritating master. Hemingway eventually made a spirited if slipshod attack on Anderson in *The Torrents of Spring* (Spring 1926), wherein he parodied Anderson's fuzziest mannerisms. The elder man's partially synthetic pose of naïveté, his imprecision, his sentimental expansiveness, his lament for dumbness were all intolerable to Hemingway, who unlike Anderson was sure he knew very well why, could he only learn to express it. The young Hemingway "was thoroughly hostile, inevitably, to Anderson's concept of unconscious art."[10]

Gertrude Stein was another matter. In time Hemingway emancipated himself from her too, beginning with a vulgar, adolescent parody that opened, "In the rain in the rain in the rain in the rain in Spain / / Does it rain in Spain / / Oh yes my dear on the contrary and there are no bullfights."[11] Hemingway struck out at her again in *The Torrents of Spring,* entitling its fourth part "The Passing of a Great Race and the Making and Marring of Americans." "Miss Stein," he told an interviewer after her death, "wrote at some length and with considerable inaccuracy about her influence on my work. It was necessary for her to do this after she had learned to write dialogue from a book called *The Sun Also Rises.*" He then added more kindly, "Here it is simpler and better to thank Gertrude for everything I learned from her about the abstract relationship of words."[12]

In that final phrase lies, I think, the main clue to Gertrude Stein's usefulness to Hemingway. She taught him to see "the abstract relationship of words." For a time he very much admired her writing, believing it to be "invaluable for analyzing anything or making notes on a person or place."[13] Even his posthumously published memoirs, *A Moveable Feast,* which contain a last supremely vicious thrust at Gertrude Stein's private life, acknowledge: "She had also discovered many truths about rhythms and the uses of words in repetition that were valid and valuable and she talked well about them."[14] He personally arranged to have a portion of *The Making of Americans* published in the *transatlantic review.* Feeling that Anderson had misunderstood and misused Gertrude Stein's theories, in *The Torrents of Spring* Hemingway made the Andersonian Yogi Johnson reflect: "There was a street in Paris named after Huysmans. Right around the corner from where Gertrude Stein lived. Ah, there was a woman! Where were her experiments in words leading her? What was at the bottom of it? All that in Paris."[15] Hemingway himself for a time found it difficult to control the more obvious influence of Gertrude Stein. In "Up in Michigan" this derivative paragraph appears:

LIZ LIKED Jim very much. She LIKED it the way he walked over from the shop and often went to the kitchen door to watch for him to start down the road. She LIKED it about his mustache. She LIKED it about how white his teeth were when he smiled. She LIKED it very much that he didn't look like a blacksmith. She LIKED it how much D. J. Smith and Mrs. Smith LIKED Jim. One day she found that she LIKED it the way the hair was black on his arms and how white they were above the tanned line when he washed up in the washbasin outside the house. LIKING that made her feel funny.[16]

Hemingway only freed himself slowly from the reiterated "liked." In two other stories in the *In Our Time* collection he aped himself, writing in "Cat in the Rain":

The wife LIKED him. She LIKED the deadly serious way he received any complaints. She LIKED his dignity. She LIKED the way he wanted to serve her. She LIKED the way he felt about being a hotel-keeper. She LIKED his old, heavy face and big hands.[17]

And in "Soldier's Home":

HE LIKED to look at them from the front porch as they walked on the other side of the street. He LIKED to watch them walking under the shade of the trees. He LIKED the round Dutch collars above their sweaters. He LIKED their silk stockings and flat shoes. He LIKED their bobbed hair and the way they walked.[18]

Equally symbolic of Hemingway's stylistic education was the inclusion of ten poems in addition to the three stories in his first book. They serve to remind us of Hemingway's early uncertainty as to whether he was more properly a poet than a prose writer. They point too to his friendship with Ezra Pound, who, in exchange for boxing lessons, helped Hemingway to see his object more clearly. John Peale Bishop reported the now familiar Hemingway remark: "Ezra was right half the time, and when he was wrong, he was so wrong you were never in any doubt about it. Gertrude was always right."[19] Fiercely dedicated to aesthetic values and a vigorous proponent of both Flaubert and James, Pound spoke and corresponded in an exaggeratedly crude version of the American vernacular. Although he has never referred to Mark Twain in his published writing, Pound's anomalous character was recently summed up by Sylvia Beach: "There was a touch of Whistler about him; his language, on the other hand, was Huckleberry Finn's."[20]

As a letter-writer Pound delivered an unequivocal series of lessons on style, which we may suppose he matched orally. Pound embodied a host of attitudes then current in Paris and his crystallization of these theories helped Hemingway master the vernacular. Initially enrolled under the banner of Imagism, Pound wrote Amy Lowell in 1914 that he "should like [Imagism] to stand for hard light, clear edges."[21] In other elaborations of his meaning one can see at once the usefulness of his theories for Ernest Hemingway's prose.[22] Writing Harriet Monroe in 1916, after making his famous assertion "Poetry must be as well written as prose," Pound summarized what he felt he had learned from such prose masters as De Maupassant, Flaubert, and Stendhal. "No book words, no periphrases, no inversions . . . no interjections. No words flying off to nothing . . . no clichés, set phrases, stereotyped journalese. The only escape from such is by precision, a result of concentrated attention to what is writing. The test of a writer is his ability for such concentration AND for his power to stay concentrated till he gets to the end" (*Letters,* pp. 48–9).

These were the very ideas needed to dissipate Anderson's murkiness. What is more, Pound also insisted upon particularity, a virtue that neither Stein nor Lardner could offer Hemingway. "Language is made out of concrete things. General expressions in non-concrete terms are a laziness" (ibid.). The whole art of writing, Pound felt, was "concision, or style, or saying what you mean in the fewest and clearest words."[23]

Exactly that became Hemingway's goal in prose. The vernacular offered new words and new rhythms whose expressive beauty had been revealed by Mark Twain. Gertrude Stein, working out of the style of Henry James, had analyzed and set forth some underlying patterns of the vernacular, and had indicated the residuum of energy remaining in a word detached from its conceptual meaning. If Hemingway desired both the word cleanly placed and the object directly evoked, then the two original masters of the American colloquial tradition, Mark Twain and Henry James, offered—either directly or through at least two practicing theorists, Pound and Stein—ways of achieving both ends, ways which often coincided. Something larger than mere eccentric theory is afoot when three writers as apparently distant as Mark Twain, Pound, and Gertrude Stein share a basic stylistic tenet. "As to the Adjective: when in doubt, leave it out." "The only adjective that is worth using is the adjective that is essential to the sense of the passage." "The first thing that anybody takes out of anybody's writing are the adjectives."[24]

The vernacular impulse we have been following is an intensifying one, and whether the intensification centered primarily on linguistic qualities as in James and Stein, or primarily on physical evocation as in Mark Twain and sometimes Anderson, the stylistic techniques for achieving intensity frequently overlapped. It only required a writer willing to submit himself to the disciplines then current in Paris for a style to emerge holding compressed within it a focused world of experience *and* a series of verbal elements formally arranged. I have not forgotten that style and literary achievement are composed of other elements, willed and fortuitous, but one is repeatedly brought to recognize that in Hemingway's case, models, tutelage, and conscious experimentation were all three pre-eminently involved in the development of his style. Its concinnity was no fluke.

II

If, as I have suggested, *Tender Buttons* is a primer of stylistic possibilities, then Hemingway's *in our time* is a deliberately composed book of stylistic exercises. It was published in Paris in 1924 at the Three Mountains Press; later it was revised, conservatively, and most of its "chapters" renumbered and inserted between the short stories in the 1925 New York collection, *In Our Time.* The original version is rich with technical demonstrations of style, and some of its chapters can stand as brilliant, independent miniatures. Only thirty pages in length, the book contains eighteen consecutively numbered chapters, hereafter designated by number. We have no specific name to give these chapters; they do not tell a consecutive story, nor do they in any way develop what we conventionally understand to be a plot, although they are both thematically and formally related. They have been called vignettes, sketches, and miniatures. Unprecedented in English prose and subsequently unimitated, these pieces served Hemingway eminently well, primarily as tests of the narrative voice. Because they so well illuminate his devoted effort to locate the pitch and tone of voice suited to his understanding of life, they deserve close attention.

Half of the chapters are told in the first person (1, 2, 4, 5, 11, 13, 14, 15, 18), and half in the third person (3, 6, 7, 8, 9, 10, 12, 16, 17). To begin with the extremes of the first-person group, chapters 2 and 5 are distinctly marked with dialect. Chapter 5 is told by a British officer whose dialectal intensifiers —"frightfully," "absolutely," and "topping"—establish an ironic distance between the reader and the event that occasions the officer's schoolboy enthusiasm: the successful placement of a barricade across a bridge. The whole chapter reads:

It was a frightfully hot day. We'd jammed an absolutely perfect barricade across the bridge. It was simply priceless. A big old wrought iron grating from the front of a house. Too heavy to lift and you could shoot through it and they would have to climb over it. It was absolutely topping. They tried to get over it, and we potted them from forty yards. They rushed it, and officers came out alone and worked on it. It was an absolutely perfect obstacle. Their officers were very fine. We were frightfully put out when we heard the flank had gone and we had to fall back.[25]

The British voice was useful to Hemingway beyond mimicry because of the opportunity it gave him to hold his material far enough off to see and exhibit it without emotional distortion. But he could hardly base his career on a British dialect; consequently, he abandoned it.

Chapter 2 is American colloquial speech, pocked with slang expressions, grammatical mistakes, and syntactical expansiveness. In part it reads:

The kid came out and had to kill five bulls because you can't have more than three matadors, and the last bull he was so tired he couldn't get the sword in. He couldn't hardly lift his arm.

Other idiomatic terms in 2 such as "crazy drunk," "slug," "puked," and "hollered" not only create the style but also provide the excuse for it. And so long as the expedient of an assumed character was needed to justify the vernacular, then we know that Hemingway had not yet liberated himself from the need to appeal to realism for sanction to use the vernacular.

Charles Fenton has said that Chapter 4, like 5, was taken by Hemingway "directly from post-war conversations with his friend Dorman-Smith, a professional English soldier. The clipped upper-class diction of Sandhurst was unmistakable and deliberate" (p. 238). Chapter 4, the briefest of the vignettes, is considerably less radical in its dialect than Chapter 5, with fewer eccentricities of speech, and is the more interesting as a consequence.

We were in a garden at Mons. Young Buckley came in with his patrol from across the river. The first German I saw climbed up over the garden wall. We waited till he got one leg over and then potted him. He had so much equipment on and looked awfully surprised and fell down into the garden. Then three more came over further down the wall. We shot them. They all came just like that.

Just three words are used in a British manner: "young" as applied to a name, "potted," and "awfully." Yet an American could use each of them in this way without strain or affectation. In other words, Hemingway had begun to work back toward one of the voices we have since come to associate with the young Ernest Hemingway.

In Chapter 1 (quoted in full on page 175), the other first-person chapter with a particular linguistic identity, the bulk of the paragraph is a discursive, repetitive reminiscence ending on the observation, "That was when I was a kitchen corporal." The tone of this chapter is anecdotal, the product of an uncomplicated American mind. It is no instance of a man compressing an account in order to keep his sanity, such as we sometimes associate with Hemingway's prose, but rather the bemused reminiscence of a simple soul. The repetition then points first to character—even though this is at best shadowy —rather than to formal structure. But a reversal of this emphasis could be quickly effected. In the meantime, neither Chapter 1, 2, or 5 is free of eccentricity in diction. Chapter 4 (which may be British) is still unsteady but closing in on the needed neutral voice.

Three of the other five first-person chapters of *in our time* (11, 13, 18) are the words of a quiet, cool observer, who impassively reports the details of an incident. Each exposes a character to a low-keyed and rather sympathetic irony. Chapter 11, long enough to be retitled "The Revolutionist" and offered as a short story in *In Our Time,* recounts the meeting of the speaker with a pleasant, devoted agent of world revolution. The narrator speaks but once. Asked how the movement is going in Italy—" 'Very badly,' I said." He does, however, make aloof, somewhat condescending judgments of the revolutionist: "a very nice boy and very shy," "I took him with me," "He thanked me very much." These I take to be the sentiments of Hemingway the foreign correspondent, wise in the ways of world politics, friendly but unwilling to engage himself. Altogether, the voice forms a familiar part of the Hemingway literary personality.

It was used again in 13 where a bullfighter disgraces himself in the ring and later admits in a matter-of-fact tone, "I am not really a good bull fighter." The change in voice between an American dialect and this one is clearly demonstrated by comparing the last line of Chapter 2 with the first line of 13.

He sat down in the sand and puked and they held a cape over him while the crowd hollered and threw things down into the bull ring.

The crowd shouted all the time and threw pieces of bread down into the ring, then cushions and leather wine bottles, keeping up whistling and yelling.

The latter version eliminates the slang "hollered" and replaces it with "shouted." It builds up the vagueness of "things" into the particularity of "pieces of bread," "cushions," and "leather wine bottles." Hemingway also executes a technical trill in the Stein manner with the participle-gerund phrase, "keeping up whistling and yelling." Such a phrase indicates that here he is working to perfect the powers of style rather than seeking realism. He does this by filling in, strengthening, and emphasizing some elements, while underplaying the obtrusive signs of the vernacular. He is moving away from extremes toward Malcolm Cowley's "middle American style."[26]

Chapter 18 is the wry account of a chat with the king of Greece. The narrator devotes most of the paragraph to what the king said. At the same time, the first-person permits Hemingway to modulate the observations at the end.

The king was working in the garden. He seemed very glad to see me. We walked through the garden. This is the queen, he said. She was clipping a rose bush. Oh how do you do, she said. We sat down at a table under a big tree and the king ordered whiskey and soda. We have good whiskey anyway, he said. The revolutionary committee, he told me, would not allow him to go outside the palace grounds. Plastiras is a very good man I believe, he said, but frightfully difficult. I think he did right though shooting those chaps. If Kerensky had shot a few men things might have been altogether different. Of course the great thing in this sort of an affair is not to be shot oneself!

It was very jolly. We talked for a long time. Like all Greeks he wanted to go to America.

The success here is not primarily technical—although the dialogue is experimentally rendered. Rather it lies in the calm, worldly view provided of the king. Neither thrilled nor cynical nor denunciatory, the narrator is dispassionately agreeable. "It was very jolly."

The third-person narratives of *in our time* undertake to solve the problem of stabilizing colloquial prose from the opposite direction: instead of throttling down the obtrusive colloquiality of the first-person, they try to loosen up the lines of standard prose. Three of Hemingway's experiments, however, must be counted as failures. Chapter 8 is the cynical account of a soldier under fire praying and promising Christ, "I'll tell everyone in the world that you are the only thing that matters." Delivered from danger, "he never told anybody." Such cheap purchase of irony remained one of Hemingway's enduring weaknesses. Chapter 9, which tells of the shooting of two Hungarian thieves by a detective whose sole justification for the murders is his certainty that they were "wops" is also mechanically ironic. Finally, Chapter 10 (since reprinted as "A Very Short Story") mixed the lyric and satiric modes in a sketch of hospital lovers separated at the last by woman's fatal inconstancy. Hemingway later lopped off the sardonic Flaubertian echo in his ending: "A short time after he contracted gonorrhea from a sales girl in a loop department store while riding in a taxicab through Lincoln Park." Then he expanded the story into *A Farewell to Arms*. It is significant that Hemingway rarely used dialect or the satiric mode again in his fiction.[27] Of the ten new stories introduced in *In Our Time* (counting "The Big Two-Hearted River" as a single story) none is in dialect and only one—"Mr. and Mrs. Elliot"—can be regarded as satiric in intent.

Three of the third-person vignettes, like three of the first-person ones, are distinguished by the factual journalistic flavor of their prose. Chapter 3 describes the evacuation of refugees through Thrace; Chapter 6, the execution of six cabinet ministers; and Chapter 17, the hanging of a man in an American county jail. No narrator explicitly appears and no emotion is expressed, although the very baldness of the style generates it by implication.

The first paragraph of Chapter 17 reads:

They hanged Sam Cardinella at six o'clock in the morning in the corridor of the county jail. The corridor was high and narrow with tiers of cells on either side. All the cells were occupied. The men had been brought in for the hanging. Five men sentenced to be hanged were in the five top cells. Three of the men to be hanged were negroes. They were very frightened. One of the white men sat on his cot with his head in his hands. The other lay flat on his cot with a blanket wrapped around his head.

Eccentricities of diction have been eliminated from this account, as well as names and dates, the irrelevant particularities of journalism. Objective reportage of this sort remained one of Hemingway's favorite tools for rendering otherwise intolerable scenes. Moreover, it contributed to his determination to control the vernacular. The reader cannot really distinguish the journalistic chapters written in the third person from those written in the first. One is not often aware of a particular speaker in these sketches free of dialect and illiteracies, which means that the speaker can now be manipulated for special emphasis. He can enter and withdraw silently, commenting and reacting at need. When Hemingway tried to explain to Edmund Wilson why he had inserted the chapters of *in our time* between the stories of more conventional length included in *In Our Time,* he described an impulse similar to this subtle tonal mobility. The alternating effect would be, he wrote, "Like looking with your eyes at something, say a passing coast line, and then looking at it with 15X binoculars. Or rather, maybe, looking at it and then going in and living in it —and then coming out and looking at it again."[28]

While he was learning to write a prose that could employ a form of colloquial speech remaining at a fairly constant level, with or without an announced narrator, Hemingway also had to learn how to construct a prose with sufficient internal coherence to resist the corrosion of time and how to develop sufficient internal complexity to redeem that prose from the curse of over-simplification. Answers to these problems were available but had to be recognized as answers. As we have come to see, similar stylistic conditions are visible in both branches of the vernacular. These are, first, fragmentation of syntax causing concentration on the individual word, and second, many kinds of insistent repetition. In the first case, new sources of diction, odd conjunctions of words, isolation of single words and phrases by means of syntactic adjustments and of punctuation, and even repetition itself all helped to bring new, unusual pressure to bear upon the single word. As for repetition, although it was originally used in conversations for ease of speaking and for emphasis, writers imitating those conversations soon found its aesthetic uses to be manifold.

These practices were hardly visible, however, until Gertrude Stein highlighted them. The help she gave Ernest Hemingway was comparable to that a confirmed abstractionist might give a young "realistic" painter by teaching him to recognize the formal elements underlying the compositions of his favorites. Once Hemingway knew what to look for, he could find examples aplenty, even in his own early prose. As far back as November 1916 in a high-school short story, he had written this passage of dialogue:

"Yes. He was a bad Indian. Up on the upper peninsula he couldn't get drunk. He used to drink all day—everything. But he couldn't get drunk. Then he would go crazy; but he wasn't drunk. He was crazy because he couldn't get drunk."[29]

This dialogue bears a remarkable resemblance to Hemingway's later work, but close as it is, it has still to meet the problem of transferring the characteristics of this talk over into narrative prose without bringing the talker with it. Once the older writers had brought Hemingway's attention to this problem, he began to experiment. The balance of his laboratory work involved isolating, refining, and harmoniously joining those elements native to the American vernacular. To do this he drew extensively on examples afforded by the past.

III

Hemingway's experience as a journalist and his colloquial facility assisted him as he moved toward his finished style. So extensively was he trained and exercised on the Kansas City *Star* and Toronto *Star* that Charles Fenton confidently maintained, "The principal instrument of his literary apprenticeship was journalism" (p. ix). It is a reporter's distance that dominates the treatment of the Greek evacuation and the two execution scenes of *in our time*. The Greek refugee sketch was in fact originally a cabled story for the Toronto newspaper.[30] On the other hand Hemingway also came at his spare prose by means of colloquial imitation, as in his early pastiches of Lardner, and his reproductions of British and American slang in *in our time*. He sought to retain the best of both approaches, to maintain what was most distinctive and least eccentric about each, and to work out a more highly charged synthesis of the vernacular than current practice offered.

Hemingway recognized that journalistic prose lacked durability. "In writing for a newspaper you told what happened and, with one trick and another, you communicated the emotion aided by the element of timeliness which gives a certain emotion to any account of something that happened on that day; but the real thing, the sequence of motion and fact that made the emotion . . . was beyond me and I was working very hard to get it."[31] The journalistic habit of close dispassionate observation was to be kept, but it would be controlled by an aesthetic demanding even more stringent precision.

Certainly Hemingway discovered the principal components of that aesthetic in the colloquial tradition. In *in our time* we can observe him testing techniques even as he does voices. Gradually he evolved a synthetic style that fixed a group of related and carefully tested elements into a new and brilliant mosaic. Ford Madox Ford once described Hemingway's words as being like "pebbles fetched fresh from a brook. They live and shine, each in its place. So one of his pages has the effect of a brook-bottom into which you look down through the flowing water. The words form a tessellation, each in order beside the other."[32] Ford's metaphor is an apt one, for by stressing the colloquial emphasis upon the word, Hemingway brought his prose to a point of unparalleled verbal individuation.

This concentration upon the word was made possible by Hemingway's modifying his diction, adjusting and paring his qualifications, and varying his rhythm so that attention was focused on the separate verbal units in the sentence. And furthermore, unlike Anderson, Hemingway paid the strictest attention not only to the units as devices for telling a story, but also to the relations and patterns existing among them.

As the first step in outlining the verbal tesserae on his page, Hemingway resolutely eliminated abstractions. He depended almost completely on concrete objects for the body and movement of his prose. If there was meaning, the thing, the object, the image had to supply it. No meaning existed apart from this world of particulars. This was matched by the rigorous exclusion of all but the most essential qualification. Even the minimally used adjectives and adverbs were sometimes translated into active dependent clauses. Given this bareness, Hemingway found it useful to introduce emotional overtones into his prose. For this reason he retained that laconic narrator whose understated reactions were paradoxically expressed by colloquially overstated adverbs— "very nice," "very funny," "awful," and "plenty." If the scene was devilishly horrid, as in the executions, then evaluative comments became extraneous. But sometimes a slight touch of the brush humanized the scene. The talk with the Greek king is "very jolly." The brave, naïve revolutionist is "a very nice boy." This restraint reminds us of Huck crying "a little" over the body of Buck Grangerford, "for he was mighty good to me." Similar as the understatement may be, however, a wide web of experience intervenes between the two examples. Huck's boyish earnestness invests his restraint with sincerity. He cannot and need not be more explicit. Hemingway's laconism on the other hand is the result of rigorous control. He will not be more explicit. Although the formal appearance in *Huckleberry Finn* and Hemingway may be similar, the emotions covered by the simple expressions come from quite different sources. When the narrator in Chapter 5 says of the barricade,

They rushed it, and officers came out alone and worked on it,

the word "alone" conceals yet admits the narrator's professional knowledge that because the barricade was so good, the soldiers would refuse to rush it again. This obliged the officers to emerge. Behind that technical knowledge is elation over the success of the barricade coupled with admiration for the officers.

Even as he creates dynamic contrasts between the spare substance of his prose and his occasional emotional interjections—"Their officers were very fine"—so Hemingway deliberately alternates specific names, titles, foreign words, and exotica, and very ordinary nouns and pronouns. This passage drawn from Chapter 13 shows him handling both Spanish and English words. The italics here are Hemingway's.

Finally the bull was too tired from so much bad sticking and folded his knees and lay down and one of the *cuadrilla* leaned out over his neck and killed him with the *puntillo*. The crowd came over the barrera and around the torero and two men grabbed him and held him and some one cut off his pigtail and was waving it and a kid grabbed it and ran away with it.

The insistent use of the nomenclature of the bull ring here threatens self parody, but we can see that Hemingway's intention is to variegate the prose surface. "Puntillo" is italicized and "barrera" is not. "Pigtail" is one word, but in the same clause "some one" is made two. And the vagueness of "crowds," "men," "kid," and "it" is set next to the specificity of "knees," "neck," and "torero." Simple as the words themselves are, their relationships and increments are intricate. Evidence of similar tinkering is visible in the verbs. Chapter 10 begins,

They whack whacked the white horse on the legs and he knee-ed himself up.

After this initial experimentation the chapter proceeds with perfectly commonplace verbs: "twisted," "pulled," "hauled," "swung," and "hung." When the scene was republished in *In Our Time* Hemingway dropped one "e" from "knee-ed" as well as the hyphen, and added a hyphen to "whack whacked." His conservatism reduced the force of the original sentence:

They whack-whacked the white horse on the legs and he kneed himself up.

(Much later, in *Across the River and into the Trees,* a book marked by a desperately radical style, Hemingway reversed himself once more, referring to a soldier's "puttee-ed legs."[33]

These examples of variation in treatment of words are the key to the durability of Hemingway's style. Rather than depend on a mechanically simplified diction and syntax, he created a dynamic complex of words in which the various elements were determined quite as much by reference to one another as they were by reference to some observed reality off the printed page. Chapter 1 shows this very well:

Everybody was DRUNK. The whole battery WAS DRUNK GOING ALONG THE ROAD IN THE DARK. We WERE going to the Champagne. The lieutenant KEPT RIDING HIS HORSE OUT into the fields AND SAYING to him, "I'm drunk, I tell you, mon vieux. Oh, I am so soused." We WENT ALONG THE ROAD all night IN THE DARK and the adjutant KEPT RIDING UP alongside my kitchen AND SAYING, "You must put IT out. IT is dangerous. IT will be observed." We were fifty kilometers from the front but the adjutant worried about the fire in my kitchen. It was funny GOING ALONG THAT ROAD. That was when I was a kitchen corporal. (capitals added)

The repetition, while useful here as a binding device and as ironic commentary, is not obtrusive, nor is it merely a reminder of the speaker's lack of sophistication or a rhetorical trick of emphasis. Here the lieutenant will keep riding out and talking to his horse, the adjutant will keep riding up and talking to his kitchen corporal, and the formal similarity of their actions reminds us that a common condition of war causes both the lieutenant's erratic behavior and the adjutant's nervous fussing.

Other and different instances of repetition appear in other chapters, all inventive. In the execution of six ministers (chapter 6), we are told that they were shot "against the wall of a hospital." The soldiers futilely try to hold one of them, sick with typhoid, "against the wall," and while these efforts are being made, "the other five stood very quietly against the wall." In a scene described in some ten lines, this discreet repetition keeps both the impending execution and its incongruous location against the wall of a hospital before the reader. So too there is an inevitable cross-relationship set up between this chapter and the next, which begins, "Nick sat against the wall of the church." He, soldiering, has been shot in the spine. Civilian or soldier, hospital or church, men end suffering against the wall. Hemingway's point is made quietly with the signals of language.

Another favorite device of Hemingway's also appears in Chapter 6—the repetition of numbers with different meanings.

They shot the six cabinet ministers at half-past six in the morning. . . .

Chapter 9 begins similarly:

At two o'clock in the morning two Hungarians got into a cigar store at Fifteenth Street and Grand Avenue.

The slightly off-center repetition is retained in the next sentence where "Fifteenth Street" is no longer a place, but an adjectival specification.

Drevitts and Boyle drove up from the Fifteenth Street police station in a Ford.

Prepositions are also repeated in proximity with shifting meanings. The repeated preposition, like the repeated number, forces the reader alert, even as it furnishes a substratum melody. In Chapter 4, a shot German "fell DOWN into the garden. Then three more came over further DOWN the wall." Down down the wall they came, twice and in two senses. Chapter 8, the account of a soldier praying under fire, contains a close parallel to this. After the deliberately uncapitalized plea for mercy, "please please dear jesus," the account continues,

The shelling moved further UP the line. We went to work on the trench and in the morning the sun came UP and the day was hot and muggy and cheerful and quiet. The next night back at Mestre he did not tell the girl he went UPstairs with at the Villa Rossa about Jesus. (capitals added)

The simple distinctions in meaning of a word like "up" had been lost in prose before this, lost in the flood of rhetoric; but here they are seen, felt, and used, I think, consciously. Indeed, since elegant variation was possible in most of the quoted instances, we must take Hemingway's repetitions to be either deliberate or unusually careless. Believing the former, I argue their intention is to afford variety within the severe limits of the simplest sort of syntax and diction. The subtle success of the technique illustrates how Hemingway applied what he had learned from Gertrude Stein about "the abstract relationship of words."

Several other stylistic observations arise out of this same paragraph. Hemingway has capitalized "Jesus" in the last quoted sentence, to indicate, economically, that there the name occurs outside the essentially disbelieving mind of the soldier who prays "please please dear jesus." Also, by technical means he has contrasted the frenetic, jammed, tumbling words of prayer under fire:

Oh jesus christ get me out of here. Dear jesus get me out. Christ please please please christ.

with the relaxed and syntactically expansive details of the day following the shelling:

hot and muggy and cheerful and quiet.

Both procedures force the reader to proceed as deliberately as a motorist on an unfamiliar detour. Stendhal, one of Hemingway's acknowledged favorites, once commented in this connection: "I had the audacity to despise elegance of style. I saw the young apprentice fully occupied in avoiding ugly endings to sentences and strings of awkward sounding words. On the other hand he constantly altered the details of circumstances that were difficult to express."[34] Although consciousness of style is everywhere in *in our time,* Hemingway's first concern was to render "the way it was," that favorite expression of his, and first cousin to Gertrude Stein's (and Henry James's) "things as they are."

One more instance of repetition contrasts usefully with Sherwood Anderson's problem concerning apples and other round objects in "Paper Pills." In a work as short as *in our time* (eighteen chapters on thirty pages), some carry-over of images may be expected. Chapter 4 begins,

We were in a garden at Mons.

There it is that, as the Germans come over the wall, they are shot. Chapter 18, on the other hand, begins,

The king was working in the garden.

We are then introduced to a time-serving, good-natured cynic who "like all Greeks . . . wanted to go to America." There is a planned cross reference, I think, between the two scenes, not unlike that between the men standing with their backs to the hospital wall waiting to be shot, and the wounded soldier against the church. This is made possible by the brevity and simplicity of the book, and is cued by the evident resemblance of the phrases "in a garden" and "in the garden." Both phrases appear in the first sentence of their chapters. In one we find men at work, bodies thumping to the garden floor. In the other, a genial conversationalist is said to be "working," also in a garden; but *he* has time for a whiskey and soda. The implicit irony of this comparison I take to be central to Hemingway's understanding of the actual nature of our time.

Chapter 7 also plays a variation on repetition. With Nick seated and Rinaldi "face downward against the wall," Nick's head is described taking three different positions, each one part of a slow, pained movement. Between the moves of his head, the scene is elaborated, Nick's thoughts are rendered and Nick himself addresses a few words to Rinaldi. The varied repetitions occur this way:

Nick looked straight ahead brilliantly.

Nick turned his head carefully and looked down at Rinaldi.

Nick turned his head carefully away smiling sweatily.

The fighting has moved on—"Things were getting forward in the town"— leaving this backwash of the battleline, a hot still pool of misery without movement except Rinaldi "still in the sun breathing with difficulty" and the slow, controlled head-turning of a man hit in the spine. Down to the side. Back again. Hemingway draws attention to this first by the slight oddness of the original adverb, "brilliantly," which is connected with the sun and heat but also has a thin wash of irony over it. Nick's head movement is then indicated by a phrasing repeated but slightly and pertinently varied. This verbal and syntactic care emphasizes the delicate, economical movement of a man injured and in shock.

Hemingway also learned to take full advantage of prepositions. Mark Twain's careful management of them created the impression of vivid directional movement in *Huckleberry Finn:* "I went straight out in the country as much as a mile, before I stopped; then I doubled back through the woods towards Phelps's" (ch. 31). A preposition points a direction or locates an object. At times Hemingway's prose became a series of arrows rhythmically pointing now this way, now that. He relied especially upon prepositional intensity for the difficult job of describing movement through towns and across landscapes. So in *The Sun Also Rises:*

Down below there were grassy plains and clear streams, and then we crossed a stream and went through a gloomy little village, and started to climb again. We climbed up and up and crossed another high Col and turned along it, and the road ran down to the right.[35]

Hemingway's poetic evocations of movement depend upon the careful placement of his nouns, participles, and conjunctions. His reportorial accuracy is heightened by the purely formal relationships of the words themselves, as in the first sentence of Chapter 15:

I heard the drums coming down the street, and then the fifes and the pipes, and then they came around the corner, all dancing.

Euphony of sound—fifes, pipes, drums coming, they came around the corner
—and a subtle cadence supplements Hemingway's exposition. Significantly,
in our time contains these examples of rhyme and alliteration:

the bull only bumped him

he hung on to the horn

the bull rammed him wham

kids were in carts crouched

the flank had gone and we had to fall back

the picador twisted the stirrups straight

the horse's entrails hung down in a blue bunch

over the barrera and around the torero

the corridor of the county jail

the priest skipped back onto the scaffolding[36]

One cannot expect to find many more instances than this in so short a book.
Still, when the diction and syntax are simplified as far as they are in Hemingway, then these moments will occur more often than in standard prose. And
even if they must often have arisen spontaneously during composition, the
new, important point is that they were retained during revision.

The Villalta chapter, 14, and especially its second paragraph, is the most
successful and complex piece in *in our time*. It incorporates repetition, rhyme,
alliteration, and assonance ("snarl," "charge," "curve," "roar," and "toro"
are its central words), and a number of participles that culminate in a very fine
final pose which is at once static, yet intensely active.

If it happened right down close in front of you, you could see Villalta
snarl at the bull and curse him, and when the bull charged he swung back
firmly like an oak when the wind hits it, his legs tight together, the muleta
trailing and the sword following the curve behind. Then he cursed the
bull, flopped the muleta at him, and swung back from the charge his feet
firm, the muleta curving and each swing the crowd roaring.

When he started to kill it was all in the same rush. The bull looking at
him straight in front, hating. He drew out the sword from the folds of his
muleta and sighted with the same movement and called to the bull, Toro! Toro!
and the bull charged and Villalta charged and just for a moment they became
one. Villalta became one with the bull and then it was over. Villalta standing

straight and the red hilt of the sword sticking out dully between the bull's shoulders. Villalta, his hand up at the crowd and the bull roaring blood, looking straight at Villalta and his legs caving.

The repetition is employed here for both harmonic and symbolic purposes. For example, following the command, Toro! Toro!, Villalta moves toward the bull and at that point his name takes over to dominate the remainder of the paragraph—just as in fact he dominates the bull. The deliberateness of this cannot be denied. Next, man and beast each charge in a separate clause, and with the stroke of death "they became one." A variation then: "Villalta became one with the bull"—and the act of killing is finished. Now the "roaring" of the crowd from the first paragraph is transferred to the bull's blood, and the bull that formerly "looked at him straight in front, hating," now is "looking straight at Villalta and his legs caving." In this moment when many complicated aesthetic forces successfully interact, the literary use of the vernacular and all its techniques is fully justified.

Hemingway's mode of stylistic attack changes too often and is too clearly signalled to be accidental. I do not mean that Hemingway followed a mechanical rhythm, or that such diversity was unique to him. But Sherwood Anderson, for example, had nothing like Hemingway's variety of effect, and indeed he was only intermittently aware of the necessity of relieving colloquial simplicity with contrast. He could rapidly bore or irritate with his stretches of declarative sentences bearing simple-minded images and ideas across the page. Similarly, the prose of Lardner and Stein, was too often of a piece, unrolling long ribbons of narrative without respite. Hemingway's style was eclectic, alert for the incipient monotony that dogs the colloquial style. Without lapsing into the stylistic vaudeville of a Saroyan, he enlivened his prose by means of formal variety, and he polished his stylistic surfaces to reflect his meaning. His labor is there for all to see in that extraordinary little book, *in our time.*

IV

If all this simplification took place in narrative prose because, after decades of segregation, dialogue finally infiltrated it, then it is reasonable to assume that the dialogue of a dialogue-dominated narrative will change too, and it does. Again *in our time* furnishes us examples of a variety of possibilities in the treatment of dialogue, thus bringing us full circle.

Three Stories and Ten Poems, published earlier, showed evidence of the dialogue usually associated with Hemingway—clipped, repetitive, advancing incrementally. In "Out of Season" two men prepare to fish, and the repetition typically centers on *piombo,* an otherwise unemphasized foreign word whose definition is organically furnished.

"Have you some lead?"

"No."

"You must have some lead." Peduzzi was excited. "You must have piombo. Piombo. A little piombo. Just here. Just above the hook or your bait will float on the water. You must have it. Just a little piombo."

"Have you some?"

"No." He looked through his pockets desperately. Sifting through the cloth dirt in the linings of his inside military pockets. "I haven't any. We must have piombo."

"We can't fish then," said the young gentleman, and unjointed the rod, reeling the line back through the guides. "We'll get some piombo and fish tomorrow."[37]

The dialogue continues in this vein. It is still a little awkward, but it is new. This apparently artless kind of conversation evolved under the pressure of Hemingway's prose, and he made it his hallmark. But before he returned to work this vein, he conscientiously tried out a number of ways of recording conversations. In fact, *in our time* contains *no* instance of dialogue rendered in completely conventional form, with quotation marks and paragraph indentations. To examine the book's dialogue is to find still more deliberate experimentation, as well as to see the spoken word blending insensibly into the narrative.

The most normal arrangement of dialogue in *in our time* occurs in Chapter 17. During the moments before the hanging, a terse, unindented interchange takes place.

"How about a chair, Will?" asked one of the guards. "Better get one," said a man in a derby hat.

In Chapter 1, a similar arrangement is used, but there it is more highly formalized. The lieutenant keeps riding out into the fields and saying to his horse, "I'm drunk, I tell you, mon vieux. Oh, I am so soused," and the adjutant keeps riding up to the kitchen corporal and saying, "You must put it out. It is dangerous. It will be observed." Neither quote is indented, both are approached over almost identical phrasing, and each is dominated by repetition of subject: I, I, I, it, it, it.

In Chapter 7, the formal designation of the speaker and his action is eliminated.

Nick turned his head carefully and looked at Rinaldi. "Senta Rinaldi. Senta. You and me we've made a separate peace." Rinaldi lay still in the sun breathing with difficulty. "Not patriots." Nick turned his head carefully away smiling sweatily.

Chapter 9 reproduces the conversation of two policemen just after one of them has shot a pair of thieves. It combines three different kinds of quotations: those with no formal introduction, those introduced by dashes, and those introduced by indentation. The critical points are indicated by capitals.

Drevitts got frightened when he found they were both dead. HELL. Jimmy, he said, you oughtn't to have done it. There's liable to be a hell of a lot of trouble.
—THEY'RE crooks ain't they? said Boyle. They're wops ain't they. Who the hell is going to make any trouble?
—That's all right maybe this time, said Drevitts, but how did you know they were wops when you bumped them.
WOPS, said Boyle, I can tell wops a mile off. (capitals added)

Chapter 15 depends upon indentation and commas alone to set off its quotations, but near the end it works into a stylized frenzy of bitterness, marked by the curious locution "we kills" and the colorful phrase *"riau-riau* dancers' bulls."

Well, I said, after all he's just an ignorant Mexican savage.
Yes, Maera said, and who will kill his bulls after he gets a *cogida?*
We, I suppose, I said.
Yes, we, said Maera. We kills the savages' bulls, and the drunkards' bulls, and the *riau-riau* dancers' bulls. Yes. We kill them. We kill them all right. Yes. Yes. Yes.

In Chapter 18 banal social observations are set off simply by commas.

We walked through the garden. This is the queen, he said. She was clipping a rose bush. Oh how do you do, she said. We sat down at a table under a big tree. . . .

The brief shout Villalta gives for the bull is met in chapter 14 without fuss: ". . . and called to the bull, Toro! Toro! and the bull charged." In 13 even the comma has disappeared.

He was very short with a brown face and quite drunk and he said after all it has happened before like that. I am not really a good bull fighter.

In Chapter 8 too one enters the mind of the shelled soldier without formal warning.

He lay very flat and sweated and prayed oh jesus christ get me out of here.

No one of these instances is in itself of any great moment, but significantly they are all different. They provide an uncommonly clear view of how Hemingway publicly tested various techniques. After working out these exercises he returned to the traditional way of enclosing dialogue, and began to change reported speech from within. The strategy of revolutionizing not its presentation but its constitution turned out to be a wise one, for Hemingway needed a dialogue to match his prose. He simplified conversations, lengthened them, and extended them vertically—that is, a characteristic Hemingway dialogue is a long, often thin, vertical rectangle, rather than a square Hawthornian block. And he economized so that the very briefest statements were forced to bear his meaning, to *be* his meaning, in fact. In this respect Hemingway resembles Henry James, whose characters invested a surprising amount of feeling in innocuous-sounding chats. Carlos Baker has discussed the similarity of the two writers' dialogue, saying that "if one tries the experiment of lifting a Jamesian conversation *verbatim* from its framework, and substituting 'he saids' and 'she saids' for James's more complicated directions, the dialogue proceeds in a manner scarcely distinguishable from Hemingway's."[38] Two passages from which only brief prose parts of the framework have been excised, one from *The Portrait of a Lady* and the other from *The Sun Also Rises,* prove Baker's point:

"Well now, there's a specimen," he said to her.
"A specimen of what?"
"A specimen of an English gentleman."
"Do you mean they're all like him?"
"Oh no; they're not all like him."
"He's a favourable specimen then, she said, "because I'm sure he's very nice."
"Yes, he's very nice. And he's very fortunate."[39]

"Doesn't anything ever happen to your values," she asked.
"No. Not any more."
"Never fall in love?"
"Always," he said. "I am always in love."
"What does that do to your values?"
"That too has got a place in my values."
"You haven't any values. You're dead, that's all."
"No, my dear. You're not right. I'm not dead at all." (p. 63)

As it happens, Hemingway has on several occasions testified to his admiration for James. In *Green Hills of Africa* he wrote, "The good writers are Henry James, Stephen Crane, and Mark Twain. That's not the order they're good in. There is no order for good writers" (p. 22). Some years later in an interview with Harvey Breit, he repeated his sentiments, although he dropped Crane from the list: "As a Nobel Prize winner I cannot but regret that the award was never given to Mark Twain nor to Henry James, speaking only of my own countrymen."[40] In that statement Hemingway links the two men who I think must be linked in order to make any real sense of the genesis of modern American prose style.

It is particularly in dialogue that Hemingway emulates James. Baker has referred to a "hovering subject" as being characteristic of both men's dialogue. Their characters normally talk around, or below, or above, or beside their real subject. One convenient index of the stylistic and cultural distance between Hemingway and Mark Twain exists in Mark Twain's criticism of Fenimore Cooper's dialogue. The trouble with it, Mark Twain thought, was that "the talk wandered all around and arrived nowhere. . . . Conversations consisted mainly of irrelevancies, with here and there a relevancy, a relevancy with an embarrassed look, as not being able to explain how it got there."[41] But the use of irrelevancies in speech as a means of revelation is part of Hemingway's stock in trade. He recognized that in spoken banalities lay much of the inchoate drama of human life, and as we read his dialogue, we are always looking through it to meaning. Probably the indirect influence of Freud's work had something to do with this, but it also arose out of the habit of close observation cultivated in this century. Pedestrian exchanges were forced to represent more complicated emotional states. In "Cat in the Rain" the wife reveals her discontent by the repeated, "Anyway, I want a cat . . . I want a cat. I want a cat now. If I can't have long hair or any fun, I can have a cat."[42] And in Hemingway's later story "Hills like White Elephants" occurs perhaps the most famous instance of what F. O. Matthiessen called one of Henry James's special gifts, "the ability so to handle a conversation that he keeps in the air not merely what is said, but what isn't—the passage of thoughts without words."[43] By means of conversational trivia and without ever being directly broached, the idea of an abortion is proposed, discussed, objected to, and finally accepted.

The nature of Hemingway's dialogue also bears out the earlier contention that he wrote a style based on deliberate diversification. Unlike the highly specific narrative, his dialogue is often vague, ambiguous, indirect. It is even more truncated and narrowed than the prose. Indeed, the epitome of inexpressiveness between quotation marks is reached in the account of a Montmartre dance in *The Sun Also Rises:*

The drummer shouted: "You can't two time—"

"It's all gone."

"What's the matter?"

"I don't know. I just feel terribly."

". . . . ." the drummer chanted. Then turned to his sticks.

"Want to go?"

I had the feeling as in a nightmare of it all being something repeated, something I had been through and that now I must go through again.

". . . . ." the drummer sang softly.

"Let's go," said Brett. "You don't mind."

". . . . ." the drummer shouted and grinned at Brett.

"All right," I said. (pp. 66–7)

The drummer is understood still to be making sounds, however unintelligible they may be; but at times Hemingway's dialogue reaches a point of explicitly noted silence.

Her husband did not answer.

His wife was silent.

I don't know what to say.

I did not say anything.

Cohn said nothing.

Krebs said nothing.

Nick said nothing.

I said nothing.[44]

Hemingway's talk, pared, splintered, and adrift, marked by inarticulate emotional flareups and the verbal blur behind six dots, at last falls into silence, and a long cycle is completed. With his dialogue this study, which began with dialogue, has come full circle to discover all has changed.

The cycle began as nineteenth-century American writers sought to naturalize fictional talk, either by imitating dialects or by loosening literary representations of standard discourse. In the process they followed the bent of colloquial speech—gave it its head and let it assume its own hitherto unimaginable forms. As men like Mark Twain and Henry James learned to reproduce versions of American speech free from obtrusive regionalisms, they introduced elements of that speech into their narrative prose. Gertrude Stein extended their example. By exaggerating the characteristics of the vernacular she produced abstract patterns of words meant to cohere independently of rational meaning. Her work proved valuable, for other writers in the vernacular tradition had discovered that in using the vernacular, they were unable to free themselves from an acknowledged narrator. When they dropped the narrator, they also lost control of their prose. Guided, however, by Gertrude Stein's revelation of the underlying formal structure of the vernacular, Ernest Hemingway developed a subtle, intricate, and balanced narrative prose independent of a specific narrator. In response to the radical stylization of his narrative prose, Hemingway's dialogue then began contracting and kept on until at last it dwindled down to silence, the other side of speech. Having achieved this attenuated extreme, American prose style began to recomplicate itself, but now it possessed the considerable advantage of starting from a stabilized colloquial base.

1. Quoted in Charles Fenton, *The Apprenticeship of Ernest Hemingway* (New York: Farrar, Straus & Young, 1958), p. 59.

2. Quoted in Carlos Baker, *Hemingway, The Writer as Artist* (Princeton: Princeton University Press, 1956), p. 4 n.

3. Fenton, pp. 33, 34, 187.

4. *Death in the Afternoon* (London: Jonathan Cape, 1950), p. 10.

5. *Ernest Hemingway* (New York: Rinehart & Co., 1952), p. 160.

6. See Fenton, p. 196, and Baker, pp. 11–12, for the story.

7. Fenton, p. 149.

8. Fenton, p. 118.

9. *Collected Essays*, ed. with intr. by Edmund Wilson (New York: Charles Scribner's Sons, 1948), p. 40.

10. Fenton, p. 104.

11. "The Soul of Spain (In the Manner of Gertrude Stein)" in *Der Querschnitt* (Herbst, 1924), reprinted in *The Collected Poems of Ernest Hemingway*, "Number One of the Library of Living Poetry" (n.p., n.d.), no pagination.

12. "The Art of Fiction XXI," *The Paris Review* (Spring, 1958), 73.

13. Quoted in Edmund Wilson, *A Literary Chronicle: 1920–1950* (Garden City: Anchor Books, 1956), p. 44.

14. (New York: Charles Scribner's Sons, 1964), p. 17.

15. *The Hemingway Reader*, ed. with intr. by Charles Poore (New York: Charles Scribner's Sons, 1953), pp. 74–5.

16. *The Short Stories of Ernest Hemingway* (New York: Modern Library, 1938), p. 179 (capitals added). Passage analyed in Fenton, pp. 152–4.

17. Ibid., p. 266 (capitals added).

18. Ibid., p. 245 (capitals added).

19. "Homage to Hemingway," *After the Genteel Tradition*, ed. Malcolm Cowley (New York: W. W. Norton & Co., 1937), p. 193.

20. *Shakespeare and Company* (New York: Harcourt, Brace and Co., 1959), p. 26.

21. *The Letters of Ezra Pound 1907–1941*, ed. D. D. Paige (New York: Harcourt, Brace and Co., 1950), p. 38.

22. Note that Pound remarked in 1937 "It should be realised that Ford Madox Ford had been hammering this point of view into me from the time I first met him (1908 or 1910) and that I owe him anything that I don't owe myself for having saved me from the academic influences then raging in London." *Letters*, p. 49. Hemingway too was closely associated with Ford, especially during the life of the *transatlantic review*, but he is not mentioned in this study because I am necessarily compressing influences into a few representative figures.

23. Letter to Iris Barry, July 1916, ibid., p. 90.

24. *Pudd'nhead Wilson*, epigraph to chapter XI; *Letters*, p. 49; *Lectures in America* (Boston: Beacon Press, 1957), p. 211.

25. *in our time* (Paris, 1924), p. 13. Hereinafter identified in the text by chapter.

26. "The Middle American Style," *The New York Times Book Review*, July 15, 1945, pp. 3, 14. Cowley never makes it clear whether he intended to designate a social, geographic, or rhetorial "middle style." But he does point out the neccessity of developing this style as "a literary instrument. In a sense, Mark Twain had apologized for using it, by putting it into the mouth of an illiterate hero; it was not at all his fashion of speaking for himself." As Cowley intimates, the convention of an illiterate narrator imposes serious limitations upon the writer. He shrewdly suggests that the way out of the dilemma is "for an educated author to use this style when writing ordinary third-person narrative. That was the step taken by Gertrude Stein in her first book, *Three Lives*." This is true, if we add the important qualification that Gertrude Stein took that step with no support from Mark Twain. It was in fact the discovery of how difficult it was to establish any meaningful connection between Gertrude Stein and Mark Twain that gave the present work its final direction.

27. *The Torrents of Spring* is parody, and the chapter-end conversations of *Death in the Afternoon* are mordantly good-humored. A slight dialect (one of educational deficiency) is used in *To Have and Have Not*, and there is some imitation in it too, in "Albert Speaking."

28. Wilson, *A Literary Chronicle*, p. 48.

29. Quoted in Fenton, p. 18.

30. See Fenton, pp. 229–36 for a discussion of the story's gradual transformation.

31. *Death in the Afternoon*, p. 10. See his letter to Gertrude Stein in November 1923: "I am going to chuck journalism I think. You ruined me as a journalist last summer. Have been no good since." —Fenton, p. 160.

32. Quoted in introduction to *The Hemingway Reader*, p. xiv.

33. (New York: Charles Scribner's Sons, 1950), p. 59.

34. *On Love*, tr. H. B. V. under direction of C. K. Scott-Moncrieff (New York: Anchor Books, 1957), p. xix.

35. (New York: Charles Scribner's Sons, 1926), p. 95. By the 'thirties Hemingway had begun to press very hard on his mechanics, so that in *Green Hills of Africa* there appeared this extreme version of the same technique.

So in the morning, again, we started ahead of the porters and went down and across the hills and through a deeply forested valley and then up and across a long rise of country with high grass that made the walking difficult and on and up and across, resting sometimes in the shade of a tree, and then on and up and down and across, all in high grass, now, that you had to break a trail in, and the sun was very hot. (p. 68)

36. The quoted phrases come from chapters 16, 2, 2, 3, 5, 12, 13, 17.

37. *In Our Time*, p. 134.

38. *Hemingway*, p. 183.

39. *The Portrait of a Lady*, intr. by Fred B. Millett (New York: Modern Library, 1951), p. 90. This passage is taken from the revised edition which is somewhat more colloquial and hence more to the present point. In the third chapter of this study, however, I have consistently quoted from the original versions, because I was discussing James's gradual movement *toward* the colloquial.

40. *The Writer Observed* (New York: The World Publishing Co., 1956), p. 276.

41. "Fenimore Cooper's Literary Offenses," *The Shock of Recognition,* ed. Edmund Wilson, 2 vols. (New York: Farrar, Straus, and Cudahly, 1955), I, 592.

42. *In Our Time,* p. 123.

43. *Henry James, The Major Phase* (New York: Oxford University Press, 1944), p. 169.

44. Lines quoted appear in "The Doctor and the Doctor's Wife," *In Our Time,* p. 29; ibid., p. 30; "The End of Something," *In Our Time,* p. 40; "The Revolutionist," *In Our Time,* p. 106; *The Sun Also Rises,* p. 47; "Soldier's Home," *In Our Time,* p. 99; "The Battler," *In Our Time,* p. 74; *The Sun Also Rises,* p. 48.

HEMINGWAY AND THE THING LEFT OUT

JULIAN SMITH

HAVING LONG SUSPECTED Ernest Hemingway of omitting essential details from his stories and novels, I was not surprised by his account in *A Moveable Feast* of how he deleted "the real end [of "Out of Season"] which was that the old man hanged himself. This was omitted on my new theory that you could omit anything if you knew that you omitted and the omitted part would strengthen the story and make people feel something more than they understood."[1] I can see why Hemingway left out the old man Peduzzi's suicide—his death would have distracted our attention too far from the young American couple who seem at the story's center; moreover, it wasn't necessary to actually tell us Peduzzi killed himself. That is, Hemingway had the advantage of having written under the tension of knowing what would happen—it was the tension Hemingway valued, not the Thing that caused the tension, so he left the Thing out.

"Out of Season," the first story Hemingway wrote after the theft of his early manuscripts, marks his true professional beginning (the only stories to survive the manuscript catastrophe, "My Old Man" and "Up in Michigan," are not of the true style). It should follow that Hemingway, having so begun, continued to experiment with the technique of leaving things out. Indeed, Carlos Baker states that Hemingway excised from "Indian Camp" "an entire preliminary episode covering eight long-hand pages. This was the story of Nick Adams, a small boy afraid of the dark, firing off a rifle to bring his father and

Reprinted with permission from *Journal of Modern Literature,* I, No. 2 (Second Issue, 1970-71), 169-182.

his uncle back from jacklight fishing in the lake."[2] Hemingway seems to have reversed the technique he employed in "Out of Season": instead of building toward a moment of tension, he *started* with the tension of Nick alone and afraid on the lake, a tension later balanced by the boy's final calmness, in spite of the night's terrors, in his father's company. Having established Nick's personality, gotten him moving down an emotional track, Hemingway simply cut off the motive power, fear.

But the excision of the early scene from "Indian Camp" is the kind of editorial cut many authors make without greatly altering the effect or meaning of a story. What I mean by The Thing Left Out is illustrated in "Big Two-Hearted River," which Hemingway called a story "about coming back from the war but there was no mention of the war in it."[3] Again, the motive power, the tension, seemingly remained outside the story, but within the author's mind as he wrote. The omission is more crucial because what has been left out affects our reading. To read "Big Two-Hearted River" without reading anything else Hemingway wrote causes confusion: what is wrong with Nick? Why does he take pleasure in those simple obsessions? Not knowing the answers should not bother one greatly, for many things are unknowable, yet the reader who has read the other Nick Adams stories and knows of Nick's wounds should be much more impressed by what has been left out, impressed by the craftsmanship of a writer who has managed as a third-person narrator to avoid telling us what his hero has avoided thinking about. The effect is hard, stoic, controlled, and the reader who understands what has been left unsaid finds himself initiated into a cult.

I

Though these three stories (written in less than two years) are the only ones we positively know employ the technique of omission, it seems unlikely that other examples do not exist. I will therefore suggest that three often misunderstood stories are also built around something never clearly expressed: "In Another Country," "Now I Lay Me," and "God Rest You Merry, Gentlemen."

But first, let me cite a case in which Hemingway either passed up the chance to leave something out or put it back in at the last minute. In October, 1926, two months after his first marriage ended, he submitted "A Canary for One" to *Scribner's Magazine.*[4] In this story, a young American couple, obviously not talking to one another, share a train compartment with a middle-aged American tourist who insists on talking about marriage in general and how she broke up her daughter's engagement. The story seems at first to be

about this American lady, but the young couple become increasingly important until the last sentence when the husband, who narrates, tells us "We were
returning to Paris to set up separate residences." I don't think Hemingway
worked up here to the kind of WOW ending he disclaimed in *Death in the
Afternoon*. Rather, writing under the effect of his own recent separation,
writing from personal experience and perhaps even for himself, he felt no need
to say what was wrong, or was incapable of revealing the problem as he wrote.
But when he submitted the story for publication, he did not, I speculate, have
sufficient faith in the terrible finality of the true end: "We followed the porter
with the truck down the long cement platform beside the train. At the end was
a gate and a man took the tickets." So he put back the thing left out by adding
that O. Henry last sentence.

     He was far bolder with "In Another Country," submitted the following
month and printed beside "A Canary for One" in *Scribner's Magazine*. So
much has been omitted that the young American narrator, who as in "Canary"
is the secret center of the story, has frequently been ignored or relegated to a
minor position ("the central figure was an Italian major"; "It is the major's
pain that the story is about"; "the story centers around [the major]")[5] or falsely
identified as Nick Adams (Philip Young and others). He is not Nick Adams,
but like the narrator of the companion story, anonymous. Nick Adams is
Hemingway's adolescent alter ego; Hemingway, unsettled by the end of his
first marriage, I suggest, developed two new avatars, both young, both American, both in Europe, and both bereft of love. At the end of "A Canary for One"
we are informed directly of this loss of love if we have not understood it in
the story; "In Another Country" seems to be about a middle-aged Italian
major whose wife has died of pneumonia, but is actually about the young
American who witnessed the major's loss without realizing he was about to
suffer a similar loss.

     What has been left out of "In Another Country" is the dead wench
alluded to in the story's title taken from Marlowe's *The Jew of Malta* by way
of T.S. Eliot's "Portrait of a Lady":

> Thou hast committed—
> Fornication: but that was in another country,
> And besides, the wench is dead.[6]

If we read Hemingway's story as it has generally been read, the "wench" is
the major's wife. Such an identification is doubly inappropriate because it puts
the emphasis right back on the major in spite of the fact that the narrator has
been carefully characterized long before we meet the major and because "com

mitted fornication" connotes an illicit act, whereas the very proper major was
married. It is our nameless young narrator, looking back to "a long time ago"
when *he* was in another country, who has committed fornication with a
"wench" now dead.

.That my reading may make "In Another Country" seem an early version
of *A Farewell to Arms* should be obvious: the narrator anticipates Frederic
Henry and the offstage "wench" his mistress, Catherine Barkley. Carlos Baker
dates the start of *A Farewell to Arms* as early March, 1928, and states Hemingway wanted to use the "in another country" quotation for an epigraph.[7] I
wonder if Hemingway had a hand in choosing the direct translation of Marlowe's words for the title of the German edition of the novel, *In Einem Andern
Land.*

Although there are only these two peripheral connections between the
story of 1926 and the novel begun less than two years later, the direct connections are far more numerous. The narrators, young Americans attached to the
Italian army, are both equally interested in medals, both wounded in the leg
and afflicted by a knee that won't bend. Both walk across Milan from their
hospital quarters to another hospital for mechanical therapy—and both stop
to drink at the same place before returning to their hospital. The first words
of the story summarize perfectly the mood of the last half of the novel following Henry's farewell to arms: "In the fall the war was always there, but we
did not go to it any more." Hemingway achieves the same kind of removal
from warfare through the novel's first sentence by ignoring the war entirely:
"In the late summer of that year we lived in a house in a village that looked
across the river and the plain to the mountains."

It would be an easy matter to insert "In Another Country" either after
the marriage conversation at the end of Chapter XVIII or between Chapter
XXI, in which Catherine announces her pregnancy, and Chapter XXII, in
which Henry loses his chance to go on leave with Catherine and is sent back
to the front. The story fits so well into the novel that it seems The Thing Left
Out. But though the novel does not need the story, the story needs the novel
if it is to be read with any understanding of the narrator's reason for telling
it. It is of course impossible to know how much of the story line for the novel
Hemingway had in mind when he wrote "In Another Country"—quite likely
he was not even thinking of a full novel but of a hero very much like himself
and in love, like his younger self, with a nurse.

He also knew that something would have to happen to the love affair. But
what?

In 1924, in what has been called the starting point for *A Farewell to Arms,*

Hemingway tried to fictionalize his unsuccessful courting of Agnes von Ku-
rowsky, the American nurse he met in Milan. In the bitter result, "A Very
Short Story," a nurse writes her suitor that she has decided to marry a mature
Italian officer instead, for "theirs had been only a boy and girl affair." But such
a commonplacely unromantic end to the affair is not appropriate to the autumnal mood of "In Another Country"—nor would it have been appropriate, I
believe, to the mood of Hemingway right after his separation when, as he
hinted at the end of *A Moveable Feast,* he felt morose and guilty for having
ruined his first and most idyllic marriage.

At this point it would be well to quote the marriage conversation in "In
Another Country";

"Are you married?" [asks the major]
"No, but I hope to be." "The more of a fool you are," he said. He seemed
very angry. "A man must not marry."
"Why, Signor Maggiore?"
"Don't call me 'Signor Maggiore.' "
"Why must not a man marry?"
"He cannot marry. He cannot marry," he said angrily. "If he is to lose
everything; he should not place himself in a position to lose that. He should
not place himself in a position to lose. He should find things he cannot lose."

For some reason the narrator's odd answer to the first question, that he
"hopes" to be married, has gone unnoticed. Young American males do not
hope for marriage in general or as a future condition; if anything, they may
hope for the opposite. In addition, the way the narrator patiently asks why a
man should not marry, the way he later asks "But why should he necessarily
lose it," suggests that the narrator, who has trouble speaking Italian with the
intensely precise major, is making more than polite small talk, that his interest
is highly personal. The major breaks off the conversation, goes into another
room, makes a telephone call, and returns with the news that his young wife
has died.

Had Hemingway incorporated "In Another Country" in the middle, say,
of Chapter XIX of *A Farewell to Arms,* it would have ominously foreshadowed
Catherine's death. Let us try such an interpolation. After the major's wife dies,
Henry returns to Catherine, where, following his return in the novel itself from
therapy, we find this dialog:

"I'm afraid [says Catherine] of the rain because sometimes I see me dead
in it."
"No."

"And sometimes I see you dead in it."

"That's more likely."

Perhaps Hemingway was remembering "In Another Country" as he wrote these lines; what has been left out is that they form a terrible coincidence after the conversation with the major. Or take this fragment from Chapter XXI:

"They won't get us," I said. "Because you're too brave. Nothing ever happens to the brave."

"They die of course" [says Catherine].

None of this, however, is proof that the story's narrator has lost his wife, fiancée, or mistress to death. Proof I cannot give; I can only assert that "In Another Country" becomes an even more impressive story if you will read it as I do. For instance, the major is obviously a "tutor" figure similar to the many tutors encountered by Frederic Henry—as such, he teaches *not* that one should not marry, but how one should accept the loss of one's wife: one returns to what one has been doing, even if it is something as ridiculous and futile as mechanotherapy for a ruined hand. Such a message would be intolerably commonplace if purely abstract, but Hemingway-Henry-nameless narrator is pulling it out of his memory at a time when it is a useable truth following the loss of his own "wife." At the same time, by dwelling on the major's loss rather than his own, the narrator shows he has learned well the major's stoic philosophy.

II

Though it is the second story in *Men Without Women,* "In Another Country" is actually the first to state the men-without-women theme. The nominal lead story, "The Undefeated," about bullfighting, was probably placed first to capitalize on the recent popular success of *The Sun Also Rises.* Further evidence that "In Another Country" is the real beginning of *Men Without Women* is to be found in the fact that it is counterpointed by the last story, "Now I Lay Me," also narrated by a young American in the Italian army who has also been wounded and who also has a conversation about marriage. But whereas in the first story the narrator wants to marry and is warned not to, in the second the narrator, who seems unwilling to marry, is advised to do so by his orderly, John.

"Now I Lay Me" ends with the narrator's confession that the orderly came "to see me several months after and was very disappointed that I had not yet married, and I know he would feel very badly if he knew that, so far,

I have never married. He was going back to America and he was very certain about marriage and knew it would fix up everything." Richard B. Hovey lumps this with three other Hemingway stories about "a bachelor hero so reluctant to marry that he cannot even contemplate the possibility except with doubt and apprehension" and asserts that the narrator's "efforts to cope with his trauma require a fuller inquiry, but for the moment it is enough to note the story's obvious moral: that marriage is no help for a man who has come too close to death."[8] I have taken Professor Hovey's comment because it comes from one of the fullest and most recent readings of the story and because it so well represents the tendency of much Hemingway criticism to reduce a story to an "obvious moral."

Very little in this or any other Hemingway story is as obvious as it seems. Earl Rovit calls the orderly "a wounded fellow soldier" when it is not at all evident he is wounded and when it is absolutely certain that he is not a "fellow" soldier but a subordinate; Rovit also calls the story "a direct recounting of [Hemingway's] convalescence in Milan after the Fossalta wound"[9] despite the first words of the story ("That night we lay on the floor in the room and I listened to the silkworms eating"—odd place to convalesce, on the floor of a silk worm house) and the later information that the setting is only "seven kilometres behind the lines" (Milan was far from the front). Rather, it should be clear that the narrator, who has "been wounded a couple of times," is back at the front between woundings.

Criticism of "Now I Lay Me" is abundant and becoming increasingly synoptic. Its popularity with critics probably results from its openness to psychological interpretation: the narrator, who can't sleep partly for fear of dying before he wakes, first occupies his mind by fishing the big two-hearted rivers of imagination, then begins to remember the running warfare between his parents and his own childish involvement in that warfare. Joseph DeFalco, taking the psychological reading to its outer limits, pontificates thusly: "As he lies in bed at night unable to sleep, a willful precipitation of regressive infantile reveries marks him as suffering from some acute mental disorder."[10] The first thing wrong here is that the narrator is not in bed; he's on a blanket spread over straw on the floor. Secondly, things other than "acute mental disorder" keep one awake—dripping faucets, fear of the police, debt, mosquitoes, straw bedding. And why must childhood memories be labeled "willful precipitation of regressive infantile reveries"? That kind of talk gives us all a bad name.

Not enough attention, on the other hand, has been given to the nagging little questions raised by the story. What exactly does the first sentence mean? "That night we lay on the floor in the room and I listened to the silk-worms eating." The first two words alone offer enough problems to distract us from psychological readings. What night? Why is he *listening* to rather than merely *hearing* the silk-worms? Why does he mention "we" and not tell us who "we" are until the second half of the story? My point is that the story has still not been read carefully at the first level of meaning, the literal.

A prime example of this neglect is that no one, to my knowledge, has explained the narrator's double insistence that "I had not yet married" and "so far, I have never married." The narrator, called Nick by his hen-pecked doctor father, seems almost certainly Nick Adams, but we know from "Cross Country Snow," published in January, 1925, over two years before "Now I Lay Me," that Nick Adams is already married. There are several unsatisfactory ways around this problem. We could say that although the story was published after "Cross Country Snow" and although the narrator seems to be speaking of his present condition, that he is actually speaking prior to the time we meet him in the later story. We could say that Nick of this story is not Nick Adams, or that though generally consistent in his treatment of Nick, Hemingway cannot be held to consistency at the expense of effect. Or perhaps "Cross Country Snow" itself was a false direction in the history of Nick Adams and Hemingway changed his mind later and unmarried him ("Fathers and Sons," 1933, is the only other story in which we see Nick has ever been married). Or the narrator may be lying, or Hemingway may be ironically purging himself of his first marriage ((apparently composed at about the time of his second marriage in May, 1927, the story may reflect his temporary unmarried state).

The trouble with all these suggestions is that they are too far from the story itself. Ideally, the reason for Hemingway's decision to arbitrarily change facts in the biography of Nick Adams and to end with "he was very certain about marriage and knew it would fix up everything" should be found within the story, but since it cannot be found, clearly something has been left out. If we read "Now I Lay Me" as an extension of "In Another Country" and as an early effort by Hemingway to fictionalize and romanticise his unsuccessful courtship of an American nurse in Italy, we might get this kind of plot line: the narrator of the first story disregards the major's advice, seeks to marry, but like Frederic Henry loses his fiancée-mistress; following his loss, not having deserted the Italian army at this stage in Hemingway's thinking, he returns to the front where we see him sleepless in the summer, half a year or more after the time of the first story, and in no mood to think of marriage, for marriage will no more cure his inner wounds than will the therapy machines cure the major's.[11]

Unfortunately, such a reading does not explain the presence of the narrator's highly specific memories of his father's psychological emasculation: how "after my grandfather died'we moved away from that house and to a new house designed and built by my mother" (the mother, on the death of the patriarch, usurped the male role of architect and builder); how his mother burned his father's collection of phallic snakes and equally phallic Indian artifacts—arrow heads, stone axes, skinning knives, and tools. Professors De Falco and Hovey see the narrator as psychically emasculated, Hovey calling Nick's memories of Mom-the-destroyer "the prototype of Nick Adam's first 'wound'—the child's fear of emasculation. This long-established and buried trauma has been revived with terrible power through the physical battle wound. That somehow this is the earliest memory, dredged up through so much pain, indicates that in Nick Adams the fear of castration is stronger than in most men."[12] Why does the narrator dwell on memories that suggest fear of castration, and what has this preoccupation to do with the fact John "was very certain about marriage and knew that it would fix up everything"? I suggest the story concerns something that literally cannot be "fixed up" by marriage, that the narrator has been sexually wounded, and that his memory of his father's symbolic castration is selective, not random, highly personal, not removed. In short, I am suggesting he is closer to Jake Barnes, the sexually wounded narrator of *The Sun Also Rises* (1926), than to Nick Adams.

The many similarities between the narrator of "Now I Lay Me" and Jake Barnes might be explained away as further evidence that Hemingway himself is the common denominator among his heroes and that they do not resemble each other as much as they resemble Hemingway. Hemingway, Jake, and Nick of "Now I Lay Me" are all young Americans from the Midwest who served in the Italian army; all three are wounded and hospitalized in Milan's Ospedale Maggiore; all love fishing; Hemingway and Jake are reporters, Nick says he wants to be a reporter. More specifically, Nick and Jake are afflicted by a common insomnia during which Nick remembers his childhood and Jake remembers being hospitalized in Milan; neither can keep his mind from "jumping" around. Jake is a Catholic and Nick says Catholic prayers; Nick attempts to pray for his family, Jake prays for his friends and himself. In short, *The Sun Also Rises* shows Jake Barnes seven or eight years after his wound; "Now I Lay Me" shows someone with a similar but much newer wound who has not yet made adjustments.

Though "Now I Lay Me" was published a year after the novel, it may be a fragment excised from an early version or a scene Hemingway meant to write, a scene showing young "Jake" adjusting to the new knowledge that he cannot have an ordinary marriage, all the while inflicted with the gratuitous advice that marriage "would fix up everything," a spurious message echoed in Brett Ashley's famous last words to Jake: "we could have had such a damned good time together." But, granted my suspicions are correct, why has Hemingway taken a scene from Jake Barnes' life and given it to Nick Adams? Simply because Jake is Nick, sharing the same wounds, the same experiences, even the same friends. Bill, Nick's friend and advisor in "The End of Something" and "The Three Day Blow" (1925) shows up a year later in the novel as Bill Gorton, Jake's old friend. Nick's Bill and Jake's Bill are both based on Hemingway's friend (and best man at his first wedding) William Smith.[13] If Nick's friend Bill appears in *The Sun Also Rises,* can Nick be far behind?

In an article on the real-life sources for *The Sun Also Rises,* Bertram D. Sarason summarizes the "biographical" interpretation of Jake's wound as representing "imaginatively the blockade to a love affair with Lady Duff Twysden (the Lady Brett Ashley of the novel) which had to be foregone because of Hemingway's loyalty to his wife."[14] I think, however, that Jake's wound is just as much a part of Hemingway's romantization of his "affair" with the nurse who declined to marry him, thus inflicting a psychic wound as debilitating as the physical one. Jake's first conversation with Robert Cohn about Brett Ashley may show our author's old love wound festering and that Hemingway may have combined Duff Twysden and the nurse:

"Have you known her a long time?" [asks Cohn]
"Yes," I said. "She was a V.A. D. in a hospital I was in during the war."
"She must have been just a kid then."
"She's thirty-four now."

Hemingway's real nurse, born in 1892 like Duff Twysden and Brett Ashley, was also thirty-four in 1926, the year the novel appeared. Note too the similarities between Brett Ashley and Catherine Barkley: both are British and older than the narrators, both once cared for the narrators as V. A. D.'s, both lost lovers to the war before they met the narrators. Hemingway's romantization of his adolescent affair in these two stories and two novels had day-dream alternatives: on the one hand the hero cannot marry because the girl dies; on the other the hero cannot have a normal marriage because of a sexual wound.

III

If Jake Barnes's experiences are reflected in one story published after the novel, it should not be surprising to find them in another. Such, I think, is the case with "God Rest You Merry, Gentlemen" (1933). The narrator, a former cub reporter from journalist Jake Barnes' hometown, Kansas City, tells about an extremely religious youth who demanded to be castrated in order to escape sexual desire. Turned down, and not knowing what castration entailed, he cut off his penis. I think what has been left out of the story is that the identically mutilated Jake Barnes, and not an anonymous narrator, is remembering an incident that meant nothing to him at the time it occurred but later came to have a terrible relevance. Like "Now I Lay Me," "God Rest You Merry, Gentlemen" may also have been excised from an earlier mental version of *The Sun Also Rises;* if nothing else, both stories share titles calling upon divine aid in gaining the peace so sought after by Jake Barnes:

Now I lay me down to sleep,	God rest you merry, gentlemen,
I pray the Lord my sould to keep;	Let nothing you dismay . . .
And if I die before I wake,	Oh, tidings of comfort and
I pray the Lord my soul to take.	joy. . . .

Though "God Rest You Merry, Gentlemen" has been mostly ignored, there seems a hierarchy of misreadings: at the highest level of misunderstanding, critics discussing the boy who mutilates himself fail to notice the two doctors who tell the narrator about the boy. Since the boy is not even a character in the story, this reading is patently misguided. Closer to the truth comes the larger group of critics who find significant the conflict between the competent Doc Fischer and the incompetent Doctor Wilcox. Neither reading, however, explains the presence of the narrator, for the story could be told by one of the doctors or in the third person. Instead, Hemingway devotes the first hundred and fifty words to memories of the narrator, memories seemingly irrelevant to the story, and later goes to great trouble to characterize him.

The first mistake made by those who do notice the narrator is to call him Horace, the nickname used by the ironic Doc Fischer ("you don't mind me calling you Horace, do you?"). The Roman Horace was everything young Hemingway aspired to be: poet, satirist, and stoic. It is a fine name for a young Jake Barnes, a gift from the sophisticated Doc Fischer to a young aspirant who takes pleasure in false sophistication, as when he tries to interpret *"Dans Argent,"* the motto on a racing car: "this I believed to mean the silver dance or the silver dancer, and, slightly puzzled which it meant but happy in the sight of the car and pleased by my knowledge of a foreign language, I went along the street in the snow." The second mistake is to underrate the narrator, as does Peter L. Hays who says "Horace is a perfect Hemingway persona, an accurate but impartial observer," but condemns him as "none too intelligent"[15] partly on the basis of his weak French. The point should be clear: the narrator has over the years acquired sufficient true sophistication, so much so he can now speak objectively of his youthful naïveté, just as Jake Barnes can tell us straightforwardly and with great dignity of his adult humiliations and cruelties.

Indeed, I can think of no Hemingway character better qualified than Jake to speak the first sentence of "God Rest You Merry, Gentlemen": "In those days the distances were all very different, the dirt blew off the hills that have now been cut down, and Kansas City was very like Constantinople." Here are the poles of Jake's existence, K. C. and Constantinople—when he was young Kansas City was the center of the world, civilization amid wilderness, a metropolis where one found *"Dans Argent"* on the hood of a car. "In those days the distances were all very different" because he had a different spatial, temporal, and intellectual scale of reference.

To see the story as about anyone but the narrator is to negate all the narrator tells us about himself, to make him superfluous. Yet on the evidence within the story, he seems totally unnecessary, and the story seems lacking in focus. Once again I am thrown back to the conclusion that Hemingway has left out the narrator's identity and his reason for telling the story. At the same time, I admire the story for its incompleteness, for it is tense, beautiful, and passing strange as written. Still, I want to know why things are as they are in the story; why, for instance, the ending dribbles away in a pointless argument between the two doctors in which the incompetent Wilcox can do no more than ineffectually and irrelevantly attempt to turn Doc Fischer's Jewishness against him.[16] I conclude that the narrator has managed to distract us from himself so we will not bother to ask too many pointed questions about him; I also conclude that the ending is dramatically realistic—at the time it happened the boy's self-mutilation was little more than an agent for increasing the tension and conflict between the two doctors and the narrator remembered the incident in that context. Jake Barnes tells us the story from a personal context, but has left out that context.

If I have gone too far with some of my readings, I repent. But I think it better to err in the direction of seeing Hemingway as too coherent than to accuse him, as some readers of all the stories discussed have, of lacking focus, of introducing irrelevant characters and incidents, of, in short, not knowing his business. Instead, I here assert that through omission Hemingway has succeeded in the goal he stated in *A Moveable Feast:* to "make people feel something more than they understood."

1. (New York: Scribner's, 1964), p.75.
2. Carlos Baker, *Ernest Hemingway: A Life Story (Scribner's, 1969, p. 125.*

3. *A Moveable Feast,* p. 76.

4. For dates and details of composition and submission, I am indebted throughout this paper to Professor Baker's biography.

5. See Carlos Baker, p. 177; Philip Young, *Ernest Hemingway: A Reconsideration* (Pennsylvania State University Press, 1966), pp. 58–59; Leo Gurko, *Ernest Hemingway and the Pursuit of Heroism* (New York: Crowell, 1968), p. 181.

6. For Hemingway's debt to Eliot and Marlowe, see Phyllis Bartlett, "Other Countries, Other Wenches," *Modern Fiction Studies,* III (Winter 1957–58), 345–349.

7. Baker, p. 190.

8. *Hemingway: The Inward Terrain* (University of Washington Press, 1968), p. 8.

9. *Ernest Hemingway* (New York, 1963), p. 79.

10. *The Hero in Hemingway's Short Stories* (University of Pittsburgh Press, 1963), p. 105.

11. Further evidence of a relationship between these two stories is found in the fact that a "near-final draft of what became 'Now I Lay Me' " was originally titled "In Another Country —Two. A Story." See Philip Young and Charles W. Mann, ed., *The Hemingway Manuscripts: An Inventory* (Pennsylvania State University Press, 1969), p. 44.

12. *The Inward Terrain,* p. 52; see also DeFalco, p. 113.

13. See Donald St. John, "Interview with Hemingway's 'Bill Gorton,' " *Connecticut Review,* I, ii (1968), 5–12, for an identification of Smith and Gorton.

14. "Lady Brett Ashley and Lady Duff Twysden," *Connecticut Review,* II (April 1969), 6.

15. "Hemingway and the Fisher King," *University of Kansas City Review,* XXXII (March 1966), 226.

16. *The Sun Also Rises* and "God Rest You Merry, Gentlemen" are the only works in which Hemingway has important Jewish characters—perhaps he is making up for his anti-semitic portrait of Robert Cohn by the extremely sympathetic portrayal of the tutor-figure Doc Fischer. Hemingway goes out of his way to avoid stock characterization by making Fischer thin and blond and the Christian Wilcox short and dark.

THE MARINATING OF
FOR WHOM THE BELL TOLLS

LINDA WELSHIMER WAGNER

THERE IS EVIDENCE that most of Hemingway's successful fiction has under-gone not only serious and major revision, but long periods of pre-writing. As early as 1936 Hemingway was planning to write Santiago's story; *A Farewell to Arms* was in process nearly ten years. Contrastingly, *To Have and Have Not* began as a long story and accidentally grew into a novel, as did *Across the River and Into the Trees.* Hemingway's own amazement at the completion of the

Reprinted with permission from *Journal of Modern Literature,* II, No. 4 (Nov. 1972), 533–546.

latter novel testifies to the very brief time between the story's inception and its finish.[1] A revealing comment on Hemingway's method of working is inherent in Max Perkins' story of asking Hemingway why he did not write about life in the Cape Sable waters. " 'Maybe sometime,' said Ernest, pensively. 'I don't know enough about it yet'. . . . He did know, thought Perkins, but it would not emerge in written form until it had marinated a long time in the depths of his subconscious."[2] As this anecdote illustrates, Hemingway's usual approach was to have his story so well in mind—at least in character and intent, if not in plot—that the writing of it was almost always "right."

No major Hemingway novel so well reveals this process of gradual mastery of possible materials as *For Whom the Bell Tolls*, the 1940 book which was written only after Hemingway had explored its themes, and established prototypes for many of its characters, in his NASA columns, five short stories, a movie scenario, and *The Fifth Column* (his only play). The setting for each is the Spanish Civil War, the vantage point usually Madrid. Because Hemingway as early as 1937 announced that he was planning to write a novel about these war experiences, it is plausible to consider this work—done from the fall of 1937 to the spring of 1939—as presaging *For Whom the Bell Tolls.*

Perhaps the most surprising point about the writing here considered is that it is not the novel in miniature. *For Whom the Bell Tolls* represents Hemingway's views once he had come to know the war intimately. At first, however—as his NASA dispatches clearly show—he had forgotten what war is like. The earliest impression of his dispatch coverage, beginning in March of 1937, is understated surprise, replaced quickly by less understated horror. Then as Hemingway learns about the Loyalist methods of survival, his horror at war turns to admiration for the people involved, and that admiration deepens until it is almost worship. Finally comes the disillusionment with the mechanics of the cause, its politics, leaders, and the damning lack of concern for the common people.

In light of this progression in Hemingway's attitudes, it is revealing that *The Fifth Column,* his play, was written after he had been in Madrid only six months. Some elements in the drama suggest that war is still somewhat glamorous to him, and the flip attitudes and stock triangle situations seem appropriate to an almost romantic view of the conflict. Living in the Madrid Hotel Florida, with drinking buddies, girls, and the "fiesta" atmosphere[3] was hardly Robert Jordan's experience with Pablo's band. In fact the cast Hemingway has assembled is more nearly a continuation of the writers and society fops of *To Have and Have Not* than forerunners of the Loyalist peasants. (Indeed, the key to the tone of much of the play seems to lie in the dialogues about hoarded food and supplies, reminiscent of "home-front rationing" woes.)

Dorothy Bridges, "a bored Vassar bitch" and a magazine correspondent, prefaces her statements with "Darling," and changes lovers in the course of the play to end up with the counterspy posing as playboy Philip Rawlings. Although Hemingway presents her as heroine, Dorothy's vapid conversations and materialistic interests make her less than sympathetic. If this is the best Hemingway could do with an American girl as heroine, his choice of the Spanish Maria for *For Whom the Bell Tolls* was probably wise.

Rawlings is the embryonic Jordan, though—with less introspection possible in the dramatic format—not such a convincing hero. Rawlings too comes from living a very private life to caring a great deal for Dorothy, but eventually he breaks with her because of his love. As he says bitterly to Max, "We're in for fifty years of undeclared wars and I've signed up for the duration."[4] There is no place in his life for marriage; but before his renunication of that possibility, he does tell Dorothy, "I'd like to marry you, and go away, and get out of all this" (p. 58).

Rawlings' personal dilemma—facing a genuine love for the first time in his life—is played against his professional activity, capturing a civilian leader of the Fifth Column insurgents within Madrid. Hemingway gives full play to the successful capture scene, and consequently drains off that plot-oriented tension. The play lacks dramatic intensity because the high point of the espionage has passed, and we care relatively little about Rawlings' relationship with Dorothy. (In *For Whom the Bell Tolls* the plot is reversed: Jordan's romance is successful, whereas his professional endeavor brings him death.)

Pilar's account of the way the various men of their village met death at Pablo's hands is foreshadowed here when Rawlings talks with the executioner about the ways men die. Again, Hemingway's interest in man facing death is evident; but he chooses not to have Rawlings meet his own. The choice— dramatically—may well have been a mistake. The essential conflict of romance vs. opposing duty is the basis of both the play and the novel, yet because the materials are treated so differently, the effect is quite dissimilar. Once Hemingway had opened the play with jocular comments and minor characters whose roles could only be comic (the hotel manager is a stamp collector with a voraciously hungry mother-in-law), building toward tragedy was almost impossible. Perhaps for that reason he so clearly creates mood in the first chapter of *For Whom the Bell Tolls,* placing Pilar's reading of Jordan's palm very early in the novel.

Other elements of the novel have their inception in the five short stories written after the play. "The Denunciation" treats of man's loyalty to his own code of conduct, a more important concern than any political affiliation. Just as in *For Whom the Bell Tolls*, Jordan blows the bridge for the people of Spain —and much more immediately for Maria, Pilar, and Pablo's band—so Enrique in "The Denunciation" would overlook the fact that one of Chicote's customers is a Fascist. Enrique would not himself denounce Luis Delgado, but he gives the proper phone number to the waiter who has talked with him about such an act. Enrique's hypocrisy is the issue here: at first he is angry because Delgado has returned to the bar and thus put everyone in awkward positions, although he also understands the reason for the man's return:

All we old clients of Chicote's had a sort of feeling about the place. I knew that was why Luis Delgado had been such a fool as to go back there. He could have done his business some place else. But if he was in Madrid he had to go there. He had been a good client as the waiter had said and we had been friends.[5]

Then he remembers what a good loser Delgado had been years before in a shooting match. Realizing his own involvement, he sees that he could have discouraged the old waiter, instead of giving him the information he needed. And finally, with a rather strange sense of exoneration, he calls the executioner and asks that he, Enrique, be named as informer instead of the old waiter. Unless one understands Hemingway's conviction that human relationships are the most essential supports a man has—and that those between man and man, man and chauffeur, and man and waiter have particular intensity—Enrique's act has little significance.[6] The gesture is similar to Jordan's allowing Pablo to pretend that he has not killed his men at the end of *For Whom the Bell Tolls*. Man has so little to believe in; another man does not take any dignity from him.

In "The Butterfly and the Tank" Hemingway relates a simple but tragic incident he had already mentioned more briefly in *The Fifth Column*. A half-drunk young civilian was squirting people in Chicote's Bar with a cologne-filled flit gun, and as tempers rose, he was himself killed. In the travesty of justice that resulted, the man responsible for his death walked out while the rest of the bar patrons were held long hours for questioning. The incident prompts the narrator to think about the political issues of the story; that is, would it be maligning the Loyalist side to write about their mock-justice? And, in a larger sense, he considers the death of this Pedro as another senseless debt to the hysteria of war, "the deadly seriousness that is here always," in the words of the old waiter. Hence, the waiter's title for the story, as he describes the young man: "His gaiety comes in contact with the seriousness of war like a butterfly . . . and a tank" (pp. 108–109).

The attitudes of the narrator in this story parallel those of Jordan in the novel. Both men are already aware of the travesty of some wartime justice, and each has seen more than once that it is the poor who get the bad deals. It is Pedro who pays for the edgy tempers of war, Pedro who wears no undershirt and whose soles are worn through. The extension of this realization forms the theme for "Night Before Battle," the most powerful story of the five, in which Hemingway questions the military strategy of the Peoples' Army, and defames the authority which plans such wars. Written in October of 1938, just a few months before he began *For Whom the Bell Tolls,* "Night Before Battle" is also Hemingway's tribute to the men he most admired, the tank drivers who did their best in Spain, but against frightening odds.[7]

By centering on Al Wagner, the tank commander who knows the coming attack will fail, Hemingway can use the vernacular to make Al's discussion of the debacle more readable ("Listen the whole thing is just as crazy as a bedbug. Why do they want to make a frontal attack against positions like those? Who in hell thought it up?"). Throughout the evening, narrator Hank and Al mix with other soldiers and fliers who are playing craps in Hank's room, so that attention is always on the men who do the fighting, not those who make the plans. Al is killing the night bit by bit, trying whatever will keep him from thinking. For, as he says, "I don't mind dying a bit . . . Only it's wasteful. The attack is wrong and it's wasteful . . . If we had tanks that were a little bit faster the anti-tanks wouldn't bother them the way it does when you haven't got the mobility." Al is concerned not only for himself. The other tank men know what he does, and his problem will be to make them attack. "I can make them start all right and I can take them up to where they will have to quit one at a time" (p. 117).

As in *For Whom the Bell Tolls,* Hemingway establishes the conflict in the opening of the story as Al describes the impossibility of it all, and tells Hank that he thinks he will die during the attack. This plot line is unresolved because the story ends before daybreak, but it serves to color the other actions within the story: the gambling, the search for love, the drinking—all are more understandable in this desperate atmosphere. The real climax of the story occurs when the balding drunk riding the elevator with six bottles of champagne turns out to be a pilot-hero who has miraculously lived through the adventure he tells. The whole scene with Baldy Johnson changes the direction of the story by emphasizing that war is not rational, that chance plays a major role.[8] Underlying even this episode is Al's tense recognition of his "duty" ("my duty is to do what I'm ordered to do"), and his thoughts about the coming "blood bath."

"Under the Ridge," the fourth story, is an expansion of Al Wagner's quandary about the recalcitrant soldiers. What should be done? Is a dead man good for anything, even encouraging discipline? Hemingway explores that problem here, but also gives the reader some insight into the feelings of the native Spaniards. Here the narrator Henry is also unaware of what has happened, and the story of Paco eventually comes from the bitter Extremaduran who distrusts all foreigners, but especially the Russian battle police. (The fact that several of these stories were told to Hank, and the fact that throughout them the narrator has the same name, or is unnamed, suggests that the group might well have been intended for a unified collection, perhaps a Winesburg at war.)

Paco had some months before shot himself in the hand in order to leave the front. After an amputation and recovery, he is brought back to his former brigade at mealtime and, summarily, to everyone's horror, shot in the head. This "lesson" occurs the evening before the battle now in progress, which the Loyalists have again lost because of inadequate arms and men as well as poor strategy. As Hank watches the dying battle, in progress, he sees a tall middle-aged Frenchman walk away from it, and soon sees him hunted down and shot —thirteen times—for his cowardice. But as Hemingway concludes, "The nearest any man was to victory that day was probably the Frenchman who came, with his head held high, walking out of the battle" (p. 151).

The more complicated structure of this story and the narrator's role in it convey its ultimate meaning. Section I gives the somewhat humorous animosity of the Extremaduran to all foreigners. Section II presents the Frenchman's proud desertion and his execution. In some of his best writing in the story, Hemingway exonerates the Frenchman; but, although his sympathies are with the deserter, he tries to conclude that "In war it is necessary to have discipline" (p. 147). The dour Extremaduran checks his glib assurance, however, by pointing out, "There is one kind of discipline and another kind of discipline." And then he breaks his silence and tells the story of young Paco, reinforcing the apparent inhumanity of the Russian "blood hounds" who serve as executioners. By ending with the pathos of this story, Hemingway has effectively undermined his own argument for discipline.

It is evident that *For Whom the Bell Tolls* contains many of the same attitudes and premises that have been operative in the play and the republished short stories. Hemingway's decision to make the novel one of people, one of human relationships, must have been made on the basis of his own loyalties during the two years he was in Spain. The political systems are rotten, but the people who believe in them are, or can be, magnificent. By making *For Whom the Bell Tolls* nearly apolitical, Hemingway created an image that would relate to all wars, all conflict.

Even the most apparently slanted of Hemingway's Spanish Civil War writings, his text for *The Spanish Earth,* the movie designed to raise funds for the Peoples' Army, had its moments of impartiality. Just as Hemingway shows the human side of the Fascists in the novel, so the cameras focus on Italian dead during the film, and the text reads, "These dead came from another country. They signed to work in Ethiopia, the prisoners said . . . The Italians lost more killed, wounded and missing in this single battle of Brihuega than in all the Ethiopian war."[9] This excerpt, besides commenting on the misuse of, again, the common people's trust, also includes a mention of Hemingway's reading letters of some of the dead soldiers, "We took no statements from the dead but all the letters we read were sad."

Such inclusion is characteristic with the theme of the film, for it does not berate political philosophy; instead it nearly ignores it. The film is a study in faces—soldiers', workers', women's, men's, children's; pained and happy; angry and sad; gaunt and prosperous—and the text opens with that emphasis, "The Spanish earth is dry and hard and the faces of the men who work on that earth are hard and dry from the sun." Centering on the right of the people to own land, to improve that land by irrigation, the film shows the physical waste of the autocratic political system. Hemingway's oblique treatment of the political issues throughout the novel reminds one of his censure of Tolstoy as philosopher instead of writer, "his ponderous and Messianic thinking was no better than many another evangelical professor of history and I learned from him to distrust my own Thinking with a capital T."[10]

And so Hemingway succeeded in writing a propaganda film which was amazingly free of propaganda; the word *fascist* did not appear anywhere in the narration, and even the commentary about the hired mercenaries is sympathetic to their "cause," a way of earning a livelihood.

The last use of the Spanish Civil War before he began *For Whom the Bell Tolls* is the short story which Mary Hemingway excluded from publication in *The Fifth Column* collection. "Nobody Ever Dies" is the closest story to the novel. Published in March, 1939 (written in the fall of 1938), in *Cosmopolitan,* it is the longest of the five stories and the least polished. But its roughness probably stems both from Hemingway's strong convictions about its theme and the wide range of material within the story. In it he creates the prototypes for both Robert Jordan and Maria, as lovers persecuted by the Cuban secret police after their activities in Spain. Jordan is again named Enrique, and is described on the first page as "a young man of about 28, thin, dark, with circles under his eyes and a stubble of beard."[11] Horribly wounded in battle, he has a hole in the small of his back a man could put his fist through (Regler's wound). His greatest parallels with Jordan are his tough, intellectual response to life, and his amused shock at the way the Spanish people carry on the war.

Jordan is also somewhat intellectual, but in *For Whom the Bell Tolls* Hemingway puts the discussion of his "coldness" in Pilar's words ("The boy is smart . . . Smart and cold. Very cold in the head"). Because we know that Pilar likes Jordan, the condemnation is not harsh—his intellect is more a foil to her own gypsy reliance on instinct, and even mysticism. Also, because we are given many monologues for Jordan, we know that much of what appears as coldness is really discipline. We are thus conditioned to think of Jordan's intellect as a positive force, especially when it is tempered by his very real love for Maria. But in "Nobody Ever Dies" we have only a brief dialogue between Enrique, the political machine, and Maria, who rather naturally loved her brother. She has just discovered that Vincente has been killed, along with many other friends, and is anguished by her grief. Enrique says coldly,

> It does no good to discuss it. They are dead.
> But it is not only that Vincente is my brother. I can give up my brother. It is the flower of our party.
> Yes. The flower of the party.
> It is not worth it. It has destroyed the best.
> Yes. It is worth it.
> How can you say that? That is criminal.
> No. It is worth it.
> She was crying now and Enrique went on eating. Don't cry, he said. The thing to do is to think how we can work to take their places.

The choppy, slow sentences; Enrique's eating; his complete political bias certainly load our reactions in Maria's favor. Unfortunately for our view of the hero, Hemingway later in this scene also has him deal in abstractions like "romanticism," "terrorism," and something labeled "revolutionary adventurism." We are with Maria as she screams, "You talk like a book . . . not like a human being. You have a dry heart and I hate you."

One of the implausibilities of the story comes then, as Enrique (hurt by her words) shows her his wound: she begs forgiveness, and he melts. The character reversal is too fast—and too much—for us to accept. Enrique is the man who, two pages before, had been saying things like "where you die does not matter, if you die for liberty." But, in terms of plot, the reversal is necessary because on the next page Enrique is shot, and Maria captured by the Cubans. Their threats of torture only bring out Maria's bravery as she gains strength from all the dead. Her promise that she will not talk, that she will live through the dead, gives Hemingway his title; it also gives him reason to picture this

Maria as another Jeanne de Arc. Since we have seen her only as a girl grieving for a brother, this concluding extension of her character is too melodramatic to be effective.

Hemingway often praised himself for knowing when to revise and when to cut. In creating the metamorphosis of Enrique into Robert Jordan, he has changed many traits to make the young American less objectionable. But some basic parallels remain. Jordan, like Enrique, believes in the cause, but he has a sense of humor to go with his belief (as Jordan mused, he fought so that "there should be no more danger and so that the country should be a good place to live in. That was true no matter how trite it sounded" (p. 162). And their thoughts about a man's doing the impossible are almost identical: Enrique says, "Some things we had to do were impossible. Many that looked impossible we did." And Jordan, introspectively, "should a man carry out impossible orders knowing what they lead to? . . . Yes. He should carry them out because it is only in the performing of them that they can prove to be impossible. How do you know they are impossible until you have tried them?"

In the short story, with Enrique's death on no field of battle, Hemingway seems impressed with the irony of it all, with the discrepancy between the glorious sound of the man's words and his final act, crawling painfully through the dusty weeds. The glory is reserved—though arbitrarily—for Maria, whose trial is yet to come (in *The Spanish Earth,* a recurring image is the "enduring bravery" of the Spanish women). Maria's simplicity of both speech and action are admirable. While her saintliness may be an exaggeration, Hemingway tries to build the impression through the use of the Negro informant who rides with her, fingering his blue voodoo beads but still afraid ("they could not help his fear because he was up against an older magic now"). The primitive posed against the saintly provides at least a colorful closing image; and in some ways suggests Hemingway's slight definition of "religion" as simply "love lived."[12]

This phrase is an apt description of the Maria of *For Whom the Bell Tolls* as well. Although she has already had her torture at the hands of men, she is forgiving enough to love one of them again. Maria embodies all the qualities Hemingway considered virtues—she has a great capacity to love, she is gentle and soft spoken, she does not demand anything, and she has been tested and still maintains a stable "perspective," with help from Pilar.[13] With Pilar's obvious approval of Jordan, and with everyone's recognition of the danger ahead, Maria's love for Jordan is quite plausible.

Hemingway was careful to place the Jordan-Maria relationship in its proper context. It has been initiated and fostered by Pilar. Her anger in the forest as she speaks of her age and resultant ugliness, her immediate trust of and admiration for Jordan suggest that theirs is also an enduring bond. Pilar dominates the story partly because of her physical power, still in evidence with Pablo; she has gone through life as the mistress of some truly great men, and she responds to Jordan on these same quasi-sexual terms. Pilar's character must be a genuine amalgam, possibly growing from that of Marie Morgan in *To Have and Have Not,* enlivened by bits of the minor characters Anita in *The Fifth Column* and Manolita in "Night Before Battle," but surely one of Hemingway's more inventive and consistently-done women. She is the realization full blown of the enduring Spanish women from his film, and one of her best scenes is her introspective questioning of that very endurance: "neither bull force nor bull courage lasted, she knew now, and what did last? I last, she thought. Yes, I have lasted. But for what?" (p. 190). She is also, in a way, a tribute to Hemingway's own maturity.[14] For once, he seems to enjoy having a woman as leader. In her struggle with Pablo, Pilar wins when she needs to win, but she always leaves the door open for Pablo. When he is ready to act like a man, she will give back his place, and assume her more culturally appropriate one. Maria is not the only woman in *For Whom the Bell Tolls* who knows how—and when—to be submissive.

The character of Robert Jordan is the most predictable in the novel. A kind of dogged Al Wagner, with his real but realistic devotion to duty, Jordan also has the humane convictions of the Extremaduran, the bravado and capacity for love of Philip Rawlings, and the respect for the simple verities of Hank. Like Jake Barnes, he eventually becomes the fully matured Hemingway hero —and, for a while, an uninjured one. He deserves the love he finds with Maria.

Jordan too understands Pablo. Consequently he does not kill him, either in the struggle for leadership or after his sabotage. Pablo has found something to love in the horses and resents being dragged into more danger; he has been too long in the war. In the character of Pablo Hemingway makes his strongest condemnation of the war itself, for he presents Pablo as nearly sympathetic. The war has made him what he is, and what he is now is not good; but Pilar stays with him, as does the band, because of the man he once was.

Making Pablo a strong person has the same effect as making the scenes at Gaylord's more than just local color. Because Jordan is not the non-thinker he would like to be, he has to remember how this all began; his conversation with General Golz in Chapter I gives us a perfect reading of the situation, and subsequent references to Gaylord's and headquarters only reinforce that dismal opening. Most masterful touch of all is the last headquarters scene (Chapter 42) when we see the powerful but insane André Marty pocketing the crucial message from Jordan. Marty's confrontation with Karkov brings to a head all the cryptic statements scattered throughout the novel. The attack will be a blood bath, and very few at Gaylord's will care. This kind of structured, insistent emphasis reminds one of the opposite effect an outright diatribe would have had. As Hemingway wrote in 1942, "Screaming, necessary though it may be to attract attention at the time, reads badly in later years."[15]

That Hemingway did know this—and did know why his characterization in the novel was more effective than that in *The Fifth Column* and the intervening short stories—is all part of the great writer's equipment. Since every novel, every piece of writing, is a new experience, there are times when the writer cannot follow precedent but must eventually trust his intuition. Former practices, like logic and "rules," are sometimes inadequate. With *For Whom the Bell Tolls,* or more generally, with all the Spanish Civil War materials, Hemingway had admitted that the scope of the subject baffled him: "In stories about the war I try to show all the different sides of it, taking it slowly and honestly and examining it from many ways. So never think one story represents my viewpoint because it is much too complicated for that."[16]

As this summary of these separate stories has indicated, Hemingway is obviously interested in several themes: (1) the qualities of the common soldier, and of the Spanish peasant; (2) the relationship of the soldier to the military powers, and the peasant to his rulers; (3) the milieu of war, and the acts it causes; (4) the conflict between private lives and public duty; and (5) Hemingway's most enduring theme, that of love, whether it be for person or for country.

Given this variety of thematic interests, it comes as no surprise that there are several stories within *For Whom the Bell Tolls.* Some critics, however, have objected to the epic nature of the novel; most recently, Chaman Nahal writes, "there are three distinct stories in *For Whom the Bell Tolls* which have no true bearing on each other. First, there is the story of Robert Jordan and Maria. Then we have the story of Pilar and Pablo. Last, there is the story of the Russians, which includes men like Golz, Kleber, Hans, André Marty and Karkov."[17] Perhaps the thematic issues are clearer if we identify these three stories not in Nahal's terms but rather as (1) that of the lovers, Jordan and Maria; (2)that of the Spanish people; and (3)that of the political and military machine. The second story, that of the Spanish people, is in some ways the most important single element in the novel because in that story Hemingway captures the spirit of the country trying to free itself through the conflict. Pilar and Pablo are important characters not because of what Nahal calls their "love-hate relationship" but because they each represent facets of the peasant mind—the gypsy set against the cunning, Pilar's endurance juxtaposed with Pablo's pathetic realism. But all the other peasant characters are important too

—Anselmo, El Sordo, Augustin, Fernando, Rafael—each character comes through as an individual, and we receive a wide (and pleased) understanding of the real people involved in this—or any—civil war.

It is because we have this deep compassion for the Spanish people, Loyalist and Fascist alike, that the other two "separate" stories have such impact. The victims of their own commanders, the people live in hovels while Gaylord's operates like a resort hotel; they give their lives instead of verbiage. And similarly, Robert Jordan's love for Maria is also clearer since she too represents the native element he so much admires; she has also been victimized by the war machine, yet even the threat of new danger does not frighten her. And had Jordan not admired both the peasants and Golz's acute military mind, his own dilemma would have been less tortured. Indeed, rather than finding these story lines separate, it is difficult to imagine *For Whom the Bell Tolls* without any one of them, especially since they all meet—and find resolution—in the bridge.

Clearly, Hemingway has accomplished successfully the "complicated" business of retelling the story of the Spanish Civil War. "I try to show all the different sides," he had written, in explaining the several short stories and drama; and, as the single pieces show, there were for Hemingway many sides, many components. One can only surmise that the eventual scope and balance of *For Whom the Bell Tolls* might well have been less successful had Hemingway not had the chance to pre-write in the shorter works. Or as he himself explained what might have been the process: "From things that have happened and from things as they exist and from all things that you know and all those you cannot know, you make something through your invention that is not a representation but a whole new thing truer than anything true and alive."[18]

1. See Carlos Baker's *Ernest Hemingway, A Life Story* (Scribner's, 1969) for specific accounts of the way each novel came to be written; and also Hemingway's *Paris Review* interview, p. 233, in *Writers At Work,* Second Series, ed. Malcolm Cowley (The Viking Press, 1963).

2. Baker, 208.

3. See Hemingway's March 18, 1937 dispatch (p. 258) in *By-line: Ernest Hemingway,* ed. William White (Scribner's, 1967).

4. *The Fifth Column* in *The Fifth Column and Four Stories of the Spanish Civil War* (Scribner's, 1969), 80. Hereafter cited in text.

5. "The Denunciation," ibid., p. 100.

6. For positive views of this relationship, see "A Clean, Well-Lighted Place," *The Sun Also Rises,* and *To Have and Have Not.* Part of Cantwell's malaise in *Across the River,* in contrast, may rise from his difficulties in some of these same relationships.

7. Hemingway states this admiration more directly in his introduction to *Men at War* (Crown Publishers, 1942), 11–12.

8. Somewhat reminiscent of Faulkner's 1934 war story, "Turn About," this part of "Night Before Battle" also includes some references to the drunken Baldy writing for a Mississippi paper, and having trouble telling his story "straight."

9. *The Spanish Earth* (Cleveland: The J.B. Savage Co., 1938), 46.

10. *Men at War*, 10.

11. "Nobody Ever Dies," *Cosmopolitan* (March 1939).

12. "A Man's Credo," *Playboy*, X, No. 1 (January 1963).

13. That Hemingway turned to Spanish women for his heroines makes sense. Dorothy Bridges was a disaster; throughout his work no female character had been well drawn, except Brett Ashley, and she was consistently misread. By using first Maria and Pilar, and then the Italian Renata, Hemingway was both protecting himself from charges of unreality by his largest reading public, the American; and he was also freeing himself of one obstacle in creating women characters— his feeling for his mother. The farther he was culturally from the white, middleclass America of "Soldier's Home" and the Nick Adams stories, the more easily he could forget the stereotypes he found there.

14. See Alan Holder's essay, "The Other Hemingway," *Twentieth Century Literature,* IX (1963), 153–157.

15. *Men at War*, 9.

16. Baker, 337.

17. Chaman Nahal, *The Narrative Pattern in Ernest Hemingway's Fiction* (Rutherford, New Jersey: Fairleigh Dickinson U. Press, 1971), 132.

18. *Writers at Work*, 239.

ERNEST HEMINGWAY, A CRITICAL ESSAY

NATHAN SCOTT, JR.

THE WORLD, as it is rendered in Hemingway's fiction, is a world that is touched by glory—and a certain kind of piety becomes, therefore, a basic norm of human life. But it is a glory that is, as it were, *unexplained,* for it is fully countered by its opposite, in the power of blackness, the blackness which (as Melville said of Hawthorne's) is "TEN TIMES BLACK." And Hemingway does in many respects stand very near the center of that tradition in modern literature which is prepared, in effect, to testify—again, with Melville—that, "though in many of its aspects this visible world seems formed in love, the invisible spheres were formed in fright." Like the Conrad of *The Secret Agent* and the Kafka of *The Trial* and the Moravia of *The Time of Indifference* and the Camus of *The Stranger,* Hemingway situates the representative personages of his fiction in—to take a phrase from Camus' *The Myth of Sisyphus*—"a

Reprinted with permission from Nathan Scott, *Ernest Hemingway, A Critical Essay* (Grand Rapids, Michigan: William B. Erdmans, 1966), 19–29.

universe suddenly emptied of illusion and light," where every type of consolatory transcendentalism appears to have lost its persuasiveness and cogency. But he is also like these artists in feeling, as Conrad once remarked, that what is "so hopelessly barren in declared pessimism is just its arrogance." So, unlike, say, the Hardy of *Jude* or the Dreiser of *Jennie Gerhardt*—but in very much the manner of *The Trial* or of Camus' *The Plague*—Hemingway does not give himself to vague, showy speculations about Truth and about the terrible Enigma Behind It All: his characteristic manner is, rather, one of close-lipped reticence and reserve, and he has no great penchant for the rhetoric of metaphysical nihilism. But, nevertheless, a "blackness, ten times black," is there, in the fiction—and a powerful expression of it is to be found in one of his most famous short pieces, the story in *Winner Take Nothing* (1933) called "A Clean, Well-Lighted Place."

The clean, well-lighted place is a Spanish café on the terrace of which an old man sits drinking brandy late one evening, as the two waiters look on from within and talk about their patron.

> "Last week he tried to commit suicide," one waiter said.
> "Why?"
> "He was in despair."
> "What about?"
> "Nothing."
> "How do you know it was nothing?"
> "He has plenty of money."

Then the old man whose despair is unassuagable by money or by any of the largesse normally adjudged by the world as good fortune calls for another drink. And then he calls for still another. But, this time, the younger waiter who is eager to close up for the night and get home to his wife refuses to serve him. His partner, after the old man's departure, asks him, with a touch of masculine irony, if he is not a little apprehensive about getting home before the hour at which his wife usually expects him, but the young husband says, "No. . . . I have confidence."

> "You have youth, confidence, and a job," the older waiter said.
> "You have everything."
> "And what do you lack?"
> "Everything but work."

" 'I am of those who like to stay late at the café, " says the older waiter. " 'With all those who do not want to go to bed. With all those who need a light for the night.' "

The younger man, though, being full of confidence, is given no purchase in his own experience on what his elder colleague is getting at: so the older man patiently explains that this café where they work is a clean and attractive place, pleasant and well-lighted, and he is always reluctant to close up, he says, simply " because there may be some one who needs the café, " who needs the comfort of its cleanliness and light. And, after the younger waiter has bade him goodnight, he thinks to himself, as he darkens the café and prepares to leave, that his own need for a light in the night is prompted not by anxiety about any particular or specific thing.

It was not fear or dread. It was a nothing that he knew too well. It was all a nothing and a man was nothing too. It was only that and light was all it needed and a certain cleanness and order. Some lived in it and never felt it but he knew it all was nada y pues nada y nada y pues nada. Our nada who art in nada, nada be thy name thy kingdom nada thy will be nada in nada as it is in nada. Give us this nada our daily nada and nada us our nada as we nada our nadas and nada us not into nada but deliver us from nada; pues nada. Hail nothing full of nothing, nothing is with thee. He smiled. . . . Now, without thinking further, he would go home to his room. He would lie in the bed and finally, with daylight, he would go to sleep. After all, he said to himself, it is probably only insomnia. Many must have it.

Now it is this blackness beyond a clean, well-lighted place—this "nothing full of nothing" that destroys "confidence," that murders sleep, that makes the having of plenty of money a fact of no consequence at all—it is this blackness, ten times black, that constitutes the basic metaphysical situation in Hemingway's fiction and that makes the human enterprise something very much like a huddling about a campfire beyond which looms the unchartable wilderness, the great Nada. And it can, I think, be said that the principal presupposition guiding Hemingway's performance as a writer is the assumption that the reality with which the artist is properly engaged is that of the campfire, for it is the campfire—in its sequestered isolation, in its marooned desolateness—which is felt to be the essential human reality.

Indeed, it is just this determining slant of Hemingway's vision that establishes the fundamental character of his moralism. For, everywhere in his fiction, one senses an obsession with the importance of behaving well—around the campfire. And what is entailed here is at once an ethic of conduct (which is mimetically developed in the dramatic situations of the novels and stories) and an ethic of style, for the artist himself.

The style is, of course, universally recognized today as one of the important innovations of twentieth-century literature and as itself one of the great responses of that literature to an age of war and homelessness and broken faith. And it is in his role as stylist that Hemingway has been felt to be one of the principal *directeurs de conscience* for a generation whose wise men often say, in effect (with Yeats):

> Things fall apart; the center cannot hold;
> Mere anarchy is loosed upon the world.

Indeed, the style is now so famous and so familiar a way of dealing with modern experience that, at this late date, no extensive description of it is necessary. It is a prose, suffice it to say—aggressively colloquial and nonliterary in its rhythms and textures—whose great intention is to get straight "the facts of the matter." Typically, the sentences are short and declarative, the usual limit of syntactical complexity being the statement which is compounded of two independent clauses yoked together by a conjunction. As the late Joseph Warren Beach once remarked, it is a style "with no legato, no holding over of the effect with the blurring of the pedal": it resists whatever might hint of fanciness and "fine" writing: everything must have edge, must be kept lean and stripped and simple, for the style wants rigorously to avoid any strategem of diction or syntax that might have the effect of interposing intrusive qualifications and refinements between the reader and the immediate actuality which he is being invited to contemplate. It is a style that does not want to reach beneath the surfaces of things but which wants, rather, to restrict itself to the bare statement of this-and-that-and-this-and-that: the trick, as Hemingway felt and often said, was to get the thing "the way it was."

As he said of his early newspaper experience in the book on bullfighting of 1932, *Death in the Afternoon*: "In writing for a newspaper, you told what happened, and with one trick or another, you communicated the emotion aided by the element of timeliness which gives a certain emotion to any account of something that has happened on that day. But the real thing, the sequence of motion and fact which made the emotion and which would be as valid in a year or ten years or, with luck and if you stated it purely enough, always, was beyond me and I was working very hard to get it." But already, when he came to the writing of *In Our Time*, he had found what was to become his characteristic way of catching the right "sequence of motion and fact"—as in, for example, the following passage in "Big Two-Hearted River":

He came down a hillside covered with stumps into a meadow. At the edge of the meadow flowed the river. Nick was glad to get to the river. He walked upstream through the meadow. His trousers were soaked with the dew as he walked. After the hot day, the dew had come quickly and heavily. The river made no sound. It was too fast and smooth. At the edge of the meadow, before he mounted to a piece of high ground to make camp, Nick looked down the river at the trout rising. They were rising to insects come from the swamp on the other side of.the stream when the sun went down. The trout jumped out of water to take them.

Or here, again, is a passage bearing the same signature, from that section of *The Sun Also Rises* which is devoted to the journey of Jake Barnes and Bill Gorton by bus from Pamplona to Burguete:

The bus climbed steadily up the road. The country was barren and rocks stuck up through the clay. There was no grass beside the road. Looking back we could see the country spread out below. Far back the fields were squares of green and brown on the hillsides. Making the horizon were the brown mountains. They were strangely shaped. As we climbed higher the horizon kept changing. As the bus ground slowly up the road we could see other mountains coming up in the south. Then the road came over the crest, flattened out and went into a forest. It was a forest of cork oaks, and the sun came through the trees in patches, and there were cattle grazing back in the trees. We went through the forest and the road came out and turned along a rise of land, and out ahead of us was a rolling green plain, with dark mountains beyond it. These were not like the brown, heat-baked mountains we had left behind. These were wooded and there were clouds coming down from them. The green plain stretched off. It was cut by fences and the white of the road showed through the trunks of a double line of trees that crossed the plain toward the north. As we came to the edge of the rise we saw the red roofs and white houses of Burguete ahead strung out on the plain, and away off on the shoulder of the first dark mountain was the gray metal-sheathed roof of the monastery of Roncevalles.

One sentence gives you a fact, and the next another, and the next another; and they curtly move along, with a kind of terse telegraphy that stabs out at you with a remarkable power. It is a language whose poised and chilly laconicism suggests the impassiveness with which the great looming blackness just beyond the human campfire needs to be faced, if the self-containment which is the mark of man's dignity is not to be surrendered. When the writer insists on simply being attentive to what happens, on simply looking and noticing and reporting, on simply getting the thing "the way it was," "with nothing that will go bad afterwards," it is his way of suggesting, through his own practice as an artist, how one ought to behave around the campfire. As Philip Young has remarked, "The intense simplicity of the prose is a means by which the man says, Things must be *made* simple, or I am lost. . . ." You need to learn to look at the world straight and "true," Hemingway is saying—with no glossing of the facts, and with no grumbling—if you are to learn to confront the truth of your own precarious human existence. The "economy" of the language says you had better not take on more than you can really manage. And the style is "tense," as Professor Young reminds us, "because that is the atmosphere in which the struggle for control takes place, and the tension expresses the fact.

But Hemingway's moralism is expressed not only in his own style as an artist but also in the strict discipline of conduct to which he holds the people of his fiction accountable. And, at the level of manners, this is a discipline which is an exact analogue of that which is regarded as guaranteeing the writer's own integrity. Mark Schorer (in his widely known essay, "Technique as Discovery") has called it a "morality of the stiff lip," and Hemingway himself described it as "grace under pressure"—and either formula can serve as an admirable summary of that ideal of honor and code of conduct in which the controlling ethical norms of Hemingway's fiction are lodged. Edmund Wilson (in *The Wound and the Bow*) named the decisive principle here as one of "sportsmanship"—which suggests, perhaps in a more immediate way, the actual quality of the virtues and vices that the fiction brings into play. For it is indeed something like the discipline of the sportsman which is held up as emblematic of how a man ought to behave. Rinaldi and Frederic Henry in *A Farewell to Arms;* Harry Morgan in *To Have and Have Not*; Robert Jordan in *For Whom the Bell Tolls*; Santiago in *The Old Man and the Sea*; Wilson the hunter in "The Short Happy Life of Francis Macomber"; Jack, the old prizefighter, in "Fifty Grand"; the old matador, Manuel, in "The Undefeated"; Colonel Richard Cantwell in *Across the River and into the Trees*— all these (and many others who might also be cited) are men of a certain high kind of chivalry and of a most rigorous honesty, men who do not funk out in the moment of peril, who bear pain with reticence and dignity, who do not whine when defeated: and whatever it is that they do—whether it be bullfighting or fishing or prizefighting or hunting lions in the African bush or blowing up bridges as a military saboteur—is done with consummate skill and with pride of craft. These are men indeed who "carry" themselves in a way that bespeaks the high regard that they have for simplicity of life and precision of speech and consistency of conduct: they are tough and competent: they can be counted on in a tight squeeze, and they do not cheat or squeal or flinch at the prospect of danger, for in them conscience—at least through certain limited ranges of moral experience—is developed to a very fine point.

But then—opposed to the Rinaldis and the Jordans and the Santiagos—there are the messy people, the people who have never learned how to behave with decency and dignity, or with a modicum of competence; and there is a large gallery of these anti-heroes in the novels and stories. One thinks, for example, of the Mr. Johnson in *To Have and Have Not* who engages Harry Morgan over several days to take him out in Morgan's boat to fish the stream off the Havana coast. Throughout much of this time he sulks because nothing is caught. But then at last, on the eighteenth day, he hooks and fights and, through his own carelessness and stupidity and clumsiness, loses a great black marlin. And not only does he lose the fish but he also loses Morgan's gear, the rod and reel and line, worth nearly four hundred dollars. But, having made a fool of himself, instead of simply settling his bill and calling it quits, he stingily boggles at reimbursing Morgan for the lost tackle. Finally, though, they do, with much grumbling on Johnson's part, agree to a total figure covering eighteen days out on the stream and the lost gear, and Johnson promises, after docking and going to a bank, to return with the money—but, instead, he catches a plane for Miami and absconds.

Or, again, the portrayal of Robert Cohn in *The Sun Also Rises* makes another study in bad form. Cohn is a fawning, bathetic oaf who is filled with self-pity because of Brett's refusal of his love and who wants all his friends to know how painfully hurt he is by his chosen lady's rejection of him. And, in the design of the novel, the messiness of Cohn is beautifully juxtaposed against the splendidly integral and unpretentious manliness of the young matador, Pedro Romero, whose incorruptible simplicity is offered, presumably, as an example of the kind of strength and dignity that are achievable in the carefully codified life. In Hemingway's mythology, it is, of course, the bull ring where, of all places, a man is least able to get away with faking and where, as he stands exposed to the immediate threat of violent death, his stuff is put to the crucial test and is revealed as either genuine or false. And here is his description of Romero's style: he says:

Romero never made any contortions, always it was straight and pure and natural in line. The others twisted themselves like corkscrews, their elbows raised, and leaned against the flanks of the bull after his horns had passed, to give a faked look of danger. Afterward, all that was faked turned bad and gave an unpleasant feeling. Romero's bull-fighting gave real emotion, because he kept the absolute purity of line in his movements and always quietly and calmly let the horns pass him close each time. He did not have to emphasize their closeness. . . . Since the death of Joselito all the bull-fighters had been developing a technic that stimulated this appearance of danger in order to give a fake emotional feeling, while the bull-fighter was really safe. Romero had the old thing, the holding of his purity of line through the maximum of exposure. . . .

It is a wonderfully appealing picture that is drawn, of probity and honor and good faith. And one feels that, for Hemingway, Romero is an example of something finer and more important even than rectitude in the bullring —that, in the completeness with which this young matador's manhood has been steeled by a difficult and dangerous discipline, we are expected to behold an image of that by which we can alone hope to resist the subversive power of Nada. Indeed, it is to be remarked that, in his encounter with the young Spaniard, Cohn is utterly bested. He discovers that the boy is sleeping with Brett and goes to his room to thrash him—which he is able easily to do, having become a skillful boxer as a Princeton undergraduate. But, though he knocks the matador down repeatedly, Romero each time gets up without uttering a single cry of pain, until Cohn himself is finally routed by the boy's stamina and begins to weep. Cohn knows, in other words, how to handle his fists: but, here, he is pitted against a deeper strength: so he caves in and makes the "bad show" of himself which, according to Hemingway's lesson, is to be expected of the undisciplined man. " 'That's quite a kid,' " says Bill Gorton—to which Mike Campbell replies: " 'He ruined Cohn.' "

Or, still again, if we turn to the collection of Hemingway's stories that appeared in 1938 *(The Fifth Column and the First Forty-Nine Stories),* we may find in "The Short Happy Life of Francis Macomber" yet another example of the "ruined" man, of the man who, having failed to internalize within himself an exacting standard of honor, inevitably caves in under the pressure of the slightest adversity. There does, of course, finally come a time when this young American sportsman, Francis Macomber, appears to have won the necessary virtues, under the guidance of the hunter Wilson; but, throughout most of the story, he is constantly failing all the crucial tests. He is a man of wealth who has been able to acquire a fashionable wife, but, in their relation, he is without any authority, and his wife does not, therefore, trouble to conceal either her sexual infidelity or her contempt for his lack of force. And, as the story opens, Macomber has "just shown himself, very publicly, to be a coward": in a hunting expedition on the Tanganyika plains, he has run away from a charging lion, and, as Wilson explains, this is something that one simply does not do —"You know in Africa . . . no white man ever bolts." And not only has he turned heel and fled in panic but, on returning to their camp, he makes things even messier by apologizing and by asking Wilson not to tell anyone about the incident. "Now what in hell were you going to do about a man who talked like that," Wilson wonders, as he thinks about the whole episode which "had been about as bad as they come."

Nor is this the end of Macomber's indiscretions. For, on the next morning, another lion is tracked down, and, after being hit by a shot of Macomber's, it runs back into the tall grass. Now, of course, this last stage of the hunt is an exceedingly tricky and dangerous business, for, as Wilson says, in the appraisal of things that he gives to Macomber, " 'You can drive an unwounded lion—he'll move on ahead of a noise—but a wounded lion's going to charge. You can't see him until you're right on him. He'll make himself perfectly flat in cover you wouldn't think would hide a hare. . . . Somebody bound to get mauled.' " And, indeed, Macomber would very much like to avoid the encounter. So he proposes that the native "boys" be sent in after the beast. But Wilson has to remind him that they are not adequately armed for this "sort of a show," that to send them in would in effect be to slaughter them. And so Macomber proposes that the lion, then, be simply left in the grass—which immediately makes Wilson feel "as though he had opened the wrong door in a hotel and seen something shameful." And he has to explain to Macomber that they cannot merely pretend that the animal has not been hit, for they know that it is wounded and is therefore suffering: so it is unthinkable that they should simply walk away to leave it to die only after protracted agony. And, furthermore, were the lion to be left in the grass, someone else might run onto it unawares. Thus it is that he forces him to realize that there is nothing left to do but to go in and finish the job. But, then. when they do finally track the beast down, Macomber loses his nerve and bolts in panic, leaving Wilson to kill the charging animal.

Now, to be sure, Macomber does eventually learn how to behave with courage and honor in an extreme situation. On the following day they are hunting buffalo, and all at once he is no longer afraid: he hits a buffalo and can barely wait to go into the grass after it: the excitement and the danger now bring the good thing, the great wonderful thrill of the hunt: it is, Hemingway explains, the "sudden precipitation into action without opportunity for worrying beforehand" that brings this about with Macomber. Now the fear is "gone like an operation. Something else grew in its place. . . . Made him into a man. . . .No bloody fear." But his "happy life" is short, for, when he goes in after the buffalo, his wife shatters his skull with a shot ostensibly aimed at the charging beast but aimed unconsciously, one suspects, at Francis, whose sudden access to manhood this woman (with her own real need for the kind of husband she has had) finds insupportable. Yet, even so—as Cleanth Brooks remarks of the story (in *The Hidden God*), in a marvelous act of recollection of an eighteenth-century poem—"One crowded hour of glorious life/Is worth an age without a name."

IV. The Work, Studies of Individual Novels

MR. HEMINGWAY'S DRY-POINTS

THREE STORIES AND TEN POEMS. *By Ernest Hemingway. 12 mo. 58 pages. Contact Publishing Company. Paris. $1.50.*

IN OUR TIME. *By Ernest Hemingway. 12 mo. 30 pages. The Three Mountains Press. Paris. $2.*

EDMUND WILSON

MR. HEMINGWAY'S poems are not particularly important, but his prose is of the first distinction. He must be counted as the only American writer but one —Mr Sherwood Anderson—who has felt the genius of Gertrude Stein's Three Lives and has been evidently influenced by it. Indeed, Miss Stein, Mr Anderson, and Mr Hemingway may now be said to form a school by themselves. The characteristic of this school is a naïveté of language often passing into the colloquialism of the character dealt with which serves actually to convey profound emotions and complex states of mind. It is a distinctively American development in prose—as opposed to more or less successful American achievements in the traditional style of English prose—which has artistically justified itself at its best as a limpid shaft into deep waters.

Not, however, that Mr Hemingway is imitative. On the contrary, he is rather strikingly original, and in the dry compressed little vignettes of In Our Time has almost invented a form of his own:

They shot the six cabinet ministers at half-past six in the morning against the wall of a hospital. There were pools of water in the courtyard. There were dead leaves on the paving of the courtyard. It rained hard. All the shutters of

Reprinted with permission from *The Dial*, LXXVII, No. 4 (Oct. 1924), 340–341.

the hospital were nailed shut. One of the ministers was sick with typhoid. Two soldiers carried him downstairs and out into the rain. They tried to hold him up against the wall but he sat down in a puddle of water. The other five stood very quietly against the wall. Finally the officer told the soldiers it was no good trying to make him stand up. When they fired the first volley he was sitting down in the water with his head on his knees.

Mr Hemingway is remarkably successful in suggesting moral values by a series of simple statements of this sort. His more important book is called In Our Time, and below its cool objective manner really constitutes a harrowing record of barbarities: you have not only political executions, but criminal hangings, bullfights, assassinations by the police, and all the cruelties and enormities of the war. Mr Hemingway is wholly unperturbed as he tells about these things: he is not a propagandist even for humanity. His bull-fight sketches have the dry sharpness and elegance of the bull-fight lithographs of Goya. And, like Goya, he is concerned first of all with making a fine picture. He is showing you what life is, too proud an artist to simplify. And I am inclined to think that his little book has more artistic dignity than any other that has been written by an American about the period of the war.

Not perhaps the most vivid book, but the soundest. Mr Hemingway, who can make you feel the poignancy of the Italian soldier deciding in his death agony that he will "make a separate peace," has no anti-militaristic *parti pris* which will lead him to suppress from his record the exhilaration of the men who had "jammed an absolutely perfect barricade across the bridge" and who were "frightfully put out when we heard the flank had gone, and we had to fall back." It is only in the paleness, the thinness of some of his effects that Mr Hemingway sometimes fails. I am thinking especially of the story called Up in Michigan, which should have been a masterpiece, but has the curious defect of dealing with rude and primitive people yet leaving them shadowy.

In Our Time has a pretty and very amusing cover designed from scrambled newspaper clippings. The only objection I have to its appearance is that the titles are throughout printed without capitals—thus: "in our time by ernest hemingway—paris." This device, which used to be rather effective when the modernists first used to use it to call attention to the fact that they had something new to offer, has now grown common and a bore. The American advertisers have taken it over as one of their stock tricks. And it is so unsightly in itself that it is rather a pity to see it become—as in the case of Mr Hemingway's book and Mr Hueffer's "transatlantic review"—a sort of badge of everything that is freshest and most interesting in modern writing.

THE SHOCK OF VISION: AN IMAGIST READING OF *IN OUR TIME*

RICHARD HASBANY

The age demanded an image
Of its accelerated grimace. . . .
Ezra Pound

SOURCE AND INFLUENCE STUDIES are valuable only if they make the reader more sensitive to the author's goals and techniques. Numerous studies deal with the influences on the young Ernest Hemingway, and they are very useful in helping us view his early work. But I would like to suggest that they have left uncredited one movement that probably helped shape and inform the earliest major collection of stories, *In Our Time*. The movement was imagism, and the recognition of its possible influence in the conception of *In Our Time* may perhaps lead us to a new, more satisfactory reading of that work.

The standard list of literary influences on Hemingway is well known but perhaps useful to review. Hemingway remarked to Frank Mason in 1922 that he was intending to model his career after Sherwood Anderson's.[1] His admiration for Anderson's "simply written" stories is most transparent in the story, "My Old Man," and it is very possible that the idea of the unified short story anthology for *In Our Time* was first excited by *Winesburg, Ohio*. But Anderson's letters of introduction to Stein and Pound were probably his greatest service to the young author, for these two broadened and deepened Hemingway's understanding of perceptions and the precise imagistic techniques that might best render those perceptions of reality.

Stein's technique of rendering subjective states of characters through repetition, or insistence as she labeled it, is evident in the early stories of her frequent visitor. The repetitious phrase of Stein captures a rhythm of imprecise thought and perception, of the mind hitting and missing and hitting again what it really sees and truly feels. It creates a sense of the reader's entering the character's mind and remaining there in nearly motionless, directionless hovering as that mind is in the process of perceiving the present or recalling the past. The technique and effect is seen in Hemingway's "Cat in the Rain," and "On the Quai at Smyrna." In the latter, insistence is used to show us how the sights and sounds of the quai have become recurring and haunting images in the mind of the officer. So, it is probably through Stein that Hemingway began to recognize the power and importance of the single, repeated word—its possibilities as a plastic and emotionally suggestive object.

There is another sense in which Stein led Hemingway to a recognition of the importance of the single word. Her comment about those first stories Hemingway gave her to read is justly famous. "There is a great deal of description in this, she said, and not particularly good description. Begin over again and concentrate, she said."[2] It is probable that Stein intended "concentrate" to mean condense—make things concise and clear, not work harder as Charles Fenton would have it.[3] If this was not her intent, it was her, and Ezra Pound's, most important effect.

A great body of esthetic writing experience and theory filtered its way to Hemingway through his reading and through Stein and Pound. From these two tutors came the French traditions based in Flaubert and the Parnassians and their descendants that combine exactness and suggestiveness. George Wickes sees Flaubert's unemotional, matter-of-fact manner influencing Stein in her *Three Lives*. It is likely that these qualities were promoted by Stein in her talks with Hemingway; it is certain that they did find their way into his work. And behind Pound's penciled comments and crossed-out adjectives lies Flaubert's doctrine of *le mot juste*.[4] Pound was very much involved with Flaubert's work in those early years of the 1920's, praising and defending it in the "Paris Letters" for *The Dial*.[5] Also lurking behind the deletions was the non-French and certainly important Mark Twain for whom, to paraphrase, the difference between the almost right word and the right word was the difference between a lightning bug and lightning.

The right word obsession led to precision. But the right word meant even more than this. For Pound using the right word was the means of keeping a language alive and keeping man and institutions human. "The *mot juste* is of public utility. . . . We are governed by words, the laws are graven in words, and literature is the sole means of keeping these words living and accurate."[6] Pound's view probably reinforced Hemingway's own sense of the important relation of an esthetic verbal work to its time. Certainly this linking of disciplined precision with presentation of images that speak with urgency to their time is seen in *In Our Time*. And further reinforcing the emphasis on precision that Hemingway heard propounded by Pound came the always socially relevant content and exactness of technique of Chekhov and Turgenev, authors Hemingway read in books from the shelves of Sylvia Beach's Shakespeare and Co.[7]

Add Cézanne to journalism, Stein, Pound, and the Russian authors and we have the influences that are generally credited for exciting in Hemingway a passion for exactitude, visual presence, emotional control, and relevance to the conditions of contemporary life. After a close reading of *In Our Time*, however, the reader may sense the possibility of another influence making itself subtly felt. The almost subliminal presence one may feel is that of the imagist, those theories and poets who seemed to appear and then pass without causing a first magnitude impression on the current of literature. They deserve, implies Stanley Coffman in the title of his fine study of them, only a chapter in the history of modern poetry.[8] Perhaps it is not strange, then, that they are never mentioned in relation to Hemingway or to the fiction of the period. Yet Pound, so important for and influential on Hemingway in those first Paris years, had been deeply immersed in the imagist movement. He joined in 1909 the informal dining and talking club containing the prime mover and theorist of imagism, T. E. Hulme. It was Pound who first used the term "imagiste" in the November, 1912 issue of *Poetry,* and it was Pound who gave the loose guidelines of the group in 1913.[9] It is true that Pound moved from imagism to vorticism and other "schools" around 1914, but Pound's work seems to reflect the continuing and strong influence of imagist do's and don'ts. The Chinese works of *Cathay* (1915) and the haiku-like poetry of *Lustra* (1916) show the continuing importance of the clear visual image in Pound's work. *Hugh Selwyn Mauberley* (1920) seems to evidence the oblique influence of the imagists. So it is likely that the thinking of the imagist poets was made available to Hemingway through Pound in 1922–1924. These were the years of composition of the *In Our Time* pieces.

Hemingway was aware of what the contemporary poets were doing, and this is not surprising when we recall that he liked to think of himself as a poet. His first book was *Three Stories and Ten Poems* (1923). It is certain that Hemingway had read all of Eliot; he did not judge the poems great, but he saw them as perfect in their way.[10] Their "way" in "Preludes" and *The Waste Land* and others shows the poet working to evoke an emotional response in the reader through the objective correlative, the objective presentation of states and things. It is possible to see the objective correlative as a concept based ultimately in the ideas of the imagist. Further, we must note that in 1923 Pound was promoting the work of one of the contributors to the 1914 *Des Imagistes: An Anthology*—William Carlos Williams. A volume of William's work was to be published by Contact Press at the same time as Hemingway's *Three Stories.* Exposure to imagism would have been hard to avoid.

The goals and demands of imagist writing may have appeared to Hemingway to have potential use beyond the confines of works looking like poetry.

In *Poetry,* Pound, under F. S. Flint's name, listed only three goals, the third dealing with rhythm and not vital to our discussion. "1. Direct treatment of the "thing,' whether subjective or objective. 2. To use absolutely no word that did not contribute to the presentation."[11] The "Preface" to the 1915 *Some Imagists Poets: An Anthology* expands on the Pound goals. The aims of the group were:

1. To use the language of common speech. . . .

. . . .

4. To present an image. . . . We are not a school of painters but we believe that poetry should render particulars exactly and not deal in vague generalities. . . .
5. To produce poetry that is hard and clear, never blurred nor indefinite.
6. Finally most of us believe that concentration is the very essence of poetry.[12]

As if to underscore the fact that these goals do not refer only to poetry, despite the use of the word "poetry" in nearly every item, the 1915 *Anthology* contains several prose pictures by Amy Lowell. They are much like the interchapter sketches of *In Our Time* except that they are less exact, less controlled. Certainly none of the dictums stated in these two landmark declarations are in opposition to Hemingway's art, and indeed the dictums provide the best terms for discussing his work.

The basis for all the imagist doctrines can be found in the writings of T. E. Hulme, the man who started the "Poet's Club" in 1908. Here the first imagist poems were read and discussed; the Club is a kind of predecessor to the dining and talking group that Pound joined the following year. Though Pound must have known of Hulme's thinking and may have passed it on to Hemingway in some form, it is not so important that Hemingway knew these speculations and writings of Hulme's as it is to see that the two men were attempting the same things in their writing.

Hulme's speculations on the nature of language and poetry form a philosophic ground for the practical pronouncements of imagism that came later. Hulme's goal was a metaphoric, thingy use of language that would escape reductive abstractions and pass beyond logical perception, and instead would give the reader a perception of a finite but complex actuality. Most things can be separated and analyzed. As each part is separated and scrutinized, said Hulme, the relationship of the parts becomes clear. Such separation is the process of explanation and abstraction. A rose is petal A joined at the base to petal B joined at the base to petal C etc. But that sort of perception is the perception of abstractions, not of the real thing. In literature it is the kind of perception fostered in the careful psychological or ideological logic of the well-constructed plot, the Ibsenite exposition. This is the kind of exposition Hemingway carefully avoided in trying to create his sense of life in our time. He apparently saw that a different, non-abstract and non-analytical method must be employed.

For Hulme (and for Hemingway in *In Our Time*) escape from logical exposition came through the image—the focussing in on the thing itself, avoiding statements which suggest articulation of parts. In the image an intuitive perception of the complex interpenetration of parts is achieved rather than an understanding of spatial and time relationship of parts in an $A+B+C$ kind of relationship. Pound succinctly states this quality of the image in his short definition of the image in *Poetry*.

An "Image" is that which presents an intellectual and emotional complex in an instant of time. . . . It is the presentation of such a "complex" instantaneously which gives that sense of sudden liberation; that sense of freedom from time limits and space limits; that sense of sudden growth, which we experience in the presence of the greatest works of art.[13]

If the things that the writer or poet is describing, or "making" as Hemingway would insist, has time as one of its complex of interpenetrating parts, that is sequence as in a story, then more than a single image is necessary to create the intuition of meaning. "No image can replace the intuition of duration, but many diverse images, borrowed from very many different orders of things, by the convergence of their actions, direct consciousness to the precise point where there is a certain intuition to be seized."[14] What Hulme is speaking of here is obviously juxtaposition of images, or *superpositioning* of them to use Pound's term for his method in "In a Station of the Metro."

In short then, if we try to summarize what underlies the seemingly simple pronouncements of the imagists of 1913–1915 we find several complex principles of perception that are applicable to any writing, not just to poetry. The goal is to evoke a non-abstract and not necessarily intellectual response from the reader by making a startling presentation of a thing. The thing may be an object or an action, and it is startling for it is presented in naked fullness at once. The reader may never have really confronted a thing before without aid of abstract categories to "explain" it. In imagist work he must respond intuitively to that confrontation; he must respond in non-intellectual and non-categorical ways. Adjuncts to this underlying theory of writing are organic unity, of course; the avoidance of superfluities; and the use of any techniques such as refrain that help to present the thing and make the reader "see." If this is the basis of imagism, and I believe it is, then Hemingway's *In Our Time* must be called an imagist work.

The early reviewers saw something unique in the work. Edmund Wilson's review of the Three Mountains Press edition in *The Dial* pictured Hemingway as strikingly original. "In the dry compressed little vignettes of *In Our Time* Hemingway has almost invented a form of his own:. . ."[15] But Wilson does not try to analyze or define exactly what this new form is. Paul Rosenfeld caught another of the essential qualities of the work, juxtaposition, but he did not speculate on the source of the technique or its uses.[16] It was the unnamed reviewer of the New York *Times Book Review,* however, who came closest to describing the essentially imagist quality of the book. The reviewer echoes the "Preface" to the 1915 imagist *Anthology* when he labels Hemingway's language "hard and clear," and when he says that Hemingway's "prose seems to have an organic being of its own."[17] He reminds us of Pound's definition of the effect of the function of the image in *Poetry,* 1913, and of Pound's warning to writers not to be "viewy." "The items which make up the collection of *In Our Time* are not so much short stories . . . as preludes to a mood, composed with accurate and acute finesse to converge in the mind of the reader. Mr. Hemingway is oblique, inferential, suggestive rather than overt, explicit, explanatory."[18] Finally the reviewer goes to the source of the energy of the book, and he finds it where T. E. Hulme found the source of all language's energy.

Here is an authentic energy and propulsive force which is contained in an almost primitive isolation of images, as if the language itself were being made over in its early directness of metaphor. Each story, indeed, is a sort of expanded metaphor, conveying a far larger implication than its literal meaning.[19]

This unnamed reviewer almost said it all. He sees nearly every poetic, imagist technique in *In Our Time,* yet he never explicitly declares any link between Hemingway and that school. We, then, will simply take the short step that this reviewer did not take.

Hemingway confronted several problems in composing *In Our Time.* He was using various material that had been published before in both newspapers and books.[20] Further, he evidently wanted to evoke a feeling for the realities of contemporary life—to suggest the raw facts and the zeitgeist of living in the world of 1900–1925. How to give a unity to disparate forms and subjects, news releases about refugees, short stories about horse racing, that was his problem.

It was obviously a more difficult problem than Anderson faced in *Winesburg, Ohio* where only one genre and a single setting were used. That he strove consciously to achieve some kind of unity and form is confirmed by Clinton Burhans Jr. in his persuasive essay.[21] But the exact nature of the book's overall unity may be difficult to define.

There is the unifying thread of Nick Adams growing up. This thread is essential but does not bind together the total work. There are the thematic threads of war, violence, sports, love, and marriage. The recurring subjects or themes are again essential but somehow partial. There is the possibility of an argumentative thread, i.e., the presentation of a problem and a resolution to that problem. This is the kind of unity that Burhans proposes. But can we accept the idea that Nick and other characters in the book really come to any resolutions, come to grips with the horrors of life in their time? George and Nick in "Cross Country Snow" do indeed accept responsibility of marriage and school, but they accept it without joy.

> "Maybe we'll never go skiing again, Nick," George said.
> "We've got to," said Nick. "It isn't worth while if you can't."
> "We'll go, all right," George said.
> "We've got to," Nick agreed.
> "I wish we could make a promise about it," George said.
>
> . . . .
> "There isn't any good in promising. . . ."[22]

There is a pervading sense in the passage of the ambiguous value of responsibility and of how uncertain are the possibilities for things that make life worth living. Rather than acceptance and resolution of tension, there is a tired, slightly bitter cynicism.

In the final short story, "Big Two-Hearted River," we leave Nick avoiding the swamp and retreating to his camp and his womb-like tent just as he has retreated from society and personal horrors. He is conscious of just holding on to himself (a phrase that occurs often in Hemingway) and is evading threats, though in an oblique way he may be preparing himself to meet them later. The Greek King in "L'envoi" has not really come to grips with the facts of his situation. In short, Hemingway has created a world in which resolutions and points of repose are most difficult, though not absolutely impossible to achieve in face of the given realities. What can answer to the realities of "Indian Camp" and Chapter XIV wherein the bullfighter, Maera, is killed? Almost nothing can, suggests Hemingway, except perhaps not thinking about those realities and coming to some kind of a separate, subjective peace. Certainly Pound would have advised against seeking to give broad solutions and make things pat in a work of art. In his 1922 "Paris Letters" about Flaubert, Pound discusses the human situation and the great and less great writers who investigate it. In the discussion's categories Hemingway seems closer to the writer of the first magnitude than to the provincial writer.

With any provincial writer there is an 'answer' . . . a touch of kindness, the payment of the installment due on the mortgage, et. cetera; but with Flaubert, with the writer of first magnitude there is no answer, humanity being what it is, and the given character moving inside its own limitations there is *no* easy way out; . . . the impass is a biological impasse. Human capacity, perseverance, endurance continuing static, it will continue to be an impasse.[23]

It is the feeling of impasse rather than the feeling of deliverance through possible solution that is the dominant emotion evoked by *In Our Time.* The unity is not of a logical kind—from problem to resolution, even ambiguous resolution. If there is any unity it is a unity of impression. He uses the imagists' technique of images juxtaposed to create in the end one vast image wherein, to use T. E. Hulme's words, "many diverse images . . . by the convergence of their actions, direct consciousness to the precise point where there is a certain intuition to be seized." It is the unity of a precise point when a reality, a truth is perceived that Hemingway is striving for. He tries to juxtapose thirty-two separate pieces, each a kind of image in itself, into a total image. Such a task is difficult, but Hemingway succeeds remarkably well. To mark his success we must first look at individual pieces to see if they do indeed work as images, and to see then how imagistic and other poetic principles operate in the book as a whole to give it the kind of unity and organic form we have been discussing.

Because of their brevity and spareness, the interchapters of *In Our Time* seem most closely to approach what is traditionally considered an image. But even they seem very different from images unless we recall that Pound allows the image to be a thing objective or subjective. A "thing" is not necessarily an object, and Hemingway need not describe a pear or a wheelbarrow. He may try to present an action or emotion nakedly seen but suggestive to sub-levels of consciousness. The kind of action and emotion that the reader is to confront varies according to the point of view of the piece. Although there has been little discussion of Hemingway's use of point of view in *In Our Time,* such a consideration is relevant for us here. He uses both first person and third person points of view, and with both he is trying to create an expanded image of some kind. In the first person chapters and stories he presents the subjective emotions of the narrator—an image of an emotion created by presenting what that character perceives, those actions that have combined to create the emotion. In presenting the thing, the emotion, Hemingway has exercised an imagist poet's discriminating selectivity. He must lay bare only the objects and actions that cause an intuitive perception in the reader.

In Chapter I we see Hemingway working to create just such an "image" of emotion through a first person sketch. The narrator is a Nick-like character recalling a complex of actions as he and his battery march to the front. The description is slight. The only conventionally descriptive elements other than the possessive adjective "my" are the two predicate adjectives "drunk" and a prepositional phrase that functions as an adverb. The picture relies upon the selection of facts that the narrator makes, and the facts he presents are actions. The battery marches in the dark. The lieutenant rides his horse into a field and confides to the horse how drunk he is. The adjutant warns the narrator to put out his kitchen fire even though the battery is fifty kilometers from the front. That is all. We are given actions that seem to occur almost independently of each other. They are not necessarily sequential, and there is little or no cause-and-effect relationship between them. They are simply juxtaposed and presented to us. Because of the essence of the actions and the juxtaposition of them, a complex perception is evoked—and it is the perception of the emotion of the narrator. His only comment is the inarticulate "It was funny going along that road." (p. 13) He does not tell us what to think, probably because he cannot. Instead he has brought us to the emotion that he feels—the rather bemused perception of danger and fear driving men to half-comical and irrational behavior.

Three other chapters are in strict first person point of view; "L'envoi," and "On the Quai at Smyrna" use a more complex first person wherein a reporter gives us the words of another character. Chapter III and IV present us with two subjective images. Chapter III is similar in technique to Chapter I; it presents the actions as the narrator selectively saw them. Through his selection and nearly naked presentation we enter his mind. He and others shoot Germans as they (the Germans) come over a garden wall. The visual image is clear, but seems to lack emotional suggestiveness or complexity unless one sees the emotional importance of two or three details that the narrator reports. "He [the German] had so much equipment on and looked awfully surprised and fell down into the garden." (p. 33) The narrator has perceived a human quality in the German when he notices that look of surprise. What is his reaction to this human quality? He never says. "We shot them. They all came just like that." (p. 33) Does the last sentence imply that they all looked surprised, that the narrator saw a common humanity in each? Is there a feeling of guilt implied in the very spareness and reticence of the piece? The selection of details suggests something hidden, something that teases and causes complex response on the part of the reader. We look into the mind of a man reminiscent of Nick, a sensitive man experiencing an *almost* conscious recognition of the painful proximity and ambiguity of life and death, guilt and innocence. Forced by war to kill, his defenses begin to work, and he tries to repress and banish all emotion from his words. Yet he is haunted by that look of surprise in a garden. The soldier's ambiguous and unverbalized perception, insistently implicit in his concrete report of object and action, is exactly the "intellectual and emotional" complex that the imagist sought to create.

But Chapter III does not stand alone. It must be read in relation to Chapter IV in which a similar situation occurs. The enemy in Chapter IV must climb over a wrought iron grating that the new narrator and his compatriots have jammed across a bridge. Here, in contrast, the narrator's emotions are made explicit. This British soldier obviously enjoys the action of war, respects courage, and generally sees the affair as a game of movable pieces. "It was absolutely topping. They tried to get over it, and we potted them from forty yards. . . . Their officers were very fine. We were frightfully put out when we heard the flank had gone, and we had to fall back." (p. 43) When this piece is read as being consciously juxtaposed to Chapters I and III, the meanings of all three expand to include, among other things, an ironic comment on the British attitude toward war.[24] What is being developed is not a series of isolated images, but a complex of images of men at war. The man at war is many things —bemused, a victim of ambiguous but real guilt, and a man engrossed, totally at ease, and professionally cold. A larger unity is emerging—a single encompassing image of the complexity of the human response to the action of war. Through juxtapositioning of single images there is developing the convergence Hulme posited.

Later inter-story sketches become more complex presentations. They tend to have more narrative development. An example is Chapter XIII where the narrator shows us a bullfighter drowning his fear of fighting that afternoon by drinking and dancing in the procession. The two other fighters for the day try to stop him. They cannot. They will have to fight his bulls for him.

"Yes," Maera said, "and who will kill his bulls after he gets cogida?"
"We, I suppose," I said.
"Yes, we," said Maera. "We kill the savage's bulls, and the drunkard's

bulls, and the riau-riau dancer's bulls. Yes. We kill them. We kill them all right. Yes. Yes. Yes." (p. 150)

The uncommented-on actions lead to the final uninterpreted words of Maera. The reader perceives in the dramatic actions and statements some deeply felt tension and emotion. But it is an ambiguous emotion. The words of Maera communicate something, but we are not sure what. Bitterness? Disgust?

The ambiguity of the dramatic presentation is made perhaps more complex by the following sketch in which Maera is gored and killed by a bull, presumably that same afternoon. There is no reference made to the events of the morning and no condemnation of the fighter who forced the other two to fight more bulls than they were supposed to have fought. The death of Maera is presented in vivid images, but it is this imagery's juxtaposition to the previous chapter that creates a suggestive complexity. Maera's death gives the words that ended the previous sketch new possibilities of meaning—bitterness, hatred, or a premonition and resolution. Maera perhaps senses himself to be a predestined victim, yet he goes on to face the trial of the bullfight. Without comment Hemingway suggests a complex story of cowardice and irresponsibility evoking bitterness, courage, and a horrible yet tragic death. Not once does he resort to the "abstract counter" Hulme warns against. It is important to notice that the theme of man's emotional reaction to imminent or present violence has been continued from the first chapters of the book but has undergone variations in setting and kinds of violence.

We have been dealing mainly with the first person sketches in order to illustrate the concept of the expanded, subjective image. The same kind of image is evident in the third person sketches and in the stories. In these pieces the actions are presented objectively and are juxtaposed without comment so that any emotional response and perception of meaning is experienced without authorial prompting. The specific methods of objective presentation vary. In "Cat in the Rain" images become symbolic.

The American wife stood at the window looking out. Outside right under their window a cat was crouched under one of the dripping green tables. The cat was trying to make herself so compact that she would not be dripped on.

"I'm going down and get that kitty," the American wife said.

"I'll do it," her husband offered from the bed.

"No, I'll get it. The poor kitty out trying to keep dry under a table."

The husband went on reading, lying propped up with the two pillows at the foot of the bed.

"Don't get wet," he said. (p. 118)

The cat serves obviously in the story as symbol for the wife and her feeling of being shut out of her husband's life—of being dripped on. Juxtaposed to the image of the cat's coldness and isolation is the image of the husband, self-sufficient and comfortable on the bed. The dialogue presents a dynamic picture of the relationship. The wife makes an appeal, a statement of the cat's (and her own) need for warmth. The husband only plays at responding to this appeal. The appeal is rejected and the wife is on her own. All this is done through presentation of symbolic images and dialogue of drama-like objectivity.

In "Out of Season" Hemingway treats the same kind of marital frustration, but the technique is more subtle and complex. The severely strained relationship of husband and wife is suggested most obliquely through their dialogue.

"I'm sorry you feel so rotten, Tiny," he said. "I'm sorry I talked the way I did at lunch. We were both getting at the same thing from different angles."

"It doesn't make any difference," she said. "None of it makes any difference."

"Are you too cold?" he asked. "I wish you'd worn another sweater."

"I've got on three sweaters." (p. 129)

It is as if we had casually overheard a conversation on a train; we perceive suddenly the depth of an estrangement though not the causes or details of it. The suggestion of the malaise is reinforced by the out-of-joint relationship between the Italian guide, Peduzzi, and his townspeople, by the fact that the guide and the Americans are trying to fish out of season, by the spit-rain weather, and by the wasteland imagery of the river. "They turned down the bank and Peduzzi stood, his coat blowing in the wind, gesturing at the river. It was brown and muddy. Off on the right was a dump heap." (p. 131) The juxtaposition of images creates of the relationships between men a single, over-all impression that is complex and best described by the story's somewhat metaphorical title, "Out of Season."

Such juxtaposition of traditional image and action-dialogue, or dramatic, image is the basic technique in the longer stories. The visual image of the abandoned mill town, Horton's Bay, is juxtaposed to the dramatic image of a dying youthful love affair in "The End of Something." The autumn storm of "The Three Day Blow" becomes a symbolic image of the emotional malaise of Nick, his vague sense of lost warmth and fullness because of the end of the affair with Marjorie.

So also are the images of "Big Two-Hearted River" symbolic when juxtaposed to Nick's actions. From earlier sketches and stories we know that Nick has been to war and has emerged a wounded man. Knowing this, the image of the burned out Seney and surrounding area takes on several levels of possible meaning for us. It is reminiscent of a bombed-out town where only a few foundations remain. It suggests a destructive principle existant in the world —destructive of both man and his works, and destructive of nature itself. Following the Seney image, Nick moves to the river where he sees some trout. The moment is presented matter-of-factly.

Nick looked down into the clear, brown water, colored from the pebbly bottom, and watched the trout keeping themselves steady in the current with wavering fins. As he watched them they changed their positions by quick angles, only to hold steady in the fast water again. Nick watched them a long time. (p. 177)

This and other actions seem isolated and pointless until we recognize that through skillful juxtaposition Hemingway has created in them a meaning, an interpenetrating complexity of relationships that must be grasped as a whole. Nick is running. "His muscles ached and the day was hot, but Nick felt happy. He felt he had left everyting behind, the need for thinking, the need to write, other needs." (p. 179) "His mind was starting to work. He knew he could choke it because he was tired enough." (p. 191) After these brief hints about his mental state, it becomes evident that the activities serve to keep Nick from thinking—to keep him like the trout, steady in the stream. He cannot face the swamp. He is not ready for thinking and facing things, and the story ends as it begins, with Nick evading something ugly and tragic.

Yet the story acquires great psychological complexity and tension by suggesting a paradoxically affirmative dimension to Nick's evasive actions. Nick senses that the apparently ubiquitous physical and psychic destruction is actually not universal or eternal. "Seney was burned, the country was burned over and changed, but it did not matter. It could not all be burned. He knew that." (p. 180) And because he knows that something can be saved, Nick works to save it by his evasive yet loving revelry of senses and processes. By living at a purely sensuous level, he is able to make a kind of peace with the world. He is able to live richly in a way—to affirm. " 'Chrise,' Nick said," as he eats, " 'Geezus Chrise,' he said happily." (p. 188)

He knows himself and what he can do. This fishing trip is in some ways a demonstration to himself of his abilities. He is proud and confident of his wilderness knowledge. "He did not need to get his map out. He knew where he was from the position of the river." (p. 181) "He had wet his hand before he touched the trout, so he would not disturb the delicate mucus that covered him. If a trout was touched with a dry hand, a white fungus attacked the unprotected spot." (pp. 201–202) In a wilderness context Nick is in control. He can cope. So in the lengthy catalogue-like presentation of concrete action and objects, Hemingway is creating a complex image of a man who is running from the threats of civilization and of his past experiences, but who is simultaneously confronting himself and recognizing his inability to face the swamp as yet. He accepts the present inability and lives affirmatively if precariously on the sensory level until he will feel able to risk facing the threats represented by the mysterious and tragic swamp.

The story has puzzled many readers, and Hemingway once marked and lamented the fact that no one seemed to have read it correctly. The reason may have been, and may still be, failure to read the story as one would read an imagist poem where presented objects and actions make sense through juxtaposition. In this story the juxtapositions are exceedingly subtle. We must look also outside "Big Two-Hearted River" to the other stories and to Chapter VI in which Nick is wounded. We must look, for instance, to the character of Krebs in "Soldier's Home," who at first does not want to talk about his war experiences, and who doesn't want to become involved in anything in which there may be consequences. Within "Big Two-Hearted River" itself the reader may notice the juxtaposition of statements about Nick's fear of fishing in the swamp with his obsession and enjoyment of processes and sensuous perception. The fear and enjoyment are juxtaposed to suggest a complex psychological condition, and we must perceive that condition from the facts and their positioning alone.

Such are the basic techniques of the book. There is at least one other that is essentially poetic and commonly employed by the imagist poets. The technique is that of the leit-motiv or refrain and is found in Eliot's "Preludes" and *The Waste Land,* in E. E. Cummings, in Pound, and in William Carlos Williams. A look at the use of this technique will show a carefully suggestive rather than explicit or formula-like integration of the work. What emerges is rather like a musical point-counterpoint integration. In "On the Quai at Smyrna" several themes and images are introduced which recur later in new contexts as variations on the impression of pain and horror established in this piece. The first and most obvious theme is that of the soldier recalling and dealing with war memories. Such recollections in various intensities of horror and bemusement occur throughout the book, in Chapters I, III, IV, "Soldier's Home," and "Big Two-Hearted River."

Screams are heard in this opening sketch. "The strange thing was, he said, how they screamed every night at midnight. I do not know why they screamed at that time." (p. 9) The screams do not stop here. We hear the screams of birth labor in "Indian Camp." "On the Quai at Smyrna" begins the birth theme, and birth is associated with horror and death.

The worst, he said, were the women with dead babies. You couldn't get the women to give up their dead babies. They'd have babies dead for six days. Wouldn't give them up. (p. 10)

In "Indian Camp" the birth theme converges with the screams of the opening sketch and with death so that the three become one terrible complex of realities. In Chapter II a woman is having a baby as a procession of refugees flees the advancing armies. Over her stands a young girl, crying and frightened by the events. We are forced to think of Nick, who has witnessed the event of birth in rural Michigan and who is also frightened at the juxtaposition of birth and terror and death.

In later stories variations occur on the "generation" theme. The result of intercourse in "A Very Short Story" is gonorrhea. In "Mr. and Mrs. Elliott" there is no result at all from intercourse. In "Cross Country Snow" Nick's wife is pregnant, and we see him frightened again by the fact of giving birth, because of the responsibility it forces upon him, and probably because of the pain and danger that has become inseparably linked with birth in his mind. Thus does the theme act as a refrain, always being varied but ever suggesting a single vision. The refrain haunts and forces the reader to an at first subconscious perception of what birth is made in this book—an associate of death and pain.

"On the Quai at Smyrna" ends with the image of mules with broken forelegs being thrown into the water. The image of broken animals occurs again in the book, and the note of violence and insufferable pain that accompanies this image makes a kind of crescendo. The broken animal is seen, of course, in the chapters on bullfighting. In Chapter X a horse has been gored and his entrails hang down, blood pumping from between his front legs. In Chapter XII the horror of the image reaches a climax. Though Hemingway recognized a tragic grandeur in the bullring, he saw also its ghastly literal realities. In this chapter he has created one of his more suggestive juxtaposition of images. "Villalta standing straight and the red hilt of the sword sticking out dully between the bull's shoulders. Villalta, his hand up at the crowd and the bull roaring blood, looking straight at Villalta and his legs caving." (p. 137)

There are other image patterns used as refrains that do not begin in "On the Quai," such as the rain and puddle image seen in Chapter V, "Cat in the

Rain," and "Out of Season." The important thing about these recurrent images is their cumulative effect. Images of horrible action or objects juxtaposed and repeated in different contexts creates a sense of the universal reality of that horror. Birth is everywhere accompanied by death; children are everywhere haunted by their knowledge of this fact. Life is so single mindedly awful it seems a conscious, cosmic prank; it starts in pain, is pervaded by painful initiation, dislocation, guilt, desire, fear of responsibility, and isolation; and it is always threatened by bestial violence and death. Man emerges from the carefully controlled individual images and through the cumulative effects of the juxtaposed images as a wounded creature in a ugly and treacherous world. The central image or symbol for the book, and Philip Young says for all of Hemingway's work, occurs in Chapter VI where Nick is wounded. His literal wounding merely makes concrete the metaphorical wounding he has been undergoing in every story to that point. The non-Nick stories seem to show the wounding to be a universal fact. The cosmic prank is on everyone.

So Hemingway assaults us with image superimposed on image until a new totality of insight is created from the thirty-two pieces of work he has assembled and superpositioned on each other. It is a creation of an image of a time, an image of an agonized humanity, grimacing at the reality of being in our time, and yet also the image of naivete and hope in the figures of the revolutionary and of the Greek king, who despite his house imprisonment, wants to go to America. There is no formula for the book, no problem and solution; that would be too neat to deal with the complexity of reality. That picture would be for the moralist to create. What Hemingway attempts could not be accomplished by moral or abstract words. Those could only categorize, but they could not give the vision flesh and make it real. Hemingway rose to his problem and developed a new technique, one giving remarkable sophistication to the unified short story anthology and expanding the possible uses of the imagist poets' juxtaposition-image techniques. The result is a new kind of book, a book with a central image like a vortex, turbulent and vast, drawing us in and shooting us out, evoking grimace and pain and an ambiguous though moving understanding.

1. Charles A. Fenton, *The Apprenticeship of Ernest Hemingway, The Early Years* (New York, 1954), p. 149.
2. Gertrude Stein, *The Autobiography of Alice B. Toklas* (New York, 1933), pp. 261–262.
3. Fenton, p. 147.
4. In *A Moveable Feast* it is this pruning for which Hemingway seems to remember Pound most.

5. See the following issues of *The Dial* for the relevant "Letters": LXXII (April, 1922), pp. 401–405, and LXXIII (August, 1922), pp. 332–337.

6. "Paris Letter," *The Dial,* LXII (June, 1922), p. 629.

7. Hemingway mentions the importance of the Russian authors in his interview with George Plimpton for the *Paris Review* in *Writers at Work,* second series (New York, 1963), p. 221, and in *A Moveable Feast,* p. 36.

8. Stanley K. Coffman, Jr. *Imagism: A Chapter for the History of Modern Poetry* (Norman, Oklahoma, 1951), p. 139.

9. Ezra Pound, "A Few Don'ts by an Imagiste," *Poetry,* I (March, 1913), pp. 200–206. In the same issue see F. S. Flint's "Imagisme." The guidelines given are also Pound's formulations.

10. Ernest Hemingway, "Homage to Ezra," *This Quarter,* I (Spring, 1925), pp. 221–225.

11. F. S. Flint, "Imagisme," p. 199.

12. "Preface," *Some Imagist Poets: An Anthology,* (New York, 1915), pp. vi–vii.

13. "A Few Don'ts by an Imagiste," pp. 200–201.

14. T. E. Hulme, "Romanticism and Classicism," in *Speculations,* ed. Herbert Read (New York, 1924), p. 135.

15. Edmund Wilson, "Mr. Hemingway's Dry Points," *The Dial,* LXXVII (October, 1924), p. 340.

16. Paul Rosenfeld, "Tough Earth," *New Republic,* XLV (November, 25, 1925), pp. 22–23.

17. "Preludes to a Mood," New York *Times Book Review* (October 18, 1925), p. 8.

18. "Preludes to a Mood," p. 8.

19. "Preludes to a Mood," p. 8.

20. For a good summary of the publishing history see Clinton S. Burhans, Jr. "The Complex Unity of *In Our Time,*" *Modern Fiction Studies,* XIV (Autumn, 1968), p. 313.

21. Burhans, pp. 313–328.

22. Ernest Hemingway, *In Our Time* (New York, 1925), p. 13. All quotes from *In Our Time* are from this edition and page references for subsequent quotations will be placed in parentheses following the material.

23. *The Dial,* LXXIII (August, 1922), pp. 336–337.

24. The ironic treatment of British sensibility is also evident in the reporter of "L'envoi" and to some extent in the British officer in "On the Quai at Smyrna." Hemingway's disdain of the British is suggested less subtly in a segment that did not appear in the final version of "Big Two-Hearted River." A crude British contempt for Frenchmen prompts Nick to declare, "Englishmen are a joke." See "On Writing," *The Nick Adams Stories* (New York, 1972), p. 242.

25. The first person story, "My Old Man," however, presents a problem in being more Andersonian, relaxed, and reflective than objective and terse. The action is filtered through the boy's consciousness and so is distanced from us. We are presented with a sensibility rather than with dramatic action in which a sensibility is implicitly suggested. Yet the story does fit into the complex vision of *In Our Time* both in its initiation theme and in its oblique terror at and fear of the world. "Mr. and Mr. Elliott" too seems alien to the book because of the author's sardonic tone. The actions here are presented without explicit comment, but we see the actions reported rather than seeing them performed. We see the characters made fools of by the author rather than seeing them make fools of themselves. We feel we are being presented with a judgment rather than with a thing, as that term has been used here. The judgment is only evident and not explicit, of course, and the story does fit into the book's developing theme of marriage and isolation. But the story fits better into the "personal spleen" genre, similar to *Torrents of Spring,* and might well have been deleted from the impersonal, objective presentations of *In Our Time.*

SUNRISE OUT OF THE WASTE LAND

RICHARD P. ADAMS

"YOU ARE ALL a lost generation," said Gertrude Stein. Perhaps they were. But if so they were lost together, and their togetherness is important. There has seldom been a literary generation the members of which were in closer communication than the American, French, and British writers of the 1920's. The liveliest center was Paris, where so many good Americans went before they died, but London, New York, and Chicago were not far away, and currents fed into the vortex from still more distant and unlikely places. Criticism has hardly begun to distinguish their relations.

Until it does, we cannot fully understand or properly assess the works of the period. They come, as all works do, from a context in which the mutual exchange of ideas was a significant element. The currents were often currents of influence in the strict sense. The New Criticism, still so-called, insofar as it tends to study individual works, out of context, is not an adequate method. We need to evolve and apply a procedure that will reassimilate the tradition of precise and careful scholarly investigation into a newer criticism, examining not only the inner structure of a work but all its outward relations too.

As a relevant instance, I offer a glance at Hemingway's *The Sun Also Rises* from a point of view determined by the hypothesis that it was directly and formatively influenced by Eliot's *The Waste Land*. This hypothesis has been suggested by others, but it has never been systematically applied.

Carlos Baker was one of the first to discuss the possibility of a close relationship between these works. His *Hemingway*, in 1952, called attention to the parallel between the "objective correlative" defined by Eliot in his essay "Hamlet and His Problems" and Hemingway's description in *Death in the Afternoon* of the way he learned to write. The resemblance is certainly close, and it is confirmed by further resemblances between the impressionistic or imagistic poems Hemingway published in various magazines beginning in 1923, together with the poetic prose sketches of *in our time,* and Eliot's

Reprinted with permission from *Tulane Studies in English,* IX (1959), 119–131.

"Preludes" and "Hysteria," collected in the *Prufrock* volume of 1917 and again in the *Poems* of 1920.

The parallel is in fact more extended than Baker's remarks would indicate. F. O. Matthiessen has reported a talk with Eliot about "Gerontion" that sheds further light. "His design," says Matthiessen, "is to give the *exact* perceived detail, without comment, and let that picture carry its own connotations. As he said once in conversation, the images here are 'consciously concrete'; they correspond as closely as possible to something he has actually seen and remembered. But he also believes that if they are clearly rendered, they will stand for something larger than themselves; they will not depend for their apprehension upon any private reference, but will become 'unconsciously general.' " This is not the language of Hemingway, but it is very close to his substance in the various comments he has made on the submerged seven-eighths of the iceberg, on the necessity of isolating and clearly rendering the aspects of an action that cause emotion, and on the fourth and fifth dimension that may be achieved in prose "if," as he puts it, "any one is serious enough and has luck." Hemingway's implication in all such remarks seems to me to be, very clearly, that prose, like poetry, can be symbolic; that it may be made to carry overtones of feeling and meaning, partly conscious, partly unconscious, that will give it rich and permanent esthetic value. Nothing could be much closer to the effect at which Eliot aims consistently in his verse.

This is not to suggest that Eliot was the only source of such ideas and techniques, or even the most important one. Gertrude Stein was experimenting on much the same lines, and Hemingway learned more directly from her than from Eliot. The same is true of Ezra Pound, and to some extent of Sherwood Anderson. In fact, the theory and method both, as Edmund Wilson has demonstrated, are characteristic of the romantic tradition, going back to Wordsworth, Coleridge, and the Germans. The term "objective correlative" itself was used, pretty much in Eliot's sense, by Washington Allston in a lecture probably written before 1840; and Allston's thinking was largely based on that of Coleridge. But there is further evidence that part, at least, of Hemingway's early education as a writer came from Eliot.

Another of Eliot's essays with which Hemingway's published statements agree is "Tradition and the Individual Talent." What Eliot says here about the importance of the historical sense in making a writer traditional, and at the same time "most acutely conscious of his place in time, of his own contemporaneity," is the same, in substance, as what Hemingway says in *Death in the Afternoon:* "The individual, the great artist when he comes, uses everything that has been discovered or known about his art up to that point . . . and then

. . . goes beyond what has been done or known and makes something of his own." Even their feelings about these ideas are closely similar. Eliot remarks that tradition "cannot be inherited, and if you want it you must obtain it by great labour," and Hemingway: "There are some things which cannot be learned quickly and time, which is all we have, must be paid heavily for their acquiring. They are the very simplest things and because it takes a man's life to know them the little new that each man gets from life is very costly and the only heritage he has to leave." Hemingway is not, as some might suppose, referring only to direct contact with life, for he goes on to say that "Every novel which is truly written contributes to the total of knowledge which is there at the disposal of the next writer who comes, but the next writer must pay, always, a certain nominal percentage in experience to be able to understand and assimilate what is available as his birthright and what he must, in turn, take his departure from." The difference in emphasis cannot obscure the fact that Hemingway, like Eliot, keenly feels the importance of a writer's relation to the literature of the past.

Parallels such as these—many more of which might easily be cited—are not the only evidence of Hemingway's debt to Eliot. There are a few direct references that deserve close study. The more or less fictitious "Author" of *Death in the Afternoon* at one point expresses his dislike of Humanists by saying to the Old Lady, "I hope to see the finish of a few, and speculate how worms will try that long preserved sterility; with their quaint pamphlets gone to dust and into foot-notes all their lust." The Old Lady likes the "line about lust," and the Author explains, "It came from Andrew Marvell. I learned how to do that by reading T. S. Eliot." This is not, in itself or in its context, an unmixed tribute. However, an earlier use of two other lines from Marvell's "To His Coy Mistress" in *A Farewell to Arms* is also connected with Eliot, less directly, and is less equivocal. Frederic Henry is about to leave his mistress, Catherine, to go back to the front. "Down below on the street a motor car honked.

> ' "But at my back I always hear
> Time's wingéd chariot hurrying near," '

I said.

" 'I know that poem,' Catherine said. 'It's by Marvell.' " She does not say, but we may note, that the association between these lines and "The sound of horns and motors" was first made in *The Waste Land*.

The same sort of thing happens to another quotation used by both authors. In *The Sun Also Rises*, Jake introduces Bill Gorton, the connoisseur of stuffed animals, to Brett, and says, " 'He's a taxidermist.'

" 'That was in another country,' Bill said. 'And besides all the animals were dead.' " Eliot uses a little more of Marlowe's text in his epigraph to "Portrait of a Lady":

> Thou hast committed—
> Fornication: but that was in another country,
> And besides, the wench is dead.

The reference helps, if we remember the word "fornication," to characterize Brett; but at the moment I wish only to indicate that it is a reference to Eliot as well as to Marlowe. The evidence occurs in *Across the River and into the Trees,* where the same quotation is associated not only with Eliot but specifically, though illegitimately, with *The Waste Land.* Colonel Cantwell is talking to Renata about his wife, a journalist, who is not literally dead but whose existence he prefers to ignore. " 'I told her about things once,' " he says, " 'and she wrote about them. But that was in another country and besides the wench is dead.'

" 'Is she really dead?'

" 'Deader than Phoebus the Phoenician.' " The intrusion of the sun god here suggests that the Colonel, at least, is quoting from memory and from a long time back.

There are also some evident verbal echoes from *The Waste Land* in *The Sun Also Rises,* as when Jake says to Cohn, " 'I like this town and I go to Spain in the summer-time,' " and when Brett says to Jake, " 'My nerves are rotten.' "

In spite of these indications, critics have been surprisingly cautious about suggesting anything like a direct influence. Malcolm Cowley, in his Introduction to the Viking Portable *Hemingway* (1949), pointed out the fact that Hemingway's "first novel . . . deals in different terms with the same legend that T. S. Eliot was not so much presenting as concealing in *The Waste Land.*" But Cowley shied away from the obvious presumption, saying, "I don't mean to imply that Hemingway owes a debt to *The Waste Land.*" His explanation was that, although Hemingway had read the poem, and the notes, and obviously "dealt with the same legend that Eliot had discovered by scholarship," he somehow succeeded in "discovering it for himself, I think, by a sort of instinct for legendary situations." This formula seems to have set the tone for later comments. Baker called his chapter on *The Sun Also Rises* "The Wastelanders," but his emphasis was heavily on Hemingway's difference from and independence of Eliot. Philip Young, in his *Ernest Hemingway* (1952) cited an impressively long list of parallels, but he too insisted mainly on differences. "In the poem," he said, "a message of salvation comes out of the life-giving rain which falls on western civilization. In Hemingway's waste land there is fun, but there is no hope. No rain falls on Europe this time, and when it does fall, in *A Farewell to Arms,* it brings not life but death."

Unlike these critics, I do mean to imply that Hemingway owes a debt to *The Waste Land.* He agreed with many of Eliot's principles; he used many of the some techniques; *The Sun Also Rises* was constructed by the same method and on the same myth as *The Waste Land;* I see no reason in the evidence not to suppose that we have here a typical case of direct, formative literary influence. Incidentally, rain does fall in *The Sun Also Rises;* and Tiresias, at the end of *The Waste Land,* is no more sexually potent, fertile, or hopeful than Jake at the end of his book. My theory is that Hemingway found what he needed in *The Waste Land* and took it. This is the sovereign right of genius, now as much as when Shakespeare exercised it, and I can see no reason why Hemingway or his critics need be at all embarrassed about it.

A brief digression into the literary history of the period will help, I think, to show what happened. Hemingway established his residence in Paris early in 1922. At that time he met Ezra Pound, who had recently revised and cut *The Waste Land.* He also met James Joyce, whose *Ulysses* was published February 2. In October *The Waste Land* was published, without notes, in the same issue of *Criterion* with Valery Larbaud's essay pointing out the parallels between *Ulysses* and the *Odyssey.* On December 15 *The Waste Land* appeared in hard covers, with notes. In November, 1923, Eliot's essay "Ulysses, Order, and Myth" came out in the *Dial.* Here Eliot formulated his statement on the "mythical method," maintaining that Joyce, by "manipulating a continuous parallel between contemporaneity and antiquity," had made a discovery that others would also have to use as "a way of controlling, of ordering, of giving a shape and a significance to the immense panorama of futility and anarchy which is contemporary history."

It was not, of course, a true discovery, but rather a re-discovery of the method by which art has always made sense of the disordered futility that contemporary history always seems to present. But Eliot's insistence on its value was more than justified at a time when exaggerated reverence for a naive version of scientific method in the experiments of the naturalists had demonstrated that something other than documentation was needed to give artistic form to a literary work. Now, anyone who had read as much as the first note to *The Waste Land* must have seen that Eliot had used the method himself before recommending it to others. Hemingway knew *Ulysses;* he knew *The Waste Land;* surely he must have wondered what he in turn might do by using the same mythical method.

Obviously he did not want to do what Eliot and Joyce had done, however much it interested him. His comparison of Eliot and Conrad in the *transatlantic review* for October, 1924, is indicative. "If I knew," he wrote, "that by grinding Mr. Eliot into a fine dry powder and sprinkling that powder over Mr. Conrad's grave Mr. Conrad would shortly appear, looking very annoyed at the forced return and commence writing I would leave for London early tomorrow morning with a sausage grinder." The point, I suspect, was that Conrad had used the mythical method too, but without calling attention to it; and that is what Hemingway has done.

It appears to have been another event, however, which precipitated Hemingway's beginning of the task itself. This was the arrival in Paris of F. Scott Fitzgerald, in May, 1925. *The Great Gatsby* had appeared on April 10, and copies had been sent by the author to Gertrude Stein and to Eliot, both of whom were highly pleased with it. Eliot had a personal reason to be, for *The Great Gatsby* has the same theme, uses the same imagery, and is based on the same myth as *The Waste Land.* Fitzgerald certainly knew what he had done, for he was a great admirer of Eliot, and Hemingway was certainly a good enough reader to see the point for himself, if Fitzgerald did not explain it. The two struck up a warm friendship and spent a good deal of time together that summer; and by July Hemingway was at work on *The Sun Also Rises.*

The catalytic effect I am here attributing to *The Great Gatsby,* as it must have struck Hemingway in the spring of 1925, was probably due to its clear surface and its appearance of simplicity, directness, and realism, as well as to the fact that it was a popular success. But the more important point, in the long run, is that under its surface lay the same solid structure of traditional myth that made *The Waste Land* a great and enduring work. The Grail legend, as presented by Jessie Weston in *From Ritual to Romance,* had already had a long and honorable career. As used by Eliot, it had a sharp and cogent relevance to the state of Western civilization in the 1920's. It was itself based on a much older tradition, that of the fertility cults explored by Frazer and others and referred to by Eliot in his first note to *The Waste Land* and at many points in the poem. *The Waste Land* also invokes the tradition of pastoral elegy, which is another outgrowth of the fertility cults. In effect, Eliot had written an elegy on Western civilization, only instead of rejoicing at the end for the rebirth or metamorphosis of a demigod, he remained uncertain whether any renewal of cultural fertility or creative power was possible. The structure is a truncated version of the death-and-rebirth cycle of the fertility myths, of the successful Grail quest, and of the typical pastoral elegy. The same is true, generally, of *The Great Gatsby,* as several critics have noted.

In *The Sun Also Rises* we find the same structural principle. In the beginning, as in *The Waste Land,* there is the modern city, chaotic, sterile, inorganic, and spiritually dead. Jake's encounter with Brett and her excursion with Cohn to San Sebastian are as meaningless as the sexual relations between the men and women in "A Game of Chess" and the typist and clerk in "The Fire Sermon." In the fishing interlude at Burguete, and at Pamplona during the early part of the fiesta, there seems to be some hope of regeneration and happiness, as in the "Death by Water" of Phlebas the Phoenician and the "damp gust/Bringing rain" in "What the Thunder Said." The hope, in both works, is dissipated. After the fiasco caused by Brett's elopement and Cohn's violent reaction thereto, Jake retreats to San Sebastian, the scene of Brett's affair with Cohn, where his swimming and diving suggest the death by water theme. But when he goes to Madrid to rescue Brett, he seems to be left with nothing, not even the illusion that physical potency would have permitted him felicity with her. His ultimate recourse is the typical gesture of the early Hemingway hero, withdrawal into himself, the beaten but undefeated individual, maintaining his integrity and his dignity as a man in spite of the outrageous conditions that have isolated him. The feeling is very close to that of the speaker at the end of *The Waste Land,* shoring fragments against his ruin and lacking even the energy of Jake's final sarcasm.

    The Sun Also Rises, however, is no more a simple expression of despair than is *The Waste Land.* It does embody the feeling Hemingway shared with Eliot and others that Western civilization was dying. But that feeling was not so naively entertained by these writers as it has been by some of their disciples. Both Eliot and Hemingway have remarked on this point. Matthiessen quotes Eliot as saying in 1931 that " 'when I wrote a poem called *The Waste Land* some of the more approving critics said that I had expressed the "disillusionment of a generation," which is nonsense. I may have expressed for them their own illusion of being disillusioned, but that did not form part of my intention.' " And Hemingway wrote to Maxwell Perkins on December 7, 1926, that "people aren't all as bad as some writers find them or as hollowed out and exhausted emotionally as some of the *Sun* generation." And we should always remember the second epigraph to *The Sun Also Rises,* in which the importance of a single generation, or a single cycle of any sort, is rather definitively deflated.

    Accordingly, we will find, I believe, that the Waste Land imagery of *The Sun Also Rises* is a more complex and ambiguous web of sterile and creative, good and evil, cheerful and desperate implications than has generally been seen. The most conspicuous item is, of course, Jake's wound, which has made him sexually impotent and therefore physically sterile. It is the same kind of wound which, according to Miss Weston, has imposed sterility on Anfortas, the Fisher King, and on his land, and *From Ritual to Romance* appears to be the only printed source from which Hemingway could have borrowed this image. Jake serves, as an objective correlative, in the same way that Prufrock, Gerontion, and Tiresias serve Eliot, to imply an opinion about the postwar world. As Matthiessen has noted in discussing Eliot, the device is highly effective for the concrete rendering of personal emotion through a medium sufficiently detached from the author's own experience to emerge as art rather than as historical or autobiographical reporting. That is, Jake is useful precisely because he differs from his author in important ways, and because he gets caught in situations that his author would not get caught in and is therefore free to create. Jake, not Hemingway, is the Fisher King.

Brett is not qualified to be a Grail maiden, but she has some relations to the older fertility myths. One is her interest in fortune-telling, which, according to Miss Weston's account of the Tarot cards, was originally the art of predicting "the rise and fall of the waters which brought fertility to the land." Her bathing, which is frequent and obsessive, also associates her with the life-giving water. At one point she is surrounded by the celebrants at the fiesta —"They wanted her as an image to dance around"—and they rush her into a wine shop, where they seat her on a cask and decorate her with a garlic wreath. Her pagan affinities are emphasized by the fact that she has just been excluded from a church; and even as a pagan she is debauched and debased. Cohn's equation of her with Circe is not as absurd as it may seem. She does turn men into beasts, and she feels like a bitch herself when she decides to run off with Romero.

Robert Cohn's position in the pattern of characters is that of the Grail knight whose quest, if successful, will restore the Fisher King to health and the land to fertility. But, like Perceval during his first visit to the castle of Anfortas, he fails to ask the right question. His quality is described by Jake on the occasion of his meeting with Brett: "He looked a great deal as his compatriot must have looked when he saw the promised land. Cohn, of course, was much younger. But he had that look of eager, deserving expectation." He is like Gatsby in his hopeless and irredeemably innocent infatuation, but nobody says of him, as Nick says of Gatsby, "that he had committed himself to the following of a grail," much less that he is " 'worth the whole damn bunch put together.' "

The other characters are more obliquely related to the pattern of the Grail legend and of the main action. Mike Campbell is perhaps another unworthy knight; he is less innocent but not any better than Cohn. Bill Gorton is better, and appears to be intended partly as a foil, but he undertakes no quest. Montoya seems, in similar fashion, qualified to be the wise guide of the Grail stories, but he stands aside from any action. So does Count Mippipopolous, another of the insiders who "know the values" but who are too sophisticated to try to do anything more than have a good time. Bill, Montoya, and the Count help to point the direction Jake is taking and the goal he approaches at the end, a perfect detachment from this world for which nothing can be done. This is not a death or a giving-up; it is rather the conclusion that in a dying civilization the only way a man can live is by repudiating the values of society, or making what Hemingway elsewhere calls "a separate peace."

Pedro Romero is also outside the pattern and at most auxiliary to the main action, but he has a somewhat different function. He represents a primitive and, before Brett seduces him, an unspoiled virility, proved by his love for the bulls and his skill in fighting them. Since the problem is how to be fertile and civilized, his example provides no direct solution. He can only be corrupted by his involvement with the sophisticates, as Montoya, Jake, and finally Brett realize. However, he provides an impressive standard by which to measure the other characters, and he shows that power, courage, and art are real and desirable. Whether or not these goods are accessible to civilized people, Romero makes them seem worth trying for.

The largest, most complex symbol in the book is the fiesta of San Fermin. This is a vacation from work, at least for Jake, and provides recreation in that sense. But it also suggests re-creation in the more fundamental way of the pagan seasonal festivals—specifically the midsummer celebration—which it closely resembles in certain particulars. Hemingway's detailed handling of some of these, such as the wine-drinking, the dancing, the pipes and drums, and the garlic wreaths, is neither accidental nor irrelevant. The whole experience clearly suggests the cleansing and purging of emotion, particularly of guilt, which the ancient rites effected. The focus on bullfighting, which Hemingway has elsewhere compared explicitly with tragedy, gives it added value and meaning.

Richard Ford, whose book on Spain Hemingway mentions favorably in *Death in the Afternoon,* associates modern bullfights with "the *taurobolia* of antiquity," in which "those who were sprinkled with bull blood were absolved from sin." Miss Weston mentions the *taurobolium* in connection with Mithraism, which was spread throughout the Western Roman Empire, and with the cult of the *Magna Mater,* the Attis cult, which she says is the primitive origin of the Grail legend. Frazer, in the *Adonis Attis Osiris* volumes of *The Golden Bough,* describes the Attis festival as a ritual enactment of the demigod's rebirth. "At Rome, and probably elsewhere," he tells us, "the celebration took the form of a carnival. It was the Festival of Joy *(Hilaria).* A universal license prevailed." He adds that the *taurobolium* was one of the secret mysteries of the cult, and describes it as a ceremonial baptism in bull's blood, which was supposed to insure rebirth to eternal life. Bulls' testicles were also used. "Probably," Frazer says, "they were regarded as a powerful charm to promote fertility and hasten the new birth." He believes, further, that on the climactic "Day of Blood" the novices of the Attis priesthood castrated themselves.

It seems to me very probable that Hemingway had all or most of this material in mind when he wrote *The Sun Also Rises,* and possibly more that I have not yet found. There certainly is a mystery about bullfighting in the book, and there is a cult here and elsewhere in Hemingway's works, as critics have only too often remarked, one ticket of admission to which is a passion, or *afición,* for bullfights. Montoya, who recognizes Jake as a true *aficionado,* "always smiled as though bull-fighting were a very special secret between the two of us; a rather shocking but really very deep secret that we knew about. He always smiled as though there were something lewd about the secret to outsiders, but that it was something that we understood. It would not do to expose it to people who would not understand." If this is analogous, as it seems to be, to the attitude of the pagan worshiper in the rites of sacrifice, revival of his god, and renewal of fertility in his land, his people, and himself, then certain definite consequences follow for the criticism of *The Sun Also Rises.* Our appreciation of the bullfighting scenes, the cult, and the structural pattern of the book is greatly enhanced if we understand that members of the cult are "in" on the secrets of creative activity and power which have mostly been lost in the waste land of modern civilization. Our understanding and judgment of the characters can also be sharpened if we see why their attitudes toward bullfighting are valid measures of their worth. Brett's inadequacy, for example, is devastatingly focused by the fact that she leaves the bull's ear given her by Romero, "along with a number of Muratti cigarette-stubs, shoved far back in the drawer of the bed-table that stood beside her bed in the Hotel Montoya, in Pamplona."

"San Fermin," as Jake remarks, "is also a religious festival," and the Christian, specifically the Roman Catholic aspect of it is kept in the foreground continually. Almost the first thing Jake does when he gets to Pamplona is to go into the cathedral and pray, at the same time regretting that he is "such a rotten Catholic . . . I only wished I felt religious and maybe I would the next time. . . ." The monastery of Roncevalles is a feature of the Burguete interlude, and perhaps has some analogy to the Chapel Perilous of the Grail legends. The

Christian aspect of the fiesta is used in somewhat the same way bullfighting is to undercut the character of Brett. When she succeeds in getting into a church, she whispers to Jake that it makes her " 'damned nervous,' " and the author's innuendo is almost too obvious. On another occasion she wants to hear Jake go to confession, "but," he reports, "I told her that not only was it impossible but it was not as interesting as it sounded, and besides, it would be in a language she did not know." So she goes to a nearby gypsy camp instead and has her fortune told—from any Christian point of view, the wench is dead. Hemingway at this period seems to have shared Eliot's opinion that one prime cause of sterility in Western civilization was loss of religious faith, although, like Eliot, he apparently had more desire to believe than strong conviction. Eliot's conviction has since increased, while Hemingway has said less and less about orthodox Christianity; but in *The Sun Also Rises* Christian and pagan religious feelings work together in perfect harmony.

There is some likeness between the combination of these elements in *The Sun Also Rises* and Milton's fusing of Greco-Roman with Judaeo-Christian images and references in "Lycidas," and the result is that Hemingway's book strikes a much more positive note than it would if it were merely a chronicle of despair. This effect is not accountable to the plot, or the characters as individuals, or the intellectual content; it is mainly a matter of imagery and its connotations, the submerged seven-eights of the iceberg. The ancient, traditional, and thoroughly religious rituals of the fiesta, reinforced by the fishing episode, keep Jake sane and healthy in spite of his wound and his arid surroundings; and they work in the same way, vicariously, for the reader whose ear is consciously or unconsciously tuned to receive their meanings. The sun does also rise, on the members of the cult, whose discipline enables them to be renewed, or figuratively reborn, with the season. They may not be many—they never have been—but they are always the hope of the future, the potentially saving remnant.

I have limited these remarks to the relation between Hemingway and Eliot, leaving out many other influences which are equally important, or more so, such as those of Pound and Gertrude Stein. These others, and Hemingway's literary backgrounds in general, need more study. One point at least is clear. Hemingway, as a literary artist, is not an isolated phenomenon. He has the usual ties with other writers and with a tradition. He is no imitator. He assimilates what he takes and turns it into something originally his own. But we can understand and value that something best if we know what its origins and external relations are.

HEMINGWAY'S *A FAREWELL TO ARMS:* THE NOVEL AS PURE POETRY

DANIEL J. SCHNEIDER

IN A WELL-KNOWN ESSAY[1] Robert Penn Warren has drawn a distinction between two kinds of poetry, a "pure" poetry, which seeks more or less systematically to exclude so-called "unpoetic" elements from its hushed and hypnotic atmosphere, and an "impure," a poetry of inclusion or synthesis, which welcomes into itself such supposedly recalcitrant and inhospitable stuff as wit, cacophony, jagged rhythms, and intellectual debate. The distinction between the two types, so helpful in the analysis of lyrics, may obviously be employed to advantage in the criticism of novels, and I should like to use it here to call attention to an aspect of Hemingway's art that has not received any extended comment. For if there are works, such as *War and Peace, Ulysses, Moby Dick,* and *The Magic Mountain,* whose power and beauty are best explained by their very "impurity"—novels that batten on the diversity of life and are most themselves when they are most "loose and baggy" (to use James's fine phrase)—the strength of Hemingway's novels is explained best, I think, by noting that they are in spirit and in method closer to pure lyric than to epic, and that they systematically exclude whatever threatens to interfere with the illusion of life beheld under the aspect of a single, dominant, all-pervasive mood or state of mind. They attempt to sustain perfectly a single emotion: they begin with it and end with it, and any scenes, characters, thoughts, or stylistic elements that might tend to weaken the dominant emotion are ruthlessly rejected. Consequently, Hemingway's art has both the virtues and the limitations of lyricism: maximum intensity on the one hand, extremely limited range on the other.

Hemingway's *A Farewell to Arms* is I think one of the purest lyric novels ever written. But if we are fully to appreciate its power—and the power of a number of other works by Hemingway—we are driven to examine the poetics of this lyricism[2] and to assess, if we can, the extent to which Hemingway has exploited the possibilities of the type.

Reprinted with permission from *Modern Fiction Studies,* XIV (Autumn 1968), 283–296.

I

The dominant emotion or state of mind behind the events of *A Farewell to Arms* is seldom stated explicitly. It is always there, informing every scene of the novel, lying beneath every descriptive passage and every bit of characterization, but it seldom shows, or it shows, at most, but a tiny part of itself, like the iceberg that Hemingway often took to be the apt image of his art. It is a bitterness, a disgust, a desolation of soul, a remorse of such depth and durance that it can be held in check only by dint of the severest, most unremitting self-control. When it does show itself clearly, this inner violence, as in Chapter XXXIV of *Farewell,* it is expressed in this way:

If people bring so much courage to this world the world has to kill them to break them, so of course it kills them. The world breaks every one and afterward many are strong at the broken places. But those that will not break it kills. It kills the very good and the very gentle and the very brave impartially. If you are none of these you can be sure it will kill you too but there will be no special hurry.[3]

The world's malevolence is taken for granted in Hemingway's novels. The artistic problem Hemingway faced was to find the correlatives of his bitterness —objects adequate to the emotion, techniques capable of rendering it as purely as possible. The tragic action, involving failure, humiliation, and, especially, the punishment and defeat of lovers was of course the chief means of conveying the essential vision, the essential bitterness. But a whole poetics of the novel which confines itself to the embodiment of such a state of mind had to be developed, and it is in the solution of minor as well as of major problems that the genius of Hemingway is finally revealed. His style, for example—the perfect correlative (as Brooks and Warren have shown) of his sense of the ruthless and arbitrary condition of the world that breaks and kills—becomes the perfect correlative too of the emotions of despair and bitterness. The careful selection of a dominant image and its reiteration through whole paragraphs and pages and chapters, so that the image presently becomes symbol, conveying both the central meaning and the central emotion, becomes Hemingway's fixed method. Perhaps the best analogy is found in the choice of a musical key and in the elaborate harmonization of notes always referring to the tonic. Ideally, when the writing is purest, every sentence will bespeak the central meaning and emotion. There will be no purely functional passages, no passages which merely illustrate a meaning, no characters or episodes given freedom to develop emotions outside the dominant bitterness. Everything will be converted into a symbol of the emotion. Where such conversion does not take place, the art fails and the novel becomes epic, not lyric; narrative, instead of the pure utterance of passion.

The determination to make the novel lyrical inevitably influences all of its parts. Character becomes, in one sense, unimportant. Characters exist for the sake of the emotion and, as in most lyric poems, need not be three-dimensional. Indeed, any full and vivid particularization of character is likely to work against the dominant emotion, for when a character is complex and fully realized, he is scarcely able to maintain a single, fixed emotion or state of mind. It is only rather highly generalized characters who can feel "purely." A lovely and brave young woman may function well in a lyric world. Represent her in such complicated terms as Joyce employs to depict Leopold Bloom and the emotion is adulterated by a thousand reservations and ironic complexities. Of course character cannot be *reduced* to passion: a writer like Poe frequently fails because he is so much interested in feeling that he virtually eliminates character altogether; but Poe's Gothic tales suggest the proper direction of the lyric novel: character must exist for the sake of the emotion, and wherever the variety and diversity of life threaten to dilute or dissipate the central emotion, life must be excluded from the novel. It is thus no fair criticism to say that Hemingway has created no memorable characters; the truth is that his novels necessarily reject such people. One may imagine what Hemingway would have to do with the "memorable" Buck Mulligan to adjust him to the world of *Farewell.* Much of the elan of the Joycean character would necessarily be sacrificed to the mood of the scene, and only so much of Mulligan's irreverence as would not undermine the sense of despair would be recorded. In short, what is rolicking insouciance in Joyce would become, in Hemingway, the doleful chant of "irony and pity"; the Rabelaisian humor would be infused with the central bitterness, and would scarcely be humor at all: Mulligan would become Rinaldi.

The action, too, must obviously become, as nearly as possible, simple, intellectually uncomplicated, and, in spirit if not in actual construction, akin to lyric soliloquy. An action involving much intellectual debate, analysis, repartee, or a multiplication of points of view is clearly antithetical to the spirit of Hemingway's lyric novels. For cerebration tends to destroy passion; intellectual analysis or agility introduces a note of objectivity that the lyric novel cannot tolerate, and debate might require the introduction of spokesmen whose personalities and whose mere presence could shatter the lyric mood. It is for this reason that the action of Hemingway's lyric novels approaches, whenever it can, the scene of prolonged suffering. The characteristic sources of complication are not new complications of "plot" in the sense that fresh *problems* are introduced to be debated and solved, but rather new wounds, new torments, so that bitterness deepens and grows toward a pitch of anguish and remorse. Hemingway is always reluctant to introduce actions that do not feed the dominant emotion (sometimes so close to self-pity) and in consequence his characteristic way of structuring the action of his novels is to employ a simple qualitative shift or oscillation between despair and happiness. In *The Sun Also Rises* the shifts are from Paris, to Burguete, to Pamplona, to San Sebastian; in *A Farewell to Arms* they are from the front, to the hospital, to the front, to Switzerland; disgust and bitterness, followed by a short respite, then back to disgust and bitterness again. The dominant emotion is intensified through these powerful contrasts with opposite emotions. And major form is reinforced by minor: brief scenes in which characters are represented as enjoying intensely food and drink or a lovely view or a simple physical comfort exist chiefly to heighten the sense of despair and bitterness; the interludes of normal pleasure are inevitably shortlived; by various signs we know that they will soon be over and that whatever one has will be taken away. Every meal, every sight, every sound thus comes to one as to a man about to be executed. That is one reason the descriptions of food and drink always seem so preternaturally vivid in Hemingway.

It is unnecessary to extend this poetics further at this point. We shall see, if we look closely at *A Farewell to Arms,* how thoroughly Hemingway has exploited the possibilities of his lyric form.

II

In *A Farewell to Arms* the dominant state of mind—the sense of death, defeat, failure, nothingness, emptiness—is conveyed chiefly by the image of the rain (with all its tonal associates, *mist, wet, damp, river, fog),* by images and epithets of desolation (chiefly *bare, thin, small,* and *fallen leaves),* and by images and epithets of impurity and corruption (chiefly *dust, mud, dirt,* and *disease).* Hemingway's method of working with the images is surprisingly uniform. I have already employed an analogy of music; another way of describing the method is to think of a painter working tiny patches of a dominant color over his entire canvas. Hemingway himself perhaps had both analogies in mind when he said, in the Lillian Ross interview, that he had "learned how to make a landscape from Mr. Paul Cezanne" and mentioned, in the same context, his imitation of Bach's counterpoint in the first chapter of *Farewell.*[4] The images are repeated so frequently that they begin to toll like bells in the mind. Virtually every sentence says, "Death, despair, failure, emptiness," because virtually every sentence contains an image or symbol associated with the dominant state of mind.

The novel begins with this state of mind, and it is established so firmly, through the repetition of the central symbols, that any emotions other than bitterness and despair may thereafter intrude only with difficulty. The typical procedure, as in lyric poetry, is to intensify the dominant emotion by means of a simple contrast of images. Thus the images of purity and vitality, introduced in the second sentence of the novel, are contrasted throughout the chapter with the images of dirt and failure:

In the late summer of that year we lived in a house in a village that looked across the river and the plain to the mountains. In the bed of the river there were pebbles and boulders, dry and white in the sun, and the water was clear and swiftly moving and blue in the channels. Troops went by the house and down the road and the dust they raised powdered the leaves of the trees. The trunks of the trees too were dusty and the leaves fell early that year and we saw the troops marching along the road and the dust rising and leaves, stirred by the breeze, falling and the soldiers marching and afterward the road bare and white except for the leaves. (p. 3)

Purity has been defiled, the life-force has been thwarted and defeated. The leaves are "powdered" by dust, the trunks too are "dusty"; the leaves fall "early"; and the empty road, "bare and white except for the leaves," becomes a perfect correlative of the inner desolation. The defilement and violation of life is further suggested by a reference to camouflage ("There were big guns that passed in the day drawn by tractors, the long barrels of the guns covered with green branches and green leafy branches and vines laid over the tractor" [p. 4]) and by a reference to the cartridge-boxes bulging under the capes of the soldiers "so that the men, passing on the road, marched as though they were six months gone with child" (p. 4). And these bitter ironies are reinforced by the introduction of the dominant symbol of the rain: not lifegiving rain causing the leaves to grow but the autumnal and winter rain causing them to fall, a rain associated with darkness, mud, and death:

There was fighting for that mountain too, but it was not successful, and in the fall when the rains came the leaves all fell from the chestnut trees and the branches were bare and the trunks were black with rain. The vineyards were thin and bare-branched too and all the country wet and brown and dead with the autumn. There were mists over the river and clouds on the mountain and the trucks splashed mud on the road and the troops were muddy and wet in their capes; their rifles were wet. . . . (p. 4)

The sense of failure and impotence is also reinforced by the studious avoidance of action-verbs. Almost invariably Hemingway employs the copulative *to be,* and the expletives *there were* and *there was* occur ten times in the twenty-one sentences of the chapter, six of the sentences being introduced by them. The repetitions give a sense of endless sameness and weariness: abandon hope, all ye who enter here.

The concluding paragraphs of the chapter reinforce what has already been established powerfully. The guns, the tractors, the motor-cars show a ruthless power, and it is as if life, in the presence of these overwhelming forces of death, had withered and shrunk. The "very small" king, sitting in the speeding motor-car "between two generals," becomes a fine correlative of the sense of impotence:

There were small gray motor cars that passed going very fast; usually there was an officer in the seat with the driver and more officers in the back seat. They splashed more mud than the camions even and if one of the officers in the back was very small and sitting between two generals, he himself so small that you could not see his face but only the top of his cap and his narrow back, and if the car went especially fast it was probably the king. He lived in Udine and came out in this way nearly every day to see how things were going, and things went very badly.

At the start of the winter came the permanent rain and with the rain came the cholera. But it was checked and in the end only seven thousand died of it in the army. (p. 4)

With this last paragraph the sense of doom is complete. The rain is "permanent" and the apparent consolation, the fact that the cholera is checked, is viciously undercut by the irony that *"only* seven thousand died of it in the army."

The mood of the first chapter is thus established powerfully through the proliferation of associated images, images written in a single key. But to continue in this way—that is, to continue to present events and people as the objectification of feeling through the modulation of images—would of course be to drive narrative out of the novel; there would be no "story," only bitterness distilled. Hemingway's artistic problem accordingly becomes that of presenting action and conflict in such a way that the central emotion will not be shattered by the inclusion of elements hostile to it. As I have indicated, action must be converted into passion; characters must become embodiments of the central bitterness. When it becomes necessary, then, in Chapter II, to introduce characters and to develop a scene whose essential quality is potentially uncongenial to the established emotion, Hemingway must take pains to weaken or nullify the inharmonious effects and to absorb character and scene into the dominant mood. So it is that when the priest, the captain, and the other soldiers are introduced, Hemingway guards against any dilution of the central emotion by framing the scene with a description expressive, once again, of the profound regret and bitterness:

Later, below in the town, I watched the snow falling, looking out of the window of the bawdy house, the house for officers, where I sat with a friend and two glasses drinking a bottle of Asti, and, looking out at the snow falling slowly and heavily, we knew it was all over for that year. Up the river the mountains had not been taken; none of the mountains beyond the river had been taken. That was all left for next year. My friend saw the priest from our mess going by in the street, walking carefully in the slush, and pounded on the window to attract his attention. The priest looked up. He saw us and smiled. My friend motioned for him to come in. The priest shook his head and went on. That night in the mess after the spaghetti course . . . the captain commenced picking on the priest. (pp. 6–7)

In the scene that follows, the captain's baiting of the priest takes its tone from the frame and is anything but humorous. The "good fun" is swallowed up by the pervasive sadness and bitterness, and the episode acts upon the reader in much the same way as an episode in *The Waste Land* affects Eliot's readers: dialogue, narrative, description are all viewed as expressions of the central fears and desires. The characters introduced are not important in themselves; their development as characters does not interest the writer. They are aspects of the hero's state of mind, and represent, covertly, the conflicts of his soul.

We must note, moreover, that the scene is, characteristically, short. For to lengthen any scene of this sort, in which the actions and speeches of minor characters threaten to shake our awareness of the hero's mood, would be fatal to the lyric novel. If developed at length, the scene would cease to function as the token of the hero's feelings. E. M. Forster, in his *Aspects of the Novel,* has pointed out the danger of the characters' taking the story out of the novelist's control. The minor characters, if freed from the hero's sensibility, would take the scene into their own hands. The rhythm and mood of the scene would be theirs, not the hero's, and the scene, instead of reinforcing, might easily weaken or dissipate the central emotion. Furthermore, any particularly vivid rendering of the inherent "coloring" of the events and speeches—such rendering as one finds everywhere in the novels of Dickens—might work dangerously against the emotion. Hence the scene must be reported as barely, as "objectively" as possible. Perhaps it has not been sufficiently appreciated that "objectivity," as employed by Hemingway, is more than a means of effective understatement or of being true to the facts; it is also, much of the time, a means of preventing alien attitudes and feelings from asserting themselves vigorously—at the expense of the dominant emotion of the lyric novel. Of course objectivity *also* gives an air of distance and detachment; but where the objectively rendered scene is framed by lyric passages of great intensity, the scene becomes suffused with the emotion of the antecedent lyric, and it is precisely the deadpan reporting with the recurrent "he saids" that *permits* such penetration of the emotion.

The depression of Frederic Henry continues into Chapter III, but by this time the impressions of bitterness and failure have accumulated so densely that one is ready for a shift to an opposite state of mind. Returning from his leave, Frederic finds everything at the front unchanged. He has not gone to Abruzzi, as the priest urged him to, and, as the symbolism suggests delicately, he is mired in moral filth and inertia. Rinaldi, after kissing him, says: "You're dirty. . . . You ought to wash," and in Chapter IV Frederic observes, "I was very dusty and dirty and went up to my room to wash" (p. 17). In truth he needs a kind of purification. Thus when he sees Catherine Barkley for the first time in the garden of the British hospital, the imagery hints at the purity, the Eden-like peace that Frederic most deeply craves: "Miss Barkley was in the garden. Another nurse was with her. We saw their white uniforms through the trees and walked toward them" (p. 18). But the first conversation of the lovers, with its truncated, tight-lipped exchanges, only reiterates the desperation and despair that have already pervaded the novel. Once a key word has been sounded, Hemingway modulates it beautifully in half a dozen different shadings, until the conversation, like the descriptions already quoted, becomes a refrain on the theme of failure:

"Yes," she said. "People can't realize what France is like. If they did, it couldn't go on. He didn't have a sabre cut. They blew him all to bits."

I didn't say anything.

"Do you suppose it will always go on?"

"No."

"What's to stop it?"

"It will crack somewhere."

"We'll crack. We'll crack in France. They can't go on doing things like the Somme and not crack."

"They won't crack here," I said.

"You think not?"

"No. They did very well last summer."

"They may crack," she said. "Anybody may crack."

"The Germans too."

"No," she said. "I think not." (p. 20)

Catherine here exists almost as the echo of Frederic's own bitterness and despair. She is Despair turning desperately to the religion of love. She has no past beyond the absolute minimum required for plausibility. Like another Catherine, Bronte's Catherine Earnshaw, she *is* her lover: her temperamental affinity to Frederic is so marked that their right to each other is accepted almost from the first moment of meeting. Thus she is, in a sense, not a distinct character at all but Frederic's bitterness or his desire objectified. She will presently become the peace or bliss that stands at farthest remove from the war: the white snows of the mountaintops, the idyllic serenity of Switzerland, the Beatrice of the *Paradiso.* To lose her will be to lose Love. The lyric novel requires no deeper characterization.

Once she has been introduced, Hemingway is ready to effect the first qualitative shift in the novel. He has only to bring about the circumstances that will make possible a brief interlude of love and joy—a state of mind opposite to the intolerable mood of the opening chapters. In Chapter VII Frederic returns to the front, and the sweat, the heat, and the dust are again emphasized (p. 33). References to washing or taking baths recur (pp. 36, 39), and in Chapter IX, when he is wounded, we are told that so much dirt has blown into the wound that it has not hemorrhaged much (p. 57). The form of the next several chapters, then, becomes the gradual emergence from the filth and darkness of the war into the purity and light of love. The slow healing of Frederic's wound is concomitant with a subtle, incomplete healing of his soul, and before his return to the front he will have acquired, though without fully knowing it, the conviction that neither Rinaldi, who visits him in Chapter X, nor the priest, who visits him in Chapter XI, can claim his soul: his love of Catherine is his religion. Yet this first idyll of love is by no means as pure and satisfying as the second interlude in Switzerland. It alters Frederic's disposition; it teaches him that love is possible; but it does not bring such full and radiant joy as will come later. It must, of necessity, be less complete, less satisfying, than the Switzerland episodes; if it were not, the happiness in Switzerland would be anti-climactic, and there would be no conviction that the lovers had grown emotionally and spiritually in such a way as to make the shattering of their union fully tragic. At this stage of the action Hemingway therefore wisely presents only so much of the lovers' joy as will establish a strong contrast between the old state of mind and the new. The moments of joy are intermittent. There are still, even after Frederic's recovery, many ominous suggestions of the old hollowness and despair. The ugliness of Ettore's ambition to rise and win glory in the army reminds the lovers of the world they want to forget. The rain returns and Catherine, who sometimes sees herself "dead in it," is frightened and begins to cry; in Chapter XX the dishonesty of the fixed horse-races sullies the lovers' afternoon, though they are able to outwit the world by betting on a horse they've never heard of (named symbolically "Light for Me") and Catherine says, "I feel so much cleaner." But in Chapter XXI Catherine announces that she is pregnant, and the uncertainty of the future stirs a new dread. In the next chapter the rain returns: "It turned cold that night and the next day it was raining. Coming home from the Ospedale Maggiore it rained very hard and I was wet when I came in. Up in my room the rain was coming down heavily outside on the balcony, and the wind blew it against the glass doors" (p. 142). Frederic comes down with jaundice, a physical correlative of the old sense of "rottenness," and the visit he and Catherine had planned to Pallanza is now out of the question. The old pattern of failure reasserts itself. When Miss Van Campen discovers the empty bottles in the armoire of his hospital room, his leave is cancelled.

In Chapter XXIII, the night on which Frederic returns to the front, the rain, the lovers' goodbyes, and the sense of helplessness all combine to produce a profound pathos and anguish that passes, finally, into a bitterness even more intense than that of the opening chapters. The chapter begins with Frederic's making arrangements to have a seat on the troop train held for him and with his saying goodbye at the hospital. The wife of the porter weeps. Frederic walks to a wine-shop and waits for Catherine to pass. At this point the rain of despair and death is suggested only by mist and fog: "It was dark outside and cold and misty. . . . There was a fog in the square and when we came close to the front of the cathedral it was very big and the stone was wet" (pp. 146–147). Frederic asks Catherine if she would like to go in, but she says no, and they go instead to a hotel where the furniture of vice, red plush curtains, a satin coverlet on the bed, and "many mirrors," besmirch the sacredness of their love. On their trip to the hotel the fog changes to rain, and the sense of failure and loss deepens:

"We can get a cab at the bridge," I said. We stood on the bridge *in the fog* waiting for a carriage. Several streetcars passed, full of people going home. Then a carriage came along but there was someone in it. *The fog was turning to rain.*

"We could walk or take a train," Catherine said.

"One will be along," I said. "They go by here."

"Here one comes," she said.

The driver stopped his horse and lowered the metal sign on his meter. The top of the carriage was up and there were *drops of water* on the driver's coat. His varnished hat was *shining in the wet.* We sat back in the seat together and the top of the carriage made it dark. (p. 150; italics mine)

In the hotel Catherine bursts out: "I never felt like a whore before." Frederic stands at the window looking down at "the wet pavement" until Catherine calls him back to the bed. For a time the lovers are happy in the hotel room, which, in a bitter irony, Catherine refers to as their "fine house" and their "home." But in a moment of stillness they can "hear the rain" (p. 154) and presently they must leave. The symbolic rain now finds its way into almost every sentence, as if doom were complete, inescapable:

I saw the carriage coming. It stopped, the horse's head hanging *in the rain,* and the waiter stepped out, *opened his umbrella,* and came toward the hotel. We met him at the door and walked out *under the umbrella* down *the wet walk* to the carriage at the curb. *Water was running in the gutter.*

"There is your package on the seat," the waiter said. He stood *with the umbrella* until we were in and I had tipped him.

"Many thanks. Pleasant journey," he said. The coachman lifted the reins and the horse started. The waiter turned away *under the umbrella* and went toward the hotel. We drove down the street and turned to the left, then came around to the right in front of the station. There were two carabinieri standing under the light just *out of the rain.* The light shone on their hats. *The rain* was clear and transparent against the light from the station. A porter came out from under the shelter of the station, his shoulders up *against the rain.* (p. 157; italics mine)

When Frederic enters the crowded troop-train, where "every one was hostile," the return to the old bitterness is virtually complete. He gives up his seat to the belligerent captain with the "new and shiny" scar, then stands watching the lights of the station as the train pulls out. Light has been associated from the beginning with Catherine, her white uniform and, especially, her shining hair (p. 114). Just before boarding the train, Frederic sees her face "in the light" (p. 157). But now "It was still raining and soon the windows were wet and you could not see out" (p. 159). The violence of the shift from the interlude of love to the nightmare of the war is consummately rendered in the final sentences of the chapter: Frederic is swallowed up in a hell of darkness, congestion, and hostility, and the loss of his identity as lover is complete; he sleeps on the floor of the corridor, thinking: "they could all walk over me if they wouldn't step on me. Men were sleeping on the floor all down the corridor. Others stood holding on to the window rods or leaning against the doors. That train was always crowded" (p. 159).

The world has again triumphed. Accordingly, the sense of desolation and failure at the beginning of Book Three is almost identical with that of the novel's first chapter. Once again it is autumn, and once again Hemingway uses the limited palette of key words to paint the emotion, building his opening paragraph on the adjective "bare" and on references to the rain and to "shrunken" life:

Now in the fall the trees were all *bare* and the roads were muddy. I rode to Gorizia from Udine on a camion. We passed other camions on the road and I looked at the country. The mulberry trees were *bare* and the fields were brown. There were *wet* dead leaves on the road from the rows of *bare* trees and men were working on the road, tamping stone in the ruts from piles of crushed stone along the side of the road between the trees. We saw the town *with a mist over it* that cut off the mountains. We crossed the river and I saw that it was running high. *It had been raining* in the mountains. We came into the town past the factories and then the houses and villas and I saw many more houses had been hit. On a narrow street we passed a British Red Cross ambulance. The driver wore a cap and his face was *thin* and very tanned. I did not know him. I got down from the camion in the big square in front of the Town Major's house, the driver handed down my rucksack and I put it on and swung on the two musettes and walked to our villa. It did not feel like a homecoming.

I walked down the *damp* gravel driveway looking at the villa through the trees. The windows were all shut but the door was open. I went in and found the major sitting at a table in the *bare* room with maps and typed sheets of paper on the wall. (pp. 163–164; italics mine)

The old sense of pollution also returns: Rinaldi, who fears he has syphilis, chides Frederic for trying to cleanse his conscience with a toothbrush. And the sense of impotence and failure is further objectified in Rinaldi's "You can't do it. You can't do it. I say you can't do it. You're dry and you're empty and there's nothing else. There's nothing else I tell you" (p. 174). Presently Frederic picks up the refrain: he believes "in sleep," he tells the priest, "meaning nothing" (p. 179). Then in Chapter XXVII the rains begin again:

It stormed all that day. The wind drove down *the rain* and everywhere there was *standing water* and mud. The plaster of the broken houses was gray and *wet.* Late in the afternoon *the rain* stopped and from out number two post I saw the *bare wet* autumn country with clouds over the tops of the hills and the straw screening over the road *wet and dripping.* The sun came out once before it went down and shone on the *bare* woods beyond the ridge. . . . We loaded two cars and drove down the road that was screened with *wet* mats and the last of the sun came through in the breaks between the strips of matting. Before we were out on the clear road behind the hill the sun was down. We went on down the clear road and as it turned into the open and went into the square arched tunnel of matting *the rain started again.*

The wind rose in the night and at three o'clock in the morning *with the rain coming in sheets* there was a bombardment and the Croatians came over across the mountain meadows and through the patches of wood and into the front line. They fought *in the dark in the rain* and a counter-attack of scared men from the second line drove them back. There was much shelling and many rockets *in the rain* and machine-gun and rifle fire all along the line. They did not come again and it was quieter and between *the gusts of wind and rain* we could hear the sound of a great bombardment far to the north. (pp. 185–186; italics mine)

The retreat begins, "orderly, wet and sullen," with troops marching "under the rain" (p. 188). In Chapter XXVII the word "rain" appears twenty-four times; in Chapter XXVIII, seventeen times. Chapter XXVII begins with a reference to sleep—meaning, of course, nothing—and in twelve pages the word appears, incredibly, as noun, adjective, or verb, thirty-three times. I am aware that such counting is not in itself a proof of the lyric progression of these events, but when rain means death and sleep means nothing, the recurrence of the words builds a mood of absolute hopelessness.

Moreover, because of the repetitions, a note of desperation comes to suffuse the scene: the pressure of the accumulated bitterness will become too intense, and the dominant emotion will again seek to elicit its opposite, pure peace, pure happiness, the pure joy of love. After the overwhelming development of the emotion in these chapters, Frederic's bolt for freedom cannot be far off. Hemingway can sustain the emotion for a few chapters more, but any further prolongation would make the intensity commonplace and the evil banal, meaningless. Frederic must soon fall into the hands of the battle-police. A very brief qualitative shift in Chapter XXX enables Hemingway to prolong the suffering for an additional chapter: the interlude in the barn depicts a normality, a wholesomeness and sanity that appear with great force after the nightmare of the retreat ("The hay smelled good and lying in the hay took away all the years in between. We had lain in hay and talked and shot sparrows with an air-rifle when they perched in the triangle cut high up in the wall of the barn" [p. 216]), but the war is too close, the barn provides only momentary respite, and Frederic must quickly move out into the "black night with the rain." The scene in which he confronts the battle-police occurs within four pages after the departure from the barn.

Once Frederic has fled, the lyric form of the novel is predictable: the interlude in Switzerland followed by the crushing failure in the hospital. Once again the rhythm of the novel becomes that of emergence from darkness and failure. The rain continues as Frederic crosses the symbolic Venetian plain (Chapter XXXI), as he takes the train to Stresa, and as he and Catherine lie in the hotel room there (Chapter XXXIV). In Chapter XXXV there occurs a brief interlude of sanity and peace in which Frederic trolls for lake trout with the barman and plays billiards with Count Greffi; but Chapter XXXVI begins: "That night there was a storm and I woke to hear the rain lashing the window-panes" (p. 264), and in "the dark and the rain" (p. 266) Frederic and Catherine set out for Switzerland. In Chapter XXXVII Frederic rows all night as the rain comes "occasionally in gusts" (p. 270). But when they set foot in Switzerland a second and more perfect idyll of love and purity commences.

Here again, as in the earlier interlude, Hemingway wisely guards against sentimentalizing the period of happiness. The religion of love is not enough: there is anxiety about the future, and Catherine is quick to notice that Frederic is chafing because he has nothing to do. But after the prolonged suffering and failure of the middle section of the novel, the impression of perfect joy is very strong, and the emotion is objectified in dozens of images suggesting sanity, wholesomeness, purity, and peace. Energy returns: "it was good walking on the road and invigorating" (p. 290). The snow on the mountain peaks, like the snows of Kilimanjaro, is a correlative of the sense of heavenly bliss and purity. The sun shines, and the air is "cold and clear" (p. 291). By January the winter settles into "bright cold days and hard cold nights." The snow is now "clean packed" (p. 303); the air comes "sharply into your lungs"; there is now a sense that the life-force has *not* been defeated, and the lovers see foxes; the night is "dry and cold and very clear" (p. 304).

It is not until March, when the winter breaks (Chapter XL) and it begins raining that the old failure and bitterness threaten to shatter the lovers' happiness. Then, in the magnificent last chapter, the pattern of failure is sharply reasserted in a terrible echo of Rinaldi's "You can't do it." All of Catherine's efforts to give birth to the child fail. She cries out that the anesthetic is "not working." The child is strangled by the umbilical cord; the Caesarian fails. Even Frederic's effort to say good-by fails: "It wasn't any good. It was like saying good-by to a statue" (p. 332). And so he is delivered up, once again, to the rain of death and failure: "After a while I went out and left the hospital and walked back to the hotel in the rain." The two attempts to escape the world's malice have failed, just as, in *The Sun Also Rises,* the two interludes of sanity and purity (the trout-fishing episode and the swimming episode at San Sebastian) provide only brief respite from the world; and one is left with the conviction that any further effort to escape will be crushed with equal ruthlessness.

The basic rhythm of the action of *Farewell* is thus almost identical with that of Hemingway's earlier novel, and the symbolism, too, is virtually unchanged. It seems safe to say that Hemingway had established his art in his earlier book: he had learned that lyricism was his essential talent, and he set about deliberately to apply the knowledge imparted by the earlier lessons. Over the next thirty years he was not to make any significant changes in his basic method. If there was a slight decline in his creative energy in the later books, if some of them seem mechanical, their style having become self-conscious mannerism rather than the perfect objectification of lyric impulses, the defects were scarcely so great as to impair the central vitality of his work. For he had developed his lyric art with the utmost attention to every means of rendering emotion purely. By 1929 he knew so well what he could do and how he could do it that he had reduced the possibilities of failure to a minimum. To adventure into the epic novel might have proved disastrous to an artist of Hemingway's limited powers. Provided that he confined himself to the lyric art he knew so thoroughly, he was not likely to fail. It is perhaps no small part of his genius that he seems to have recognized his limitations and to have made maximum use of the materials available to his lyric sensibility.

1. 'Pure and Impure Poetry," *Selected Essays* (New York, 1957).

2. For a sensitive analysis of the characteristics and possibilities of the lyric novel see Ralph Freedman, *The Lyrical Novel* (Princeton, 1963), Chapters 1, 2, and 6.

3. New York: Scribner Library, p. 249. Hereafter page references will be given in the text.

4. "How Do You Like It Now, Gentlemen?" in *Hemingway: A Collection of Critical Essays,* ed. Robert P. Weeks (Englewood Cliffs, N.J., 1962), p. 36.

LANGUAGE MAGIC AND REALITY IN *FOR WHOM THE BELL TOLLS*

ROBERT O. STEPHENS

IN THE OPENING PAGES OF *For Whom the Bell Tolls,* Robert Jordan begins his new assignment pondering the example of Kashkin, his predecessor in the

Reprinted with permission from *Criticism,* XIV (Fall 1972), 151–164.

partisan work with Pablo's guerrilla band. Trying to determine what had been Kashkin's flaw, he recognizes that it had been primarily a matter of language: Kashkin had talked too much of death and suicide. "You can't have people around doing this sort of work and talking like that," he concludes. "That is no way to talk. Even if they accomplish their mission they are doing more harm than good, talking that kind of stuff."[1] With such a comment, Robert Jordan demonstrates an awareness of the power of language which pervades not only the Spanish Civil War novel but Hemingway's work in its entirety, from the earliest stories to the last memoirs, in the fictional worlds of his characters and in the semi-legendary world of his own self-creation. For Hemingway and his characters must be seen as they are concerned, even obsessed, with language magic—with the tendency to presume necessary connections between words and things or actions and to assume control over events and feelings by the power of words. Whether this tendency is to be interpreted as a psychological aberration or, more probably, as a cultural pattern viewed anthropologically, it is central to the way in which Hemingway's world can be comprehended.

That such an emphasis on the reality of words operates in *For Whom the Bell Tolls* seems initially contradictory to Hemingway's practice. The well known passage in *A Farewell to Arms* on the obscenity of abstract words and the validity of only names of concrete places and things would seem, as R. P. Warren has suggested, to align Hemingway with users of exclusively empirical language. Words, according to this theory, have reference only to immediately known sensations and almost none to intellectually known concepts. But Hemingway's practice of language magic is, when seen in terms of symbolic forms, rather an expansion of this approach to language. For Frederic Henry's reliance on names of places and things is in effect a fusing of word and referent. He, like Robert Jordan, makes language a mythic and symbolic medium rather than a discursive instrument. Ernst Cassirer's distinction between the two kinds of language delineates the difference. In discursive language the word acts as symbol to expand meaning from the particular to the general and serves as an intermediate device between the two. But in mythic language the word as symbol retains its specific and particular reference; the word-symbol fuses with the object or act: "Thus, the special symbolic forms are not imitations but *organs* of reality, since it is solely by their agency that anything real becomes an object for intellectual apprehension, and as such is made visible for us. . . . The mythical form of conception is not something superadded to certain definite *elements* of *empirical* existence; instead, the primary 'experience' itself is steeped in the imagery of myth and saturated with its atmosphere.

Man lives with *objects* only in so far as he lives with these *forms;* he reveals reality to himself, and himself to reality, in that he lets himself and the environment enter into this plastic medium, in which the two do not merely make contact, but fuse with each other."[2]

Hemingway's use of such language in this novel shows Robert Jordan attempting to realize the action in terms of words and by this act to reconceive his world. He knows, as Cassirer and Whorf have postulated, that the natural world can be conceived only in terms allowed by one's language.[3] Language precedes, not follows, the apprehension of reality. The world is categorized as one's language categorizes it. And in Robert Jordan's world language deals with particulars, merging the world and the word into a fused identity. His is a pre-discursive world known not through the terminology of Marxist dialectic or of historical analysis but through mythic and creative language which makes rather than discovers reality. He is in the position of a primeval creator of his world by power of the word, and his created world is mythic, primitive, and heroic. If he finds the community of man through this emphasis on the particular, it is because he has constructed that community on the mythic, pre-discursive, pre-political level of comprehension.

To see the novel in this way is to recognize that several criticisms of the novel attribute purposes to Hemingway which were not in fact directly relevant. When Lionel Trilling, for example, says that Hemingway fails to show how Robert Jordan's fate is determined by unrecognized moral and political contradictions of the historical situation, he assumes that Hemingway attempted to depict a historical reality. When Arturo Barea castigates Hemingway for presenting not the historical Spanish Civil War but Hemingway's special vision of the war, he is correct in so noting but in error in supposing Hemingway meant to present a reportorial, true-to-custom view of Spanish mores and language. And when Robert Evans observes that Hemingway failed to present an intellectual or analytical view of the hero's predicament, he is in error in assuming the primacy of discursive over creative or mythical language in Hemingway's purpose.[4]

Rather, as Carlos Baker and Delbert Wylder among others have suggested, the world of *For Whom the Bell Tolls* is heroic and epic.[5] The realities are supernatural and imaginative as well as natural, and the historical actions of men do not explain everything. There is a great element of pre-rational awareness in the novel. There are invisible fates at work in the action and they can be accounted for only when one uses the appropriate language. To miss the language is to miss much of what is at work in the heroism of Robert Jordan.

What makes the Spanish war novel particularly meaningful as an index to such language is that it is intensified by the gypsy lore pervading the work and by the extra sensitivity of Robert Jordan to such psycho-cultural patterns because of his travel and study in Spain. That he is aware of such lore is evident in his musing about the experience and research that went into his book. "He had put in it what he had discovered about Spain in the ten years of travelling in it, on foot, in third-class carriages, by bus, on horse- and mule-back and in trucks. He knew the Basque country, Navarre, Aragon, Galicia, the two Castiles and Estremadura well. There had been such good books by Borrow and Ford and the rest that he had been able to add very little" (p. 248). Of the two primary sources mentioned, one is, to judge from the context, Richard Ford's *The Handbook for Travellers in Spain,* which went through eight editions in England by 1892 as one of John Murray's travel book series. The other is probably George Henry Borrow's *The Zíncali: An Account of the Gypsies in Spain,* originally issued in 1841 and in its ninth and definitive edition by 1901 with numerous reprintings thereafter.[6]

Borrow's accounts of gypsy origins and gypsy lore with their suggestions of cannibalism, forest life, chiromancy, and occult powers seem particularly in Robert Jordan's mind when he thinks of the hidden forces in man's archetypal mind: "Nobody knows what tribes we came from nor what our tribal inheritance is nor what the mysteries were in the woods where the people lived that we come from. All we know is that we do not know. We know nothing about what happens to us in the nights" (p. 175). Pilar's reading of Robert Jordan's fortune in his hand echoes Borrow's account of gypsy chiromancy. And Borrow's rendering of the significance of the term "Zíncali" explicates Rafael's gypsy song. Borrow explains, "They [the gypsies] likewise call themselves 'Cales,' by which appellation indeed they are tolerably well known by the Spaniards and which is merely the plural terminology of the compound word Zíncalo, and signifies, the black men." Rafael sings:

> *"My nose is flat,*
> *My face is black*
> *But still I am a man.*
>
> . . .
>
> *Thank God I am a Negro.*
> *And not a Catalan!"* (p. 60)

But Robert Jordan takes the magic-haunted world of the gypsies as a paradigm of the world at large. He follows Sir James Frazer's discovery that, "While religious systems differ not only in different countries, but in the same country in different ages, the system of sympathetic magic remains everywhere and at all times substantially alike in its principles and practice."[7] Frazer's two basic principles of imitative and contagious magic operate in Robert Jordan's world as he finds necessary connections between words and events. Jordan sees the universal applications of the lore known to the gypsies when he points out to Anselmo the correspondence between gypsy and American Indian beliefs in man's brotherhood to bears (p. 40), noted also in Frazer. He similarly sees the gypsy code extended to the Moors when he and Anselmo note that the gypsies and Moors both have secret laws that allow killing outside the tribe, laws they will not admit having (p. 40). And he sees how the magical mind works among the Navarrese when he reads the letter taken from the dead fascist cavalryman. The horseman's sister has written that the chest badge of the Sacred Heart of Jesus has talismanic power to stop bullets (p. 303).

Indeed life in the guerrilla camp exists on a different and more primitive level than that Robert Jordan has known with Karkov and Golz in Madrid. As he first enters the camp, he recognizes the difference and reminds himself, "Turn off the thinking now, old timer, old comrade. You're a bridge blower now. Not a thinker" (p. 17). His self-admonition is in effect a dismissal of that political world known through discursive, dialectical language and an embracing of a magic and mythical world known through the language which creates it. Jordan frequently contrasts the language used in the guerrilla camp with that remembered from Madrid.[8] He recognizes the ideological language of Madrid as a tissue of ready phrases inappropriate to his present circumstance. When he thinks of the betrayal of the Republic by its leaders, the phrase "enemies of the people" comes to mind, but he recognizes it as a present unreality: "Enemies of the people. That was a phrase he might omit. That was a catch phrase he would skip. . . . phrases like enemies of the people came into his mind without his much criticizing them in any way. Any sort of *clichés* both revolutionary and patriotic. His mind employed them without criticism. Of course they were true but it was too easy to be nimble about using them" (pp. 163–64). He also remembers Karkov's laughter at the communiqué from the Cordoba front demonstrating the divorce of language and reality: "Our glorious troops continue to advance without losing a foot of ground" (p. 239). Part of that remembered picture too is Karkov's cynical manipulation of terms. The party does not believe in "acts of terrorism by individuals. . . . But certainly we execute and destroy such veritable fiends and dregs of humanity and the treacherous dogs of generals and the revolting spectacle of admirals unfaithful to their trust. These are destroyed. They are not assassinated. You see the difference?" (p. 245)

All this is in contrast to the power of words operating within the guerrilla band. There, words are treated as realities rather than as symbols to be manipulated. There, the word becomes the ordering agent of reality and must be taken seriously. Robert Jordan cryptically notes that the fate of the band is decreed by words as he writes out the battle plan in his notebook: "Now it is all written out and ordered" (p. 226). Pilar and El Sordo also note that the words of such an order are the basic curse on the guerrillas. Recognizing the obscene power of such words, El Sordo quips, "That they should let us do something on paper. . . . That we should conceive and execute something on paper." And Pilar agrees, "What I would like to do is use thy orders for that purpose" (p. 152). Later, Robert Jordan realizes again the magical ordering power of such words. Anselmo's killing of the bridge sentry is justified in his eyes by Jordan's putting the instruction in form of an order. "I'm glad I remembered to make it an order, he thought. Thàt helps him out. That takes some of the curse off" (p. 410).

The operation of language magic during the three-day action follows in its particulars the outlines described by Sir James Frazer, Bronislaw Malinowski, C. K. Ogden, I. A. Richards, Ernst Cassirer and Sigmund Freud.[9] Some of the forms of language magic used include verbal catharsis, or exorcism and dissipation; the pronouncement of curses; the recognition of taboo words; name magic; phatic communion; induction; the attempt to arrive at metaphysical substantiality in words; and the construction of a future reality through language. Central to all these particular forms is the growth of a sense of community within the partisan group. And if their example is fundamental enough, their sense of community may serve to explain for whom the bell tolls.[10]

Cathartic language occurs as a means of denying existence to intolerable realities. Essential to the theory is the recognition of reality as subjective. Actions and events are real only if they are accepted as integral to one's inner life. Thus, Pilar tells Maria and Maria tells Robert Jordan that "nothing is done to oneself that one does not accept" (p. 73). But the agency of language is crucial. Denial comes out of purgative confession; experience must be made real through words before it can be exorcised. Robert Jordan understands this for himself when, after the fascist cavalry patrol has passed the masked entrance to Pablo's cave area, he feels "the need to talk that, with him, was the sign that there had been much danger. He could always tell how bad it had been by the strength of the desire to talk that came after" (p. 283). He reflects Freud's theory of art as purgation also when he thinks of his demolition work as "the constant attempt to approximate the conditions of successful assassination. . . ."[11] Then he wonders, "Did big words make it more defensible? Did they make killing more palatable? . . . But my guess is that you will get rid of all that by writing about it. . . . Once you write it down it is all gone" (p. 165).

Catharsis also works as confession for those who have experienced the atrocities of war. After young Joaquín sobbingly and convulsively relates the story of his family's execution by the fascists at Valladolid, Pilar announces the value of confession as a way of purging terror: "That you should speak. . . . For what are we born if not to aid one another? And to listen and say nothing is a cold enough aid" (p. 139). Robert Jordan further recognizes that confessional utterance has its formulaic response, which acts as a kind of litany. After such a confession, one usually responds, "What barbarians!" And he thinks, "How many times had he heard this? How many times had he seen their eyes fill and their throats harden. . . . Nearly always they spoke as this boy did now; suddenly and apropos of the mention of the town and always you said, 'What barbarians!' " (p. 134)

At the same time, Pilar recognizes that the reality of atrocities can be denied for others by her refusing to evoke horrors in words. To know intellectually that Pablo has massacred fascists at his home village near Avila is not the same as having it made real through vivid creation by words. When Robert Jordan urges her to tell of the massacre, she says, turning to Maria, "It isn't whether you can hear it. . . . It is whether I should tell it to thee and make thee bad dreams" (p. 99). Pilar reflects her relief that she did not see the end of the massacre and retrospectively thanks the drunkard who pulled her from the window of the *ayuntamiento*. If she had seen that spirit-destroying spectacle, she would have to give it reality in words too (p. 126).

Cathartic language as a denial of future or potential reality also operates throughout the novel. The guerrillas are constantly aware of the danger of a carelessly spoken allusion to death; they fear being killed by their own words. Walter Starkie reports that among the gypsies words and songs are not to be uttered vainly, for they do not fade away but remain hovering in the air, waiting for malevolent forces to use them against their speakers.[12] Thus, when Robert Jordan tells Pilar that he will take Maria away to the Republic if they are still alive after the attack on the bridge, Pilar rejects such talk and says, "That manner of speaking never brings luck" (p. 33). When he says he cannot take a woman where he goes in his work, Pilar observes, "You may take two where you go," and he in turn rebukes her (p. 89). In effect, the rebukes are attempts to cancel dangerous words. When Maria tells Jordan after their lovemaking that she has not felt the earth move as before but that "one does not have to die" every time, he quickly answers, *"Ojala no. . . .* I hope not" (p. 263). And as the guerrillas eat before the attack, Pilar tells Fernando to eat all the stew: "What does it matter if thy belly should be full? There is no doctor to operate if you take a goring." Agustín quickly cautions her not to "speak that way," but coincidentally or not, Fernando does later take a fatal wound in the groin as would a gored torero (pp. 383, 440).

Pronouncing curses is, if not identical, closely related to the cathartic use of language. Pilar demonstrates this link as she, El Sordo, and Robert Jordan discuss the plan to attack the bridge and dispute whether to retreat to the Republic or to the Gredos. As the gloom and tension build up and Jordan urges his preference for the Gredos, "the woman started to curse in a flood of obscene invective that rolled over and around him like the hot white water splashing down from a sudden eruption of a geyser," and the tension is dissipated (pp. 149–50). But beyond this is the fact that Spanish profanity constitutes a special kind of rhetoric itself, a type of verbal action dealing with the most obscene realities. "There is no language so filthy as Spanish," Hemingway observes in his authorial right. "There are words for all the vile words in English and there are other words and expressions that are used only in countries where blasphemy keeps pace with the austerity of religion" (p. 318). Agustín and Pilar demonstrate the ultimate stylization of this curse-making, indicative of the shared understanding on which it is based, when it is reduced either to unintelligibility or to such elliptical expressions as "thy mother" or to absurdity. "I un-name in the milk of their motor," Agustín cries as the fascist planes fly past, and Pilar remarks, "That is really something. But really difficult of execution" (p. 93).

Such cursing is both cathartic and a last mode of action when all other acts are futile. Robert Jordan's only recourse is to curses as action when he finds the snow falling that will either prevent or betray El Sordo's horse-stealing raid (p. 179), when he learns Pablo has stolen the exploders (p. 369), and when he realizes that the Republic is likewise betrayed by its leaders (p. 370). His curse becomes a litany of "Muck . . . Muck . . . Muck. . . ." Primitivo can likewise only curse and cry as he hears the cavalry attack and the planes bomb El Sordo and realizes he can provide no more active help (p. 297).

Making curses, however, is a two-edged sword, and those who blaspheme may bring catastrophe on themselves as well as on others by their words. Lieutenant Berrendo and the cavalry sniper sense this while Captain Mora shouts obscenities and blasphemies at El Sordo's men on the hilltop. The principle of contagion operates as they dissociate themselves from the captain and his curses. "They did not want to have that sort of talk on their consciences on a day in which they might die. Talking thus will not bring luck, the sniper thought. Speaking thus of the *Virgen* is bad luck. This one speaks worse than the Reds." And Lieutenant Berrendo feels that "this foul mouth stands there bringing more ill fortune with his blasphemies" (p. 318). The curse is indeed contagious for all concerned. Captain Mora dies by El Sordo's shot, exalted by his blasphemy, Berrendo's friend Julien lies dead on the slope, Sordo's men are fated for decapitation, and Berrendo will come into Robert Jordan's gunsight the next day.

Thus a third operation of language magic emerges—the mistake of uttering taboo words. Pilar has recognized this earlier during the massacre at Pablo's village. In this case, mockery rather than blasphemy is involved. Mockery of the foppish Don Faustino is justified, but mocking the dignified storeowner Don Guillermo Martín, whose only error is in being a petty fascist, can bring bad luck. A sense of violated order operates through language at this point: "to mock such a serious man as Don Guillermo is beyond all right," says a nearby peasant (p. 119). That taboo is linked with names becomes clear when Karkov challenges André Marty. Though the event is outside the guerrillas' world, it shows the residual influence of language magic among the cynical manipulators of words. In the Communist hierarchy Marty is presumably taboo and untouchable, but Karkov is willing to challenge that taboo and the sense of order it implies: "I am going to find out just how untouchable you are, Comrade Marty. I would like to know if it could not be possible to change the name of that tractor factory" (p. 426). He refers to the factory in Russia named after Marty, leader of an important naval mutiny years before. Thus taboo words and names are closely linked with broken order—political, military, and by implication, metaphysical. It is "not for nothing," as Karkov would say, that he has studied and admired Lope de Vega's *Fuente Ovejuna,* the primary Spanish drama of revolution and challenged order (p. 231).

A further operation of language magic, then, is that of naming. The principle involved, as Frazer has noted, is that one's name is a vital part of one's total person—equal in importance with his body and soul.[13] A sorcerer has power over one if he knows the man's name. This sense of the importance of names pervades the novel. When Robert Jordon first enters the guerrilla camp, he temporarily forgets Anselmo's name and regards the lapse as a bad sign (p. 2). The lapse functions as a true omen of Anselmo's death later as the bridge is destroyed. When Jordan asks Pablo his name, Pablo remains sullenly silent, and like the Ojibway Indians described by Frazer and known to Hemingway, he will not tell his name to a stranger but lets another, Anselmo in this case, reveal his name (p. 10). The importance of true and masked names is also evident to Jordan in the guerrilla camp as he remembers Golz's comment on their names. "You have a funny name in Spanish, Comrade Hordown." Golz hints the link between name and fate in his own case also. "Comrade Heneral Khotze. If I had known how they pronounced Golz in Spanish I would pick me a better name before I come to war here. . . . Now it is too late to change" (p. 7). That names are important for fulfilling identity can also be seen in the guerrillas' discussion on whether Jordan is *Inglés,* Roberto, or Don Roberto (pp. 67, 141, 172, 204, 210). Maria calls him *Inglés* in private and Roberto before the others. The guerrillas see him as *Inglés* the dynamiter. El Sordo begins calling him *Inglés,* shifts to *Russo,* and as he gains confidence in Jordan, calls him *Americano,* even as he shifts his language from pidgin Spanish to standard as a mark of acceptance. The guerrillas also debate whether Jordan should be called Don Roberto as an alien and perhaps fascist name, or as Fernando sees it, as a future equivalent of Comrade, once the revolution is over. Jordan similarly seeks realization of the essential Maria when he says he loves her name as well as her person and body (p. 263).

A fifth form of language magic in the novel is what Malinowski calls "phatic communion"—language used for social intercourse and a sense of group feeling.[14] It need not convey intellectual meaning or prompt reflection; rather it is a way of "binding hearer to speaker by the tie of some social sentiment or other." It is the use of language as a mode of social action and ranks with the breaking of bread together as an act of communion rather than communication. Pilar recognizes this when she tells Robert Jordan, "Every one needs to talk to some one. . . . Before we had religion and other nonsense. Now for every one there should be some one to whom one can speak frankly, for all the valor that one could have one becomes very alone" (p. 89). The statement is in consequence of her recitation of the good times in Valencia with the matador Finito. The account has no direct relevance to the three-day preparation for battle but is a way of evoking a communal experience of prewar days for the group.

Narrative is a special form of this phatic communion. Malinowski further notes, "When incidents are told or discussed among a group of listeners, there is, first, the situation of that moment made up of the respective social, intellectual and emotional attitudes of those present. Within this situation, the narrative creates new bonds and sentiments by the emotional appeal of the words. . . . In every case, narrative speech as found in primitive communities is primarily a mode of social action rather than a mere reflection of thought."[15] Thus, Pilar as leader of the group serves an important cohesive function when she tells of the massacre at Pablo's village and later when she describes the smell of death on the fated matadors Ignacio Sanchez Mejias, Manolo Granero, and Joselito (pp. 252–54). Her narrative and later her instruction on how to identify such a smell are part of her work as evoker of common culture for the group. This function of narrative-communion has not been taken into account by those critics who see the descriptions as gratuitous set pieces.

A closely related function of language noted by Malinowski is that of inductive magic. In this, the word is co-active with the gesture as part of a single process. "A word is used always in direct conjunction with the reality it means. The word acts on the thing and the thing releases the word in the human mind."[16] Malinowski describes how the Trobriand islanders use such words as an integral part of their joint actions to hunt and fish as they talk their fish or game into their traps. The physical action is completed by the verbal act. El Sordo practices this inductive magic as he talks the fascist Captain Mora into his gunsights: "This one is for me. This one I take with me on the trip. This one coming now makes the same voyage I do. Come on, Comrade Voyager. Come striding. Come right along. Come along to meet it. Come on. Keep on walking. . . . Close enough. Too close. Yes, Comrade Voyager. Take it, Comrade Voyager" (p. 319).

Robert Jordan also utilizes the elements of language magic as a means of evoking essential experience. He seeks an intuitive, metaphysical basis of reality through language in much the way Gertrude Stein does in *Tender Buttons.* Reality is imagined as residing within the word rather than beyond it. As he eats onions for breakfast after the encounter with the fascist cavalry patrol and exchanges quips with Agustín, he plays with the Shakespearean dictum that a rose by any other name would smell as sweet. "A rose is a rose is an onion," he notes in modification of Gertrude Stein. "An onion is an onion is an onion . . . a stone is a stein is a rock is a boulder is a pebble" (p. 289). In another instance he attempts to realize the essences of such words as *now, dead, war,* and *sweetheart,* particularly as they have realities in different languages: "And if there is not any such thing as a long time, nor the rest of your lives, nor from now on, but there is only now, why then now is the thing to praise and I am very happy with it. Now, *ahora, maintenant, heute. Now,* it has a funny sound to be the whole world and your life. . . . Take dead, *mort, muerto,* and *todt. Todt* was the deadliest of them all. War, *guerre, guerra, krieg* [sic]. *Krieg* was the most like war, or was it? Or was it that he only knew German least well? Sweetheart, *cherie, prenda, schatz* [sic]. He would trade them all for Maria. There was a name" (pp. 166–67). He further recognizes the identity of word and natural event, somewhat in the manner of Emerson's transcendental theory of language, when he notes Anselmo's fidelity to his assignment at the roadwatching station. "To stay in a storm in a way corresponds to a lot of things. It's not for nothing that the Germans call an attack a storm" (p. 200). And when Maria calls their sexual ecstasy *la gloria,* he glimpses the essence of that critical word: "She said La Gloria. It has nothing to do with glory nor La Gloire that the French write and speak about. . . . I am no mystic, but to deny it is as ignorant as though you denied the telephone or that the earth revolves around the sun or that there are other planets than this" (p. 380).

But if Robert Jordan senses reality in other languages, he finds English his own special language of power. Just as the primitive shaman has his special argot, often unintelligible, Robert Jordan learns that for himself, some words achieve reality only when spoken in English.[17] He is tempted to hide from himself his father's suicidal cowardice by calling his father *cobarde* but recognizes that saying the English word *coward* is the only way he can come to terms with the name (p. 338). Similarly, when Rafael says that the Lewis gun will fire as long as one squeezes the trigger, Robert Jordan has to recognize the reality in English that Lewis guns jam, run out of ammunition, and melt. He tells Anselmo that he looks into the future in English, and he later tells Pablo that he speaks English for its comforting, reassuring sound when he becomes disgusted or baffled (pp. 27, 180). For English is that special medium through which he can make and control reality. It is the matrix of his vision.

Finally, even as Robert Jordan and the guerrillas struggle to make a past and present reality through language, they are also aware that the future reality of the Republic must be a product of words as well as acts. That future, they recognize, can be flawed or strengthened depending on the words used to create it. Like primeval creators, they must use words as the agents of creation and like successors to those creators, they perpetuate creation by words. Thus, when Agustín says that after the revolution fascists should be made to jump without parachutes from airplanes and be nailed to the tops of fence posts, Anselmo rebukes him: "That way of speaking is ignoble. . . . Thus we will never have a Republic" (p. 286). Robert Jordan sees that talking of dying is not the way to make the Republic. Such talk is anti-creative, typical of the anarchists (p. 305).

In place of such false words, the future as Anselmo evokes it is one of forgiveness, reconciliation, and work. He evokes that future conditionally to avoid tempting fate. "That we should govern justly and that all should participate in the benefits according as they have striven for them. And that those who have fought against us should be educated to see their error. . . . That they should be reformed by work" (pp. 285–86). Robert Jordan's vision is of the Madrid that is to be and of Maria there. Like Anselmo's, his future is one created by word. Its proof is not in the future actualities it might denote but in its present reality as word-vision. His function, then, is not that of valedictorian of abstract phrases without concrete denotations, as Stanley Cooperman has suggested, but as a prophet whose words are self-contained in reality.[18] As he tells Maria of his love for her and "liberty and dignity and the rights of all men to work and not be hungry," he realizes it is "a complete embracing of all that would not be . . ." (p. 348). But as he lies wounded and ready to say farewell to Maria, he knows also that the words are necessary for a continued reality. "He knew there was a great hurry and he was sweating very much, but *this had to be said and understood.* 'Thou wilt go now, rabbit. But I go with thee. As long as there is one of us there is both of us' " (p. 463, emphasis mine). So at last he leaves the words of a future reality hovering in the air to achieve their latent power even as the guerrillas earlier left vain words to linger and achieve their latent result.

If, as Robert Penn Warren has suggested, there is a code for the Hemingway hero—a code based on one's sensuous perceptions and his evaluations of those perceptions—the other part of the code is the language in which it is conceived as well as expressed. The people and the places and the things, whether in Italy or France or Spain, are first words whereby they may become realities in the imaginations of the characters. Hemingway's use of language magic in *For Whom the Bell Tolls,* as indeed in his other works, sets up a kind of verbal resonance whereby the narrative action is enriched and illuminated. As Robert Jordan notes quite early, to act is not enough. Actions must occur within the context of a communal reality known through language.

1. *For Whom the Bell Tolls* (New York, 1960), p. 21. Subsequent references will be to this Scribner's Library edition and will be parenthesized within the text.

2. *Language and Myth,* trans., S. K. Langer (1946; rptd. New York: Dover, 1953), pp. 8, 10, 56–57.

3. Benjamin Lee Whorf, *Language, Thought, and Reality,* ed., John B. Carroll (1956; rptd. Cambridge, Mass.: MIT Press paperback, 1967), pp. 209–19.

4. Trilling, "An American in Spain," *Ernest Hemingway: Critiques of Four Major Novels,* ed., Carlos Baker (New York, 1962), pp. 79–81; Barea, "Not Spain but Hemingway," *Hemingway and His Critics,* ed., Carlos Baker (New York, 1961), pp. 202–12; Evans, "Hemingway and the Pale Cast of Thought," *AL,* 38 (May 1966), 172.

5. *Hemingway: The Writer as Artist* (Princeton, 1963), pp. 245–50; *Hemingway's Heroes* (Albuquerque, 1969), p. 163.

6. Ford (1796–1858) traveled in Spain from 1830 to 1833 with special stays in Granada and Seville, where large gypsy populations were located, but reflected a general contempt for Romany people, at least in his advice to British travelers. Borrow (1803–1881), on the other hand, admired

gypsy life in both Britain and Spain, traveled in Spain during the late 1830's, and made a notable career for himself as their champion in such later works as *The Bible in Spain* (1843), *Lavengo* (1851), *Romany Rye* (1857), and *Romano Lavo-Lil* (1874), a wordbook of the gypsy language. Ford, 8th ed. (London, 1892); Borrow, 9th ed. (New York, 1923). For biographical data see *The Encyclopaedia Britannica,* 11th ed., IV, 275–76; X, 643.

7. *The Golden Bough: A Study in Magic and Religion,* abridged ed. (1922; rptd. New York, 1949), p. 56.

8. This is a different concern from that of critics involved in showing Hemingway's version of Spanish and English as Elizabethan, stately, plausible, or idiomatic. See Carlos Baker, pp. 248–49; Barea, pp. 202–12; Edward Fenimore, "English and Spanish in *FWBT,*" *Ernest Hemingway: The Man and His Work,* ed., J. K. M. McCaffery (New York, 1950), pp. 205–20; John J. Allen, "The English of Hemingway's Spaniards," *SAB,* 27 (November 1961), 6–7; J. W. Beach, *American Fiction, 1920–1940* (New York, 1941), pp. 115–17.

9. *The Golden Bough,* pp. 11–59, 244–261 *passim;* "The Problem of Meaning in Primitive Languages," Suppl. I in Ogden and Richards, *The Meaning of Meaning,* 3rd ed. revised (New York, 1930), pp. 297–326; C. K. Ogden and I. A. Richards, *The Meaning of Meaning,* pp. 1–47; Cassirer, pp. 1–62; Freud, "The Relation of the Poet to Daydreaming," *Delusion and Dream* (Boston, 1956), pp. 122–23.

10. Ogden and Richards, p. 25.

11. Freud, pp. 132–33.

12. *In Sara's Tents* (New York, 1953), p. 83.

13. Frazer, p. 244.

14. Malinowski, pp. 314–15.

15. *Ibid.,* pp. 312–13.

16. *Ibid.,* pp. 310–12, 323.

17. Hutton Webster, *Magic: A Sociological Study* (Stanford, 1948), p. 94.

18. "Hemingway's Blue-Eyed Boy: Robert Jordan and 'the Purging Ecstasy,' " *Criticism,* VIII (Winter 1966), 187.

HEMINGWAY ACHIEVES THE FIFTH DIMENSION

F. I. CARPENTER

IN *Green Hills of Africa,* Ernest Hemingway prophesied: "The kind of writing that can be done. How far prose can be carried if anyone is serious enough and has luck. There is a fourth and fifth dimension that can be gotten." Since then many critics have analyzed the symbols and mythical meanings of Hemingway's prose.[1] A few have tried to imagine what he meant by "a fourth and fifth dimension."[2] But most have agreed that the phrase is pretty vague.

Reprinted with permission from *American Literature and the Dream* (N.Y.: The Philosophical Library, 1955).

"The fourth dimension" clearly has something to do with the concept of time, and with fictional techniques of describing it. Harry Levin has pointed out that Hemingway's style is lacking in the complexity of structure that normally describes "the third dimension," but that it offers a series of images (much like the moving pictures) to convey the impression of time sequence and immediacy. Joseph Warren Beach has suggested that "the fourth dimension" is related to an "esthetic factor" achieved by the hero's recurrent participation in some traditional "ritual or strategy"; while "the fifth dimension" may be an "ethical factor" achieved by his "participation in the moral order of the world." And Malcolm Cowley has also related "the fourth dimension" of time to "the almost continual performance of rites and ceremonies" suggesting the recurrent patterns of human experience, but has called "the fifth dimension" a "mystical or meaningless figure of speech."

But is the prophecy of a fifth-dimensional prose "a meaningless figure of speech"? Certainly Hemingway has often attacked the critics for indulging in grandiose abstractions. Perhaps in *Green Hills of Africa,* one of his poorer books, he may have lowered his guard and relaxed his muscles. "The fifth dimension," moreover, has no accepted meaning to modern physicists. But Hemingway's art has always been self-conscious, and in the years of his apprenticeship in Paris he often discussed this art with Gertrude Stein—a trained philosopher, and an admirer of Henri Bergson's theories of the two kinds of "time."[3] Finally, I think, "the fifth dimension" is too strikingly specific a figure of speech to be "meaningless," although it may be "mystical."[4]

Actually, the specific phrase "the fifth dimension" was used in 1931 (*Green Hills of Africa* was published in 1935), by P. D. Ouspensky, who defined it to mean "the perpetual now." Ouspensky, a mystic, was an admirer of Bergson and of William James. Bergson (also an admirer of James) had emphasized the difference between psychological time and physical time. And both these ideas go back to William James's philosophy of "radical empiricism" (that is, of "immediate" or "pure" experience), which Gertrude Stein (a former pupil of James) had adapted for literary purposes. There is strong internal evidence that Hemingway's philosophy and practice both of style and of structure have followed this pattern of philosophic ideas. His literary ideal has been that of "immediate empiricism." And his "fifth-dimensional prose" has attempted to communicate the immediate experience of "the perpetual now."

This mystical idea of a "fifth-dimensional" experience of "the perpetual now" might seem fantastic except that Hemingway first suggested it explicitly, and then practiced it consciously in his best fiction. *For Whom the Bell Tolls* embodies the idea both implicitly, in structure, and explicitly, in the speeches and thoughts of its characters. If this major novel is analyzed with this philosophic idea in mind, the structure and the purpose become unmistakabl?. The same structure (although less explicitly) informs the two great short stories which preceded this novel: "The Short Happy Life of Francis Macomber" and "The Snows of Kilimanjaro." And the writing of these three major works immediately followed Hemingway's prophecy of a "fifth dimension" to be achieved by prose.

Finally, this idea of "the perpetual now," and the philosophy of immediate empiricism which underlies it, suggest an explanation for the sharp alternation of brilliant success and painful failure in Hemingway's fictional career. In its sentimental or isolated form, this idea degenerates into "the cult of sensation,"[5] or of violent experience divorced from the routine of living. In this form it explains the frequent spectacular badness of *To Have and Have Not* and of *Across the River and into the Trees*. But when related to the routine experiences of life, which give the more "sensational" experiences both a frame of reference and a meaning, this philosophy suggests the heights to which human nature can rise in moments of extreme stress. No longer the cult of "sensation," it becomes the ideal of "intensity" or "ecstasy," and produces that telescoping of experience and those flashes of illumination which make the "short" life of Francis Macomber supremely "happy," and the snows of Kilimanjaro blindingly brilliant.

In the 1920s, Albert Einstein's scientific theory of relativity—with its interpretation of "time" as a fourth dimension necessary to the measurement of the space between the stars and within the atoms—spawned a generation of pseudo-scientific speculators who attempted to interpret the meaning of these physical theories for philosophic and literary purposes. The most spectacular (and the least scientific) of these was the Russian-born mystic, P. D. Ouspensky, who published his *Tertium Organum* in 1921, and *A New Model of the Universe* in 1931. Specifically, Ouspensky defined the "fifth dimension" as

a line of perpetual now. . . . The fifth dimension forms a surface in relation to the line of time. . . . Though we are not aware of it, sensations of the existence of other "times" continually enter our consciousness. . . . The fifth dimension is movement in the circle, repetition, recurrence.[6]

And at considerable length he analyzed and illustrated these pseudo-scientific ideas with reference to James's "moments of consciousness," Bergson's theory of time, and "the Eternal Now of Brahma." I do not mean to imply that Hemingway necessarily read Ouspensky's books, but his conversations with Gertrude Stein and her friends in the twenties might well have included discussion of them. Moreover, his specific reference to "a fifth dimension" finds partial explanation here, and Ouspensky's description of "the perpetual now" closely parallels passages in *For Whom the Bell Tolls* (as we shall see later).

With Bergson's theory of the "fourth dimension" of time, we approach firmer ground. Closer to the main stream of philosophic thought, Bergson tried to interpret Einstein's scientific theory of the relativity of time for literary purposes. In 1922 he used recent experiments measuring the speed of light, and proving that light rays are "bent" by the force of gravitation, to illustrate his own already published theories of time. If physical "time" may be distorted by motion in space and by gravitation, the measurement of psychological time may be distorted even more. Bergson had always emphasized that mechanic time could never measure the intensities of the *élan vital* in human experience, and that the human organism distorted "time" through the devices of memory and intuitional thought. Now Einstein's theory of relativity suggested that time was not a final measurement in physics, either. In human consciousness time might be telescoped, and sensation intensified, just as a passenger on a train approaching a warning signal at a road crossing hears the ringing intensified in pitch as he approaches. Again, these ideas find echoes in Hemingway's prose.

But all these ideas are speculative. The matrix from which they spring, and in which their "mysticism" finds relation to reality, is the philosophy of William James—acknowledged as "master" by Ouspensky, Bergson, and Gertrude Stein equally. Approaching philosophy by way of psychology, James had interpreted all religious and artistic experiences as empirical phenomena: he had sought to observe, report, and analyze those intense "moments of consciousness," which men of religion and of art alike have described as the most "real" and important. With James, therefore, "realism" had become psychological, and "empiricism" had expanded to include all "immediate" or subjective as well as "mediate" or objective experience. Studying under James, Gertrude Stein had developed artistic techniques for communicating this "immediate" experience in prose style. Hemingway now carried these techniques further, and incorporated their psychological and philosophic patterns (outlined by James, Bergson, and perhaps Ouspensky) in the structural forms of his fiction.

To trace the development of these philosophic ideas, and to illustrate their application to literature, a book would hardly suffice. But to summarize: A brief, immediate experience, observed realistically, is described first as it occurred "in our time"; the protagonist is intensely moved, but remains confused, so that the meaning of it all seems nothing, or "nada." But this immediate experience recalls individual memories of other, similar experiences, or historic memories of parallel experiences in the history of other nations, or mystical, "racial" memories. And these "mediate" experiences are suggested by "flashbacks," or by conversations, or by the suggestion of recurrent myth or ritual patterns. And these fragmentary remembrances of similar experiences, by relating the individual to other people, places and times, suggest new meanings and forms. Finally this new awareness of the patterns and meanings implicit in the immediate, individual experience intensifies it, and gives it a new "dimension" not apparent at the time it actually happened.

For Whom the Bell Tolls is Hemingway's first full-length novel to describe, and partially to achieve, this radical intensification of experience. Both explicitly and implicitly, it seeks to realize the "fifth dimension" of time. It consciously describes—as well as subconsciously suggests—the telescoping of time involved in this realization of immediate experience. Indeed the very explicit self-consciousness with which it describes this idea constitutes its chief fault. But, although the idea has been suggested before, its formal pattern has never been clarified.

On the surface, the novel describes the tragedy of an American volunteer, fighting for the Loyalists in the Spanish Civil War, who is sent to dynamite a bridge and does so, but is killed as a result. The action takes place in three days and involves a love affair with a Spanish girl named Maria, who has been rescued by the band of Communist guerrillas, after having been raped by the Fascists. This love affair has been criticized as irrelevant and obtrusive, but it actually forms the core of the book. And paradoxically it seems obtrusive *because* it struggles under so heavy a weight of conscious meaning.

The love affair begins immediately (and sensationally) when Maria crawls into the hero's sleeping bag the first night out. She hopes thus to exorcise the memory of the evil that has been done to her. But, even while loving her, the hero remains conscious of the passage of time, asking " 'what time is it now?' . . . It was one o'clock. The dial showed bright in the darkness that the robe made."[7] Later when he declares his love for Maria to Pilar, the gypsy mother-confessor, she warns him that "There is not much time." Because the ending is destined to be tragic, the love affair must be brief. But it will be meaningful, later.

After the second experience of love on the second day, this new meaning is suggested: ". . . and time absolutely still and they were both there, time having stopped and he felt the earth move out and away from under them." Later, thinking of this experience, the hero generalizes:

. . . Maybe that is my life and instead of it being threescore years and ten it is . . . just threescore hours and ten or twelve rather. . . .

I suppose it is possible to live as full a life in seventy hours as in seventy years; granted that your life has been full up to the time that the seventy hours start and that you have reached a certain age.

... So if your life trades its seventy years for seventy hours I have that value now and I am lucky enough to know it. ... If there is only now, why then now is the thing to praise. ... Now, *ahora, maintenant, heute.*

This telescoping of time becomes the new "value," and a universal one. Meanwhile, the hero continues to speculate about this tragic and enigmatic wisdom suggested by Pilar, the gypsy:

... She is a damned sight more civilized than you and she knows what time is all about. Yes, he said to himself, I think that we can admit that she has certain notions about the value of time. ...

Not time, not happiness, not fun, not children, not a house, not a bathroom, not a clean pair of pyjamas, not the morning paper. ... No, none of that. ...

So if you love this girl as much as you say you do, you had better love her very hard and make up in intensity what the relation will lack in duration and in continuity.

As explicitly as possible the hero develops these new "notions about the value of time," speculating that the intense experience of a perpetual "now" may equal in value a lifetime of "duration and continuity." "It was a good system of belief," he concluded. "There is nothing else than now. ... A good life is not measured by any biblical span."

In the ecstatic experience of perfect union with his beloved, time has stood still, and the value of intensity has been substituted for that of duration. From this experience has emerged the philosophy of the eternal now. Meanwhile, as the larger action of the novel approaches its climax, the hero seeks to understand the strange combination of violence and idealism which characterizes the Spanish people.

On the last night, Maria pours out to him the story of her violation. And again he generalizes:

Those are the flowers of Spanish chivalry. What a people they have been. ... Spain has always had its own special idol worship within the Church. *Otra Virgen más.* I suppose that was why they had to destroy the virgins of their enemies. ... This was the only country the reformation never reached. They were paying for the Inquisition now, all right. ...

Maybe I have had all my life in three days, he thought.

In the hero's mind, "Maria" thus becomes a symbol of the traditional mariolatry of the Spanish Catholic Church, which "the reformation never reached"; and the violence of the Spanish Civil War becomes an intensified version of all modern history since the Reformation, compressed in symbolic time. His love for this modern Maria becomes both a symbolic fulfillment of history and a transcendence of the old "time." In a flash, the immediate experience of the eternal now becomes not only a personal "system of belief," but a philosophy of history illuminating the action of the whole novel.

Shortly after, the third and final experience of love obliterates time ("the hand on the watch moved, unseen now"), the ecstasy is complete ("not why not ever why, only this now"), and this individual experience becomes one with the experience of all mystics: "It is in Greco and in San Juan da la Cruz, of course, and in the others. I am no mystic, but to deny it is as ignorant as though you denied the telephone." And this mystic transcendence of time and of self informs the final chapters of the book, as, after being fatally wounded, the hero comforts Maria: "Thou art me too now. Thou art all there will be of me" (p. 464), and accepts his own death: "He began to accept it and let the hate go out. . . . Once you saw it again as it was to others, once you got rid of your own self, the always ridding of self that you had to do in war. Where there could be no self." Thus finally the experience of "the perpetual now" leads to the mystical experience.

This intensification of experience under the emotional stress of love or war, resulting in an ecstasy transcending the traditional limitations of time and of self, and producing a "system of belief" verging on the mystical, is the subject of *For Whom the Bell Tolls,* both implicitly and explicitly. In a sense it has always been the subject of all Hemingway's fiction. But of course the emphasis has changed over the different periods of his writing, and he has developed this "system of belief" progressively.

Hemingway's early fiction, in general, described the immediate experience, of love or war, with a minimal awareness of meaning, and a minimal experience of ecstasy; therefore the experience seemed largely "sensational," and the meaning "nada." But beginning with "The Short Happy Life of Francis Macomber" and "The Snows of Kilimanjaro," his stories began to achieve ecstasy and to imagine a transcendence of the futility of the past. The sudden illumination of the vision of snow-capped Kilimanjaro prophesied the ecstasies and the transcendence of time in *For Whom the Bell Tolls.* But this novel exaggerated perhaps the author's new consciousness of meaning, and his concern with the "system" of his belief. In *The Old Man and the Sea* the idea became at last incarnated and the mysticism completely naturalized.

But the idea of the intensified experience of the immediate "now" is not simple, nor is its mysticism traditional. Hemingway himself has suggested some of the necessary qualifications: his Robert Jordan "supposed" that the final fulfillment of life in seventy hours was possible, "granted that your life has been full up to the time that the seventy hours start, and that you have reached a certain age." That is, the intensity of experience which transcends time, and achieves a new "value" or "dimension," depends upon an earlier fullness of experience of time and the appreciation of its value. The mysticism of this fifth-dimensional experience implies no denial of the old "values" or "dimensions," but rather a fulfillment beyond them. These heroes do not seek escape from time (as do the hero and heroine of Robert Penn Warren's *World Enough and Time*), nor do they build a "tower beyond tragedy" (like the heroes of Robinson Jeffers), but rather they seek the intensified fulfillment of life within tragedy.

Further, this achievement of a new dimension of experience requires maturity—the hero must have reached "a certain age." Besides having lived a full life in the past, he must have reached a turning point, or crisis of life. So Francis Macomber—a natural aristocrat who has excelled at sports in the past—confronts the final test of courage, fails, but suddenly overcomes his fear and achieves a brief ecstasy of happiness. And the autobiographical hero of Kilimanjaro—who has prospered well enough in love and in literature—sees suddenly the ecstatic vision of supreme success, as he dies.

Finally, the achievement of this new dimension of experience, whether in "prose" or in life, is exceptional—"one must have luck." So Robert Jordan "had learned that he himself, with another person, could be everything. But inside himself he knew that this was the exception." The new experience requires a fullness of past life, a certain age, and an ecstasy which is mystical in every sense.

A fourth-dimensional sense of time (Cowley and Beach have suggested) is often achieved by a detailed description of the patterns of experience which have crystallized in rituals, ceremonies, traditions, habits of action, codes of behavior. On the level of pure realism, this may be suggested by that loving description of the techniques of any work or sport which is characteristic of all Hemingway's stories.[8] The absence of this workaday realism contributes to the failure of *Across the River,* while the exact techniques of fishing make real the occasional mysticism of *The Old Man and the Sea.* On the level of art, the patterned ritual of the bullfight and the sporting code of the big-game hunter also suggest this sense of repetition in time. While on the level of religion, mythical or symbolic actions, which sometimes seem unreal or irrational, may provide the pattern. The esthetic sense of the perfect fulfillment of some pattern of action in time is the necessary precondition for achievement of the final "magic."

The "fifth-dimensional" intensity of experience beyond time may come, finally, from a profound sense of participation in these traditional patterns of life experience. Beach's description of the fifth dimension as a "sense of participation in the moral order of the world" is suggestive. "You felt an absolute brotherhood with the others who were engaged in it," observed Robert Jordan of his Spanish Civil War. Paradoxically, love and war become supremely "moral," and the intensity of the experience they offer may communicate a mystical ecstasy. If only the sensational and the violent aspects are described, with only a traditional, third-dimensional realism, "nada" results. But these violent sensations have always been the elemental stuff, both of human tragedy and of mystical transcendence. If the red slayer think only of slaying, and if the slain think only of being slain, no fourth or fifth dimension is achieved. But Santiago in *The Old Man and the Sea,* performing realistically the ritual techniques of his trade, goes on to identify the intensity of his own suffering with that of the great fish that he is slaying. And, telling his story, Hemingway has achieved that synthesis of immediate experience and mysticism which, perhaps, is "the fifth dimension."

1. See especially Carlos Baker, *Hemingway: The Writer as Artist,* Princeton: 1952, and Philip Young, *Ernest Hemingway,* New York: 1952.

2. Joseph Warren Beach, "How Do You Like It Now, Gentlemen?" *Sewanee Review,* LIX (Spring, 1951), pp. 311–28; Harry Levin, "Observations on the Style of Hemingway," *Kenyon Review,* XIII (Autumn, 1951), pp. 581–609; Malcolm Cowley, *The Portable Hemingway,* New York: 1944, "Introduction."

3. See Bergson, *Durée et Simultanéité: à propos de la théorie d'Einstein,* Paris: 1922.

4. I use the term "mystical" in its most general sense, to describe any intense experience or "ecstasy" which results in insight or "illumination." I have defined this kind of mysticism at length in my *Emerson Handbook,* New York: 1953, pp. 113–16.

5. See R. P. Warren, "Hemingway," *Kenyon Review,* IX (Winter, 1947), pp. 1–28.

6. *A New Model of the Universe* (first published 1931, rev. ed., New York: 1950, p. 375).

7. *For Whom the Bell Tolls,* New York: 1940, p. 72.

8. See Joseph Beaver, " 'Technique' in Hemingway," *College English* (March, 1953), p. 325.

THE STRUCTURE OF HEMINGWAY'S
ACROSS THE RIVER AND INTO THE TREES

PETER LISCA

WHEN *Across the River and into the Trees* appeared in September of 1950, two or three reviewers actually found it to be Hemingway's best novel, and a few judged it to be no more a failure in sensibility than his previous work. But the majority of reviewers were pitiless in their attack.[1] "The ideological background of the novel," wrote Mr. Geismar, "is a mixture of *True Romances, Superman,* and the Last Frontier. And the setting of the novel is a perfect instance of Veblen's conspicuous consumption."[2] Those voices honestly confused and cautious, like Evelyn Waugh and Malcolm Cowley, were very few.[3] The sixteen years which have passed since these reviews have seen much perceptive Hemingway criticism. But *Across the River and into the Trees* has received only glancing attention in this criticism, and there has been only one essay devoted to a formal analysis of that novel—the chapter by Carlos Baker in his book, *Ernest Hemingway: The Writer as Artist.*[4]

A study of the little criticism which has concerned itself with *Across the River and into the Trees* reveals, paradoxically, that, to a large extent, its failure to find that novel esthetically significant is rooted in a thorough familiarity with Hemingway's previous fiction. First, it escaped no critic that it was possible to draw a certain line of correspondence between that novel and preceding Hemingway novels. Just as each Hemingway protagonist prior to Colonel Cantwell had embodied the experiences of earlier Hemingway protagonists, so in this old Colonel, Richard Cantwell, were subsumed the experiences of the youth Nick Adams, the Lieutenant Frederic Henry, the expatriate Jake Barnes, the Key Wester Harry Morgan, and the guerilla fighter Robert Jordan. In fact, the Colonel not only implicitly subsumes these characters, he refers directly to their experiences as being his own.[5] Colonel Cantwell's obvious lineage has made it extremely difficult for critics to approach the novel with that freshness, that innocence, with which each new work of

Reprinted with permission from *Modern Fiction Studies,* XII (Summer 1966), 232–250.

art must first be understood before it can justly be related to other works by the same artist or in the same tradition. Into the critics' calculations about *Across the River and into the Trees* has been programmed a block of understandings and judgments about previous Hemingway materials and techniques. Secondly, in addition to this kind of warping by previous fictional materials, there is the added difficulty that just as the earlier protagonists have been accepted as transparently autobiographical, so in Colonel Cantwell it is easy to see this reference continued to include those recent events not yet attributed to a fictional character—Hemingway's experiences in World War II, his recent residence in Venice, and even his having attained the age of fifty-one years and now being seriously ill and wishing to finish one thing well before facing death.[6]

A too nearly perfect but otherwise typical example of the effect of this kind of knowledge upon the critic is provided by Nemi D'Agostino in an essay appearing ten years after the Hemingway novel. After identifying Colonel Cantwell in the usual fashion as Hemingway's "standard hero" grown old, and saying several nasty things about him, as if he had been requested to give a moral evaluation of a living person, he proceeds as follows:

Hemingway wanted to transfigure his eternal hero, making him a pathetic and solemn figure, a creature of bitter passions and childish goodness, whose solitary experience has brought wisdom, nobility, and peace. But the character he actually portrays is that of an embittered and bad-tempered old man, querulous and self-conceited to the point of parody, full of boring and depressing boasts. Indeed, there has never been such a striking contrast between Hemingway's intention and his results. Tied still to his world of desperate young men, he has only been able to fall back on his old type, in a mannered and senile version.[7]

There are few passages in contemporary criticism which so clearly and forcibly illustrate the consequences of consorting with the harlot Intentional Fallacy.

Finally, in addition to aspects external to the novel which influenced such radically false judgments as those typified by D'Agostino, the materials themselves of *Across the River and into the Trees* pose certain difficulties. It is true, as Hemingway has said, that the dignity of movement of good writing, like that of an iceberg, is due to its being seven-eighths under the surface.[8] But whereas previous Hemingway novels have presented a one-eighth above the surface so attractive and exciting as to draw popular acclaim from readers who knew nothing about the other seven-eighths, *Across the River and into the Trees* is unique in presenting above the surface an aspect not only unattractive but even repelling: a long monologue consisting of petulant or brutal personal attacks on specific, contemporary, public figures, interspersed at random throughout the account of an improbable romance between a beautiful nineteen-year-old girl of the Italian nobility and a sentimental, battered and dying, fifty-year-old American Colonel who seems clearly to be Hemingway himself; the scene set almost entirely in a hotel and restaurant, depicting no heroic action or youthful initiates into violence, or lost generations—in short a novel lacking all of the more public Hemingway qualities.

Yet, late in 1949, while revising the manuscript of *Across the River and into the Trees* Hemingway was very effusive about its virtues, claiming not only that it was superior to *A Farewell to Arms,* but perhaps his best work.[9] Later, while the first reviews were appearing, and it was becoming obvious that the critics did not at all like his new work, Hemingway was still very confident of his accomplishment:

"Sure, they can say anything about nothing happening in "Across the River," but all that happens is the defense of the lower Piave, the break-through in Normandy, the taking of Paris and the destruction of the 22nd Inf. Reg. in Hurtgen Forest plus a man who loves a girl and dies.

Only it is all done with three-cushion shots. In the last one I had the straight narrative; Sordo on the hill for keeps; Jordan killing the cavalryman; the village; a full-scale attack presented as they go; and the unfortunate inci-dent of the bridge.

Should I repeat myself? I don't think so. You have to repeat yourself again and again as a man but you should not do so as a writer.

In writing I have moved through arithmetic, through plane geometry and algebra, and now I am in calculus. If they don't understand that, to hell with them. I won't be sad and I will not read what they say. They say? What do they say? Let them say.

Who the hell wants fame over a week-end. All I want is to write well."[10]

Hemingway's insistence that *Across the River and into the Trees* was beyond the critics' ability or perhaps willingness to understand is a challenge no student of Hemingway can ignore.

The most important step toward an understanding of *Across the River and into the Trees* is to understand its narrative strategy, particularly because much of the antagonism towards that novel arises from the critical failure to grasp the identity of the narrating voice. Actually, although the novel is told throughout in the grammatical third person, only the short first chapter and the last thirty pages originate in an omniscient third person who occasionally tells us, especially in the last chapter, of things the Colonel cannot know. All the rest is narrated by Colonel Cantwell himself; but so subtly is this transition from one narrator to another managed, that apparently no critic has yet noticed it.

The novel begins with an omniscient third person description of "the shooter" before dawn in a duck boat proceeding to a blind, and the first chapter ends with this still anonymous "shooter" established in his blind and cautioning himself not to let the surly guide ruin his day's shooting. "Keep your temper, boy, he told himself." Chapter II begins: "But he was not a boy. He was fifty and a Colonel of the Infantry in the Army of the United States and to pass a physical examination that he had to take the day before he came down to Venice for this shoot he had. . . ." We do not return again to the duck hunt until Chapter XL, just thirty pages from the novel's end, at which point there begins a gradual transition once more to the omniscient third person narrator, who concludes the novel with a description of the Colonel's last few hours and his death. The intervening two hundred and seventy-eight pages make up an uninterrupted interior monologue during which the shooter recreates in his mind not only the actual events of the last two days, Friday and Saturday, since the medical exam on Thursday, but also the particular memories which had concerned him during those two days.[11]

Thus, the novel is really a first person narration of events in the past, like *The Sun Also Rises* and *A Farewell to Arms,* but disguised as third person narration through the device of using the shooter as a *persona* through whom the Colonel thinks about himself. The result is that we know the Colonel *only as he knows himself,* but with the authority and effects which accrue to the interior monologue by virtue of its disguise as omniscient third person narration. An understanding of this narrative strategy makes it obvious that the lack of difference between the sensibility of the Colonel and the narrator (for most critics a prime objection to the novel) does not indicate that the author (i.e. Hemingway personally) identifies himself with Colonel Cantwell, but only that the narrator actually *is* Colonel Cantwell. This brilliant narrative strategy is one of Hemingway's "three-cushion shots."

The second most important step toward an understanding of *Across the River and into the Trees* is to understand the actual relationship between Colonel Cantwell and Renata. Here too, Hemingway abandons the "arithmetic" of such a relationship as that of Lieutenant Frederic Henry and Catherine Barkley, or Robert Jordan and Maria, for a relationship much more complex. A good beginning towards this understanding can be made by realizing that, despite the much leered over gondola and hotel room scenes, for the Colonel his own sexual gratification is the least important aspect of his relationship with Renata. In fact, a careful reading of the love scenes reveals that he does not have complete sexual intercourse with her (pp. 152–154).[12] Whatever the difference between these lovers and those of *The Sun Also Rises, A Farewell to Arms,* and *For Whom the Bell Tolls* may be, they are all star-crossed. In *Across the River and into the Trees* Hemingway not only makes it impossible for them to marry because of the woman's family and religion (the Colonel being divorced), and not only makes it clear that the man is soon to die, but even denies them sexual fulfillment on the eve of their final separation by making that time coincide with the woman's period of menstruation (p. 110). Colonel Cantwell reassures Renata he doesn't care about their "losses," "because the moon is our mother and our father" (p. 114). They are children of mutability, and like the other children of mutability in Hemingway they make their adjustments to the *Nada.* "Don't think at all. Don't think," advises the Colonel frequently (p. 269); ". . . let's not talk, or think, about how things might have been different," says Renata (p. 210). Under these circumstances the Colonel demonstrates the selfishness of his love by expressing it as best he can—as if he had heard the priest in *A Farewell to Arms* saying to Lieutenant Frederic Henry, "When you love you wish to do things for. You wish to sacrifice for. You wish to serve." Cantwell thinks of himself as "assisting" or "[making] an act of presence, at the only mystery he believed in except the occasional bravery of man" and "knowing it is only what man does for woman that he retains, except what he does for his fatherland," until for Renata "the great bird had flown far out of the closed window of the gondola" (pp. 153–154).

The more pervasive significance of Colonel Cantwell's relationship with Renata begins with her name—"the reborn one." Simply, she is named "reborn" because she represents in the novel, and quite consciously for her lover, Colonel Cantwell's own youth. It is for this reason, and as a diminution of the sex-role, that he calls her "daughter" and once even "boy or daughter or my one true love or whatever it is" (p. 173), for through one's children one is re-born.[13] Her symbolic role is emphasized by her being nineteen years old, the exact age of the Colonel when he first saw Venice, was first wounded (World War I), and realized he was not immortal, an event he returns to several times in his thoughts and conversations. Renata is of course a Venetian. And just as it was defending that city that he was first wounded, so when he dies he leaves her a totem guardian in the form of a pin such as the old Venetians used to wear, a pin depicting their most trusted servant. In another of her aspects, Renata is the Colonel's idealized love. It is impossible to escape the allusions to Venus born out of the sea, as, not incidentally, Venice herself was born out of the sea, carried stone by stone from Torcello—a bit of history which the colonel supplies us. Renata is several times associated with sea imagery and once refers to her portrait as depicting her as if "rising from the sea without the head wet" (p. 97). Anyone who has seen Botticelli's *Birth of Venus* will recognize Renata's constantly wind-blown hair.

Finally, in still another aspect, Renata embodies the ultimate complement and resolution to her aspects of Youth (life) and Love (creation), for she is just as clearly Death and Nothingness. "She kissed him kind, and hard, and desperately. . . . He only thought of her and how she felt and how close life comes to death when there is ecstasy. . . . Yes, ecstasy is what you might have had and instead you draw sleep's other brother. . . . It [death] comes in bed to most people, I know, like love's opposite number" (p. 219–220). Although in a military metaphor the Colonel thinks of Renata's love as an armor against death, nevertheless it is she who frequently reminds him, explicitly and verbally, of his imminent death. (The Colonel himself plays continually with various images of his own death, from "sleep's brother" and Bach's *Komm' Süsser Tod* to the horrible depictions of Hieronymus Bosch.) Parallel to Renata's association with the imagery of rebirth and love is her association with the imagery of death—darkness, cold, wind. This Freudian merging of love and death is emphasized when she once, as they are making love, refers to herself as "the unknown country" and to her lover as its discoverer (p. 155).

This association of Renata with the imagery of death is of the very essence. For beginning with its title, taken from the dying words of General Stonewall Jackson, to those words repeated on the last page by the dying Colonel Cantwell, *Across the River and into the Trees* is a novel of death.[14] The Colonel remembers Gabriele D'Annunzio shouting to the Italian troops, *"Morire non e basta,"* and he makes of his last three days an elaborate ritual of preparation, for he agrees that "To die is not enough." In this preparation Renata plays a significant role, for it is she who, by encouraging and accepting Colonel Cantwell's three long confessions, absolves him. "Don't you see," says Renata, "you need to tell me things to purge your bitterness?" "I know I tell them to you," replies the Colonel. "Don't you know I want you to die with the grace of a happy death?" continues Renata (p. 240). The words "confession," "purge," and "contrition" appear frequently in relation to the Colonel's reminiscences to Renata.

Malcolm Cowley, one of the more perceptive readers of the novel, believes that this preparation for death is incomplete because in these confessions he leaves out what would seem to be his most painful memory—the scene of his demotion as a consequence of his objections to the General Staff's strategy for the Battle of Hurtgen Forest.[15] Actually, the Colonel's most painful memory is one of his own blunders in military thinking, whereby a dear friend (referred to only as "George") is killed. This memory he does not share with Renata. It is so painful that it occurs to him only in fragments and with the ending left out, but unmistakably implied (pp. 292–294). Significantly, it occurs to him only in his barrel, the last memory he has before the end of the duck hunt.

Corollary to the Colonel's desire for confession and absolution before death is his desire to extend understanding and acceptance to others. He is very much aware of his truculence, his "wild boar nature" (which has been noted by critics as a judgment against him, the novel, and Hemingway personally), and tries to balance it with kindness. The boatman, for example, without personal provocation, persists in his surliness and behaves very badly, almost ruining the day's shooting, which Colonel Cantwell knows may very well be his last. Yet the Colonel, except for muttering once in English, not only continues to help the boatman with his work, but even shares his gin with him. At the end of the shoot, when he asks the boatman why he had acted so badly, the boatman replies that he is sorry; he had acted "in anger." "I have done that myself sometimes, the Colonel thought, and did not ask him what the anger was about" (p. 297). It is Baron Alvarito, the host of the shoot, who later explains to the Colonel that the boatman had been "over-liberated." "When the Moroccans came through here they raped both his wife and his daughter" (p. 302). The Colonel had forgiven him before learning this, but now he also understands. This same reconciliation and making peace can be illustrated with Jackson, his chauffeur, of whom, it is true, he remembers some nice things, but many unflattering ones, and to whom he addresses some slight insults. Yet it is his realization that he is not treating Jackson with kindness that prompts the most bitter of his self-remonstrances in this respect. " 'I'm sorry, Jackson,' the Colonel said. 'I'm a shit' " (p. 58). The Colonel's desire to be more gentle and understanding, his "always renewed plan of being kind, decent and good" (p. 65) extends to groups as well as individuals. Now that the war is over he harbors no grudge against the Fascists or the Nazis.

This is not to say that the Colonel dies with no personal dislikes or even prejudices; his preparation for death is not perfect. He does not forgive bungling incompetence, whether political, artistic, or military. Nor does he forgive war profiteers of either side, whom he calls *"pescecani,"* sharks. But he tries as much as possible to strip all rancor from his heart, and succeeds more than did Dante, to whom in this respect the old Colonel alludes several times. " 'You sound like Dante,' [Renata] said sleepily. 'I am Mister Dante,' he said. 'For the moment.' And for a while he was and he drew all the circles. They were as unjust as Dante's but he drew them" (p. 246). Colonel Cantwell knows (and is reminded several times a day by the buzzing in his head, twinges of his heart, and spells of dizziness) that quite literally any action, any speech, may be his last; so he is trying to live every minute the best that he can. Whenever this attempt to live well is threatened by the callousness, cruelty, or stupidity of others, or by the indifferences of fate, or by his own truculent nature, he reminds himself not only to "take it easy," not to let anything "spoil it" for him, but also to be more charitable.

In addition to this level of the Colonel's conscious preoccupation, death is also implied in a variety of physical images which occur frequently in the novel. The most pervasive of these is the wind, which is used thematically in at least thirty passages. The Colonel first mentions the wind after he has settled into his sunken barrel and, looking towards the snow-covered mountains rising right out of the plain, he feels a breeze in his face and knows then that "the wind should come from there. . . ." This association of wind with snow, cold, and the mountains is repeated intermittently with other passages in which the wind grows quite strong and "lashes" the Colonel when he steps out from the shelter of the hotel or, especially, whenever he must cross a bridge. This wind is also associated with "last sunlight," "dying winter light," "late afternoon light," and the unusually high tide which coincides with the climactic gondola ride of the Colonel and Renata, making the passing under bridges uncertain and the next day flooding the square of St. Mark. The Colonel himself seems sensitive to this symbolic import of the wind, deliberately facing into it and even keeping the windows of his room wide open so that he can feel the cold wind. Although similar to the rain in *A Farewell to Arms* in its thematic function, in *Across the River and into the Trees* Hemingway manages the wind much more subtly despite its more frequent appearance and does not allow the narrator to explain the symbolism as he does Catherine Barkley. A good example of the extremely sensitive and indirect way that Hemingway manages this symbol is when the Colonel telephones Harry's Bar to see who is there before deciding whether he wants to join them. The company which the waiter describes is American and one which the Colonel wishes to avoid; he asks the bartender to call him when they leave. Then he looks out the window. "He watched a gondola working up the Canal against the wind and thought, not with Americans drinking" (pp. 72–73). In that image of the gondola beating into the wind he sees his own struggle against death, and he wants to avoid the risk that his third and fatal heart attack might come while drinking with this particular company. Wind imagery is also used throughout the love scene in the gondola passage. After the Colonel has satisfied Renata, he says to her,

"You're in the lee now," referring to the wind *and* her sexual climax. A little later the Colonel describes himself and Renata as "going with the wind now and they were both tired" (p. 159).

Colonel Cantwell's sensitivity to images of death reaches a peak in the extended passage describing his observations in the public market, making out of his reflections something like one of Shakespeare's sonnets on mutability. "A market," thinks the Colonel, "is the closest thing to a good museum like the Prado or as the Accademia is now . . ." (p. 192). He finds himself at the fish stalls and begins his observations:

. . . the heavy, gray-green lobsters with their magenta overtones that presaged their death in boiling water. They have all been captured by treachery, the Colonel thought, and their claws are pegged.

There were the small soles, and there were a few albacore and bonito. These last, the Colonel thought, looked like boat-tailed bullets, dignified in death. . . .

They were not made to be caught except for their voraciousness. The poor sole exists, in shallow water, to feed man. But these roving bullets, in their great bands, live in blue water and travel through all oceans and all seas.

A nickel for your thoughts now, he thought. . . .

There were many eels, alive and no longer confident in their eeldom. There were fine prawns that could make a *scampi brochetto* spitted and broiled on a rapier-like instrument. . . . There were medium sized shrimp, gray and opalescent, awaiting their turn, too, for the boiling water and their immortality, to have their shucked carcasses float out easily on an ebb tide on the Grand Canal.

The speedy shrimp, the Colonel thought, with tentacles longer than the mustaches of that old Japanese admiral, comes here now to die for our benefit. Oh Christian shrimp, he thought, master of retreat, and with your wonderful intelligence service in those two light whips, why did they not teach you about nets and that lights are dangerous? (pp. 192–193)

And having observed all these ways to death, he concludes, ironically, "must have been some slip-up," and proceeds to the sestet, as it were, of his prose sonnet. He neither succumbs to despair nor plans immortality in verse or progeny. "Every day is a new and fine illusion," the Colonel once tells Renata. "But you can cut out everything phony about the illusion as though you would cut it with a straight-edge razor" (p. 232). So, he buys some clams and, borrowing a knife, opens them himself because he cuts "closer to the shell" (of life) than the vendor had been taught, and eats them on the spot. When he leaves the fish market, the Colonel finds the wind so strong that it takes an extra gondolier to get him safely home.

The symbolism of boats is a natural one for the Venice setting, and Colonel Cantwell's awareness of the movement of gondolas and barges almost always carries some suggestion of his own journey toward death. The old launch with the faltering motor, which carries the Colonel into Venice from the garage Friday afternoon and back again Saturday, bears a resemblance to the Colonel which does not escape him. Nor does it escape Renata, who makes a point of preferring to take this same launch instead of a newer, more comfortable one after parting with her lover. The black, heavily loaded barge, the boat which carries the shooter to his barrel buried in the marsh, the gondola which carries the lovers, the boat traveling along a canal in the Veneto plain and seen only as "a sail in the country," and the gondola which the Colonel sees beating into the wind are similarly endowed with symbolic suggestion. This prevalence of boats underway constantly presents us with a physical analogue to the Colonel's own interior journey. The long section of the novel in which he remembers in great detail his journey from Trieste, where he is stationed, to Venice through the country of his youth, and the gondola ride down the historic Grand Canal, lined with the palazzos of the great departed, contributes importantly to this journey motif, as does the Colonel's death in the automobile on the way back to Trieste Sunday evening. The chauffeur, Jackson, who is first mistakenly addressed by Cantwell as "Burnam" (as in *Macbeth*) and whose actual name is that of the general whose remarks before his death give title to the novel, is an obvious Charon figure.

The opening chapter of *Across the River and into the Trees* and parts of chapters XL, XLI, and XLII, which conclude the duck shoot, have been regarded by those readers looking for the earlier, "precalculus" Hemingway style as possibly the only successful passages in the novel. Symbolically, these chapters are very integral, for the "frame story" of the duck shoot initiates and concludes the imagery of the death journey. It is significant in this regard that Colonel Cantwell's shooting blind is actually a barrel sunk into the marshy ground of the lagoon, a grave-like image which is emphasized by its further description as "surrounded by a sloping rim of earth that had been planted with sedge and grass" (p. 3). Thus, the Colonel re-lives his life (the novel) while he is actually physically below ground, symbolically entombed. It is also significant in this regard that the entire atmosphere of the first chapter, with its darkness, its boatman, and its silence is reminiscent of the death journey. Although it may be customary to pay Charon in coin, Colonel Cantwell instead helps him with the boat. "After all, I too am a boatman," he says. And indeed as a combat officer he has frequently been responsible for ferrying people across the River Styx. To complete these allusions, the day before the shoot Colonel Cantwell carefully selects some sausage for the boatman's dog.

After the duck shoot, riding in his car, the last thing he thinks about before writing his farewell note and suffering his fatal heart attack is that he had forgotten to give the dog his sausage. Presumably he still has it with him when he dies, and perhaps the customary gift to Cerberus will not be forgotten.

Through the specific details of the ducks themselves Hemingway associates with Colonel Cantwell some of the novel's most poignant imagery of death. To begin with, the ducks, as migratory birds, are effective symbols of man's transitory life, and bird-soul symbolism has been traditional from the sparrow in Bede's Ecclesiastical History to the swans and sea-gulls in the poems of Yeats. In *Across the River and into the Trees* these ducks come with the wind from the North, the mountains, and the cold, all established as death images, and are flying out to sea. The various details of how the ducks are tricked to their death by wooden decoys and live hens who "quacked loud in their loyal treachery" are similar to details of treachery in the fish market soliloquy. The only ducks the Colonel shoots in Chapter I are a lone pair which he drops close together, and the first ducks he kills when we return to the frame story 270 pages later are another drake and its mate, which the Colonel drops also together. (It will be recalled that in *For Whom the Bell Tolls* the final separation of the lovers is presaged by the gypsy, who walks into camp carrying two dead hares which had been caught making love in the snow.) Colonel Cantwell shoots only one other duck, his last one, a "single drake, long necked and beautiful, the wings fast moving and traveling to the sea. . . . with the mountains behind him" (p. 281). This duck falls among the decoys in the lightly refrozen water. On the way back to the Baron's villa, the boatman's retriever finds a crippled drake, only wing-tipped, and brings him in his jaws, the drake's head making "a movement without hope." This last duck is put into a sack with the live decoy hen to await an uncertain fate—either release in the spring or to become himself a decoy. One of the things the Colonel remembers about himself and Renata is that although he very much enjoys a solitary stroll through the public markets of Venice, he never goes "to where they have the wild ducks," for which Renata thanks him. "I never go there when we are not together," the Colonel replies (p. 199). In *Death in the Afternoon* Hemingway tells us that when a man is still in rebellion against death he will get pleasure from taking to himself the God-like attribute of giving it to others. As the Colonel picks up the decoys at the end of the duck shoot he knows that he has exercised that pleasure for the last time.

Just as effective as Hemingway's use of a duck shoot for the frame story is his use of Venice for the locale of the novel. As an amateur of the arts and a student of history, Colonel Cantwell not only thoroughly exploits his physical environment, but also brings into the novel a wealth of relevant historical, biographical, and literary materials. His interest in the origins of Venice, its history, the legends of St. Mark, the parallels between Othello's situation and his own, the course of Gabriele D'Annunzio's love affair in Venice, the details of Byron's stay in Venice, the failure of all three Brownings (counting their dog) to leave on the city any impression whatever: these bits of knowledge help discover for us significant aspects of the Colonel's personality. Furthermore, as the city in whose defense, as a youth of nineteen years, he received the baptism of his first wound and the realization of his own mortality, Venice has for the Colonel not only a sentimental, but a symbolic value. That he respects this symbolic value is clear from his commemoration of it, three days before his death, by digging a hole and burying his medal, the Italian pension, and, as a commentary, his own excrement "in the exact place where he had determined by triangulation, that he had been badly wounded thirty years before" (p. 18). To return to Venice is to return to the scenes of his youth, as the nineteen year old Renata symbolically attests. As the Colonel, in his parked car, suffers his fatal heart attack, it is probably of some satisfaction to him that he is dying on the same spot, almost exactly, where he was first wounded.

Beyond this private interplay between Colonel Cantwell and the setting of the novel lies the interplay between a complex of public associations with Venice and the larger materials of the novel—its theme and mood. From the time of the Renaissance and reaching its greatest intensity in the nineteenth century, Venice has held a particular fascination for the artistic, especially the literary, imagination, which has not only surrendered to that fascination but contributed to it. Thomas Mann's *Death in Venice,* which bears numerous similarities to *Across the River and into the Trees,* is the most obvious modern example of the Venetian setting used thematically.[16] But two other writers much more highly regarded by Hemingway have also used the Venetian setting thematically—Henry James and Turgenev. James, with his remarkable sense of place, has Milly Theale choose to die in Venice, where, she feels, there is so much beauty in decay; and perhaps also, like James, she considers that city "supremely as the refuge of endless strange secrets, broken fortunes and wounded hearts."[17] Less obviously, it is his residence in Venice and his contact with its past that prompts Hyacinth Robinson to renounce his anarchism in *The Princess Casamassima.* Juliana Bordereau of *The Aspern Papers,* existing only in her memories of a glorious past, lives in Venice. The example from Turgenev is even more to the point, for in his novel *On the Eve* not only does Insároff die in Venice, but his death is presaged by a sea-gull which unaccountably falls into the sea "as though it had been shot."[18]

Although difficult to state accurately, there seems implicit in the imagination's grasp of Venice some notion of its being a place where things come full circle, where opposites meet, a place for old endings and new beginnings. Each year the city is officially married to the sea. "Nowhere else," wrote Henry James, "has the past been laid to rest with such tenderness, such a sadness of resignation and remembrance."[19] It is particularly this sense of coming full circle, of opposites meeting (e.g., East and West, "the City in the Sea") that dictated Hemingway's use of a Venetian setting for *Across the River and into the Trees;* for the novel's central image, as well as the Colonel's main concern with the conduct of his last few days, is that of bringing together opposites, sometimes in reconciliation, sometimes as definition.

The most obvious of these opposites is, of course, Life and Death, which has here already been discussed in several connections. Also obvious is Youth and Age. The important transition from omniscient third person narration to interior monologue, it will be remembered, hinges on the repetition of the word "boy," and that word or "kid" or "son" appears at least a score of times. The Youth and Age contrast appears and is discussed not only in the relationship of Colonel Cantwell with Renata, whom he calls "daughter," and with his own youth, but also in his relationship with his chauffeur, the young Italian men who flaunt his age and misjudge his physical abilities, and the contrasts between the former fascists of the Colonel's age (like the waiter) and the young ones. Frequently tied in with Youth and Age are the opposites Past and Present, under which a variety of minor contrasts are ordered. These contrasts may be defined through history (usually of Venice); through the comparison of World Wars I and II (a large topic in the book); or through the bringing together in Venice itself of Doges' palaces (sometimes, like the Gritti, now a hotel) and the "ugly Breda works that might have been Hammond, Indiana" (p. 35). Still another opposite under which a variety of minor contrasts are ordered is Old World and New World. These contrasts are defined under a variety of topics, such as foods (K rations and energy crackers vs. Valpolicella and scaloppine with Marsala); museums (arrowheads and petrified fish vs. Titian and Tintoretto); architecture (moving picture palaces vs. St. Mark's Cathedral); people (the riff-raff from the American Consulate vs. Count Andrea and Barone Alvarito).

There are several other pairs of opposites elaborated in *Across the River and into the Trees,* such as Love and Hate, War and Peace, Male and Female, Competence and Incompetence, and others. One more of these pairs, Destruction and Creation, is of enough significance to merit some further discussion. The "shooter" begins his recollections with the information that to pass his

physical examination three days earlier he had taken so much mannitol hexani-
trate for his heart that the surgeon had advised, "But don't you ever run into
anything or let any sparks strike you, when you're really souped up on nitro-
glycerin. They ought to make you drag a chain like a high octane truck" (p.
9). The drug which gives the Colonel life is also a powerful destroyer. The first
thing which the shooter remembers of the Colonel's journey from Trieste to
Venice is a conversation with his chauffeur, Jackson, about the destruction of
works of art by the American bombers, and throughout the novel there is more
thinking and talking about war and art (Destruction and Creation) than of any
other topic. With few exceptions the personalities which occupy the Colonel's
mind are either soldiers or artists, and in those artists he most approves the
two approach each other. "That's from Shakespeare," he thinks, quoting from
Henry IV, "the winner and still the undisputed champion. . . . Soldiers care
for Mister Shakespeare too, though it may seem impossible. He writes like a
soldier himself" (p. 171). He associates Wagner, pejoratively, with the German
Staff's last few days in the bunkers under Berlin, "when they were all playing
at Götterdämmerung"; Bach, however, is thought of as "practically a co-
belligerent" (p. 88). Although, for a military man, the Colonel displays an
unusual knowledge and love of art, he realizes that art is only an imitation of
reality. "I love you very much because you are beautiful," he muses to the
portrait of Renata, "but I love the girl better, a million times better, hear it?"
When the Colonel dies, he leaves Renata (herself a figure of both life and death)
two gifts—a pair of shotguns and a painting.

Another facet of the Destruction and Creation theme is embodied in what
has appeared to many readers as one of the least attractive aspects of *Across
the River and into the Trees,* its constant military language. So completely
imbued is the Colonel with his *"sale métier,"* as he calls it, that he tends to
see all objects and situations in military terms. Thus a certain small church
"looks like a P 47," a makeshift bathroom is a "defensive rather than an
attacking" bathroom, a sharp reply is a "counterattack." He is being the
Colonel *malgré lui;* for it must be remembered that the Colonel is also the
narrator of the novel, except for the frame story.

This preoccupation with military language is evident even in his love
relations. When he whispers softly in Renata's ear, it is "as his whisper was
when they are fifteen feet away and you are a young lieutenant on patrol."
When he feels in good health, he is "as young as at his first attack." And this
is the imagery with which he describes the effect of Renata's love: "I feel as
though I were out on some bareassed hill where it was too rocky to dig, and
the rocks all solid, but with nothing jutting, and no bulges, and all of a sudden

instead of being there naked, I was armoured. Armoured and the eighty-eights not there" (pp. 128–129). Renata assumes this language from her lover and carries it further, as when, while lying together in the gondola, she asks, "Just hold me very tight and hold the high ground, too" (p. 153). In the same passage, wishing the Colonel to resume his fondling of her, she requests him to "please attack gently and with the same attack as before." It is particularly in these passages that the military terminology seems awkward. But in attempting to use the language of war (destruction) for love (creation) Colonel Cantwell is, though perhaps not so successfully, in the tradition of English poetry from the Elizabethans to the Cavaliers (best exemplified by John Donne) who carried their love into battle as an armor and who addressed not only their mistresses but even God in the language of war.

Standing over all the opposites that meet, for reconciliation or definition, is a symbol which is itself very much a part of the Venetian setting—the bridge, which in *Across the River and into the Trees* is used as symbolically as the bridge from which Lieutenant Henry leaps, or the bridge which Robert Jordan gives his life to destroy. By its very definition a bridge joins opposites. And as Colonel Cantwell's last few days are preoccupied with reconciliations and definitions before death, so this preoccupation is symbolized by the many bridges he must cross or under which he must travel. It is at the end of a particularly symbolic passage under five clearly particularized bridges that we come to one of the novel's most powerful images, the "two stakes chained together, but not touching," a symbol of himself and Renata in all her aspects; for just as clearly, the union of himself and Renata creates a microcosm in which is contained the entire structure of opposites which informs the novel.[20]

There is another aspect of Colonel Cantwell's death which is of some importance. Almost every reader of *The Old Man and The Sea* has noted the Christian imagery in that novel, and a few have also noted its brief, curious appearance in *A Farewell to Arms*. In *Across the River and into the Trees* this Christian imagery is most pervasive. Colonel Cantwell's right hand has been pierced twice, and it is this "true" hand which Renata prefers the Colonel to use in their lovemaking because it has been pierced "honorably." "Yes. Very honorably. On a rocky, bare-assed hill," adds the Colonel (p. 135). Renata tells him that in a dream this hand appears to her as "the hand of Our Lord" (p. 84). It is also significant that although the Colonel spends only one day in his submerged barrel he begins that day by recollecting briefly a medical examination on the previous Thursday and goes on to remember in great detail the events of the following two days, Friday and Saturday, rising from his barrel on Sunday, the third day. Although the time span of the novel cannot be identified as the Easter weekend, the Easter theme is here clearly implied. When during their last moments together Renata comments, "It is Saturday. . . . And when is next Saturday?" the Colonel replies, "Next Saturday is a movable feast," and in turn asks the head-waiter, *Gran Maestro* of their secret order, "When will next Saturday come?" The waiter replies cryptically, *"A Pâques ou à la Trinité,"* both movable feasts according to the luni-solar cycle on which the Catholic calendar is determined (p. 273). Further, the number three is insisted upon in many different and seemingly unrelated connections throughout the novel, and it has been just about thirty-three years since the Colonel was first wounded and thus baptized into his *sale métier*. When all these specific parallels to Christ are brought together (and "Christ!" is the Colonel's most frequent expletive) with those themes embodied in the symbolically named Renata ("Reborn"), it seems clear that the Christian theme is a prominent part of the novel's ritual preparation, bringing together the imagery of death and the themes of self-examination, reconciliation, and confession.

There remains one more element not yet examined here which bulks large in *Across the River and into the Trees*—its many references to history, politics, works of art, and personalities living and dead. In his conversations and thoughts Colonel Cantwell finds occasion to mention specifically Breughel, Hieronymus Bosch, Wagner, Bach, Dégas, Goya, Titian, Tintoretto, Michelangelo, Piero della Francesca, Mantegna, and a few other painters and musicians. He is even better versed in literature, bringing up by name or direct quotation an impressive number of figures—Dante, Blake, Shakespeare, D'Annunzio, Byron, Browning, Max Reinhardt, Christopher Marlowe, Rimbaud, Edgar Quinet, Verlaine, and François Villon. Other writers are alluded to, among them T. S. Eliot, Richard Lovelace, and John Donne. Some of these allusions are clear. "Deader than Phoebus the Phoenician," says the Colonel about his divorced wife, and probably about Eliot too (p. 213). Or, "I have my small necessities of honor in the same proportions as we have our great and enveloping love," the Colonel tells Renata. "You can't have the one without the other" (p. 123). Sometimes there is merely an echo, as when the Colonel hears the two young Italians talking about him; what he hears sounds vaguely familiar to the reader: ". . . they are making it pretty personal now," thinks the Colonel. "It isn't just Americans, it is also me, myself, my gray hair, the slightly crooked way I walk. . . . It is my uniform which they find to be without grace. Now it is why I am walking at this hour, and now it is their absolute security that I can no longer make love" (p. 186). Even more numerous than these artistic and literary allusions are the novel's references to historical, political, and military events and personalities, especially those related to

World War II. Ernest Udet, Pacciardi, Goebbels, Tito, Cripps, Field Marshall Montgomery, Gamelin, Generals Walter Bedell Smith, Leclerc, Rommel, Franco, Patton, Eisenhower, Bradley, Queseda, and Stilwell—these are mentioned by name.[21] Other personalities, such as President Truman, Margaret Truman, and Sinclair Lewis, are clearly identifiable.

Granted that it is perfectly normal under the circumstances (his age, situation in life, relationship with Renata, and his knowledge of imminent death) for the Colonel to bring up these references, there remains the question of their contribution to the novel. Trammeled by the biographical similarities between Colonel Cantwell and Hemingway, critics frequently have assumed that these references have no artistic function and serve only to parade the author's knowledge of the world and occasionally to vent his spleen.[22] In reality, remembering that the novel (except for the frame story) is an interior monologue and that very little happens in the present, these references to and judgments of actual personalities and events are the most important means by which we become aware of the narrator's own personality. Also, by means of these references, the world as the Colonel has known it is brought into the novel. This is particularly important because the novel is so static and because its actual duration is only one day. It is almost as if Colonel Cantwell were saying, "These are the fragments I have shored against my ruins."

Finally, remembering the Colonel's own seemingly facetious identification with Dante, it is clear that *Across the River and into the Trees* is a kind of *Divine Comedy* of our time, stressing the *Inferno,* true. Like Dante, Colonel Cantwell (who tells the novel, it must be remembered) lays out his levels of perdition. There are the Futile (e.g., Sinclair Lewis and the Brownings); the Violent (e.g., Goebbels and General Patton); the Fraudulent (e.g., Field Marshall Montgomery and D'Annunzio); and the Traitors (e.g., General Franco and Benny Myers). The circles of Gluttony, Avarice, Flattery, Thievery, Hypocrisy, and others are also filled with specific personalities. The allusions to Easter weekend would make the timing of the novel the same as that of the *Divine Comedy.* Furthermore, as Dante is guided through the *Inferno* and part of the way through *Purgatorio* by Virgil, in *Across the River and into the Trees* Colonel Cantwell guides Renata, who is, in one of her aspects, the Colonel's own youth—"reborn," through the horrors of war and its aftermath. But in her aspect of Ideal Love and her role as Confessor, it is Renata who, like Beatrice, guides the Colonel to purification.

In the light of these allusions and close parallels to the *Divine Comedy* and Christian mythology; in the light of its carefully worked narrative strategy; its ability to state symbolically with effect; its complex handling of a difficult immediate subject (the love of January and May); in the light of what Hemingway called its "calculus" and its "three-cushion shots" there can be no doubt that although *Across the River and into the Trees* has not been accorded the recognition and appreciation that has come to his other work, it is, nevertheless, Hemingway's most complex and indirect novel, a mature work of art by a master who had moved into a phase where none could immediately follow.

1. For a sampling of reviews, see Ben Ray Redman. "The Champ and the Referees," *Sat. Rev. of Lit.*, 28 Oct. 1950, pp. 15–16, ff.

2. "To Have and to Have and to Have," *Sat. Rev. of Lit.*, 9 Sept. 1950, p. 18.

3. Evelyn Waugh, "The Case of Mr. Hemingway," *Commonweal*, 3 Nov. 1950, pp. 97–98. Malcolm Cowley, "Hemingway, Portrait of an Old Soldier Preparing to Die," *N. Y. Herald Tr. Bk. Rev.*, 10 Sept. 1950, p. 1.

4. The present study is indebted particularly to Mr. Baker's work (Princeton, 1963) for several details. Other useful studies are Joseph Warren Beach, "How Do You Like it Now, Gentlemen?" *Sewanee Review*, LIX (Spring, 1951), 311–328; Horst Oppel, "Hemingway's *Across the River and into the Trees,*" *Hemingway and his Critics*, Carlos Baker, ed. (New York, 1961), pp. 213–226; Robert O. Stephens, "Hemingway's *Across the River and into the Trees:* A Reprise," *Univ. of Texas Studies in English*, XXXVII (1958), 92–101; and Philip Young, *Ernest Hemingway* (New York, 1952), pp. 87–93, passim. Although appearing too late for consideration in the present study, the book by R. W. Lewis, *Hemingway on Love* (Univ. of Texas Press, 1965) also should be consulted.

5. A. E. Hotchner reports that in 1958 Hemingway's reaction to the possibility of Gary Cooper's playing Colonel Cantwell in a film was as follows: " 'Good idea,' Ernest said to Cooper, 'You'd just be playing Robert Jordan ten years older.' "—*Papa Hemingway* (Random House, 1966), p. 202.

6. For these details of Hemingway biography see Baker, *Ernest Hemingway: The Writer as Artist*, p. 265, and the reviews by Cowley and Geismar cited above. For further details see Hotchner, pp. 24, 69, 70, 90, 107–109, 176–178, 202.

7. "The Later Hemingway," Barbara A. Melchiori, trans., *The Sewanee Review*, LXVIII (Summer, 1960), 490.

8. This image of the iceberg was first given by Hemingway in *Death in the Afternoon* (New York, 1932), p. 192, and was repeated by him in an interview published in the *Paris Review*, XVIII (Spring, 1958), 84.

9. Lillian Ross, "How Do You Like it Now, Gentlemen?" in Robert P. Weeks, ed., *Hemingway: A Collection of Critical Essays* (Englewood Cliffs, N. J., 1962), p. 18.

10. Harvey Breit, "Talk with Mr. Hemingway," *N. Y. Times Bk. Rev.*, 17 Sept. 1950, p. 14 Hotchner, p. 69, reports similar remarks Hemingway made to him in 1951.

11. It is clear from several specific references that the duck shoot is on a Sunday and that the Colonel and Renata say their farewells on the day before, Saturday, just before 2:30 p.m., and also that the Colonel arrives in Venice the late afternoon of Friday. It must therefore be an oversight on the part of Hemingway or the Colonel that at the beginning of Chapter III (Sunday) he identifies the day of his medical examination as "day before yesterday," especially since in Chapter II he correctly identifies that examination as taking place "the day before he came down to Venice for this shoot"—Thursday. See pp. 8, 12, 53, 75, 130, 142, 268–269, 273.

12. All page references are to the first edition published by Charles Scribner's Sons (New York, 1950).

13. The Colonel's family name, Cantwell, may be read either as "Can't-get-well" or "Can't-well" (verb)." The Colonel is once called Richard the Lion-hearted by Renata, which is interesting for its possible allusion to the Lions of St. Mark, patron saint of Venice, which the Colonel loves.

14. Like General Jackson, the Colonel has been shot through the right hand, has been fired upon by his own forces, and dies not of his wounds but of consequent complications.

15. "Hemingway, Portrait of an Old Soldier Preparing to Die," *N.Y. Herald Tr. Bk. Rev.,* 10 Sept. 1950, p. 1.

16. See Joachim Seyppel, "Two Variations on a Theme: Dying in Venice," *Literature and Psychology,* VII (Feb. 1957), 8–12.

17. *Italian Hours* (New York, 1909), p. 96.

18. *The Novels and Stories of Ivan Turgeniev,* vols. IV and V, Isabel F. Hapgood, trans., (New York, 1923), p. 160.

19. *Italian Hours* (New York, 1909), p. 44.

20. For a discussion of the symbolic meaning of this passage, see Baker, *Ernest Hemingway: The Writer as Artist,* pp. 278–279.

21. The novel contains the usual prefatory note in which the author indignantly asserts that "there are no real people in this volume: both the characters and their names are fictitious."

22. In her "Profile" (See note 8, above) Lillian Ross reports that when she met Hemingway in New York at the time he was revising the novel, he would occasionally burst out with the question, "How Do You Like it Now, Gentlemen?" addressed at large, and then chuckle to himself with immense satisfaction. Possibly, Hemingway had in mind the various gentlemen whom he was putting into his novel.

THE BOY AND THE LIONS

CARLOS BAKER

IN THE LIGHT of the experiment in symbolic representation which Hemingway tried in *Across the River and Into The Trees,* the meaning of the Santiago-Manolo relationship becomes clear. Renata stands, in one of her aspects, for Colonel Cantwell's lost youth. Manolo fulfills a similar purpose, and with greater success in that we do not have to overcome the doubt raised by the difference of sexes. To say this is not, of course, to discount Manolo's dramatic function, which is to heighten our sympathy for the old fisherman. At the beginning and end of the story, we see Santiago through the boy's sympathetic eyes. From the charitable and again fittingly named Martin, owner of the Terrace, Manolo brings Santiago a last supper of black beans, rice, fried bananas, stew, and two bottles of beer. On the morning of the expedition,

Reprinted with permission from *Hemingway: The Writer as Artist,* 4th ed. (Princeton, N.J.: Princeton U. Press, 1972), 304–311.

Manolo arranges for the simple breakfast of coffee in condensed milk cans, and procures the fish and sardines which Santiago will use for baits. He helps launch the skiff, and sees Santiago off in the dark with a wish for luck on this eighty-fifth day. At the end of the story, after the ordeal, Manolo brings coffee and food for the old man's waking, and ointment for his injured hands, commiserating on the loss, planning for a future when they will work side by side again. The love of Manolo for Santiago is that of a disciple for a master in the arts of fishing; it is also the love of a son for an adopted father.

But from Santiago's point of view, the relationship runs deeper. He has known the boy for years, from the period of childhood up to this later time when Manolo, strong and lucky, stands confidently on the edge of young manhood. Like many other aging men, Santiago finds something reassuring about the overlay of the past upon the present. Through the agency of Manolo he is able to recapture in his imagination, and therefore to a certain degree in fact, the same strength and confidence which distinguished his own young manhood as a fisherman and earned him the title of *El Campeón.*

During his ordeal, the two phrases, "I wish the boy was here," and "I wish I had the boy," play across Santiago's mind nine separate times. In each instance, he means exactly what he says: the presence of the boy would be a help in a time of crisis. But he is also invoking by means of these phrases the strength and courage of his youth. Soon after he has hooked his marlin and knows that he must hang onto the line for some time, Santiago says, "I wish I had the boy." Immediately his resolution tightens. During the first night he says it again, reflecting that "no one should be alone in their old age," although in this case it is unavoidable. As if the mere mention of the boy were a kind of talisman, he then resolves to eat the tuna he has caught "in order to keep strong." Later the same night, he says aloud, "I wish the boy was here," and promptly settles himself against the planks of the bow for another period of endurance. Near dawn he says again, "I wish I had the boy." Then he upbraids himself for wishful thinking. "But you haven't got the boy, he thought. You have only yourself and you had better work back to the last line now . . . and cut it away and hook up the two reserve coils." So he does exactly that.

As he summons courage to eat the raw tuna for his breakfast on the second day, he links the boy and salt in what amounts to an image with double meanings: "I wish the boy were here and that I had some salt." Then he proves to himself that he has enough of both in their metaphorical meaning to eat the tuna and renew his waning strength. While he wills to unknot the cramp, he thinks that "if the boy was here" a little massaging would loosen the forearm and maybe help the still useless gnarled claw of the hand. Yet when, soon afterwards, his great marlin breaches, Santiago summons the strength he needs to play his fish.

On the next breaching it is the same. While the marlin leaps again and again in an attempt to throw the hook, and while the old man and his line are both strained and stretched to the breaking-point, he triples the refrain: "If the boy was here he would wet the coils of line . . . Yes. If the boy were here. If the boy were here." Once more the effect of the invocation is nearly magical as if, by means of it, some of the strength of youth flowed in to sustain the limited powers of age. Always, we notice, just after he has said the words, Santiago manages to reach down into the well of his courage for one more dipperful. Then he goes on.

From this point onwards, having served its purpose, the refrain vanishes. It is not until the return voyage, while the old man reflects Job-like upon the problem of the connection between sin and suffering and while the sharks collect their squadrons in the dark waters, that the boy's image returns again. "Everything kills everything else in some way," he tells himself. "Fishing kills me exactly as it keeps me alive." Then he corrects the misapprehensions that can come from false philosophizing. "The boy keeps me alive . . . I must not deceive myself too much." It is good, at this point, that the old man has the thought of the boy to keep him alive. The sharks wait, and a very bad time is just ahead.

In the night in which he is preparing for betrayal by the avaricious sharks, Santiago has recourse to another sustaining image—a pride of lions he has seen at play on the beaches of Africa when he was a young man like Manolo. Hemingway early establishes a clear symbolic connection between the boy and the lions. "When I was your age," Santiago says, "I was before the mast on a square rigged ship that ran to Africa and I have seen lions on the beaches in the evening." Manolo's answer—"I know. You told me."—indicates not only that the reminiscence has arisen before in their conversations, but also that the incident of the lions is a pleasant obsession in Santiago's mind. "There is for every man," writes the poet Yeats, "some one scene, some one adventure, some one picture that is the image of his secret life, and this one image, if he would but brood over it his life long, would lead his soul." Santiago finds such an image in the lions of his youthful experience.

The night before his ordeal, after the boy has left him to sleep, the old man dreams of the lions.

He was asleep in a short time and he dreamed of Africa when he was a boy and the long golden beaches and the white beaches, so white they hurt your eyes, and the high capes and the great brown mountains. He lived along that coast now every night and in his dreams he heard the surf roar and saw the native boats come riding through it. He smelled the tar and oakum of the deck as he slept and he smelled the smell of Africa that the land breeze brought at morning. Usually when he smelled the land breeze he woke up and dressed to go to wake the boy. But tonight the smell of the land breeze came very early and he knew it was too early in his dream and went on dreaming to see the white peaks of the Islands rising from the sea and then he dreamed of the different harbours and roadsteads of the Canary Islands.

Santiago "no longer dreamed of storms, nor of women, nor of great occurrences, nor of great fish, nor fights, nor contests of strength, nor of his wife. He only dreamed of places now and of the lions on the beach. They played like young cats in the dusk and he loved them as he loved the boy."

Early in the afternoon of his second day out, having said his prayers and strengthened his resolution by this means, Santiago thinks again about his lions. The marlin is pulling steadily. "I wish he'd sleep and I could sleep and dream about the lions," thinks Santiago. "Why are the lions the main thing that is left? Don't think, old man . . . Rest gently now against the wood and think of nothing. He is working. Work as little as you can." Much later that day, "cramping himself against the line with all his body," and "putting all his weight onto his right hand," the old man manages to sleep. Presently then, he begins to dream "of the long yellow beach." In the dream, we are told, "he saw the first of the lions come down onto it in the early dark and then the other lions came and he rested his chin on the wood of the bows where the ship lay anchored with the evening offshore breeze and he waited to see if there would be more lions and he was happy." In his old age and the time of his suffering, Santiago is sustained by the memory of his youth and the strength of his youth. Living so, in the past, he is happy. Luckily for him, he has also the thought of the strength of the boy Manolo, a young lion of just the age Santiago was when he first sailed to Africa. These together enable him to go on.

They help in a very notable way. For the boy and the lions are related to one of the fundamental psychological laws of Santiago's—and indeed of human—nature: the constant wavelike operation of bracing and relaxation. The boy braces, the lions relax, as in the systolic-diastolic movement of the human heart. It is related, as a phenomenon, to the alternation of sleep and waking through the whole range of physical nature. But it is also a law which operates on the level of mentality, and its effects can be seen in our reactions to works of literature like this story of the acquisition and the loss of the great marlin. In its maritime sections, at any rate, the basic rhythms of the novel resemble those of the groundswell of the sea. Again and again as the action unfolds, the reader may find that he is gradually brought up to a degree of quiet tension just barely endurable, as in the ascent by a small craft of a slow enormous wave. When he has reached the presumptive peak of his resistance, the crest passes and he suddenly relaxes towards a trough of rest. The rhythm of the story appears to be built on such a stress-yield, brace-relax alternation. The impression is furthered by the constant tension which Santiago and his fish maintain on the line which joins them. Again and again one finds the old man telling himself that he has stretched the cord to a tension just short of the breaking-point. Then and only then, the stress relaxes, and the involved reader relaxes with it. This prolonged tug-of-war involves not only the fisherman and his fish but also the reader and his own emotions.

The planned contiguity of the old man with the boy and the lions pulls the story of Santiago, in one of its meanings, in the direction of a parable of youth and age. There is a distinct possibility that Hemingway, who read the whole of Conrad during the days of his writing apprenticeship in Paris and Toronto, has recollected if not the details at least the central strategy of Conrad's long short story, "Youth." For that story is brilliantly organized in terms of the contrast of age and youth. The ill-fated voyage of the barque *Judea,* out of London, bound for Bangkok, shows young Marlow, with all the illusions and prowess of his youth, side by side with old Captain Beard, the ship's master and a brave man. "He was sixty, if a day," says Marlow of the captain. "And he had blue eyes in that old face of his, which were amazingly like a boy's, with that candid expression some quite common men preserve to the end of their days by a rare internal gift of simplicity of heart and rectitude of soul." Again Marlow says, as the fated ship beats her way through a sea of trouble, that Beard was "immense in the singleness of his idea." It may of course be a coincidence that these are qualities which Santiago shares. Two "quite common men" rise to the level of the heroic through simplicity of heart, rectitude of soul, and that immensity in the singleness of their respective ideas which enables each to stick out the voyage to the end. "Do or die," the motto which adorns in flaking gilt the stern-timbers of the old *Judea,* might with equal justice be carved into the weather-beaten wood of Santiago's skiff.

Conrad's story depends for its effects not only upon the contrast of young Marlow and old Beard but also, since the story is told some twenty years after the event, upon the contrast of the aging Marlow and his own remembrance of his youthful self. The aging Santiago happily recalls the lions on the shore of Africa. The aging Marlow recollects, with mingled happiness and sorrow, that time, far back now, when the small boats from the wrecked *Judea* at last pulled into a port on the Javanese coast. "I remember my youth," says Marlow, "and the feeling that will never come back any more—the feeling that I could last for ever, outlast the sea, the earth, and all men; the deceitful feeling that lures us on to joys, to perils, to love, to vain effort—to death; the triumphant conviction of strength, the heat of life in the handful of dust, the glow in the heart that with every year grows dim, grows cold, grows small, and expires." This feeling, which Hazlitt has well described as "the feeling of immortality in youth," is closely associated in Marlow's mind with the East —"the mysterious shores, the still water, the lands of the brown nations." For me, he tells his auditors, "all the East is contained in that vision of my youth. It is all in that moment when I opened my young eyes on it. I came upon it from a tussle with the sea—and I was young—and I saw it looking at me. And this is all that is left of it! Only a moment; a moment of strength, of romance, of glamour—of youth!"

For Santiago it is not the coast of Java but that of Africa, not the faces of the brown men crowding the jetty but the playing lions, which carry the associations of youth, strength, and even immortality. "This is all that is left of it," cries Marlow of his youthful vision. "Why are the lions the main thing that is left?" says Hemingway's old man in the midst of his ordeal. For both of them, in Marlow's words, it is "the time to remember." But Santiago, luckily, is able to do more with his vision than remember it. He puts it to work once more in the great trial of his old age. "I told the boy I was a strange old man," he says. "Now is when I must prove it." And the author adds: "The thousand times that he had proved it meant nothing. Now he was proving it again. Each time was a new time and he never thought about the past when he was doing it." But if he does not, at these times, think about the past to brood upon it, he periodically calls back what it means to him through the double vision of the boy and the lions. If he can prove his mettle for the thousand-and-first time, there is no reason why he cannot prove it again and again, as long as his vision lasts.

Of how many events in the course of human life may this not be said? It is Marlow once more who reminds us of the way in which one account of one man on one journey can extend outwards in our imaginations until it easily becomes a paradigm of the course of men's lives. "You fellows know," says Marlow, beginning his account of the *Judea,* "there are those voyages that seem ordered for the illustration of life, that might stand for a symbol of

existence. You fight, work, sweat, nearly kill yourself, sometimes do kill yourself, trying to accomplish something—and you can't. Not from any fault of
yours." If it is so with the *Judea,* out of London bound for Bangkok, do or
die, it is so likewise with Santiago of Havana, bound for home, with the sharks
just beginning to nose the blood of his great fish. Do or die. In such works as
this we all put to sea, and sitting well in order smite the sounding furrows.
Santiago makes his voyage on what used to be known as the Spanish Main.
But it is also, we are persuaded, that more extensive main or mainstream where
we all drift or sail, with or against the wind, in fair weather or foul, with our
prize catches and our predatory sharks, and each of us, perhaps, like the
ancient mariner of Coleridge, with some kind of albatross hanging around his
neck.

It is provided in the essence of things, writes the stoical philosopher, that
from any fruition of success, no matter what, shall come forth something to
make a greater struggle necessary. With such a sentiment Santiago would no
doubt agree. For the second major movement of the novel confronts him with
a struggle which, though shorter in duration, is at least as intense as the fight
with the marlin just brought to a successful conclusion. This comes, too, at a
time when he has used all his strength, and as much more as he could summon,
to attain his object; when his hands are stiffening round the edges of his
wounds, when the muscles of his back and shoulders are knotted with pain,
and when his fatigue runs bone-deep.

Having secured his catch alongside, stepped his mast, rigged his boom,
and moved off with the beneficent tradewind towards the southwest and home,
Santiago enjoys (though not to the full because of his tiredness) that brief
respite which follows work well done. Side by side like brothers the old man
and the marlin move through the sea. Up to now, they have been, as Santiago
believes, friendly and mutually respectful adversaries. Now they join together
in league against the common enemy. "If sharks come," the old man has long
ago reflected, "God pity him and me." It is a full hour before the first shark
arrives.

With its arrival begins a tragedy of deprivation as piteous as that which
King Lear undergoes at the hands of his sharkhearted daughters. Lear's hundred knights, the only remaining sign of his power and the badge of his kingly
dignity, are taken from him in batches of twenty-five. A series of forty-pound
rippings and tearings are now gradually to reduce Santiago's eighteen-foot,
fifteen-hundred-pound marlin to the skeleton he brings finally to shore.

The first of the sharks is a Mako. "Everything about him was beautiful except his jaws . . . Inside the closed double lip . . . all of his eight rows of teeth were slanted inwards. They were not the ordinary pyramid-shaped teeth of most sharks. They were shaped like a man's fingers when they are crisped like claws. They were nearly as long as the fingers of the old man and they had razor sharp cutting edges on both sides." Santiago, standing poised with his harpoon, hears the clicking chop of these great jaws and the rending and tearing of the marlin's flesh just before he drives the point of his weapon "with resolution and complete malignancy" into the Mako's brain. Death is immediate but the loss is heavy. When the shark sinks, he takes with him forty pounds of the marlin, the harpoon, and all the rope. The marlin's blood will attract other sharks. But worse than this is the mutilation of the long-fought-for prize. Santiago "did not like to look at the fish anymore since he had been mutilated. When the fish had been hit it was as though he himself were hit." The process of crucifixion is now intensified.

At first sight of the second shark, Santiago utters the single word *Ay*. "There is no translation for this word," writes Hemingway, "and perhaps it is just a noise such as a man might make, involuntarily, feeling the nail go through his hands and into the wood." For some hours now, of course, Santiago's hands have shown the fisherman's equivalent of the stigmata of a saint. Both have been cut in the "working part," which is the palm, by the unpredictable lurchings of his quarry. The right hand is cut first, at a time when the old man's attention is momentarily diverted by the warbler's visit. Another of the marlin's sudden accelerations awakens him from the only sleep he permits himself. The line is burning out through his already wounded right hand. When he brings up his left for use as a brake, it takes all the strain and cuts deep.

The old man's involuntary epithet, and Hemingway's explanation of it, is fully in line with what has gone before. Throughout the ordeal, Santiago has been as conscious of his hands as any crucified man might be. He speaks to them as to fellow-sufferers, wills them to do the work they must do, and makes due allowances for them as if they were, what he once calls them, "my brothers." He also carefully distinguishes between them in a manner which should not be lost on any student of paintings of the Crucifixion. The right hand is the good one, dextrous and trustworthy. The left hand, the hand sinister, has "always been a traitor."

Our Lord might well have entertained a similar reflection about the man who was crucified on his own left. The allusions to Santiago's hands are so carefully stylized that such a statement becomes possible. On the naturalistic plane, of course, the meaning of the distinction between the two hands is apparent to all normally right-handed persons; the left is never as good as the right. But on the plane of what we have called *Dichtung,* and in the light of the tradition of Christian art as it pertains to the Crucifixion, it is clear that a moral judgment is to be inferred. Of the two who were crucified with Jesus Christ, the one on the left failed Him, insulting and upbraiding him. But the man crucified on Jesus' right hand rebuked his companion, and put his fortunes into the hands of the Savior. In paintings of the Crucifixion, as Hemingway is well aware, the distinction between the two malefactors is always carefully maintained. It even carries over into pictures of the Last Judgment, where those who are to be saved are ranged on the right hand of the Savior, while the damned stand dejectedly on the left.

Santiago vanquishes the second and third sharks, hateful, bad smelling, "scavengers as well as killers" with his knife lashed to an oar. But when the *galanos* sink into the sea, they take with them fully a quarter of the marlin's best meat. "I wish it were a dream and that I had never hooked him," says the old man. "I'm sorry about it, fish. It makes everything wrong." The fourth shark, a single shovel-nose, adds yet another degree to our sense of wronged rightness. "He came like a pig to the trough if a pig had a mouth so wide that you could put your head in it." This one breaks Santiago's knife, bearing the blade in its brain-pan as it follows the *galanos* to death.

By the time the old man has clubbed the fifth and sixth sharks into submission just at sunset, a full half of the marlin has been gouged away. "What will you do now if they come in the night?" asks the voice inside Santiago. "Fight them," says the old man aloud. "I'll fight them until I die." But when he tries to stand off a whole ravaging pack at midnight, striking at whatever heads he can see, he knows the fight is almost useless. Something seizes his club and it disappears; he hits out with the unshipped tiller until it breaks, and then lunges at another of the sharks with the splintered butt. When this one lets go of the marlin and rolls away, the massacre is ended. A few more come to hit the carcass in the night, "as someone might pick up crumbs from the table." But the old man ignores them and sails on. There is nothing left of the great fish except the skeleton, the bony head, and the vertical tail.

This story of great gain and great loss is esthetically satisfying partly because of its symmetry. Hemingway has little trouble, either, in persuading his readers of the inevitability of the process. For with so fine a prize in a tropical sea where hungry sharks constantly swim, Santiago's return with a whole fish would be nothing short of miraculous. In assessing the old man's total experience, one is reminded of the experiences of younger men in some of Hemingway's earlier novels: Lieutenant Henry's gain and loss of a new wife, for example, in *A Farewell to Arms,* or Robert Jordan's gain and loss of a new life in *For Whom the Bell Tolls.* Yet in this latter-day return to the theme of winner-take-nothing, on which Hemingway has so often and so successfully played his variations, he seems to have added a new dimension. This is the dimension of transfiguration, anticipated (it is true) in the story of Robert Jordan, but never made quite so nearly explicit as in the instance of Santiago.

Santiago's experience is a form of martyrdom. We do not object: it is his by right of eminent domain. The old man's only fault, if it is a fault, consists in doing to the best of his ability what he was born to do. When the man on the right rebuked his companion for crass raillery at the expense of Jesus Christ, he raised the essential moral problem. "We receive," said he, "the due reward of our deeds: but this man [Jesus Christ] hath done nothing amiss." Neither has Santiago, but this does not prevent his martyrdom. Tried out through an ordeal by endurance comparable to a crucifixion, he earns, by virtue of his valiance, a form of apotheosis.

His humility and simplicity will not allow entry to any taint of conscious martyrdom. "Man is not made for defeat," he says at one point. "A man can be destroyed but not defeated." His resolution is always stiffened by some such thought as this, and he acts in accordance with it. Being native to his character, these qualities of resolution and action sustain him up to that point when he knows that his only remaining recourse is to take what comes when it comes. Arrival at this point does not unbalance him. He is not a rebel, like the mariner Ahab, against the ruling powers of the universe. Nor does he imagine, as he drives his harpoon into the marlin's heart, that he is destroying anything except a prize fish with whom he has fought long and fairly. The arrival of the sharks on the scene does not surprise him. He does not expect for a moment that they will let him run their saber-toothed gauntlet unscathed. Santiago is a moral realist.

Yet he is too human not to be troubled, like Job before him, by certain moral and metaphysical questions. One is the problem of whether any connection exists between sin and suffering. "It is silly not to hope," he thinks to himself after the killing of the Mako shark. "Besides I believe it is a sin." In this way he launches himself into a consideration of the problem. At first his realistic capacity for self-criticism cautions him that this is dangerous ground. "There are enough problems without sin. Also I have no understanding of it and I am not sure that I believe in it . . . Do not think about sin. It is much too late for that and there are people who are paid to do it. Let them think about it."

The problem will not be put down so easily. "Perhaps," he speculates, "it was a sin to kill the fish. I suppose it was even though I did it to keep me alive and feed many people." After all, "San Pedro was a fisherman," and who would accuse him of sin? But once more the cautionary voice chimes in. "You did not kill the fish only to keep alive and to sell for food, he thought. You killed him for pride and because you are a fisherman. You loved him when he was alive and you loved him after. If you love him, it is not a sin to kill him. Or is it more?"

On this double allusion to pride and to love, greatest of sins and greatest of virtues, hangs the philosophic crux of the problem. Was his real motivation the blameless one of doing his professional duty and feeding people? Probably not basically. He did it for pride: to show that he was still El Campéon. "I'll kill him," he boasted during the battle. "In all his greatness and his glory . . . I will show him what a man can do and what a man endures." Yet all through the struggle he was never without love and compassion for his marlin, or for most of the lesser creatures in God's marine creation.

As in other tragic literatures, the whole process consists ultimately in the readjustment of moral proportions. What begins as a balanced mixture of pride and love slowly alters through the catalysis of circumstance. When Santiago brings his marlin to the gaff, his pride has been gone for a long time. Statements like "I'll fight them until I die," made during the encounter with the sharks, are not so much the evidence of pride as of the resolute determination to preserve something loved and earned from the distortion that comes with mutilation. The direction of the process then comes clear. Where pride and love exist together, the pride must be burned out, as by the cautery of fire. Love will remain as the natural concomitant of true humility.

Though Santiago admits to pride and lays claim to love, his moral sense is not fully satisfied by this way of resolving the problem. He looks for some other explanation of the profit-and-loss pattern. What he seems finally to settle on is the notion that he has gone, as he often puts it, "too far out." This concept of "too-far-outness" is not simply what Colonel Cantwell might describe as over-extension: lines of communication stretched past the breaking-point, possible support abandoned, danger courted for its own sake, excess of bravery spilling over into foolhardiness. It is rather what Melville described as "the intrepid effort of the soul to keep the open independence of her sea"—a willingness to take the greater risk where the greater prize is involved.

Very early in the book the contrast is established between the lee shore and the Gulf Stream. There are the inshore men, those who work within sight of land because it is easier, safer, and less frightening, and those like Santiago who have the intrepidity to reach beyond the known towards the possible. "Where are you going?" Manolo asks him, on the eve of the eighty-fifth day.

"Far out," replies Santiago, "to come in when the wind shifts." The boy hopes to persuade his father to work far out that day in order to provide help for Santiago if it should be necessary. But this will not happen. Manolo's father is plainly an inshore man, one who does not like to work far out, one who prefers not to take chances, no matter how great the potential gain might be.

Santiago does not hesitate. On the morning of the eighty-fifth day, we are told that he "knew he was going far out." This is why he passes over, even before dawn, the inshore fishing-ground which fishermen call "the great well" —an easy place teeming with provender, where thousands of fish congregate to feed and to be caught. By seven he is already so far out that only three fishing boats are remotely visible inshore; by noon only the tops of the blue Cuban hills show on the horizon. No other boats are now in sight. Here, somewhere, lurk the great fish of this September season. When Santiago is passed by a school of dolphin, he guesses that marlin may be nearby. "My big fish," he tells himself, "must be somewhere."

Even as he speaks the marlin is approaching, the lordly denizen of this farout domain. In coming there, in the process of invasion, the old man has made his choice—not to stay inshore where the going might be easier but to throw out a challenge to what might be waiting, far out and down deep at the hundred-fathom level. As for the marlin, "his choice had been to stay in the deep dark water far out beyond all snares and traps and treacheries." Yet he accepts, in effect rises to, the old man's challenge. From then on Santiago is tied by a strong line to his doom. "My choice," he reflects, "was to go there to find him beyond all people. Beyond all people in the world. Now we are joined together." The long battle is also joined. Since it came about through Santiago's free choice, he has no alternative but to accept the consequences.

These follow inevitably. For to have gone far out is to have invited the depredations of the sharks on the equally long homeward voyage. When the first three have done their work, Santiago apologizes. "I shouldn't have gone so far out, fish. Neither for you nor for me. I'm sorry, fish." When the mutilation has developed to the point where he cannot bear to look at it, he apologizes again. "You violated your luck," says his speaking self, "when you went too far outside." Inshore again, with the marlin destroyed and the old man's weapons gone, there is another dialogue of the soul with itself. "And what beat you?" "Nothing," answers the second voice. "I went out too far." Urged on by pride, by the love of his trade, by his refusal to take continuing bad luck as his portion, and by a resurgent belief that he might win, Santiago made trial of the impossible. In the tragic process he achieved the moral triumph.

It is not necessarily a Christian victory. Yet it is clear that Hemingway has artfully enhanced the native power of his tragic parable by enlisting the further power of Christian symbolism. Standing solus on the rocky shore in the darkness before the dawn of the fourth day, Santiago shows the wounded hands. Dried blood is on his face as from a crown of thorns. He has known the ugly coppery taste in his mouth as from a sponge filled with vinegar. And in the agony of his fatigue he is very much alone. "There was no one to help him so he pulled the boat up as far as he could. Then he stepped out and made her fast to a rock. He unstepped the mast and furled the sail and tied it. Then he shouldered the mast and started to climb."

Once he paused to look back at the remains of his fish. At the top of the hill "he fell and lay for some time with the mast across his shoulder. He tried to get up. But it was too difficult and he sat there with the mast on his shoulder and looked at the road. A cat passed on the far side going about its business and the old man watched it. Then he just watched the road." The loneliness of the ascent of any Calvary is brilliantly emphasized by the presence of the cat. The Old Masters, as Auden wrote long ago, were never wrong about suffering. "How well they understood its human position; how it takes place while someone else is eating or opening a window or just walking dully along . . . They never forgot that even the dreadful martyrdom must run its course anyhow in some corner, some untidy spot where the dogs go on with their doggy life"—and where the innocence of ignorance never so much as bats an eye. The cat on the far side of the road from Santiago is also proceeding about its private business. It could not help the old man even if it would. Santiago knows and accepts this as he has accepted the rest. There is nothing else to be done—except to reach home, which he manages at last to do, though he has to sit down five times to rest between the hilltop and the door of his shack.

On the newspapers that cover the springs of the bed, and below the colored chromos of the Sacred Heart of Jesus and the Virgin of Cobre, the old man now falls heavily asleep. He sleeps face down with his arms out straight and his body straight up and down: cruciform, as if to sum up by that symbolic position, naturally assumed, all the suffering through which he has passed. *In hoc signo vinces.* Santiago has made it to his house. When Manolo looks in next morning, he is still asleep. There is a short conversation as he drinks the coffee the boy brings, and they lay plans for the future even as they allude laconically to the immediate past. "How much did you suffer?" Manolo asks. "Plenty," the old man answers. Outside, a three-day blow has begun. Inside the shack, the book concludes, the old man falls again into the deep sleep of renewal, of diurnal resurrection. "He was still sleeping on his face and the boy was sitting by him watching him. The old man was dreaming about the lions." In my end is my beginning.

INDEX

abstractions, 14–5, 44, 47, 49, 52, 67–8, 89, 94, 136, 145, 149, 173–74, 207, 227–28, 267

Adams, Nick, 2, 85, 88, 99, 106–8, 122, 133, 135–36, 140, 162, 188–90, 195–97, 212n, 230ff., 288

adjectives, use of, 13–4, 16, 161, 165, 173, 225

Adrianople, 14

aficionado, 59–60ff., 110, 135–36

Alger, Horatio, Jr., 53

allegory, 132, 145–46, 150–51

alliteration, 179

Allston, Washington, 242

American language, 42ff., 52, 215ff., 222

"American loneliness," 138–39

Anderson, Maxwell, 75

Anderson, Sherwood, 9, 16, 18, 19n, 40, 47, 57, 161–63, 166, 177, 180, 222, 224–25, 230, 242

Anfortas, 248

Antheil, George, 13

anticlimax, 15

anti-hero, 218

Arnold, Matthew, 89–90

art as religion, 1, 17–19, 37

Asch, Nathan, 32

Asselineau, Roger, 7n

Auden, W. H., 318

Austen, Jane, 142

Babbitt, Irving, 43

Bach, Johann Sebastian, 29, 255, 293, 303

"Bad art" defined, Pound, 17

Baker, Carlos, 4, 6, 42, 47, 70, 103, 128, 140, 162, 183, 188, 191, 241, 244, 268

Barbusse, Henri, 48–9

Barea, Arturo, 70–1, 268

baseball, 132, 135

Bates, H. E., 123, 127

Baudelaire, Charles, 37

Beach, Joseph Warren, 215, 280, 286–87

Beach, Sylvia, 8, 20n, 165, 225

Beard, Charles A., 23

Beebe, Maurice, 6

Bel Esprit, 10

Benson, Jackson, 5

Bergson, Henri, 131n, 280–82

Bessie, Alvah, 70

Bhagavad-Gita, 121

Bird, William, 9, 10, 13, 59, 77–8

Bishop, John Peale, 9, 16, 163, 165

Blake, William, 303

Borrow, George Henry, 269

Bosch, Hieronymus, 29, 30, 293, 303

Botticelli, Sandro, 293

boxing, 9, 165

Brahma, 281

Braque, Georges, 28

Brecht, Bertolt, 154, 156

Breit, Harvey, 18, 184

Breughel, Pieter, 29, 303

Bridgman, Richard, 4

Brontë, Emily, 260

Brooks, Alden, 23

Brooks, Cleanth, 221, 253

Brooks, Van Wyck, 50

Browning, Robert, 303–04

Bruccoli, Matthew J., 5

Bryer, Jackson, 6

bullfights, 15, 21–3, 45, 58–68ff., 109, 132–34, 148–50, 217–19, 223, 249, 286

Burguete, Spain, 110, 154, 216, 247, 250

Burhans, Clinton, Jr., 230

320